Praise for prior parenting and family-formation books by Randall Hicks:

"A must read. Every nuance in the world of adoption is explored and clearly explained. This book nails down the realities of how adoption works – and more importantly, how to succeed."

—*Colleen Quinn, Past President*
American Academy of Adoption Attorneys

[Starred review] "A brilliantly lean book . . . enthusiastically recommended."
—*Library Journal*

"Educational and empowering. No-nonsense, matter-of-fact advice while using a compassionate approach."

—*Publishers Weekly*

"Showers the anxious parent with information on methods and resources."
—*Booklist*
American Library Association

Featured in the television media:

CBS This Morning, The Today Show, Sally Jessy Raphael, John & Leeza from Hollywood, Mike and Maty, PBS and more.

And the print media:

The New York Times, The Los Angeles Times, Chicago Sun-Times, San Diego Union-Tribune, Orange County Register, Parents.com and more.

ADOPTING

IN

AMERICA

How to Adopt Within One Year

6th Revised Edition

RANDALL B. HICKS

Attorney at Law

WORDSLINGER PRESS
San Diego, California

[1]Book reviews on front and back covers are from either reviews of this, or earlier, editions. Cover-cited press/TV coverage includes author appearances and/or recommendations/references to Randall Hicks's multiple adoption/parenting books.

Published by WordSlinger Press
9921 Carmel Mountain Road #335
San Diego, CA 92129

ISBN: 978-0-9839425-5-9 (hardcover)
ISBN: 978-0-9839425-4-2 (trade paperback)
ISBN: 978-0-9794430-7-7 (e-book)

Library of Congress Cataloging-in-Publication Data

Names: Hicks, Randall, 1956- author.
Title: Adopting in America : how to adopt within one year / Randall Bruce Hicks, Attorney at Law.
Description: Revised 6th edition. | San Diego, CA : WordSlinger Press, [2017] | Revised edition of the author's Adopting in America, 2012. | Includes index. |
Identifiers: LCCN 2017033942 (print) | LCCN 2017037978 (ebook) | ISBN 9780979443077 (ebook) | ISBN 9780983942559 (hardcover : alk. paper)
Subjects: LCSH: Adoption--United States. | Adoption--Law and legislation--United States.
Classification: LCC HV875.55 (ebook) | LCC HV875.55 .H53 2017 (print) | DDC 362.7340973--dc23
LC record available at https://lccn.loc.gov/2017033942

10 9 8 7 6 5 4 3 2 1

Table of Contents

INTRODUCTION

This 2018-19 edition is the 6th edition of this book, going back to its debut in 1992. It was such a revolutionary book when it was released that it was promptly featured on many national TV shows: *The Today Show, CBS This Morning*, and too many to fully list that have since gone off the air, like *Sally Jesse Raphael, John and Leeza from Hollywood, Mike & Maty, The Home and Family Show*, and more. No other "how to" adoption book can say that. My "style of teaching" is to be very blunt and not dance around tough subjects to be "politically correct." I will give you the unadulterated realities of adoption and show you the same strategies I've used with my clients to create more than 1,000 successful adoptions in my 31 years of being an adoption attorney, doing independent, agency and intercountry adoptions

I want to show you how to adopt quickly.

The key to success in any endeavor is *knowledge*. Adoption is no different. I will give you that knowledge in an easy-to-understand, step-by-step approach. In addition to the basic knowledge you'll need, I'll give you a strategy for success. And not just success, but quite possibly *quick* success. I promise to give you more information than you thought was possible about how to succeed at adopting a child. This is true whether you wish to adopt a newborn child, an older child, a child with special-needs, or do an intercountry adoption. Some of these strategies you won't find anywhere else. But don't take it on faith. Before you even finish this

Introduction, you will see adopting within one year is not an exaggeration. It is accomplished by countless adoptive parents.

I want to show you how to adopt safely.

Every endeavor in life has risks, and adoption is no exception. I believe the biggest key in avoiding a failed adoption is to never start a risky one. Will there still be risks? Yes. Adoption is fraught with emotions, for both you and the birth family, so risks can't be eliminated entirely. However, I'll show you the red flags to watch out for to greatly minimize risk, and allow you to proceed into your adoption with confidence.

I want to show you how to adopt ethically.

Although this is a "how to" and "strategy" book, make no mistake that I believe the most important thing in every adoption is to not just doing it legally, but with high morals as well. Shortcuts backfire. Illegality corrupts. Immorality taints. Run from people who tell you otherwise. Adoption is how you bring your child into your home. His or her unique adoption story will be a part of your family history, to be lovingly shared with your child as he or she grows. You want to look back on how each step was accomplished with pride. Your adoption can be, and should be, one of the most wonderful and rewarding journeys of your life.

I want you to go into your adoption plan with high confidence.

The subtitle: *How to Adopt Within One Year,* is not just a catchy phrase. The real numbers of adoption show adopting within a year is not only possible, but accomplished by countless families nationwide. Unfortunately, there are no government statistics regarding how long adoptive parents wait to adopt. (Instead, governmental research is focused on the waiting time for the children—not the adoptive parents—such as how long foster children stay in foster care before being adopted).

But statistics are available. The highly respected *Adoptive Families* magazine (AdoptiveFamilies.com) did a recent survey of its readers' adoption experiences. In its 2016 report of adoptions completed in 2014-2015, their readers reported that:

- 68% of those selecting independent adoption had a baby placed with them within one year. Most of those were within six months.
- 63% of those adopting through a private adoption agency had a baby placed with them within one year. Most of those were within six months.
- 64% of those adopting a waiting child through a public agency or adoption exchange had a placement within one year. The majority were within the first six months.

These impressive numbers can be tricky to interpret, however. Be aware that this quick success is what is experienced by those who actually *had* an adoptive placement. It does not include those who have not yet successfully adopted, and are still awaiting a placement. When considering unmatched/waiting adoptive parents, there is no possible way to determine what their waiting time will be. Still, to see the very fast success of the many families who are actually adopting shows how quick results in adoption is indeed not just possible, but actually happening every day.

The advice and information in this book can help you be one of those successful families. Success in any endeavor usually goes to those with the most knowledge, and who work the hardest to use that knowledge. There is no reason that can't be you.

—Randy Hicks, Adoption Attorney

CHAPTER 1

ARE YOU READY TO ADOPT?

Your readiness to adopt is the first critical step in your adoption. If you are not emotionally ready, all the knowledge in the world won't make adoption the right family-building option for you. Instead, it will be the proverbial "house built on sand," destined to fail. You owe it to yourselves, and your future child, to be sure you are ready.

Readiness to Adopt

People often confuse being ready to *adopt* with being ready to *parent*. They are two vastly different things. Adoption means a full recognition that you are making someone else's biological child your own, as if born to you. Adoption can't be a healthy option if an adoptive parent views the lack of their own biological connection with a child as a negative characteristic. The biological diversity of an adopted child must not just be accepted, but embraced. As stated by two of the nation's leading authorities on the subject, Lois Ruskai Melina and Sharon Kaplan Roszia in *The Open Adoption Experience*:

> Children reflect both nature and nurture, though the exact interplay between those factors is still a mystery. Consequently, the child has a connection to both the birth parents and the adoptive parents, because each has made a significant contribution to the child's

development. This dual responsibility for who a child is and who he becomes also creates a connection between birth parents and adoptive parents . . . Through them, a human life is created and nurtured . . .

As an adoptive parent, you must recognize that your child may look different from you (even if of the same ethnic group), or genetically be pre-disposed to different interests and skills. Of course, even biologically conceived children often have interests different from their parents or siblings, or don't look alike. Oddly, those differences are never questioned in biologically created families, just taken for granted as an extension of each person's individuality. In adoption, however, some people examine such differences with inappropriate scrutiny.

Another issue related to readiness to adopt, assuming you are adopting due to infertility, is that you have come to terms with infertility. For this reason, counseling is a normal and highly recommended part of the infertility/adoption process. For some, it is hard to give up the dream of a biologically conceived child, while others have little difficulty with the concept of adopting a person who is genetically from another family. For those who have difficulty abandoning the dream of their own biologically conceived child, it is critical to come to terms with this issue before starting an adoption. To not do so would be like marrying one person while you are still in love with someone else. Everyone will suffer as a result, no matter how good your intentions.

Readiness to adopt means you have to look into more than your heart. You have to look into your mind. Are you adopting because you want to be a parent? To have a family? If so, those are natural, healthy reasons to adopt. Some adoptive parents, however, are motivated by the desire to "save a child." Yes, this is a good-hearted motivation by likely a wonderful person. It is the wrong reason to adopt, however.

Let's use marriage as an example again. If you were to marry someone to "save" them, perhaps from a life of loneliness and poverty, think how doomed that marriage would be. Either consciously or unconsciously, you would expect gratitude, and you would not get it. Instead, you would eventually get resentment. You'd feel they were ungrateful, and now we've got two people feeling resentment.

Adoption is no different. The fact may be—particularly in older child and intercountry adoption from some impoverished nations—that you are physically "saving" a child from a poor start in life and giving them a brighter future. Adoption, however, is about creating a family—a parent and child relationship—not living an act of charity. There are many honorable and much-needed ways to help children besides adoption, such as foster parenting, mentoring, volunteering time, and donating money. So, leave adoption for true family creation, not human charity.

Talking to Your Child about Adoption

You might be asking a valid question right now. Why is there already a subsection about talking with your child about adoption when you don't even have a child yet? Good point. There are several reasons to bring it up now, however. First, let's look at the practical side of the issue. If you are planning a newborn adoption, where the birth mother will likely be meeting with you prior to deciding if you are the right parents for her baby, a common question for a birth mother to ask you is, "How are you going to tell your child that s/he's adopted?"

If this is a question to which you've never given any thought, and you stumble out something simplistic and antiquated about the child "being special," you will likely not impress that birth mother. In fact, many birth mothers have already been given information, or met with a counselor, and learned about how and when adoption should be discussed with a child, meaning she already knows what the answer to this question should be.

You want her to look at you as more than nice people who will be great parents, rather who will be great *adoptive* parents. That means you took the time to be ready for these issues because you care about the subject, not left it to deal with at some uncertain point in the future. Failure to fully educate yourself in such vital issues means you might not be "birth mother ready" when you are selected by a birth mother, and she may come away unimpressed after meeting you. The result is she might select another adoptive family and you've lost what should have been your placement.

The second reason is that you owe it to your future child to do this kind of thinking in advance. It's just what adoptive parents do. It's part of the appropriate fantasy every future parent has, whether that family is created biologically or through adoption. As we look forward to parenthood, we all have fantasies about our child taking their first steps, playing catch on the lawn, opening presents at Christmas or Hanukkah, and sitting on grandma or grandpa's lap to hear the same stories we were told as children. The only thing different is that adoptive parents need to have a few additional stories, and talking to their child about how they entered the family is one of them.

Here is the introduction to a children's book, *Adoption Stories for Young Children*. Although it is a picture book for children, the first page is for parents regarding this very important topic.

Some adoptive parents feel very comfortable in discussing adoption with their child, while others have some anxiety. All adoptive parents, however, have one thing in common. They understand that not only does their child need and deserve knowledge of how their family was created through adoption, but also that his or her knowledge must be provided in a way which will give their child the pride and self-respect every person needs as a foundation in life.

What do you say and when do you say it? Every child—and family situation—is different, but there are many common themes which the adoption community has come to embrace. The practice followed by some parents many years ago of hiding any information about adoption until the child was "old enough" has been rejected. Although that policy may have been followed with good intentions, many problems resulted. Many children would accidentally learn from others they were adopted, instead of from their parents, creating confusion and parent-trust issues. (Think of all the people that will know your child is adopted. All your relatives. Most friends and neighbors. Should everyone know but the child him/herself?)

These children may end up learning they were adopted from people other than their own parents, causing them to perhaps think their parents' silence was due to embarrassment about the adoption, creating shame in the child, unjustly believing something must be "wrong" with adoption.

Now, openness is embraced. Although your child grew in your heart and not physically in your body, you don't want to deny your young child the great joys every child feels when hearing about your anticipation of his or her arrival into the family, and how cherished and important a part of your family s/he has become. How your child views him or herself—and adoption itself—will depend almost exclusively upon you.

If you are adopting a newborn, talking about adoption starts at birth. True, the baby won't understand you, but that doesn't stop you saying "I love you," does it? You say "I love you" because you enjoy the giving and receiving of emotion the words bring. You don't wait until you are sure your child can understand the meaning of those words. Using the word "adoption" in a context such as, "The day we adopted you was the happiest day of our lives," makes the word a comfortable part of your family's vocabulary for when the time comes that the words are understood. And your child will know, even before the word "adoption" has any meaning, that it must be a "good" word, because mom and dad are always smiling when they say it.

That does not mean you have to volunteer that your child is adopted to everyone you meet. Not at all. A lot of family information stays private, whether your child came to you via conception or adoption. But you do want your child to know you are comfortable with, and proud of, your family's adoption story, to be shared at appropriate times.

Learning about adoption is a gradual process, like many things we need to teach our children about, such as "the birds and the bees" and "stranger danger." We don't sit down our babies or toddlers and give them a detailed lecture on those subjects. Neither do you do so when discussing adoption. Instead, you slowly lay the groundwork, and give information as your child is mature enough to understand it.

When you are adopting an older child, either in a domestic or intercountry adoption, they will enter your home knowing they are adopted. In these cases, the focus is on why you have brought them into your home, and that you are going to be their parent forever. Many older children come from disrupted families, often filled with unreliable— sometimes even abusive—parents. Even if they were raised in foster care, they may have been moved often, making it more difficult to form normal attachments. For these older children the simple passage of time, and trust in you through good times and bad, are key elements in these children understanding and accepting the true permanence of an adoptive placement. (This issue will be discussed in more detail in chapters focused on adopting "waiting" children.)

Regardless whether you are adopting a newborn or older child, it will be helpful to your child to know of other adoptive parents and adopted children, to be aware there are millions of other people out there who entered their family in just the same way. Some of these people will be your friends and neighbors, or people in your community like your dentist or minister. It can also be some of the many public personalities, such as adoptive parents Steven Spielberg (director), Magic Johnson (basketball player), and actors like Tom Cruise, Nicole Kidman, Brad Pitt and Angelina Jolie, who are all very public about their adoptions.

Famous adoptees (adopted persons) include Aristotle (philosopher), Charles Dickens (writer), Edgar Allen Poe (writer), Faith Hill (country singer), George Washington Carver (inventor) and Mark Twain (writer). And why stop there? The Bible tells us Moses was adopted, not to mention Jesus (born to Mary but not conceived by Joseph and Mary—raising God's child as their own).

The comics give us Superman, a superhero adopted by his Earth family. Even two U.S. presidents were adopted via stepparent adoption (William Clinton and Gerald Ford).

This knowledge creates the subtle message, allowing your child to think: "I'm not different. I'm like everyone else. I just entered my family differently than some, but exactly like many others.

This chapter is short, but don't think that is because these issues are not important. To the contrary, they are critical to your long-term success, and that of your family. One book can only do so much, however, and the goal of this book is to help you adopt. Issues related to emotional readiness to adopt and talking to your child about adoption are best covered by those who specialize in those fields. These subjects need, and deserve, entire books to adequately cover them. By touching upon these subjects, however, it is hoped you can see their importance, and that you will choose to explore them. A small investment into an adoption library may be the best money you will spend in your entire adoption. Visit Adoption101.com for a list of recommended adoption books in all categories (as well as a list of famous adoptees, adoptive parents and birth parents).

CHAPTER 2

THE FIFTEEN—YES, *FIFTEEN!*—TYPES OF ADOPTION

The normal approach in teaching you about adoption would be to start off by giving you a detailed outline of how each major type of adoption works: independent, agency (including adoption *exchanges* for waiting children) and intercountry. The problem with that approach is it encourages you to only learn more about the type you have already decided is right for you, rather than learning there are other options which might be just as good, or even better. So the following overview is to tempt you to expand your horizons, and with it, your chances of success.

The exciting news is that wherever you live—a small town in Alaska with no adoptive placement options, an east coast state where independent adoption is not permitted, or a region with no qualified adoption attorneys or agencies—it makes no difference. You are not limited by your city, county, or even state. Your only limitation will be how open you are to explore new options that may be different from your initial concept of how adoptive matches are made.

Of the fifteen sub-types of adoption, eleven involve domestic (American-born) children and four are intercountry. Before we review these sub-types, however, it will be helpful to have a basic adoption vocabulary.

Domestic adoption: Adopting a child born in the United States.

12

Intercountry adoption: Adopting a non-American citizen, usually parentless and living in an orphanage-type situation.

Birth mother: The biological mother of the child being placed for adoption.

Birth father: The biological father of the child being placed for adoption.

Birth family: A general term referring to all biological relatives of the child, such as the birth parents, siblings, grandparents, et cetera.

Adoptive parents: The parents who will be adopting the child and becoming the child's legal and permanent parents.

Adoptee: The child being adopted.

Networking: The outreach effort to find women with unplanned pregnancies who might be considering adoption, and in turn have them consider you as adoptive parents. You can network on your own following the suggestions in this book, or rely upon your adoption attorney or agency to do it based on their special relationships with healthcare professionals and others, leading to referrals.

Interstate Adoption: Many adoptions "cross" state lines, where the child was born in one state, but is being removed to be adopted in a different state. This is very common, but requires compliance with the Interstate Compact for the Placement of Children (the ICPC). Each state requires certain forms be completed, and a home study done, prior to approving the child being taken out of the child's home state for purposes of adoption.

Independent adoption: An adoption typically overseen by an attorney, and who in many cases helped "match" you with a birth mother, then doing the legal work required thereafter. Virtually all independent adoptions involve only newborns.

Private adoption agency: Private agencies can elect to serve the general public, or a selected group (usually based upon religious affiliation). They can help match you with a birth mother and perform your home study, as well as other functions. Many private agencies handle both newborn adoptions, as well as being certified as foster family agencies, where they assist in the placement of waiting children presently in foster care.

Public adoption agency: Virtually every county in the nation has a governmentally operated adoption agency. Although most county adoption agencies handle some newborn adoptions, they have the primary duty of finding homes for waiting children, virtually all of them dependents of the court due to their removal from their biological parents who were unable to care for them. Usually the agency's services to adoptive parents are free, or at a very minimal cost, to encourage the adoption of the waiting children presently under the county's supervision in foster care.

Exchanges: Each state has a program to find homes for the children in foster care awaiting adoptive homes. These are called adoption *exchanges.* There are also adoption exchanges which cover multiple states, and there is one nationwide exchange.

Waiting children: Most of the children immediately available for adoption are those already born but with no available adoptive home. These are the "waiting children" of the American foster care system. Many of these children are already legally freed by the court for adoption.

Okay, you've got the basic lingo. Let's take a quick look at the fifteen types of adoption. Thereafter, we have an entire book together to look at them in more detail, analyze the pros and cons, determine which methods are right for you, and map out a strategy for a quick, safe, economical and ethical adoption.

Independent Adoption via an Attorney Located in Your Home State

You select an attorney located in your home state. He or she helps match you with a birth mother by showing your photo-resume to women contacting his/her office, or supervises your networking efforts, then does the legal work thereafter all the way through finalization of the adoption in court.

Your home study is done by an agency, social worker or state adoption office, depending upon the regulations of your state. (All states permit independent adoption except: Colorado, Connecticut, Delaware, Massachusetts and North Dakota.) In Chapter 3 we will be exploring independent adoption in great detail. Chapter 15 provides a state-by-state review, detailing the exact laws and procedures governing independent adoption in your state.

This is a great method if:

- Your state has a large enough population base resulting in a sufficient number of birth mothers making adoptive placements. (And if not, the attorney might use out-of-state networking efforts.)
- The qualities you possess as adoptive parents are those local birth mothers will find appropriate for their expected child. (For example, if you are Catholic and live in a state like Utah, with a predominately Mormon population, the birth mothers will most likely be Mormon, and less likely to pick you as non-Mormon.)
- Your region or state has attorneys who are well qualified and with reasonable fees.
- Your state's laws are fair to adoptive parents and not unduly restrictive.
- You are seeking to adopt a newborn.

Independent Adoption via an Attorney Located Outside Your Home State (An "Out-of-State" Adoption)

Instead of hiring an attorney who is located within your home state, you select one out-of-state. This could be in a neighboring state, or across the country. This attorney will usually be networking in his or her state for birth mothers, with the baby generally born in the attorney's state.

Does this mean you have to stay six or eight months out of state with the baby until the adoption is completed? Not at all. When the child is born, after the necessary interstate approval, you return home with the baby, later finalizing the adoption in your home state's court. You would be using a second attorney (a local one in your region), for the legal aspects of the adoption in your home state, as primarily your home state's laws will apply. In addition to the more detailed information about out-of-state independent adoption in Chapter 3, the state-by-state review in Chapter 15 gives each state's unique laws and procedures, allowing you to learn about the laws and procedures in other states to determine the most advantageous ones in which to possibly start your adoption.

This is a great method if:

- There are not sufficient birth mothers in your state, perhaps due to a low population, or adoption is not a promoted or popular option.
- You live in a state that you feel is over-represented with waiting adoptive parents compared to the placements available.
- There are not enough well-qualified attorneys in your state in helping to create adoptive matches.
- You wish to adopt within your ethnic or religion, but believe there are few birth mothers to select you in those groups.
- Your state might be satisfactory, but you want to expand your options by including efforts in additional states.
- You don't mind traveling out of state, typically one or more times (to meet the birth mother, and later for the birth).
- You are seeking to adopt a newborn.

Independent "Non-Resident" Adoption

This is one of the most important types of adoption, and one of the least known. As with the above type of adoption, it involves hiring an attorney in a different state from your own. However, instead of finalizing the adoption under your own state laws and in your local court, *you complete virtually the entire adoption in the attorney's state, where the child was born, under that state's laws.*

As with out-of-state adoption, discussed above, you can bring the child back to your home state after birth and reside there. Although most courts do have the requirement that the adoptive parents and child appear at the final hearing, many courts will waive this obligation if the adoptive parents live out-of-state and will permit your appearance by phone or just by your attorney.

Since about everything is done according to the laws of the state of birth, you often won't need an attorney in your home state as with out-of-state adoption. The only service usually needed in your home state would be a local agency doing your home study, and reporting that you are caring for your child properly.

About half the states in the country permit non-residents to adopt in their state, only requiring that the baby be born there. These states are: Alabama, Alaska, California, Hawaii, Iowa, Indiana, Kansas, Maine, Maryland, Michigan, Missouri, New Hampshire, New Jersey, New Mexico, New York, North Dakota, Ohio, Pennsylvania, South Carolina, Texas, Utah, Virginia, Washington and the District of Columbia. Chapter 3 provides more information about this critically important type of adoption, and the state-by-state review in Chapter 15 details the laws of the above 24 states which permit non-resident adoption.

This kind of adoption is ideal for adoptive parents for the same reasons as those listed above regarding "out-of-state adoptions," as well as the following:

- The laws of a particular state are attractive to you, as the birth state's laws will almost exclusively apply when you are also finalizing there.

- Adoption costs in your state are extremely high, and some of them can be reduced or avoided by completing the adoption in another state.
- Your state's adoption laws are unfair toward adoptive parents (such as giving the birth mother too long to change her mind and reclaim a child), which can be avoided by an out-of-state birth.
- You don't mind traveling out of state, as you will normally travel to meet the birth mother for your initial meeting, as well as return for the birth.
- You are seeking to adopt a newborn.

Private Adoption Agencies Located in the Adoptive Parent's Home State

This is one of the most popular types of newborn adoption in the country. You select a private adoption agency located in your home state. The agency will help match you with a birth mother, or supervise your efforts to do so, do your home study, take the birth mother's relinquishment and write a report for the court recommending the granting of the adoption.

The agency will either have an in-house attorney do the legal work needed through finalization in court, or most likely, refer you to a local attorney to do so. This method is very similar to an independent adoption via an attorney in your home state, except you are selecting an agency, rather than an attorney, to be the primary entity. Chapter 5 explores the dynamics of an in-state agency adoption. Chapter 15 reviews the laws governing agency adoption in each state.

This is a great method if:

- Your state has agencies that are well-qualified, reasonably priced, and you meet their eligibility requirements.
- Your state has a large enough population base in your region resulting in sufficient birth mothers making adoptive placements (assuming you are seeking a newborn).

- The characteristics you present as adoptive parents are those which local birth mothers will find appropriate for their expected child, such as religion and ethnicity.
- Your state's laws are fair to adoptive parents and not unduly restrictive.
- You are seeking to adopt a newborn (although most private agencies also do placements of waiting children).

Private Adoption Agencies Located Outside the Adoptive Parent's Home State

Instead of hiring an agency located within your home state, you can select one out-of-state, either in a neighboring state, or thousands of miles away. This is very similar to an independent out-of-state adoption, except you are retaining an agency rather than an attorney. The agency will usually be networking in its state for birth mothers, meaning the baby will likely be born in the agency's state.

The out-of-state agency will also usually be responsible for taking the birth mother's relinquishment. You can bring the child home shortly after birth, process the adoption primarily under your home state's laws, and finalize it in your local court.

You will retain a second adoption agency, this one in your home state, to do your home study and prepare the final report to the court recommending the adoption. In this type of adoption, you are finalizing the adoption under your home state's laws, despite the child being born in another state. Chapter 5 gives more details about how out-of-state agency adoption works. Chapter 15 explains the laws within those states.

This is a great method if:

- There are not sufficient birth mothers in your state, perhaps due to a low population, or adoption is not a promoted or popular option.
- You live in a state that you feel is over-represented with waiting adoptive parents compared to the placements available.

- You are not pleased with the qualifications or fees of agencies in your state regarding the costs and services in helping to match you to a birth mother.
- You belong to an ethnic or religious group and want to adopt a child matching your characteristics, but they are under- represented in your state, meaning few birth mothers to select you.
- Your state's adoption laws are unfair toward adoptive parents.
- Your state might be satisfactory, but you want to expand your options by including efforts in additional states.
- You are seeking to adopt a newborn (waiting children will be available as well, but as will be seen, they can be viewed and considered via your in-state agency).

Private Agency "Non-Resident" Adoption

Just as non-resident adoption can be done with attorneys, it can also be done via adoption agencies. You retain a private adoption agency located in another state, and finalize the adoption there, under that state's laws, where the child was born or the agency having custody of the child is located.

It is not required that you stay in the child's birth state during the entire adoption. Instead, after interstate approval, you can return home with your child until it is time to finalize the adoption, when you normally return to the birth state (or ask that your court appearance be waived due to the distance, and in most states this is granted).

Usually the only services required within your state will be a home study by a local agency or social worker and their supervising of the placement between birth and finalization.

Thirty-one states and the District of Columbia permit non- residents to adopt in their state in an agency adoption, a few more than in independent adoption. These states are: Alabama, Alaska, Arkansas, California, Colorado, Delaware, District of Columbia, Hawaii, Iowa, Illinois, Indiana, Kansas, Louisiana, Maine, Maryland, Massachusetts, Michigan, Missouri, New Hampshire, New Jersey, New Mexico, New

York, North Dakota, Ohio, Oregon, Pennsylvania, South Carolina, Texas, Utah, Vermont, Virginia and Washington.

There are actually more than 31 states permitting non-resident adoption when done by agencies, if the agency has *legal custody* of the child, as opposed to the child simply being born in their state. Chapter 5 gives more information on this popular type of adoption and the state-by-state review in Chapter 15 provides the laws and procedures of each of the above states.

This kind of adoption is ideal for adoptive parents for the same reasons as those listed above for out-of-state adoptions, as well as the following:

- The laws of a particular state are attractive to you, as the birth state's laws will almost exclusively apply when you are also finalizing there.

- Adoption costs in your state are extremely high, and you wish to reduce or avoid some of them by completing the adoption in another state.

Public/County Adoption Agencies

Almost every county in each state has a public adoption agency to serve both the children and adoptive parents in their region. This "public" or "county" agency is primarily supported by taxes, and their services to adoptive parents are either free, or virtually free. Although sometimes newborns are available via this method, in most cases the county adoption office has the imposing duty of finding homes for the waiting children in their care. Many of these children have been involuntarily freed through the courts due to inappropriate parenting, including neglect, abandonment and abuse.

There are also occasionally healthy newborn placements. These usually come about when a woman gives birth with no desire to parent and has made no advance adoption planning with an adoption attorney and agency, so the hospital calls the county agency. (Those "last minute" adoption situations also occur in independent and private agency adoptions.) For more information about adopting through your local public agency please refer to Chapter 5.

Adopting via your county agency means you can also be part of the adoption exchanges (discussed momentarily), which is the huge benefit of this type of adoption. (Some private agencies also work with adoption exchanges.)

This is a great type of adoption if:

- You like the procedures of your local county adoption agency, as there will be only one "public" option in your county. Some are excellent while some are overly bureaucratic. (You can't "shop" for a public agency outside your county and go to the county "next door" like you can with private agencies.)
- You are looking for a free adoption, or one which has very minimal costs.
- You are seeking an older child, a sibling group, a child with special-needs and/or a child of an ethnic minority, as many, but not all, children will be in one of these groups.
- You are interested in receiving a monthly stipend to help you raise your child (often available with children having some sort of special-need, but this might only be their age or being part of a sibling group).
- You possess the emotional qualities necessary to provide the extra nurturing a child from a disrupted family will require if you are adopting a waiting child.
- You are open to a child who has been exposed to drugs during the pregnancy. (Only some, not all, fall into this category—and be aware this issue can arise in independent or private agency adoptions as well, just normally not as often.)
- Your income is limited and other adoption options are outside your needs.

Adoption Exchanges

In addition to each county serving their own local children, there are state and regional adoption exchanges, as well as one national one. They list waiting and special-needs children in an effort to find homes. Best of all, if this adoption route is right for you, it is basically a *guaranteed way to adopt*. Not only that, but do it quickly, and at no cost.

In an effort to find the best homes for these waiting children, some exchanges welcome adoptive parents from any state, not just the state in which the child is located. For example, this would allow a Texas child to be matched with the perfect family who lives in New York. (As will be discussed more in Chapter 5, however, the system does not always work as well as it should in interstate situations.) Although it is true that most of the children served by exchanges have been deemed to have special needs of some type, it may not always be a physical or mental challenge, as you may initially imagine when hearing the term "special needs."

Some of the children have received that designation for no reason other than their age being past the toddler years, being part of a sibling group to be adopted together, or being of an ethnic group for which there are not enough adoptive parents. This is one of the most viable adoption programs, serving both you, and the waiting children, yet it is ignored by most adoptive parents without giving it a chance.

Yes, some adoptive parents can only imagine themselves with a newborn, but there are many adoptive parents who will be perfectly content to skip over those challenging first two years of babyhood. There are countless rewards in those early years, but also countless sacrifices. And although many fear adopting a waiting child means a child with "problems," this option should not be so quickly dismissed.

A very sensible and persuasive argument is that when adopting a waiting child, *you know who they are*. What does that mean? Well, consider this . . . You first learn all about them. Then, you meet them. You get to know them. They stay with you to be sure the fit is right before moving forward and eventually adopting. So, you *know* the person you are adopting. Are they quiet or loud, healthy or sick, intellectual or an athlete, an introvert or an extrovert, prefer to read or to play in the dirt . . .

Compare this to when you conceive a child yourselves or adopt a newborn. The reality is like all parents, you cross your fingers and hope all will be fine with your child (emotionally, physically, intellectually), which you may not know for many years. But when adopting a waiting child, much of their personality is already formed for you to see. To repeat, *you know who they are*.

Think of all the people who spend $40,000 or more to adopt a waiting child overseas via intercountry adoption, a child who has likely faced some of the same family disruption as a child here in America and presently in foster care. (There is virtually no such thing as a newborn adoption when adopting via intercountry adoption—although China does have placements of children under age two—most foreign countries now place children well past toddler years or only with special-needs.)

But for some reason, many American families prefer intercountry adoption despite the fact that similar adoptive placements exist right in their own country (with none of the worries about a child learning a new language, adjusting to a new culture, and the complicated and expensive bureaucracy of intercountry adoption). Often this is because they didn't know the true nature of intercountry adoption and the domestic exchanges before committing to intercountry adoption.

As discussed in more detail in Chapter 5, each state has its own adoption exchange. There are also regional exchanges and one national exchange. Generally, the exchanges charge no fees. Most exchanges have photo-listings so you can see the actual children available online right from your home. In fact, you could do it right now if you want. Each state exchange website is listed in the state-by-state review in Chapter 15 (although not every state lists their exchange and you have to navigate through the state adoption website first). Some states allow online viewing by anyone, and some permit it only after starting to work with an adoption agency. The national and regional exchanges, and their phone numbers and websites, are listed in Appendix A.

Be aware that not all children are viewable, however, rather only a small number. To see all the children, you must work through an agency. This is because some children have not yet had the court grant permission to post their photos online.

This kind of adoption is ideal for the same reasons as those listed for public/county adoptions, as well as the following:

- You want a virtually guaranteed way that you can successfully adopt.
- You don't mind traveling several times to another region or state to meet, and slowly bond with, a possible child, if you elect to work with a child outside your county or state.

The Foster Parent Short-Cut

In the above two types of adoption (local county agencies and exchanges), the children are often legally free for adoption when they are shown to you. This also means they were either relinquished at birth, or the child is older and has been waiting in foster care for an adoptive home.

You can sometimes get to the "front of the adoptive parent line" by being a foster parent, caring for a child who may not yet legally be free for adoption. This often means the birth parents still have their parental rights yet have been denied custody, and it is believed the child is destined for adoptive placement.

For example, the birth mother may have abandoned the baby in the hospital, or been under the influence of drugs at the time of birth, requiring the county agency to step in and take care of the child. If the birth mom wasn't then ready to give up her parental rights, the court will give the birth parents a limited time to prove they can be adequate parents and regain custody, but if they fail to do so, will terminate their parental rights. While this is happening, the child is in foster care, with a family potentially like you.

The foster parent short-cut can be emotionally risky, as only some placements starting out as foster care turn into adoptions. Some of these children will be reunified with their birth parents. Chapter 5 provides more information about fost-adopt placements.

This kind of adoption is ideal for the same reasons as those listed for public/county adoptions, as well as the following:

- You have the emotional constitution to be content with helping a child by giving him or her a loving home as a foster parent, knowing it may not turn into an adoptive placement as hoped.

- You feel you want to live with a child for an extended period and see if the family emotionally gels as you anticipate, prior to moving into adoption planning.

- You want to adopt a newborn but can't afford the cost of an independent or private agency adoption. (Most all placements via this method are waiting children, however.)

Identified Adoptions

An "identified" adoption is a hybrid between an independent and a private agency adoption. Some people call them "designated" adoptions. These are adoptions where the adoptive parents like some elements of an attorney-initiated independent adoption, but also likes the formality of an agency adoption, and combines the best elements of the two.

In the most typical identified adoption, the adoptive parents retain an attorney to help find a birth mother and do the legal work, then when a birth mother is "identified," they use a private agency to provide counseling to her, assist with her relinquishment of parental rights, conduct the adoptive parent home study, supervise the placement and write the final report to the court. (In a fully independent adoption, these functions might be done by a state adoption office. Identified adoptions refer to when a private agency is used.)

This type of adoption can be combined with other sub-types of adoption. For example, you might select an out-of-state attorney to help find a birth mother and get the adoption going, but hire an agency in your home state to do the rest and complete the adoption in your home state as an agency adoption. In so doing, you've now created a hybrid of sorts: an "identified out-of-state adoption." When you include the many hybrids possible, there are actually more than fifteen types of adoption available to you. Identified adoptions are discussed in Chapters 5.

This is a great option for you if:

- You want the flexibility of the characteristics of both independent and private agency adoption.

- You want the option to do an in-state, out-of-state adoption or non-resident adoption, determined mainly by the laws of the state where you elect to hire your adoption agency and/or attorney.
- You seek to adopt a newborn.

Facilitators

A facilitator is not so much a type of adoption as it is a method to start a newborn adoption, which can be completed as either an independent or private agency adoption. A facilitator is a person or business being paid a fee for adoption services, but which is not a licensed attorney or agency. They are the subject of a great deal of controversy.

Some consider facilitators as "infantpreneurs," profiting from the placement of children, because unlike attorneys (who do legal work, are qualified to explain the legal process to you, and make needed court appearances) and agencies (who can take relinquishments, do home studies, supervise placements and write final court reports) facilitators are not licensed to do *any* of those things. In fact, some states make it a crime to facilitate an adoption for a fee. And even if a state permits facilitators, some attorney and agencies will not work on an adoption initiated by a facilitator.

Most would agree a facilitator's primary function is to "find birth mothers" (usually via yellow page and internet ads). Those who support facilitators argue they are a viable, although often expensive, route to finding a birth mother. Also, remember that once you find a birth mother via a facilitator, you will still need to complete your adoption via either the independent or agency adoption method, and select an attorney and/or agency to assist you with those legalities, so you will have those costs as well.

Those who detest facilitators cite that many clearly attempt to mislead birth and adoptive parents by using a name which makes them sound like they are an actual adoption agency, which they are definitely not, having met none of the requirements to be an agency, and their ads often obscure the fact they are only a facilitator.

Many facilitators also have the bad reputation of making any placement, regardless if there are many red flags, as it means they get paid, while ethical attorneys and agencies might recommend to the adoptive parents to not even start the adoption. Because of this, many facilitators require you to use only their "approved" attorneys or agencies, whom the facilitator has found will not discourage the adoptive parents away from an adoption that more cautious attorneys or agencies would. (Sadly, not all attorneys or agencies are ethical and/or qualified.)

For more information about facilitators, and the potential risks in using them, please refer to Chapters 6 and 8.

This might be an option for you if:

- The state in which you are working permits facilitators and does not make their services a crime.
- You are comfortable with the facilitator's methods of networking for birth mothers.
- You understand the risk of working with an entity not licensed as an agency or attorney.
- You understand that besides paying a facilitator, you will still normally need an attorney and/or agency to complete the adoption.
- You don't mind that the facilitator is perhaps charging a fee equal to more than an agency or attorney, to do less work, and not be licensed or trained for most of the jobs that must be done.

Private Adoption Agencies with Intercountry Adoption Programs in the Adoptive Parent's Home State

Some of the private adoption agencies in your home state will offer intercountry adoption programs rather than domestic placements. A few agencies do double duty, handling both domestic and intercountry adoptions, although most intercountry agencies focus only on that specialty.

You will find that each intercountry agency normally has specific countries from which it makes adoptive placements. One agency might have a program only in China, while another might work in multiple countries, like Ethiopia and Ukraine. Hiring an in-state intercountry agency means that one entity can handle your domestic requirements such as your home study, as well as supervise the overseas portion of the adoption.

Although there are more than 1,200 agencies in the United States, only a small number are approved for intercountry adoption. Chapter 7 provides detailed information about this option.

This is a great method if:

- You want to adopt a non-newborn (most from 3-7 years of age, depending upon the country).
- You want one agency to do everything: your pre-placement home study as well as the intercountry aspects of the adoption.
- Your state has qualified intercountry agencies with programs in the country of interest to you, and you meet the eligibility requirements of the agency.
- You are comfortable adopting a child where sometimes little medical history is available.
- You are willing to travel to the child's country one to three times and stay there in total for at least several weeks (although a few countries use escorts to bring the child to you).
- You understand that your child will initially speak another language and not know English.
- You are aware that at the time of the placement your child will usually be ten percent underweight, and about two months per each year of age regressed in physical and emotional development compared to other children due to lack of sufficient stimulation and nurturing in orphanages. (Many of these children can and will quickly catch up to similarly aged children, however, if there are no other health factors causing the lack of development.)

- You understand a child raised in an orphanage or similar institutional setting may suffer from some degree of attachment disorder due to lack of prior nurturing, or bonding with a parenting figure.
- You want a "closed" adoption, as usually you will have no contact with the birth family.

Private Adoption Agencies with Intercountry Adoption Programs Outside the Adoptive Parent's Home State

As with domestic adoption, you might find that the agency with the best program, working in the country from which you want to adopt, is located in another state. No problem. In fact, this is very common, especially in intercountry adoption. The out-of-state agency will handle the intercountry aspects of your adoption (which is the critical part of an intercountry adoption), and will ask an agency in your local region to do the required pre-placement home study and post-placement supervision (if required by the foreign country). For more information on out-of-state agency intercountry adoption, please refer to Chapter 7.

The factors favoring this kind of adoption are the same as those listed above for private intercountry agencies within your state, with these additional considerations:

- You feel there are no qualified intercountry agencies in your home state with programs in the countries of interest to you, or you don't meet their eligibility requirements.
- You don't mind working with two agencies: one to do your pre-placement home study, and one to handle the intercountry aspects of the adoption.

Adoption Attorneys with Intercountry Adoption Programs in the Adoptive Parent's Home State

Most all intercountry adoption programs are operated via private adoption agencies. Still, there are some attorneys who operate intercountry programs. To some degree, every intercountry adoption is an "agency adoption," as each country requires a pre-placement agency home study, and most require a few post-placement visits as well.

When we talk about intercountry adoption programs, however, we are talking about much more than locating a child, such as: satisfying our federal laws governing intercountry adoption and immigration, preparing a dossier to present overseas, having translators and drivers in the child's country to guide you during your visit, and much more. It could be argued that attorneys can do some aspects of the process as well, or better, than agencies, such as the legal and immigration aspects. For more information on intercountry adoption please refer to Chapter 7, and the attorney biographies in the state-by-state review, which list which attorneys practice intercountry adoption.

The factors favoring this kind of adoption are the same as those listed above for private agencies within your state, with the addition of the following:

- You will be working with two entities: a local agency to do your pre-placement home study and any post-placement reports, and the attorney for the intercountry aspects of the adoption.

Adoption Attorneys with Intercountry Adoption Programs Outside the Adoptive Parent's Home State

You might like the idea of working with an attorney outside your home state if he or she has an excellent intercountry program in the country you prefer. This is usually no problem. You will need an agency in your local region to do the required home study, but the out-of-country work required in the intercountry program can be done equally well whether you select someone in, or out of, your home state. After all, most of the work in the adoption will likely be occurring 6,000-10,000 miles away, in the child's country, so having an attorney in another state is usually not a big factor.

The factors favoring this kind of adoption are the same as those listed above for out-of-state intercountry and in-state attorney intercountry adoption. Chapter 7 provides more information.

*　　*　　*　　*　　*

So, there you have it . . . fifteen distinct types of adoption—more actually—when you count the many possible hybrids. And we've only touched the tip of the proverbial iceberg in learning about them. As you can see, there are many, many doors open to you. To find the right door, however, we need to explore each method in depth.

We will be doing that by devoting individual chapters not only into independent, agency and intercountry adoption, but additional chapters describing how to find the right attorney or agency. So much time is spent on this issue because success in adoption means not only finding the right method to accomplish your personal goals in adoption, but also the right professional to help you make that method successfully work for you.

CHAPTER 3

INDEPENDENT ADOPTION

Independent adoption is also referred to as *private, direct* or *open* adoption. How popular a method is it to adopt a newborn? Statistics are tricky because the federal government, and most states, only keep records of placements made through public or private agencies. In some states which do keep records (such as California), the vast majority of newborn adoptions are via independent adoption. But other states show private agencies as the most popular route.

Which is actually more popular is not really important. What is important is selecting the method in which you feel most comfortable.

Why independent adoption is popular with both birth mothers and adoptive parents can be seen in its characteristics. In some ways, it is very similar to private agency adoption, but in others it is distinctly different. The most popular elements of an independent adoption are:

- Almost all adoptions involve newborns.
- A pre-placement home study is not required in all states.
- There are usually no formal eligibility requirements.
- There is less bureaucracy.
- A match can sometimes be made faster than via agencies because attorneys generally network more aggressively for birth mothers

(although there are a small number of states which do not permit attorneys to help match birth mothers with adoptive parents).

Forty-five states permit independent adoption, while five require all adoptions to be done via only the agency method. Those states are: Colorado, Connecticut, Delaware, Massachusetts and North Dakota. (Note these states still have many adoption attorneys in them, as their services are still needed, even in agency adoptions.)

Here are the basic steps in an independent adoption:

1. Retain an adoption attorney (preferably one who has their own outreach program to find birth mothers to create adoptive matches and/or who has experience advising adoptive parents on the networking strategies for you to employ on your own).

2. Wait for the attorney to create an adoptive match for you (or find a match through your own networking efforts, supervised by the attorney).

3. Have your attorney screen the birth mother to be sure it looks like a safe placement, and examine the case for potential legal problems.

4. Have a pre-placement home study done if one is required by your state. Your state law may provide that the home study be done by a social worker, adoption agency or state adoption office. Most states require you to have the home study in place when the child is placed with you, but some states only require it after placement, before final court approval granting the adoption. See Chapter 15's state-by-state review.

5. Get to know your birth mother personally so she has confidence in you, and you in her.

6. Help her with medical and other pregnancy-related expenses, assuming she has any, if permitted by your state.

7. Be present at the hospital to share the birth experience.

8. Bring home the baby from the hospital.

9. The birth mother consents to the adoption (a small number of states require this before the child is released to you from the hospital, but most take the consent after hospital discharge).

10. The birth father consents to the adoption, waives notice, or has his rights terminated because he can't be found or fails to object. (Some states permit this to be done pre-birth.)
11. Do your post-placement visits to supervise the placement (usually two visits in six months in most states).
12. Have your attorney complete all necessary documents and satisfy all legal obstacles to make sure the child is fully free for adoption.
13. Go to court to finalize your adoption.
14. Receive a new birth certificate naming you as the child's biological parents, as if you gave birth to him or her, and naming the child as you've chosen, regardless of the name given on the original birth certificate.

There are a lot of choices in how you do an independent adoption. That, in fact, is one reason for its popularity. The fact it is flexible, however, does not mean it is simple. To the contrary, there are many potential false steps in every adoption. Becoming aware of independent adoption's ins and outs and how to best use its flexibility to serve your goals is an important step to achieving success.

Eligibility Requirements

Asking what the requirements are for independent adoption is a bit of a misnomer. Why? Because there usually are no requirements. The restrictions commonly seen in some agency adoptions, such as your age, marital history, sexual orientation, religion, financial status, number of children and proof of infertility, have little relevance in independent adoption. This is because there are usually no agency or governmental guidelines which must be satisfied.

Instead, the birth mother personally selects the adoptive parents based upon factors she deems important. If she elects to choose a single woman as the adoptive parent, fine. If she wants to choose adoptive parents where both are over fifty years of age, fine. If she chooses an adoptive family where the adopting father is Caucasian and Jewish with two children from a prior marriage, and the adoptive mother is African-American, Catholic and restricted to a wheelchair, fine. And the same regarding same sex couples. It's like choosing a spouse; everyone is attracted to different kind of people. (A bonus flowing from the long-time flexibility of independent adoption is that it has forced the agency adoption world to reevaluate their guidelines, and now many agencies are much more flexible.)

Does this mean anyone can adopt via independent adoption? No. You still have to be approved via a home study pursuant to the state's guidelines, but the state requirements will almost always be very basic, generally establishing two things: 1) your present and past life indicates you can and will be good parents (including fingerprinting to confirm no improper issues in your past); and 2) you were honest in telling the birth mother about yourself, so she can make an informed consent about who is adopting her baby. We will discuss the home study in more detail shortly.

The Role of the Adoption Attorney

An attorney . . . do you need one? And if you do, does it have to be an adoption specialist? That's up to you. Technically, you can do an independent adoption without an attorney, just like you could try to do any type of legal action on your own, whether it be a divorce or forming a corporation. You could find your own birth mother, make sure there are no legal obstacles or risks (and solve them if there are), do all the routine legal work required, select a proper agency or social worker as required in your state to do your home study, prepare your final documents and finalize your adoption in court. Yes, it's possible, but do you want to try? The creation of your family is on the line. Legal issues in adoption are actually incredibly complex.

Some adoptive parents think of adoption attorneys only as a route to be introduced to a birth mother to select them as adoptive parents. That is *one* valid reason for selecting one. Sometimes, however, finding a birth mother is the easiest part of your adoption. The real work is in screening potential adoptions, looking for legal risks (outlined in Chapter 12), noting red flags indicating risks beyond legal issues (Chapter 10) and doing the legal work needed in the adoption. By the time you've finished this book you will see how much analysis and work goes into each adoption, and why the chances of your adoption being successful increase dramatically with a qualified adoption attorney at the helm.

As you learn more about independent adoption, you will see it is the adoption attorney who makes things happen in an adoption, and helps make them happen when and how they are supposed to. Because finding the right attorney is so important, Chapter 4 details forty-four individual steps and inquiries leading to finding the right attorney to best serve your unique needs.

The Home Study

The home study required in an independent adoption is usually considered less intrusive and time-consuming than in a typical agency adoption. Here's why. In agency adoptions, there are always two stages in a home study: pre-placement (before a child is placed with you), and post-placement (after a child is placed with you). In independent adoptions, however, approximately half the states do not require a pre-placement home study. The state-by-state review tells you which states waive this requirement. By comparison, a few states require the pre-placement home study, but do not require any post-placement supervision at all, allowing finalization within weeks. (This is rare, but it does demonstrate how different each state can be.) These states are Hawaii, Mississippi and Wyoming.

The fact that no home study is often required before a child is placed with you, and only occurs post-placement, might sound quite odd. The rationale behind it makes sense, however. In an agency adoption, the birth mother is technically placing her child with the agency, and the agency uses its judgment to place that child with selected adoptive parents. Whether or not the birth mother had a role in selecting the adoptive parents, it was the agency that officially made the placement, making the agency legally responsible. To protect itself (and the state which licenses it) from that liability, a home study is their safeguard.

In independent adoptions, it is usually the birth mother who is personally—and legally—making the placement, based upon her judgment of the adoptive parents, not those of an intermediary agency. Even if she perhaps met the adoptive parents through an attorney, as is typical in independent adoption, it is the birth mother who is the "placing person." Not an agency. Not the attorney. Because a third party (the agency) isn't legally placing the child, rather the birth mother is doing it herself, many states feel a pre-placement home study need not be required, just as the birth mother could choose a long-term babysitter without state intervention. Except for the rare exceptions made by the three states mentioned above, other states always require the post-placement supervision and investigation by an agency.

As a practical matter, it is very, very rare for adoptive parents in an independent adoption to be denied due to their home study. Virtually all adoptive parents know from the beginning what their home study will entail for them, and don't attempt to start a process they know will not be approved. Plus, it also helps that the standard is very basic, simply showing that nothing indicates you will not be a secure and loving parent, and you were honest in describing your life situation to the birth mother, without the sometimes subjective approval of a private agency.

Each state has different regulations and procedures regarding who may perform an independent adoption home study. In some states a special state adoption office, usually a division of its Social Services office, has been staffed to perform all independent adoption home studies. Other states allow private agencies, social workers, or people approved by the court to perform it.

Home study fees vary. If a pre-placement home study is required, the cost may range from state to state between $500 and $3,000 and usually takes three to twelve weeks to complete once started. The post-placement is more lengthy (usually six months) and frequently costs $1,000 to $7,000. Most fall in the middle. (Agency fees will usually be higher if it is a full agency adoption and it is the agency, not the attorney or the adoptive parents, doing the networking and creating the adoptive match. But now we are discussing the agency's role in an independent adoption.)

A typical independent adoption home study will include the following:

- Your completion of forms describing your life history (health, employment, marital history, existence of other children, religion, age, religion, et cetera.). Unlike a private agency, however, which may exclude you based upon your answers, the independent adoption home study entity is simply collecting the information to provide to the court, and share with the birth mother when appropriate.

- You will be fingerprinted for a criminal and child abuse check.
- A basic physical, usually with your personal physician. (If you have a physical impairment, or one spouse has a reduced life expectancy, this will not necessarily disqualify you in an independent adoption, but is a fact which will usually need to be shared with the birth mother.)
- Several letters of reference from friends/neighbors, whom you select.
- Verification of marriage (if married).
- Verification of the existence of health insurance, or a plan to deal with medical costs if you don't have insurance.
- Verification of employment. (The issue is simply that you can meet your family's needs, not reach a designated high income level.)
- Proof that any prior marriages were terminated by a court of law (via a certified copy of the divorce decree).
- Verification of assets and facts regarding any past bankruptcies. (The only concern here is if you show an inability to properly manage your resources, which could therefore put your family at financial risk. A prior bankruptcy, followed by financial stability, would rarely be seen to demonstrate financial instability.)
- Inspecting your home. Unlike becoming a foster parent, or even an adoptive parent in an agency adoption, an independent adoption home study in most states will usually not need to meet the same safety levels imposed upon foster or agency adoptive parents. The reason traces back to the rational that in those placements the agency is usually liable for any injuries to the child which might result from an accident. In independent adoptions, the birth mother is making the placement directly, usually without an intermediary taking over her role as the "placing person." For example, in a foster parent home study, the agency might require the adoptive parents to have latches on all toilets and cabinets, even if the child to be placed is, at present, a baby and unable to move from his or her crib. In an independent

adoption, many states will only require that the adoptive parents make changes which are necessary for the child's safety at the present time, and simply recommend alterations to be considered when needed as the child grows. This is closer to the decision-making adoptive parents have the freedom to make when conceiving a child themselves.

And when the child is born, these additional functions:

- Home visits by your social worker. Most states require between two and three visits, usually over a six-month period. If a pre-placement home study is required, both adoptive parents must usually be present at home at the same time. In the post-placement supervision period, both adoptive parents and the child are usually expected to be present. In almost all cases these visits are by appointment, not "surprise" visits.
- Reports from your child's pediatrician that you have been properly caring for the child.

The Children Available

Virtually all children available through independent adoption are newborns. They are of all ethnic groups, typically mirroring the ethnicity of the community in which the birth mother's live. If you live in a region which is mainly Caucasian, most birth mothers will be Caucasian, meaning Caucasian placements. If your region is predominantly Hispanic, expect most of the placements to be Hispanic.

It is understandable why so many adoptive parents select independent adoption as their chosen method of adoption, but why do so many birth mothers do so? There are several reasons. Some birth mothers may feel a stigma about approaching an adoption agency and feel better about contacting a private attorney. (This stigma is unfair to most agencies, as the majority are staffed by non-judgmental, caring people, but sadly the stigma still exists in the minds of some birth mothers.) Also, adoption attorneys are often more aggressive in their networking efforts to reach birth mothers, resulting in more referrals. Lastly, independent adoption has the reputation of being more open and direct, which is pleasing to most birth mothers.

What about drug usage by the birth mother? Many say that drug usage by birth mothers in independent adoption and private agency adoption is rare, but common in public agency adoptions. This statement is not entirely true. Sadly, drug usage has permeated society, and in particular, some of the women who are most likely to place a child for adoption. Namely, this is low income women living "on the edge," which is exactly why they recognize they can't parent and choose adoption.

It is true that there are more babies born with drug exposure in public agency adoptions as it is the county agency's job to be available for such situations (such as when a child is held at the hospital due to a positive drug screen when there is no existing adoption plan in place). But any adoption attorney or private agency that tells you there are absolutely no drug-exposed births in independent adoption is not being honest, or is tremendously inexperienced. Overall, however, you will find drug issues in newborn adoption arising less in independent and private agency. Drug usage is discussed more in Chapter 10, as well as some encouraging information about why fears over drug exposure are often greatly exaggerated.

Waiting for a Child

There is no absolute guarantee of adopting quickly, even in an independent adoption. For some lucky couples the waiting time can be only a few weeks or months (and we will be talking in this book about how to maximize your chances to be one of them). One reason for this quick success is that there are usually no waiting lists employed in independent adoption, where the adoptive parents must wait to get to the top of a list to be considered for an adoptive placement. (Notably, most private agencies have also discarded the "waiting list" philosophy and instead usually focus on giving the birth mother the widest possible selection of adoptive parents.)

Instead, most independent adoption attorneys show all their waiting adoptive parent families and leave the decision of who is the best family completely up to the birth mother (assuming the adoptive parents want to be shown to that particular birth mother). Also reducing the time for a placement is that many states do not require a pre-placement home study, allowing you to start the process instantly, rather than wait to complete a home study.

Even if you live in a state which requires a pre-placement home study for independent adoption, you can still normally start networking for, and meeting, birth mothers immediately. You would just concurrently start the pre-placement home study, as typically it must only be completed before a baby is placed with you. Even if you met a birth mother almost immediately, she will likely not be due before you could complete the home study. (Compare this to most agency adoptions where you usually cannot start working toward a birth mother match until the pre-placement home study is complete.)

As stated above, some adoptive parents do get selected by a birth mother within just months. In the author's personal experience in 31 years as an adoption attorney, and handling more than 1,000 adoptions, this does indeed happen more than just occasionally. But it is also true that some families are at the opposite spectrum of the "luck" roll of the dice, and don't get picked for one year, or two. And it's possible they will not get picked at all. Most adoptive families find success somewhere in the middle time-wise, six to eighteen months, assuming they selected the right attorney and are properly networking.

The best example is to equate it to marriage. Some people find the right spouse when they are young (a short wait) and others equally deserving of finding a spouse do not do so until they are older. And for some, it never happens at all. There is a lot of luck in success in adoption, but as in all things, people can go a long way in making their own luck by doing everything the right way from the start.

Regardless of these variables and the non-guaranteed nature of life (and adoption), people still want statistics. Accordingly, here is a helpful one from *Adoptive Families* magazine:

In a 2016 survey of their readers who completed independent adoptions in 2014-2015, the responses showed that 68% adopted within less than one year, and the majority of those were within the first six months.

Those are extremely encouraging numbers. Be aware, however, that this is the waiting time for those who actually adopted. It does not factor in those who tried but did not yet succeed. Still, the quick success time of those that did adopt is very impressive and encouraging, showing what is happening for countless families across the country.

The Openness of the Adoption

Many people think of independent and "open" adoption as being synonymous. This is confusing as *open* adoption is a vague term and can mean many things. When used to describe independent adoption, it usually refers at minimum to the fact most all adoptive parents and birth mothers meet in person (or at least by phone if they live in different states, but personal meetings are strongly recommended and are the norm), and share first, or more commonly both first and last, names. Each state has different requirements and traditions about openness. The state-by-state review in Chapter 15 tells you what to expect in each state. Western states learn toward full name disclosure and more pre-birth face-to-face contact than in some eastern or southern states.

For birth mothers, personally meeting and selecting you can be emotionally rewarding to her as she can develop complete confidence in you as adoptive parents, greatly enhancing her likelihood of placing the baby for adoption as planned. She can visualize you as the child's parents and the child being nurtured by you. She can also take pride in her active role in personally creating your family, rather than relinquishing that role to an agency.

You also benefit from becoming acquainted before the birth. You can learn more about your child's biological mother in person (and hopefully the birth father and their extended families as well), rather than reading about her from an impersonal written analysis. You will be able to share important information with your child about how the adoption occurred and why his or her birth mother felt adoption was her most loving option for the child—issues of great importance to a child as he or she grows. You might even take pictures of you and your birth mom together to one day share with your child, showing it took all of you to create your family

(and the birth father too, if he is one of those rare birth fathers who wishes to be involved in the process.)

A small number of states allow for confidentiality in independent adoption, as is done in some agency placements. Usually this is done by the use of an intermediary, such as an attorney, who will provide information about the birth mother and adoptive parents to each other, allowing each individual to withhold their identities if they so desire. This practice is rare, however, and even when states permit it, the birth mother and adoptive parents often voluntarily opt for sharing full identities.

This open relationship can continue post-birth. The overwhelming majority of post-birth arrangements call for the birth mother to receive pictures of the child and updating letters from you once or twice a year (often the child's birthday and Christmas) and a promise from you that you will be raising your child with the knowledge that he or she was placed with you out of love by their birth mother. It is not uncommon for the birth mother to give you a photo of herself, and perhaps a letter to the child describing why adoption was the best way to show her love.

Sometimes, even if you and your birth mother have become well acquainted before the birth, some birth mothers elect to have complete privacy after the birth and wish no further contact. Not all are comfortable with openness.

An equally small percentage will wish to stay in contact with you, but expand that contact to what is usually called "cooperative adoption." A less technical term would simply be "a very open adoption." This would be where you and the birth mother agree that not only will you send pictures and letters, but maintain a face-to-face relationship, perhaps getting together from one to several times a year. Some adoptive parents embrace this openness, while others feel uncomfortable. About 5% of newborn adoptions fall into this category.

Cooperative adoptions are *not* co-parenting. Not even close. For those who select it, it is closer to the situation of having a distant relative whom you see once or twice a year. (And remember, the birth parent has given up all their parental rights, you just choose to stay in contact, so there should be no fear over it.) Supporters of very open adoptions point out that a child can never have too many people love them, and with all the other people in a child's life—you as Mom and Dad, countless relatives, neighbors, teachers, et cetera—doesn't it make sense for a birth parent to have a little contact as well? (Cooperative adoptions can be done in a private agency adoption as well, not just independent.)

Talking about the issue with an adoption counselor, as well as your attorney, and reading the many books on the subject (see recommended books at Adoption101.com) will help you determine what is right for you and your child. The subject of very open adoptions is often somewhat terrifying for people new to the world of adoption. In fact, if most new adoptive parents were to be completely honest, they would say they want to adopt a baby and never have to think about the birth family again . . . that it's a "complication" they don't need. Surprisingly, though, the more adoptive parents learn about it, the more they tend to embrace it, and lose the fear they previously had.

Regardless of what you decide, the degree of openness your adoption will have should be discussed with your birth mother before the birth to be sure you all have matching expectations. To learn more about openness in adoption, The Donaldson Adoption Institute has many insightful articles on the subject, found at AdoptionInstitute.org.

Fees and Costs

There are several areas of possible expenses in an independent adoption. The major ones are:

- Attorney fees.
- Home study costs.
- Possible medical and pregnancy-related expenses for the birth mother.
- Travel costs for you if your birth mother is out-of-state.

An attorney is usually considered a necessity in an independent adoption as there is no adoption agency overseeing the entire process. Even if adoptive parents find their own birth mother, there are many legal issues to be addressed requiring an attorney's skill and knowledge. Although the attorney's degree of involvement will vary from case to case, thus affecting the cost of the adoption, most adoption specialists charge between $1,500 to $11,000 to handle all aspects of an uncontested, independent adoption, depending upon many factors.

For example, if both birth parents are not available to consent, perhaps the birth father was a one-night stand and unfindable (discussed in Chapter 12), then the required legal action to terminate their rights will add a few thousand in fees.

There are some attorneys who charge well over $11,000, even in an uncontested case, but be advised that this does not always mean they are better attorneys. Sometimes it means just the opposite—just as some of the most expensive cars are the least reliable—they are just glitzy. Using the recommendations of Chapter 4 will help you determine if a super high-priced attorney is indeed amazing, or one with questionable ethics who overcharges and over-promises results.

The three biggest factors in attorney fees are the extent of the services offered, their location and reputation. Attorneys in more populated cities and highly commercial states tend to have higher fees than their small town counterparts. And, of course, attorneys with established reputations and a history of success, like in any profession, are going to charge more than those lacking those qualities. Also, some attorneys expend a great deal of time and money in networking and outreach efforts to locate birth mothers, who in turn select their waiting clients. This can greatly increase the attorney's overhead costs, so expect to pay in the higher end of the fee range, or even a few thousand dollars more, if your attorney is also performing that service.

For their fee, an adoption attorney will typically do the following:

- Fully educate you on the laws and procedures in adoption, and advise you on how to plan a successful adoption.
- Use an established outreach program to find birth mothers, or advise you how to effectively do it on your own.
- Screen birth mothers to eliminate inadvisable situations.
- Help advise you on how to work with the birth mother and handle emotional issues that can arise.
- Obtain necessary background and health information about the birth parents.

- Provide physician, counseling and hospital referrals to the birth mother.
- Examine the case for potential legal or practical difficulties.
- Attempt to contact the birth father and give any legal notices required.
- Handle any legal problems that may arise, particularly complicated issues than may arise, like the Indian Child Welfare Act and the Interstate Compact (discussed in Chapter 12).
- Help the assigned social worker process the home study by providing what is needed.
- Manage an attorney-client trust account to provide expenses to the birth mother or other parties (doctors, landlord, et cetera) on behalf of the adoptive parents.
- Prepare the necessary legal documents and make sure the birth mother properly executes her consent to adoption.
- Appear in court with you to finalize the adoption.
- Make sure the correct paperwork has been done to generate an amended birth certificate for the child.

Expenses for the birth mother may exist. If she needs assistance with expenses related to the birth, such as her medical costs or her living expenses, you can usually assist her by paying some or all of those expenses. Such assistance allows a birth mother to stay in her own residence when she would otherwise be short on rent, rather than relocating to an agency-style maternity home which may not be comfortable for her. Or she may be without a place to stay and you can help get her into an apartment.

Each state has different regulations regarding what assistance may be provided and for how long. A small number of states forbid adoptive parents to provide any expenses other than medical and legal costs, not permitting help with such expenses as food and rent. Generally, however, if the expenses are pregnancy-related, they are permitted. Financial assistance can usually be provided not only during the pregnancy if she is unable to provide for herself, but also after the birth for a month or two, while she recuperates.

Of course, in some cases, there may be no pregnancy-related expenses at all. For example, if a birth mother has health insurance (perhaps through her parents' policy or her own employment) or state-provided Medicaid, there may be no medical costs for the you. It is actually very common for there to be no medical costs as most birth mothers are so poor they are either already on public assistance, or they can qualify for it, meaning they are eligible for the state Medicaid. (The fact she plans to place the child for adoption should not affect her Medicaid eligibility.)

Regarding living costs, although some birth mothers are impoverished and desperately need financial help to pay for basic food and rent during the latter stages of the pregnancy, there are many birth mothers who require absolutely nothing. They have adequate employment, receive public assistance, or live with their parents, the result being they have no expenses.

Other less substantial expenses may involve the purchase of some maternity clothes, and arranging for adoption counseling to prepare for the birth and adoption experience. These expenses usually total several hundred dollars each.

Many adoption professionals estimate the total cost of most attorney-assisted independent adoptions, including attorney fees, home study fees, medical and living expenses (if any), and every other possible cost, to range between $7,000 and $40,000. That's a big range, but costs vary in so many areas. Most fall in the middle. A birth mom might have $5,000 in medical costs, or none (most have none). She might have no living costs, or she could have $1,500 a month for five months (just as an example, most are in the middle). You might have no travel costs or spend thousands if she is out of state. Your attorney might cost $2,000 or $15,000. There are so many variables. (As discussed in Chapter 10, a birth mother with extremely high living costs might be a red flag for reasons besides the high cost itself.)

Particular expenses, as well as suggestions to reduce or eliminate such critical expenses as medical costs, will be addressed in subsequent chapters.

Bringing the Baby Home

One of the nicest parts about independent adoption is that it normally allows you to bring the baby home directly from the hospital. There is virtually never an intermediate foster parent placement while you wait for the birth mother's consent to become irrevocable, or other procedural steps to be satisfied. (The popularity of immediate placements in independent adoption has caused many private agencies to duplicate the practice of immediate placement in their adoptions.) Most states allow the birth mother to release her child directly into your physical custody immediately upon the hospital's discharge of the baby, usually when the baby is one to three days old.

A small number of states have requirements before you can take custody of the child from the hospital, such as a court order. This is rare, however, and even when it is required, it is designed to occur very quickly so as to not delay placement.

There is a great benefit to you in taking your baby home immediately. Every new parent, adoptive or otherwise, knows the early days of a child's life are precious and irreplaceable. Naturally, the child also benefits from being with you immediately as his or her future parents, rather than foster parents. But there is also a disadvantage. There is always a possibility you will bond to a child the birth mother has not yet permanently released for adoption and that she may seek to reclaim.

This is because often the child is released from the hospital before the consent to adoption is signed, as many states require a specific number of days to pass before the consent can be signed, or she has to be discharged from the hospital. (In most states, the consent is signed within just a few days of birth. The state-by-state review in Chapter 15 details the laws of each state.

Identified adoptions

An *identified* adoption (sometimes called a designated adoption) is a hybrid of an independent and an agency adoption. Sometimes adoptive parents like some aspects of an independent adoption and other aspects of an agency adoption. Combine them, and what you have is an identified adoption.

An identified adoption typically involves your selection of an adoption attorney to network for birth mothers, screen potential birth mothers, help create your adoptive match, then refer the birth mother to an agency to provide counseling, do your home study, and perhaps witness her consent if permitted by that state's laws. Depending upon the laws and procedures of your state, the attorney and agency will divide their legal duties to you. Essentially, identified adoptions start as an independent adoption, but are finalized as an agency adoption.

What is the advantage of this type of hybrid adoption? Usually it is increased speed and/or safety. Let's say for example that you think an attorney will be more effective in quickly matching you with a birth mother, and spotting potential legal risks in the adoption. This makes independent adoption attractive. But maybe you live in a state which has different procedures in how a birth mother gives up her rights in each type of adoption, and agency relinquishments are faster. You want to reduce the at-risk time you face post-birth, so you want to complete the adoption as an agency adoption. Presto, a hybrid: identified adoption. In some states, this can be a major advantage, while in most it makes no difference in terms of how quickly and safely things can be done. It will be the job of your attorney to explain if this is a benefit in your particular state.

Working with an out-of-state attorney

The majority of adoptive parents will do every aspect of the adoption in the state in which they live. This is true whether they are doing an independent or agency adoption. They will hire an attorney there, the birth mother will live and give birth there, and the adoption will be finalized in their local court. If you live in a state with great attorneys from whom to choose, good adoption laws making you feel secure, and a sufficient number of birth mothers in your region or state, why leave your own state?

Many adoptive parents aren't so lucky. What if you don't like what the local attorneys have to offer? Perhaps there are few adoptive placements in your region or state. Maybe you are concerned that your state has laws which give a birth mother an excessively long period in which to change her mind. Or could it be that your state is fine, but you want to expand your options to increase the likelihood of being picked for an adoptive placement quickly. Clearly, there are many reasons to either do your adoption out of state, or work in both your home state and another state concurrently. Let's look at the two primary ways to do this.

Interstate adoption: finalizing in your home state. Let's say you've found a highly recommended adoption attorney, but he or she is located in another state. Does that mean you can't work with that attorney because you are in a different state? No. In fact, it is getting more and more common to have an interstate aspect to your adoption. For example, you can hire the out-of-state attorney to help you find a birth mother and create your adoptive match, arrange for birth mother counseling, assist with her signing her consent to adoption, and have the child discharged directly to you from the hospital.

Then, very shortly after birth, when the initial paperwork is done and you get interstate approval to bring the child across state lines (discussed in Chapter 12), you return home. Depending upon the laws of your home state, you would have an in-state attorney and/or agency. The agency would do your home study and write the final report to the court to complete the adoption, and the attorney would do any legal work needed in your home state. Doing an adoption involving two states sometimes creates a conflict between state laws, although rarely does this become a problem. This issue is discussed in Chapter 12.

A twist on the above is if a birth mother who selects you is located out of state, but perhaps the birth mother doesn't wish to stay in that state. Perhaps she has no place to live and has recently lost her job. To get to know you better and have you close for the moment the birth occurs, you can discuss having her relocate for the birth to your home state. After the birth, she may return to her original state, relocate elsewhere, or decide she likes what your state has to offer and stay.

In an adoption such as this, your local attorney and/or agency would be performing all the needed legal functions, other than the initial act of creating the adoptive match. Depending upon the facts of your case the attorney can also determine if the Interstate Compact would apply. (Technically, it may still apply if she gave birth in your state but relocated there specifically for the adoption. Many factors are at issue. Discussed in Chapter 12.)

You might worry that using an attorney out-of-state, and another attorney or agency in your home state, would double the cost. That is not true, however. As discussed in more detail in Chapter 4 and Chapter 9, many attorneys and agencies only charge for the services they perform. Accordingly, if they are dividing their duties, their fees should be proportionally less. Not every adoption professional will work that way, but most will.

Interstate adoption: non-resident adoption. Some adoptive parents want to do virtually the entire adoption outside their home state. You might choose to do this because your state allows a birth mother a long time to change her mind and the birth state's laws only permit a few days to do so. Maybe you recognize birth mothers are more likely to start adoption planning if you are permitted to help them with their pregnancy-related costs, and your state does not permit them, but the laws of the birth state do. Or perhaps your adoption can be finalized in court much faster out-of-state. Adoptions might be extremely expensive in your state as compared to another. For these reasons, you might want to adopt from a state permitting independent non-resident adoption.

Many states permit independent non-resident adoption. They are: Alabama, Alaska, California, Hawaii, Iowa, Indiana, Kansas, Maine, Maryland, Michigan, Missouri, New Hampshire, New Jersey, New Mexico, New York, North Dakota, Ohio, Pennsylvania, South Carolina, Texas, Utah, Virginia, Washington and the District of Columbia. You can learn more about each state's laws and the attorneys and agencies within that state in the state-by state review.

A non-resident adoption is basically just like the interstate adoption discussed above. You selected an out-of-state attorney to help match you with a birth mother. That attorney, however, continues to do virtually everything in the adoption, rather than transferring everything to your home state. After creating the adoptive match, he or she can make sure the child is placed with you directly from the hospital, arrange for the birth mother to sign her consent to adoption, do the legal work and finalize your adoption in court. An agency in your home state will only be needed to do your home study and any required post-placement supervision as required by the laws of the state of where the child is born.

Although normally it is required for the adoptive parents to appear at the final court hearing, meaning the adoptive parents and child would have to travel back to the birth state if finalizing under their laws, most states have laws allowing the court to waive your personal appearance due to the cost and inconvenience of distant travel. Instead, the attorney appears in your place, or you appear by telephone.

As will be discussed in Chapter 12, the technical rules of the Interstate Compact (getting permission from both states before the child can leave the state), apply whenever the child is crossing state lines, in other words, the birth is in one state and the adoptive parents live in another state. So, it is applicable whether you finalize out of-state, or in-state, if the child crossed state lines. The difference is mainly a question of which state law applies.

Choosing between the types of interstate adoption. Adoptive parents are often confused when understanding the differences between the two types of interstate adoption mentioned above, and how you choose one. There really is no need for confusion, nor is a decision made in advance which type of interstate adoption you will do. It happens like this:

- You've chosen your attorney and started your networking plan.
- If you find a birth mother in your home state, you do an adoption in your home state.
- If she is in another state, however, you and your attorney analyze the case and the laws of her state compared to your state. Only then do you decide if you can and should adopt in her home state under her state's laws (if it permits non-resident adoption), or finalize in your home state under your state's laws.
- The bottom line is that you simply have options as to which way you elect to go, but you won't make a decision until you've been chosen by a birth mother.

When Independent Adoption is Not Permitted in Your State

Five states do not permit independent adoption, requiring that all adoptions be completed only by agencies. These states are Colorado, Connecticut, Delaware, Massachusetts and North Dakota. If you live in one of these states you either must do an agency adoption in-state, or work with another state.

If you elect to do an out-of-state adoption, you may still be able to initiate the adoption with an attorney, as long as your home state completes it as a full agency adoption. Because each region within these states may differ on this policy, however, it is best to check with the agency which will be doing your home study and writing the final report to the court, to be sure they foresee no problems with your plan.

Alternatively, you can do a non-resident adoption, which will virtually eliminate your state and its laws from the adoption. Even there, however, the out-of-state authorities will want to see a home study of you from an agency in your area, so check in advance to be sure they will cooperate in that plan. Usually, there are no problems.

CHAPTER 4

SELECTING THE
RIGHT ATTORNEY

Here's what most people do to find their adoption attorney:

They go online and select a lawyer conveniently located.

And there you have the reason why most people fail at adoption, or take longer to succeed than they should have.

Think about it. Did you buy your house down the street from your mom and dad's place? Did your find your career job around the corner from your high school? Likely the answer is "no." So why would you think the best attorney for you, and your unique needs, would just happen to be right in your area?

That doesn't mean there isn't a well-qualified adoption attorney right in your region, and you might actually be hiring one of them. For most people, however, if that is the beginning and end of their search, the adoption is doomed from the start. Let's look at why that is, and what the right approach is.

Let's start with the basics of why you need an attorney. The attorney's role is to explain every aspect of the adoption process to you in advance so you fully understand what is ahead, then guide you through it. If you are planning a traditional *agency* adoption, you may not need an attorney at all, or for only certain services, depending upon the state in which you complete your adoption. However, if you are like the majority of adoptive parents seeking to adopt a newborn through *independent* or *identified* adoption, the selection of your adoption attorney is critical.

In addition to their obvious legal function, many adoption attorneys also have a network of sources leading to birth mothers being referred to their office, creating adoptive matches as well. Simply doing one of these two functions is of great importance. Doing both is monumental, making the selection of your attorney likely the most important decision in your adoption.

You might already have a "general practice" attorney in mind to assist you. This might be an attorney you previously used for a non-adoption purpose, such as drafting a will. Or perhaps a friend has recommended their family law attorney who does "some adoptions on the side." In most cases hiring such an attorney is a mistake. We live in an era of specialization. The world in general, and law in particular, is so complex it is almost impossible to be a "jack of all trades." Not a good one anyway. Would you consider consulting a dermatologist for a bad back? Or an orthopedic surgeon to examine your eyes? So why would you trust the formation of your family to someone who "dabbles" in adoption?

Finding the right attorney is not a difficult task if you know how to approach it. There are specific steps to follow to find not just a great attorney, but one who is right for your unique needs and desires:

1. Compile a list of possible attorneys.
2. Fine-tune your list.
3. Ask specific questions to the attorney to test their knowledge.
4. Test the attorney's knowledge.
5. Determine if their personality and approach to adoption matches yours.

Compile a List of Possible Attorneys

There are tens of thousands of attorneys in the country, and several hundred who specialize in adoption. It is best to start with a wide net, and narrow it down to find an attorney not only well qualified, but with whom you feel personally comfortable. You may be looking only for an attorney in your home state, or in states other than your own. Regardless of whether you hire one, or more than one, to start your adoption quest, let's look at creating your list.

Only consider attorneys in your preferred states. Your selected states from which to adopt will be unique to you and different from other adoptive parents. You might live in a well-populated region in a state with advantageous adoption laws and a good percentage of birth mothers. If so, you will likely select an attorney in your home region and state. Another adoptive family may live in a state with very poor adoption options, so they've selected several states they feel are best for them, and will consider attorneys in those states.

To determine the right states for you, consider the many in-state and out-of-state options discussed in Chapter 2, and the information provided in the state-by-state review in Chapter 15. Depending upon where you live, and the kind of adoption you want, different states will be best for you. It is within only these states that you need focus your search for the best attorneys.

Consider members of the American Academy of Adoption Attorneys (AAAA—referred to within the adoption profession as "Quad A). This membership organization has more than three hundred members nationwide and is limited to attorneys with demonstrated skill and expertise in adoption. The completion of fifty adoptions, twenty of them within the last two years, is a minimum requirement to become an AAAA member. Most have completed hundreds of adoptions, however. Members are listed in the state-by-state review, including their biographies detailing information about their background and experience, as well as contact information. The AAAA website is adoptionattorneys.org (but it does not include the biography information obtained and listed in Chapter 15).

Sometimes people fear a "specialist" will charge more. This can be true (although it is usually well worth it for the extra knowledge and experience), but the reverse is also true. Often hiring a specialist is actually less expensive. This is because a non-specializing attorney will not know the needed procedures and documents to prepare, and will charge you for that research time. The experienced adoption attorney typically already knows the needed information and has prepared the required documents hundreds of times, meaning less work hours are required, and less time for which you are billed.

Are there good adoption attorneys who are not in the AAAA? Certainly, yes, but the AAAA remains an excellent starting point. It is there you will find most of the nation's premier adoption attorneys. The AAAA is not one of those membership organization where attorneys pay a fee just to get a fancy plaque for their wall. There is a great deal of information-sharing between members, and attendance at periodic national educational conferences is required. Some attorneys apply for membership but are denied due to not meeting AAAA standards.

What if there isn't an AAAA member in your area, or you don't feel the closest member is right for you, but you want an AAAA attorney handling your adoption? Don't worry. First of all, as was discussed in Chapter 2, you don't necessarily need an attorney to be located right in your home area, or even in your own state. True, you will likely be finalizing your adoption in your local courthouse, unless you do a non-resident adoption, but that is the simplest part of the entire adoption. It's the equivalent of the "graduation ceremony" after years of college. The difficult work is in getting there. The smart thing to do is to find the best attorney for you, whether they are close or distant. Then if need be, that attorney can use another attorney right in your hometown to make the final court appearance, often at a small fee.

Check online for "adoption attorney" and check your local Yellow Pages under "adoption," or perhaps "attorneys – adoption/family law." Although many of these attorneys may lack the qualifications you need and deserve, you might get lucky and find an excellent attorney who is not an AAAA member. Both the internet and Yellow Pages have no screening mechanism regarding "quality" so you will find the best and the worst, listed side by side. The following pages will help you distinguish them.

Join or visit local adoptive parent support groups. Many of the people attending these meetings have "been there, done that." They've completed the process you are just starting. They can tell you about their experiences with local attorneys, both good and bad, and perhaps some outside your region as well. To find out if there is an adoptive parent support group in your area, try calling local adoption agencies and attorneys who might know of some.

Also listing adoptive parent support groups in each state is the Child Welfare Information Gateway's site: childwelfare.gov. Click "State Resources" from the top bar then from the dropdown menu select "National Foster Care and Adoption Directory." Then select the state of interest to you, and under the heading "Support Groups" click the box for "Kinship, Foster Care and Adoption Support Groups," then click the "Go" button. Listed will be both private groups, as well as private adoption agencies that have support groups. You can also find online discussion groups at the AdoptiveFamilies.com. In the second row of options on the menu bar you will see "Groups." After clicking on that, you will see many different online groups from which to choose. You can also find online support groups at Adoption.com by clicking "Community" then "Groups." (Websites are constantly redesigned and updated, so the above "first click here, then click there" directions might not be accurate in the future. But if you explore the sites, you should find their listings of groups.)

For more information about AdoptiveFamilies.com and the Child Welfare Information Gateway, please see Appendix B.

Join Resolve, or attend one of their meetings. Resolve is a very established and respected national infertility organization with regional chapters throughout the country. Part of their focus on infertility includes adoption. Many of their members are in the process of, or have completed, an adoption, and can talk about attorneys they used. To find a Resolve chapter near you, visit resolve.org.

For more information about Resolve, please see Appendix B.

Call your local bar association. Some bar associations have referral services based upon the attorney's specialty. Although this will possibly lead you to a good attorney, be aware that a local bar association "referral" is not as impressive as it may sound. Most local bar associations are merely associations which attorneys pay a fee to join. Many of the attorneys being "referred" to you have done nothing more than fill out a form to be included in their list of recommendations. There is usually no requirement of demonstrating expertise or experience in adoptions. It is often the equivalent of an internet or yellow page ad. Still, it is worth checking into when starting your list.

Call your local court. Each court has a different department which accepts Petitions for Adoptions (the document which starts the legal process in court) for filing. In some states, this might be the probate court, or perhaps the family law court. Call the court's main number and ask to speak to one of the clerks who handle the filing of Petition for Adoptions.

When you reach the correct person, explain that you are planning to adopt and are compiling a list of possible attorneys. Ask which attorneys file a lot of Petitions within your county. Some clerks (especially if you are calling small-town courts rather than hectic, big-city ones) will be willing to share some names with you, and some won't. Remember, although the cases filed are confidential, you are only asking for the names of attorneys they see a lot in court on adoption-related matters. There is nothing confidential about that. The clerk's only remaining concern will be if he or she will be perceived as giving a recommendation (which they are barred from doing) by passing along some names. Explain that you are not asking for a recommendation, simply the names of attorneys who are busy in their courthouse doing adoptions. There is about a chance someone will be willing to give you a name.

Talk to other adoptive parents. The more you start talking about adoption, the more you will find that people you already know have adopted. Often they have not previously volunteered the information to you, as there was no need to do so. But upon hearing you share that interest, they are happy to share their adoption experiences. There are millions of successful adoptive parents out there. You will find them everywhere: at work, in your neighborhood, at your place of worship. Ask who their attorney was, and other attorneys they've heard about from their friends who have adopted. Generally, adoptive parents tend to know a lot of other adoptive parents.

Talk to any attorneys you know. You may have used an attorney to draw up a will, handle a car accident, a prior divorce, or whom you just know socially. Although they may know nothing about adoption law, they may know of other attorneys who specialize in adoption. Sometimes these referrals are more to "friends" than necessarily the best attorney. Still, sometimes these leads can be viable.

Visit *AdoptiveFamilies.com.* Adoptive Families (formerly Adoptive Families of America) offers a great magazine and website, as well as an annual adoption report. Both the website and annual publication have a state-by-state listing of adoption attorneys.

Talk to people you know in the healthcare industry. Adoption attorneys constantly work with doctors, counselors and hospitals regarding the care of the birth mothers they are working with. For this reason, some health-care professionals may be able to tell you about attorneys with whom they have had contact in prior adoption situations.

You will be surprised how quickly you can compile a list of possible adoption attorneys, and how large the list becomes. Don't worry if it seems unmanageably large. We will be paring it down fairly quickly.

Fine-Tune Your List

Okay, you've got the list. What now?

Depending upon the scope of your search, you might have only a dozen attorneys on your list, or more likely, many times that, and they will be located in one or several states. Now it's time to visit their websites. If they don't have a website, and a good one, that is a major concern. So many adoptions are started from internet searches, not just by adoptive parents, but more importantly, by birth mothers. If you can't find the attorney online, how will a birth mother?

Call the office and see if additional information is available by mail, or if it is all on the website, regarding the attorney's qualifications, experience and fees. You want to learn as much as you can.

To fine-tune your list, and make it a manageable size, we now need to do some fact-finding. Just because an attorney does some adoptions, perhaps even specializes in it, does not mean he or she is the right attorney for you. Different qualities are important to different people, and the best adoption attorney for one adoptive family may not be the best one for you. Here are some recommended steps to take, or questions to ask, to narrow down your list:

- Examine the website and/or written information provided by the attorney. Is it clear and concise? Does it give you bona fide information about the adoption process, the attorney's qualifications and the likely fees? Or is it a "puff piece" featuring a cute baby on the cover of a brochure or website, but little hard information? If the attorney can't provide you with professional, clear information to convince you to become a client, imagine how bad he or she will be once you've become a client and they've already got your money. Also, you are seeing your first sample of the attorney's work product. Is it well written, neat and professionally presented? If not, why would you expect their court documents prepared on your behalf, or correspondence to important people in your case, to be any better?

- In your initial phone call to the attorney's office, do you get a good feeling from the phone receptionist, secretary or answering machine message? Professional and friendly? Remember, this will be the same person or message a potential birth mother will likely get on the phone in her initial call. If the person or message is not warm and friendly, why would a birth mother be interested in staying on the line to speak to the attorney? That would mean fewer birth mothers to be considering you as adoptive parents through that office. During business hours, an actual receptionist—not an answering machine or service—is preferred, as most birth mothers will not leave a message on a first call. She'll just call someone else and that possible birth mom is forever lost.

- Call the state bar association where the attorney practices, or visit the state bar website. (Each state has a mandatory state bar association.) Records are available to the public regarding any discipline against the attorney for inappropriate conduct or malfeasance. Discipline by the state bar can result in disbarment, temporary suspension of the attorney's license or a public reprimand. Even the least severe discipline, a public reprimand, is seen as a quite serious among most attorneys. Be aware, however, that a "clean record" for an attorney is only confirmation he or she has not been disciplined for something. An attorney may still be a very poor practitioner, yet manage to have not committed any indiscretions requiring sanctions by the state bar.

Don't be surprised if you quickly eliminate half the attorneys you are considering just from the steps above. Does this surprise you? Sadly, the legal profession is no better than similar fields. Think of all the doctors you've met whom you didn't really care for and would not trust to treat you again. How about all the bad teachers you've had in your life? Attorneys are no better or worse. Just be glad you can quickly eliminate some and not waste more of your time on the ones not right for you.

Specific Questions to Ask the Attorney

Now it's time to pare down your list to just a few attorneys, and hire the right one. Some of the following questions may be answered by the attorney's advance materials you have received or read on their website, or provided by other materials, such as their biographies in the Chapter 15 state-by-state review. Some questions, however, you will have to personally ask the attorney in a phone call or in a personal consultation. For adoptive parents seeking an attorney to provide legal services and help them be matched with a birth mother to start a newborn adoption, all the following questions will be relevant. If you already have your own birth mother, or don't feel you will need an attorney's guidance in being selected by one, some of these questions will not be necessary.

- *How many years have you been an attorney?* There is no perfect answer here. For example, an attorney with forty years experience is impressive, but are they so advanced in years that a birth mother will not be able to relate to them? What about an attorney with only a few years experience? Likely they are younger and can work more effectively with seventeen-year-old birth moms, but do they possess enough experience? So, what's the correct answer? It's a combination of things and requires answers to the next few questions, so keep reading.

- *Is your practice limited to, or does it primarily consist of, adoption?* The more specialized an attorney is, the more likely he or she is to be up to date in every aspect of adoption law, on both the state and federal level, as both can impact your adoption. If an attorney handles only a few adoptions a year, as well as a few dozen bankruptcies, some divorce work, and the occasional drunk driving case, they show an admirable diversity, but will he or she have the same depth of knowledge as the attorney who focuses exclusively, or primarily, on adoption? (Let's revisit the comparison of doctors and attorneys. If you needed surgery on your spine, would you go to a general practitioner also who delivers babies, and helps the local teenagers with their acne? Likely no. You'd be seeking a specialist.) In almost every case, the more specialized the professional is, the better trained they are within that narrow specialty. A general practice attorney who confidently tells you: "Adoptions are simple; there's no need to specialize in them," is only proving to you how little he or she knows about the field, and what can potentially go wrong. They just don't know enough to know it. In a few moments you will be give some "test questions" to ask the attorney, as a way to determine their knowledge.

- *How many adoptions have you done in your career?* The years of experience are important, as is their degree of specialization in adoption. More important than both, however, is the numbers. Does this mean more is always better? Not necessarily, as long as the attorney has completed a significant number of adoptions to have sufficient experience. You will find some attorneys, particularly those in major metropolitan areas, who have completed hundreds and hundreds of adoptions, maybe even more than a thousand. That's impressive. However, that by itself does not make the attorney better than one who has completed only one hundred. That is still an impressive number of adoptions, and enough to have seen most possible situations come up, and have experience handling them.

- *How many adoptions do you complete each year? How about last year?* You will find that most adoption specialists complete from ten to seventy adoptions a year. Generally, the larger number is for attorneys in large cities. A high number of adoptions each year, particularly the most recent year, is impressive. As you will see in the next few questions, however, that information by itself can be misleading.

- *How many adoptive parents do you work with at one time waiting to be matched by a birth mother? Is there a maximum number you work with at one time? How many do you have at this moment?* These questions are all related, and critically important if you are looking to your attorney for his or her birth mother matching skills. Let's say attorney "Bob" completes sixty adoptions a year, and he works with one hundred adoptive parents at one time waiting to be matched with a birth mother. Attorney "Susan" only completes twenty, but she limits her number of clients waiting for a match to ten. Mathematically, Susan actually has a more successful ratio, as her clients on average are waiting six months for an adoptive match, while Bob's clients are averaging a wait of almost twice that long. Plus, assuming Susan isn't filling her time with other non-adoption cases, her smaller caseload may indicate she has more time to work on each case, and to get to know each client. (Sometimes bigger is better, and sometimes it isn't. There is no simple answer, which is why there are so many factors to consider.)

- *What is the average wait of your clients for an adoptive match? What is a soonest versus longest estimate of waiting time to be picked based upon prior clients?* On your own, you can "do the math" of a typical waiting time for an adoptive match based upon the attorney's estimates of the number of adoptions done annually divided into the waiting number of clients. Still, it is helpful to hear it from the attorney. For example, if the attorney does fifty adoptions a year and works with one hundred waiting clients (100 divided by 50 = 2), that tells you the average wait is about two years. If that same attorney tells you his clients' average wait is five months, something is wrong. Either the attorney is not being honest about some of those figures, or there is an explanation for the disparity. Ask the attorney to explain any confusion.

- *Are most of the adoptions you help arrange "open" or "closed?"* Sometimes the issue of an adoption being open or closed is due to state law on the subject. Other times, it is due to mindset of the attorney who consciously or subconsciously feels one type of adoption is best, and that feeling is picked up by birth mothers and adoptive parents working with him or her. As a general rule, most newborn adoptions in the United States are to some degree, open. Usually this means meeting in person, and sharing identities. Slightly more open will include the adoptive parents sending the birth mother an annual picture and updating letter about the child until adulthood. Still more open might be where it is agreed the birth mother will have some continuing face-to-face contact with you and the child. Make sure that the attorney's philosophy, and his or her typical cases, matches your preferred degree of openness.

• *Do some adoptive parents who hire you never get picked by a birth mother, or have to wait several years? Do you find these adoptive parents have any qualities in common (age, ethnicity, religion, having existing children)?* There are two reasons to ask this question. One is that if the attorney finds some families don't get picked by a birth mother, or have a much harder time being picked, you want to know if you fall into that category. For example, if you are a Hispanic couple seeking a Hispanic child, and you are hiring an attorney who is in a predominantly Caucasian region, there will be fewer birth mothers of your ethnicity to select you. It would likely make more sense for such couples to select an attorney in a border state, like California or Texas, with a higher percentage of Hispanics. This would make more sense than hiring an attorney in Idaho, for example. The same issue can arise regarding religion. Parts of Utah would be an example of this, where the Mormon religion is quite prevalent. A non-Mormon family would likely find that attorneys practicing in Utah would be less effective for them. America is a very homogenous nation, however, and many adoptions cross cultural and ethnic lines. Still, the reality is that many birth mothers and adoptive parents' first choice is to stay within their ethnic group. If an attorney isn't suited for your particular individual characteristics, best to know it right away. The second reason to ask an attorney if some of their clients don't get picked is to judge their honesty. The reality is that some adoptive parents desiring a newborn child won't get picked by a birth mother, just as some wonderful people out there will never find the love of their life and get married. Life is not always fair. It is reasonable to think that if an attorney tells you *every* client gets picked, this either means he or she has only handled a small number of adoptions over a short period of time, or the attorney is exaggerating his or her success. So, there is nothing wrong with an attorney telling you some adoptive parents don't ever get picked. It is to be expected. The key is how often does it happen and why. (Later we will discuss strategies to increase the chances you will not end up in the small percentage of adoptive parents who do not succeed.)

- *Does the state in which you practice allow attorneys to find birth mothers for adoptive parents and create a "match"?* Several states either bar attorneys from "finding" birth mothers to create an adoptive match, or may permit it but forbid the attorney to charge for it. Some states limiting this are Connecticut, Georgia, Illinois, Maryland, Minnesota, New Jersey and New York. If you live in one of these states (and plan to finalize your adoption in your home state, as most do) it should not discourage you if your attorney can't introduce you to birth mothers. Although it is great when an attorney has the added benefit of finding a birth mother for you, let's not forget that an attorney's primary role—and a critical one— is to give you legal advice at all stages of your adoption. This is an especially important role in your home state. If you want an attorney to be networking for you, in addition to your own networking efforts (or in place of it), you can consider retaining an out-of-state attorney in addition to your home state attorney, as discussed elsewhere in this book. And remember, even if the attorney can't network for you, he or she can supervise *your* efforts, and screen any potential birth mothers you find.

- *What methods do you use to find birth mothers, or to help us do it, resulting in a birth mother selecting us?* There are many strategies you, as well as your attorney, can use to find women facing unplanned pregnancies and desiring to start an adoption. Later, we will discuss some successful networking methods, including some unusual ones. Every attorney has their favorite methods, and you need to make sure you agree with the methods your potential attorney plans to use. Some attorneys practice in states where it is not legal for them to attempt to find birth mothers (the state-by-state review tells you which these states are). Accordingly, in those states, the attorney will give you advice on what techniques he or she thinks is best. You will want to make sure that you see eye-to-eye on the methods to be used, as either you, or the attorney, may not feel comfortable with some types the other plans to use. Some networking strategies are very aggressive and public, which some adoptive parents might find uncomfortable. There are also many subtle and more private techniques. Regardless of the kind of networking campaign you plan to employ, you want to make sure the attorney shares your view.

• *What percentage of the birth mothers you find are in-state, as compared to coming from another state?* If you don't care which state your birth mother resides in (affecting your travel costs, easy access to the birth mother pre-birth and at birth, and the state law which will apply), this may not be an important issue for you. However, if you are retaining an attorney in, let's say Washington, because you want a Washington birth mother, or you want to do a non-resident adoption there, why would you want to retain an attorney who finds all his or her birth mothers via a method leading to out-of-state birth mother contacts, such as the internet or out-of-state Yellow Page ads.

• *When birth mothers contact you, how are we and other adoptive parents shown to her, giving us a chance to be selected?* Some attorneys show all their waiting adoptive parents, while a small number may favor those who have waited the longest, showing those families at the exclusion of his or her newest clients. Others only show a few adoptive parents, selected to match characteristics of the birth mother. (Most adoption professionals believe the best approach is to show every adoptive family to every birth mother, unless the birth mother has characteristics not desired by the adoptive parents: ethnicity, drug usage, projected expenses, open or closed adoption, et cetera.) The reason favoring that wide approach, rather than the subjective thinking of the attorney selecting the "right" families, is it assumes the attorney knows what the birth mother is truly looking for. The reality, however, is that often opposites attract. The "spark" of attraction is impossible to define. Furthermore, the more adoptive families the birth mother has to choose from, the more likely she can be truly happy with her decision. For example, is she more likely to find a family she truly likes, and therefore will follow through on her adoption plan, if she chooses from only two families . . . or from twenty? Obviously, twenty. What would our chances to be a successful marriage if we had only two or three prospective spouses from which to choose? Adoption is no different. So be cautious of attorneys who severely limit who he shows to birth mothers.

- *What percentage of your clients find a birth mother through your efforts, as compared to your clients finding a birth mother on their own?* If one of the key things you hope to accomplish in hiring an attorney is to have his or her help in finding a birth mother to in turn select you as adoptive parents, you will want to know how effective their efforts are. For example, an attorney may complete a very impressive forty adoptions a year, but if eighty percent of the adoptive parents found their own birth mother, it is not as impressive as an attorney completing twenty-five, all of which resulted from his or her own birth mother networking efforts. (Although this might mean the attorney is still very valuable as his or her advice may have led to the adoptive parents' success.)

- *Does your fee include your networking efforts to help us get picked by a birth mother, or is it a separate fee?* If the attorney is networking for birth mothers, leading them to contact his or her office to in turn select one of the waiting adoptive families, a lot of time and money is being expended by the attorney in that effort. This might take the form of mailings to health care professionals, yellow page advertising, internet promotion, contributions of time and/or money to organizations which indirectly leads to referrals, et cetera. Just like with any attorney expenses, these costs are passed on to you as the client benefiting from those efforts. The question is if it is part of their standard fee, which includes their legal work, or a separate fee specifically designated for networking. (It does not matter which of the two payment options the attorney uses. What does matter is that you know what you are paying for.)

The issue of networking, and its costs, is discussed in more detail in Chapter 8.)

- *Can we be listed with other attorneys and/or agencies while we are working with you, and proceed with whichever attorney or agency finds an adoptive placement first?* The goal of every adoption agency and attorney should be to help you adopt. To that end, if you wish to hire more than one attorney or agency to obtain your goal as quickly as possible (see Chapter 9), you need attorneys who will work within that philosophy. Most all will be agreeable. Some attorneys, however, require you to only work with them. They are making themselves the central person in your adoption, however, which is to be avoided.

- *Do we pay for your services as we work through the adoption, or do we pay it all in advance?* Some attorneys, especially in matters like criminal cases, charge their entire fee in advance, or require a retainer for their anticipated total fee, then bill against that and return any unused portion. Adoptions tend to be billed differently. For example, if you are waiting to be matched with a birth mother, it is not yet even known if you will *have* an adoption. For that reason, many adoption attorneys charge their fee in stages, or hourly against a reasonable retainer amount, so you are only paying for the services as they are provided. (Some adoption attorneys may charge their entire fee in advance, but you should only accept such a fee arrangement if the unused portion is held in a trust account and any unused portion will be returned to you with a written accounting of all expenses.) Be very cautious of attorneys who require a disproportionately large payment, compared to other attorneys, in advance, particularly if it is non-refundable. While you might be led to think that paying more means you are getting more, this is often not the case. Often you will find the best, and most ethical, attorneys charge the most reasonable fees.

- *What are typical birth mother expenses we will be expected to pay?* Almost all states allow adoptive parents to help the birth mother with the pregnancy and adoption-related expenses. Often this includes medical bills, and the birth mother's living costs while she is incapacitated due to the pregnancy. Some birth mothers have few, or no, expenses (they have insurance and are employed, or live at home), while others may have significant expenses. This question is important because some attorneys either practice in an area with a higher cost of living, or choose to operate their practice in a way which results in higher birth mother costs. As a general rule, expenses for a birth mother ranging from a few hundred to several thousand for total living costs during the pregnancy is not unusual. (When you get into significantly higher amounts, however, it is a sign for potential caution. For example, does the attorney "bribe" birth mothers to work with him or her by offering them an ocean view condo (at your expense) at double the rent of a typical apartment? Does the attorney entice out-of-state birth mothers to travel to meet with you by providing them a first class plane ticket rather than coach? Needless to say, such behavior is not conducive to a successful adoption, or finding the right kind of birth mother.)

- *What is the fee for your initial consultation?* Some attorneys offer free consultations. You know this because you see them offered on TV for personal injury cases, right? Other attorneys charge you for their time, and considering legal fees range from $150 to $350 hourly depending upon where in the nation you live, a two-hour consultation with an adoption specialist will cost you approximately $300 to $700. A good consultation will completely educate you about the adoption process, not just the basic legal aspects. This would include: strategies to be used to find a birth mother, screening birth mothers, what happens when meeting a birth mother in person, the hospital experience, potential risks (the birth mother's time in which to change her mind and revoke her consent, et cetera), birth father's rights, permitted expenses, interstate adoptions, the Indian Child Welfare Act, the home study, finalization in court and the federal adoption tax credit. The initial consultation will let you determine if you like the attorney. Does he or she explain things thoroughly? Can you imagine the attorney meeting with birth mothers and making them comfortable? Let's get back to the enticement of free consultations. Sounds good, and in some cases, it may be. Generally speaking, however, while some attorneys, such as personal injury attorneys, are in the habit of offering free consultations, well-qualified adoption attorneys—or any specialist for that matter—are not. Usually free consultations are offered only when the attorney's practice is lacking in clients (not that they'd admit that's the reason). Think about it. Would a successful and established heart specialist, copyright attorney or dental surgeon sit down with you and spend two hours of their day for no compensation? And then do it again for the next family after you? And the family after that? No. You generally get what you pay for. Well-qualified professionals get paid for their time, and to expect otherwise is not reasonable. However, a few free moments on the phone of "free time" with the attorney before scheduling a consultation is not too much to ask.

- *Do you encourage counseling for birth mothers?* Placing a child for adoption will be one of the most emotional moments of a birth mother's life. The more prepared she is, the more likely it is she can make the placement as planned and handle the emotions of birth. Some state laws require counseling, and some do not. If an attorney feels counseling is not important, or in any way discourages birth mothers from receiving it, this likely indicates a lack of not only empathy, but a basic understanding of the emotions at work, and the making of a successful adoption. Accordingly, you may wish to not consider an attorney who diminishes the importance of counseling and discourages birth mothers from receiving it.

The answers to these questions should give you an excellent idea of the full scope of the attorney's services, fees, personality, and view of adoption. Do they match your vision of how an adoption should be handled? Do they make you feel comfortable and confident? Likely your list of possible attorneys is getting smaller and smaller, and those on it are getting better and better.

Test the Attorney's Knowledge

No . . . by the above subtitle of "Test the Attorney's Knowledge," it is not being suggested that you hand your prospective attorney a #2 pencil and a written exam. Nor should you be obvious, and perhaps offensive, that you are testing the attorney's knowledge. But what it is being recommended that you do is ask about certain areas likely to arise in an adoption, which are normal questions to ask. The key here is that by the time you have finished this book, you will be savvy enough to know a good answer from a bad one. You would be amazed how many attorneys claim to understand adoptions, but have no real understanding of issues like the legal issues that arise in every adoption, but the attorney needs to know enough to look for them.

Let's say you've narrowed down your list to just a few attorneys. It's now time to meet them in person (or do a Skype or phone consultation if they are distant and you don't want to travel) to see if you want to work with them. (You might get some to speak to you on the phone if you explain you've read their materials and just have a question or two. For more than that, however, you will need to schedule a consultation.)

Here are some recommended questions:

- *I've heard about something called the Indian Child Welfare Act (ICWA). Can you explain what that is?* As we will discuss later in Chapter 12, this is a federal law (and some states have their own state version of the ICWA—meaning there are *two* ICWAs to be concerned with). The federal ICWA provides that if a child is a member of an Indian tribe, or even potentially eligible for membership, the tribe must be given notice and certain procedures followed. If the attorney is unfamiliar with the Indian Child Welfare Act, or says it never applies in their state, beware. More and more adoptions are at least potentially touched by the Indian Child Welfare Act, such as where the birth parent is not actually a member, but has a small degree of tribal heritage which could make them a member. The issue is not always obvious, where a birth mother looks like Pocahontas or has a name like TV movie character name like *Running Bear*. To the contrary, she might look like Taylor Swift and have a name like *Debbie Smith*. Noncompliance with the Indian Child Welfare Act can potentially invalidate an adoption, a high cost to pay for an attorney's ignorance. It is not necessary for the attorney know every aspect of the law off the top of his or her head, but should have some familiarity with the law.

- *We may do an interstate adoption. Can you explain to me how the Interstate Compact works?* As we will discuss in Chapter 12, many adoptions are interstate, where you live in a different state than that of the child's birth or residency. The Interstate Compact for the Placement of Children (ICPC) provides that prior to a child being transported across state lines by adoptive parents, certain requirements exist, such as you having a completed pre-placement home study and approval from both states' Interstate Compact administrators. About twenty documents make up an ICPC packet. This is fundamental knowledge every attorney should have.

- *What are the birth mother and birth father's rights? Can they change their minds, and if so, for how long?* These issues are the most fundamental and important of all, so the attorney should know these issues frontwards and backwards regarding their own state. Do not, however, expect them to know this information for other states without some research, however, as each state has different laws.

- *Is there a federal tax credit for adoptive parents?* If the attorney does many adoptions, he or she should certainly know about the federal tax credit. (It is much better than a deduction; it is a dollar for dollar elimination of tax owed.) The amount of the credit, and income eligibility, changes each year. For 2017, if the adoptive parents have a modified adjusted gross income of $203,540 or less, they are eligible for a tax credit of $13,570 per child adopted. The income can actually go up to $243,540, but the credit is proportionally reduced when income exceeds $203,540. It is not reasonable to expect an adoption attorney to know the detailed tax repercussions of adoption. That is for a professional tax advisor. However, they should know the existence and basics of the tax credit. (More on the federal adoption tax credit in Chapter 13.)

The above questions are just a sampling of what an attorney needs to know, but they are diversified enough to give you an idea of an attorney's knowledge. Those particular questions may not even be applicable to your individual adoption, but it doesn't matter, as they are an excellent indicator of what your attorney knows, or doesn't know. If he or she is ignorant about these issues, the same is likely true regarding other important adoption issues. If you find you know more than the attorney simply by reading this book, look for another attorney.

Determine if the Attorney's Personality and Approach to Adoption Matches Yours

Doing an adoption is a very emotional process, with many highs—and potentially—some lows. Although high legal qualifications are mandatory in the attorney you choose, it is not enough. You want someone who views adoption the same way you do. Like a marriage, you need to be on the same page for things to go smoothly.

Remember, you've got an entire nation of attorneys out there. Tens of thousands of them in fact, with several hundred being adoption specialists, offering the exact service for which you are looking. And if you end up not being satisfied with the attorney options, there are more than a thousand licensed private adoption agencies to choose from, as discussed in Chapters 5 and 6. Your options are limited only by your own time and effort.

CHAPTER 5

AGENCY ADOPTION
& ADOPTION EXCHANGES

There are two basic types of adoption agencies: *private* and *public*. Despite sharing the term "agency" adoption, they are actually often quite different. This is true in the services they offer, the fees they charge, and the children they place. In fact, many private agency adoptions are more like independent adoptions than they are like public agency adoptions, at least for newborn placements.

A common question, which can't accurately be answered, is "Which is the most popular method to adopt a newborn . . . private agency or independent?" The reason it is not answerable is the federal government, and most states, do not keep records on the number of independent adoptions to accurately compare the two. Most government statistics are kept only on the placing of children out of foster care.

Some states, which do keep records of newborn placements show more placements by private agencies, while other states show more by independent adoption. In a recent survey by *Adoptive Families* magazine of its readers completing newborn adoptions, it showed more were completed by private agencies. However, because in so many adoptions both an adoption agency and an attorney play a role, it can be difficult to differentiate them. It is public agency adoption that is significantly different from both of them—in procedures, costs, and the children placed—while private agency and independent adoption are in many states almost identical, just different entities doing the same thing.

In Chapter 2, we briefly looked at fifteen different types of adoption. Of those, nine types are fully, or partially, agency adoptions:

- Private adoption agencies performing services in your home state. (You are matched with a birth mom, or a waiting child is placed with you, from within your home state, and one agency can perform all needed services.)

- Private adoption agencies located outside your home state, but able to create matches for you, with the adoption to be finalized in the court of your home state. (Example: you find a birth mother in a state other than your own, so you retain an agency to counsel her and take her consent/relinquishment there, and retain an agency in your home state for your home study and arrange post-placement supervision and writing the final court report to approve the adoption.)

- Private adoption agencies located in states permitting non-residency adoption, allowing you to retain an out-of-state agency and finalize the adoption in the state where the child was born and finalized under that state's laws.

- Identified adoptions, where an attorney and agency are working together, using elements of both independent and agency adoption.

- Public adoption agencies.

- The foster parent short-cut (can be done via both the public agency or private agencies which are *foster family agencies*, working with the county to make placements).

- State, regional or national adoption exchange.

- Intercountry adoption by agencies located in your state.

- Intercountry adoption by out-of-state agencies.

To better understand these many options, we need to explore how agencies work, and how they can best be used to help you accomplish your adoption goals. But first let's see how they differ.

Comparing Private and Public Agencies

Private agencies are privately-operated businesses. (Most states require them to be non-profit, and we'll discuss this later, but the reality is their employees still need to be paid and there is overhead to cover, so they have still have fees, and sometimes those fees are large, particularly when doing a newborn adoption.) They are licensed by the state(s) in which they operate to conduct adoptive parent home studies and/or place children for adoption. Some agencies only do one or the other, but most do both. Some additionally help match adoptive parents with birth mothers, creating adoptive matches, and may even actively network and advertise to make birth mothers aware of their existence.

Although some private agencies only do newborn adoptions (where the child was voluntarily relinquished through their agency), many are also licensed as *foster family agencies*. This means the agency works hand-in-hand with the county or state adoption agencies to find homes for waiting children presently in foster care or group homes. This can include not just local children, but beyond, as we will discuss in upcoming pages when we talk about *adoption exchanges*. For these waiting-child adoptions, the private agency fee is usually free or very low. In some states, the fee may be refunded when an adoption from foster care is finalized. For newborn non-foster care adoptions, however, private agency fees can range from modest to very expensive. So, basically:

- Waiting child/foster care adoptions = free or very low cost
- Newborn adoptions not from foster care = similar costs as independent adoption

Most private agencies only do domestic adoptions, but some do intercountry placements (discussed in Chapter 7). Some do both. Some only do home studies and make no placements at all.

Private adoption agencies are principally supported by the fees they receive from adoptive parents, or by public funding that is received upon finalization of a waiting child adoption in which the private agency assisted.

More than 1,200 licensed adoption agencies exist in the United States. Listing them within this book is not practical given the frequent changes of addresses, phone numbers and websites. Fortunately, a fairly current listing of every adoption agency in the nation can be found at childwelfare.gov. In the top menu bar click "State Resources," then from the dropdown menu select "National Foster Care & Adoption Directory." Then, click on the state you desire and under the heading "Licensed Adoption Agencies" click the box next to "Private Domestic Foster Care and Adoption Agencies." Your state adoption office website (provided in Chapter 15) will also usually list all licensed adoption agencies within the state.

Public adoption agencies are completely different than private. Public agencies are operated by the county or state in which they are located and are supported by tax dollars. The exclusive function of public agencies is to find homes for children for whom the county or state has assumed responsibility. These agencies, usually referred to as *county* or *public* adoption agencies, are a branch of your state social services department. You can find your local public adoption agency in several ways. The state-by-state review provides each state's central adoption office, most of which will list the public adoption agency serving your area. You can also check online, or in your local phone book and look under government listings for your county under "adoption."

Although public adoption agencies are licensed to accept birth mothers' relinquishment of newborns, meaning they do get occasional newborn placements, their most important function is to find homes for "waiting" children (in foster care and in need of an adoptive home due to the inability or inappropriateness of returning them to their birth family). Ages, ethnicity and potential special-needs vary. Sometimes this means the child has an emotional or physical challenge, but sometimes "special-need" only means the child is of an age or ethnic group, or be part of a sibling group to be adopted together, which makes finding an adoptive home more challenging.

Free seminars. A nice thing about adoption agencies, both public and private, is that they typically offer free seminars to learn about their services. Compare this to attorneys, who will almost always charge you for a lengthy initial consultation. One difference for the distinction, however, is that the typical agency free seminar is in a group setting scheduled at a time dictated by the agency, while attorney consultations are private and scheduled at a time convenient for you. Some private adoption agencies offer private consultations like attorneys; and a few may even charge an "intake fee" or "consultation fee" for this service. When you attend agency seminars, you should bring a question list (see the next chapter) so you leave fully informed. The seminar is your chance to learn exactly what their services are, and what they can and cannot do for you, as well as at what cost.

The Agency's Licensing Status. Both public and private agencies are licensed by the state, and a failure to perform their services properly can result in license revocation, so they take their duties seriously. Unlike facilitators, who are by and large unregulated, most states require each agency to satisfy numerous demanding requirements. Agencies are each licensed to do different things. Virtually all are licensed to perform home studies. Some will be licensed to perform either domestic or intercountry home studies, while a small number does both.

Domestic agencies may also be licensed to take legal custody of children for the purpose of placing them for adoption, acting as a state-approved intermediary of sorts between the birth mother and adoptive parents. Agencies that do home studies *and* make adoptive placements are often called "full service" agencies. In some states all agencies are full-service, while other states issue separate licenses for each permitted service. For these reasons, you need to ask each agency:

1. Are they licensed by the state as *an adoption agency*? (You want to make sure you are not calling a facilitator which employs a name that implies they are an adoption agency—discussed below.)
2. Are they licensed to perform services in your county? (Many states require agencies to be approved on a county-by-county basis, with some being statewide.)
3. What services they are permitted to perform? Ask specifically about home studies, post-placement supervision, foster family services, domestic or intercountry services, to the extent some or all of these pertain to your adoption plans.

Clearly, there is no benefit to you in hiring an agency if they can't perform the duties you need done, so the above are threshold questions. The first inquiry about asking if they are "licensed as an agency" may sound unnecessary, but that is not the case. The reality is that you must verify the agency you are considering is licensed as an actual *licensed adoption agency* by the state in which it operates. Some individuals or organizations use names which sound like adoption agencies, when in fact they are not. Instead, they are generally what is referred to as *facilitators*. Facilitators are those who render the limited service of finding a baby for a fee. Chapter 8 addresses the risks of facilitators.

Religious Affiliation. Private agencies can be divided into *denominational* and *nondenominational* categories. Denominational agencies are those affiliated with a particular religious faith. Generally, these agencies are easy to recognize based upon the agency's name (e.g. Catholic Family Services, Church of Jesus Christ Latter Day Saints Social Services, Jewish Family Services, et cetera.).

An important fact about denominational agencies not known by most people is that some denominational agencies do not require adoptive parents to be of the faith with which the agency is affiliated. In fact, some state laws may forbid them from doing so. This may be beneficial when you live in a region with few agencies, or if you find the policies of one particular agency match your desires, even though the agency is affiliated with a different religion.

Public adoption agencies are different. They are forbidden to have any religious ties, or to use religion to determine the general eligibility of adoptive parents. Religion can still be a factor in child placement, however, as where an older child will benefit from being with an adoptive family which shares the child's existing religious beliefs.

Eligibility Requirements of Adoptive Parents. Each agency, whether private or public, sets eligibility requirements for you as adoptive parents. These can vary from state to state, and even from agency to agency within a state. Speaking very generally, however, here are some typical guidelines and factors used by many agencies:

- Age. Be of an age that indicates you will "be there" through the life of a child until he or she reaches adulthood, and that you can handle the emotional and physical demands of parenting. Some states do not allow any specific age limit, while others allow agencies to impose a maximum age, for example, no more than 40 or 45 years older than the child. More recently, however, many agencies are eliminating age restrictions, taking more of a "whole person" view of the adoptive parents when seeking the right match for a child's needs.

- Marital Status. The days are gone when single persons could not adopt. Today, many single women adopt, and even some single men elect to do so. From a practical perspective in a newborn adoption, many birth mothers lean towards a couple rather than a single parent, but at least the days of rejecting or barring single parents just for being single are basically gone.

- Length of Marriage. Some agencies impose a minimum length of marriage, such as two years, just to confirm relationship stability before adding a child into the household mix. Some agencies do not have this requirement, and some states do not allow such requirements due to prohibitions against marital discrimination.

- Number of Prior Marriages. Some agencies may require a therapist's evaluation of relationship stability if there is a history of multiple marriages. This policy may vary by state or agency.

- Suitability of Home and Bedroom Situation. The days of requiring home ownership are largely gone. Usually renting either a house or apartment is acceptable, as long as the housing will be safe and appropriate for a child. Many state laws require that children over a certain age (typically one or two years) may not sleep in the parents' room; also, older children (usually five and up) may only be allowed to share a room with children of the same gender. Some state laws and some agency policies also limit the number of children to a room - usually two or three at the very most. An agency social worker will visit your home to make sure it appears safe for a child. These visits are almost always by appointment; "surprise" visits prior to placement are more myth than reality. The agency has the right to require certain safety precautions prior to a child being placed (safety gates, et cetera).

- Adoptive Parent Health. Be of reasonably good health with the expectation to live at least until the child becomes an adult, and not have any contagious diseases which could put a child at risk.
- Infertility. In the past, some agencies required the adoptive parents to prove they were infertile if seeking to adopt a newborn. The agency's goal was to eliminate improper motives, such as a woman's desire to not gain weight during a pregnancy, or having a "save a child" mentality which will result in the unreasonable expectation in a child to be grateful for being adopted
- Number of Children in the Home. Some states or agencies may limit the number of children in the home, although this is becoming far less common, especially when adopting waiting children.
- Child Care. Some agencies still require one spouse to be a full-time, stay-at-home parent, although most have eliminated this requirement so that both parents can be employed. Many agencies, however, encourage one stay-at-home parent as one of many factors contributing to the best interests of a child, rather than being placed into daycare.
- Criminal Record or Child Abuse History. This is a serious issue. In fact, most state's fingerprinting is in such depth that it will show even sealed and expunged adult criminal records. This does not mean that you can't adopt if you have made a mistake in your life. If a crime was of a non-violent nature (e.g. shoplifting or intoxication), and it was an isolated incident and many years have gone by without a repeat of such behavior, it can often be exempted. If the conviction was for a felony or a violent crime, however, that single offense will almost always disqualify you from adopting. Note that every adult in the household must be fingerprinted, and any disqualification of another adult household resident based on that person's criminal record or child abuse record will also prohibit you from adopting as long as that disqualified person resides with you.
- Financial Stability. To confirm your ability to manage your financial resources well and thus provide for the child, the agency

will require some confirmation of your past and current financial situation, including but not limited to employment verification, tax returns, copies of bank statements, et cetera. Normally a single bankruptcy, if followed by a significant period of financial stability to show it was an aberration, will not be deemed a reason to deny you. Current financial distress or a history of repeated financial problems, such as bankruptcies or repossessions, can lead to denial.

Remember, these are *general* requirements. Your state, or certain agencies within your state, might be stricter or more lenient. Also, be aware that even within a single agency, their requirements might differ. Because they recognize the difficulty of finding homes for waiting children, many of the eligibility requirements (other than a criminal background) might be more flexible when adopting a child out of foster care. For example, the agency will often allow adoptive parents to have more than a forty year of age differential. Single parents are also considered where they otherwise might not be. In fact, some states report one of every five agency adoptions is by a single parent. Couples who already have several children, or who are not infertile but wish to adopt, are often also not just considered, but welcomed.

If you find the agency you hoped to work with, but it will not work with you because you do not meet their requirements, it's no cause for concern. You still have tons of options. You can work with more flexible agencies within your state. You can work with an out-of-state agency. Or, you can do an independent or intercountry adoption.

Fees and Costs. Like other businesses, private adoption agencies offer services for a fee and must make a sufficient revenue to remain in operation. Most states require private adoption agencies to be operated on a *non-profit* basis. The term "non-profit" causes confusion for many who mistakenly believe that the employees are working for no pay, as dedicated volunteers. To the contrary, however, virtually every key employee is earning a salary, just as they would at any job. The designation of a business as non-profit is principally a tax designation, and may reflect state or federal (or both) tax exempt status. Only a federally-exempt non-profit has IRS 501(c)(3) status such that donations are federally tax-deductible.

A small number of states permit private agencies to be operated on a *for-profit* basis. As long as the agency is licensed by the state as an adoption agency, there is usually little difference between the services of a non-profit and for-profit agency, although some view non-profit agencies as more altruistic and reliable. Often, for-profit agencies charge higher fees, as they are solely supported by the fees earned from adoptive parents, and are legally responsible to their shareholders for earning a profit.

Fees can vary tremendously among private agencies. Depending upon the type of agency, the services being offered, and the state in which it is located, agency fees in a newborn adoption may range from $500 to $40,000. Key distinctions are if the agency created the adoptive match or if the adoptive parents came to the agency with an existing adoptive match made on their own (or via an attorney). Between those extremes, the more realistic averages when including help in locating a birth mother fall between $5,000 and $28,000. Some agencies don't use flat fees and instead adjust their fee based upon your income and use a sliding scale. This sliding scale fee typically varies from 8% to 12% of your joint pre-tax annual income.

The fee usually covers the adoptive parent pre-placement home study, pre-adoption education and counseling, matching you with a birth parent, advising the birth parent(s) of their options, taking the birth mother's relinquishment (and birth father's if he is available), completing the post-placement supervision and evaluation of the adopted child's progress in your home, and writing the final court report to recommend that the court grant the adoption.

Not all agencies offer these complete services, however, so inquire carefully with each agency you are considering. Usually a portion of the agency fee is paid when the pre-placement home study is started, with the balance due when the child is placed in the adoptive home. Most all private agencies request additional funds from you if you are doing a newborn adoption and the birth mother needs assistance with her medical expenses or other birth-related costs, just as in independent adoption.

Other agencies may include such costs in their agency fee and forbid any such expenditures directly by you. Usually these more restrictive agencies refuse to incur many pregnancy expenses, however, and offer little flexibility to a birth mother. For example, if she needs a place to live, they are more likely to insist she stay in their maternity home, rather than rent her own apartment. Many birth mothers don't like this kind of rigidity and will go to an attorney or to a more flexible agency.

The same fee flexibility can be seen in the agency's networking services, if offered. Some agencies will include birth mother outreach efforts in their flat fee. Others will make it a separate optional program. It doesn't matter which method is used, as long as you know what you are getting for your money.

Public agencies have a completely different fee structure than their private counterparts. Like other government services, operating expenses of public agencies are paid out of taxpayer funds. Thus, many offer their services for free, while some may charge a very minimal fee, often $500 or less. Given the cost of providing adoption services, these public agencies basically underwrite the adoptions because:

1. Virtually all of the children are presently in foster homes, and the children would benefit from a permanent adoptive home.
2. Most of the children waiting for placement are in a hard-to-place category, including but not limited to age, ethnicity, medical challenges, emotional or mental disabilities, or membership in a sibling group to be adopted together.
3. Keeping children in foster homes until adulthood costs the government far more money than underwriting adoptions.
4. In the long run, adoption benefits not just the child, but all of society, because children who age out of the system without a permanent family are far more likely to become impoverished, become involved with the criminal justice system, develop substance abuse problems, and have psychological and emotional issues that last a lifetime.

Adoptive parents often wonder if they can get a "free" home study from a public agency, then use it toward an independent or private agency adoption, thereby saving themselves the cost of the pre-placement private agency home study. The answer is almost always "no." Remember, the entire purpose of the public agency financially underwriting adoptions is to encourage adoption of the children in their care who desperately need homes. To provide their manpower and services at no cost, only to have adoptive parents turn around and use those services for a private newborn or intercountry adoption, would not serve the purpose for which the public agencies exist.

In addition to the lack of any significant fees, public agency adoptions almost never include any costs associated with a birth mother's medical or living expenses. This is due to the fact most children come into the county agency system after being removed by CPS from their birth families, and parental rights are thereafter involuntarily terminated. Even the few voluntary newborn adoptions handled by public agencies usually forbid payment by the adoptive parents for a birth mother's pregnancy expenses. This usually means the public agency will help the birth mother become eligible for government aid to cover her costs (such as Medicaid, welfare, food stamps). If they can't meet her needs they will usually direct her to a private agency or attorney where such expenses can be legally provided.

Other factors limit adoptive parents' ability to work with a public agency. Adoptive parents cannot "shop" for public agencies like they can with private agencies, because virtually all public agencies will only accept applications from people who reside within the county or territory where that agency is located. Also, public agencies will normally refuse to provide services to prospective adoptive families who have located a birth mother on their own and who want the public agency to handle the adoption in order take advantage of the low public agency fee. This is because their function is to find homes for children for whom they are already responsible.

The Home Study. All agency adoptions, whether they are through a private or public agency, require a home study. This is a pre-placement evaluation before the child enters your home to confirm you will be appropriate parents for the type of child you hope to adopt. (The agency will consider the needs of a newborn versus an older child, and one in excellent health versus a child with special needs.) The satisfactory completion of the pre-placement home study is a prerequisite to having a child placed in your home. Parenting classes are almost always required, as they should be, to prepare you for the unique challenges of adoption, in addition to those of parenting.

An agency social worker will be assigned to do the pre-placement home study and will want to have several meetings with you, some of which will be in your home. Home visits are required to see the potential environment for a child. These visits are almost always arranged by appointment, not "surprise" visits.

The vast majority of agency social workers are friendly professionals who are anxious to help you succeed at adoption, although a very small number may be judgmental and take advantage of the power they have over whether a child will be placed with you. To avoid such an unpleasant experience, a list of suggested questions to ask potential agencies is provided in Chapter 6.

Because most agencies operate with almost unlimited discretion regarding with which of their waiting families they will place a child for adoption, it is important to show the agency you are among the best waiting adoptive parents. Many adoptive parents waiting for a placement do not realize in many ways they are "in competition" with the agency's other waiting adoptive parents. To impress your agency, and make them be extra-motivated to specifically help you, consider doing these simple things:

- Return your required paperwork quickly, and complete it accurately and thoroughly. You'd be surprised how many people take weeks or months to return their applications or subsequent paperwork, or who try to negotiate with the agency about whether certain paperwork is "really required." If they ask for documentation, give it to them without complaining.

- When setting appointments with the social worker, whether at your home or their office, don't ask the social worker to alter his or her busy schedule to fit yours. Show the meeting is important to you by agreeing to the soonest time they have available. Reschedule any conflicting and less important matters. They will think, "If you can't prioritize your life around a planned adoption now, how can you do it when a child's life will require it tenfold?"

- Attend all seminars offered by the agency to teach you about adoptive parenting and related issues. This includes non-mandatory seminars as well. They have valuable things to teach you about the uniqueness of parenting through adoption. Go because you want to, not because you must. Participate cheerfully and whole-heartedly.

- When asked by the agency why you wish to adopt, be honest regarding your motivation, instead of saying what you think they want to hear. For example, many social workers report that they question the motivations of adoptive parents who profess to be interested in adopting only out of humanitarian desires to make a home for a child. This motivation may be one of many appropriate factors when discussing adoption, particularly concerning waiting children/special-needs children. Even in those cases, however, most social workers feel the primary motivation for adoptive parents should be the desire to share their love with a child and the satisfaction of being a parent, acknowledging you have emotional needs as well.

- Read recommended books regarding adoption and share what you learned with your assigned caseworker, and others on the agency's staff you deal with. It is tremendously impressive to the caseworker if you have read respected adoption books, especially if you have done so voluntarily before the agency even begins your home study. Your advance reading shows you are strongly motivated and truly desire to learn all you can about the most important thing in your life—your planned adoption. Adoption101.com has a helpful list of recommended adoption books in all adoption topics.

These basic suggestions toward establishing a beneficial relationship with your agency may seem absurdly simple. Surprisingly, however, many caseworkers complain that many of their agency's waiting families fail to show their sincerity and readiness to adopt by such simple acts. Remember, an agency's goal is to find the best homes for the children they place. The more educated and prepared you show yourselves to be will not only impress your agency, it will prepare you to be a better parent. Make their discretion benefit, not hurt, your chances to adopt quickly.

After a child is placed with you, the agency in almost every state is required by law to complete post-placement supervision to ensure the child is being cared for properly. Depending upon your state, this is usually two to three visits, usually spaced out over a period up to six months (but in some situations, monthly). As with the pre-placement evaluation, normally there are no "surprise" visits, but rather scheduled appointments, sometimes in your home and sometimes in the agency's office. For newborn placements, pediatrician reports will be requested, and for older children, the agency worker will probably be required to speak privately with each to child to ask about the placement, and how the child feels about the planned adoption.

Usually there is little difference between a private or public agency home study. The only exception is usually time (and cost, as public agencies are usually free). In most cases, private agencies can start and complete your home study faster than public agencies. This is just the reality between the private and public sector. The people employed in your local public adoption agency may be extremely hardworking and dedicated, but as part of a governmental office, they will have a higher level of bureaucracy to work through.

Another reason for this is that because public agencies are offering their services for free, or close to it, they don't want to start home studies until they are sure you plan to stick to your decision to adopt through the public agency (and not stop the process after many hours have been spent by the agency on your behalf). This means they often "put you through the paces," to test your mettle before they begin. That, in turn, often means a longer wait to start a home study. Still, if they offer the services you want, it will be worth the wait.

So far, we've only discussed home studies as they relate to agency adoptions. Considering this is a chapter on agency adoptions, that makes sense. You should be aware, however, that in most states, private agencies can perform home studies for independent adoptions cases as well. This usually occurs in an "identified" adoption (discussed in Chapters 2 and 3), where the placement begins via an attorney and is then converted to an agency adoption. For this reason, many agencies have different fee structures, to distinguish such adoptions from ones where the agency helped create the match and spent additional time and effort in that part of the adoption. For this reason, you need to be very specific when you call agencies to inquire about home study services and fees.

The Children Available. The children available for adoption through private agencies handling domestic adoptions range in age from newborns to older children and are of all ethnic groups. Some of the adoptive parents retaining private agencies, however, will do so with the goal of adopting a newborn, often of their same ethnic group. However, more and more private agencies are now mainly handling the adoption of waiting and special-needs children. The adoption of these latter two groups usually comes from a collaboration with county/public agencies with the private agency, as described momentarily.

Public agencies handle the vast majority of children in the *waiting* and *special-needs* categories. A "waiting" child refers to a child who has already been born and awaiting a home, likely living in foster care (either with a foster family or in a group home). Although all children in the foster care system are *waiting* children, not all waiting children are designated as special-needs. For example, a healthy young child would be termed "waiting," but not "special-needs."

A special-needs child is usually a child the agency feels may require extraordinary parenting due to a physical, emotional or mental challenge. But this is not always true. Kids designated as "special-needs" may also include children without disabilities, but who fall into a category the agency believes will make an adoptive placement difficult to obtain. Some prefer the term *hard-to-place* for children in this category as more accurate. This could include a large sibling group to be adopted together, a child over a particular age and children of certain ethnic groups where there is a shortage of adoptive parents. Later in this chapter we will discuss why the "special-needs" designation can be important.

Waiting for a Child. Here is the bottom line:

- If you are adopting a newborn, you are typically waiting for a birth mother to select you. You have no power over how quickly you adopt, other than how hard you work at it, as it is up to a birth mother to select you. She holds the power. Not you.

- If you are adopting a waiting child, the children are waiting for you to select them. This can eliminate a great deal of the wait-time (although you must still be selected by the public agency, and to some extent, your private agency, as a good fit for the child).

Historically, agencies maintained waiting lists. Adoptive parents would wait their turn to reach the top of the list for their turn to adopt, and waiting several years was not uncommon if a newborn or very young child was desired. Waiting lists have largely been discarded, however, and now most all agencies will now only consider which of their available adoptive parents could most effectively meet the needs of the child to be adopted and the desires of the adoptive parents.

If the child is a newborn, and the birth mother has relinquished the selection of the adoptive parents to the agency, the agency will additionally try to honor any specific requests from the birth mother regarding the kind of adoptive parents she would like the child to have. However, the vast majority of newborn adoptions with agencies, at least those by private agencies, are more like independent adoption, where there is direct contact between the birth mother and the adoptive parents. You are waiting for a birth mother to select you. Public agency newborn adoptions, however, tend to be closed.

Historically, if you were working with an agency, the birth mother matches could only come via the agency, not due to your own networking or other outside efforts. This was partially due to the agency tradition of not sharing identities between birth mothers and adoptive parents, which could not exist if you found the birth mother on your own. That has all changed and most agencies strongly encourage you to network and find a birth mother, at which point they can get involved in obtaining health histories, offering counseling, et cetera. Most agencies also support you concurrently working with an attorney to find a birth mother, and review the case to make sure there are no legal obstacles. Of course, some agencies are also active in networking and create many adoptive matches directly.

Depending how aggressively you network, and the degree of luck that always plays a role, and the success of your agency in networking to create adoptive matches, you might be matched with a birth mother in months. But it can also take years. Or it can never happen. The number of doors you open regarding the type of situations you will embrace (age, ethnicity, et cetera) will dramatically affect the number of birth mothers considering you.

Adoptive Families magazine surveyed its readers in 2016 for adoptions completed in 2014-2015. The responses showed that 63% adopted within less than one year, and the majority was within the first six months. Those are extremely encouraging statistics. Be aware, however, that this is the waiting time for those who did adopt. It does not factor in those who tried but did not yet succeed. Still, the quick success time is very impressive and encouraging.

Waiting time to adopt through public agencies depends upon the type of child you hope to adopt. If you are interested in adopting a waiting child, often there is a substantially shorter waiting period for the placement, because there are more children awaiting an adoptive home than there are available adoptive parents. Once you complete the agency home study and any required parenting classes, you can immediately start considering available children. With the combination of the home study and parenting classes often done within six months or so in most states, that means you are considering children only six months after starting the process.

The *Adoptive Families* magazine survey showed that in public agency placements from foster care of the child they ended up adopting, 64% were placed within one year, and the vast majority of these in the first six months. Finalization of the adoption was reported to be slower, but the placements were impressively quick.

With newborn placements, however, public agencies normally have a much longer waiting time than private agencies or independent adoption. This is because few birth mothers elect to place with their local public agency (they often view it as a "county facility" like a welfare or public health office), and instead prefer the private sector. Also, in many regions, a significant percentage of the few newborn placements that do end up being handled by public agencies are those involving substantial drug abuse during the pregnancy.

In fact, this is often why the public agency is involved, because Children's Protective Services (CPS) was contacted by the hospital at birth due to the positive drug test and the child was not permitted to leave with the birth mother. Prenatal drug usage can occur in any type of adoption, but is more commonly found in the placements finding their way to public agencies. However, sometimes a woman will just give birth with no prior adoption planning, with no positive drug screen or other risk factor requiring CPS intervention, but simply the desire to voluntarily relinquish almost immediately, at which time the public agency may be contacted to assist her. In other words, drug-free newborns can originate from the county agency. They are a rarity, however.

Unlike private agencies, public agencies will normally not allow you to find your own birth mother, either on your own or through an attorney, then have the agency perform the home study and needed services. For example, if you were waiting with your local public agency in good faith for an adoptive placement, and before it occurred you were approached about a voluntary adoption, the agency will usually decline to have any role. This is because, as was alluded to before, their role is to find homes for the waiting children they are dedicated to serve. They will normally refer you to a private agency or attorney to complete that adoption, and will terminate your pending public agency application or home study.

The Openness of the Adoption. Decades ago most private and public agencies arranged only closed adoptions, while independent adoption was viewed as the "open" adoption alternative. Now private agency adoptions of newborns are usually open as well. Agency adoptions are usually closed.

A closed adoption is one where the adoptive parents and birth mother would never meet and identities were not disclosed. Although the term "open adoption" can mean many things, normally it refers to an adoption where the birth mother and adoptive parents personally meet and exchange some personal information before the birth to be sure each wishes to go forward, or they agree to some level of contact after the placement, or both. In the adoption of waiting children, the birth parents' rights may have been terminated, but in some cases there might be relatives whom the agency thinks will be best for the child to stay in contact with (perhaps a grandparent who has had a long-term relationship, but can't parent the child).

The openness of a private agency in a newborn adoption will vary from agency to agency and from state to state, and also will reflect the desires of the birth and adoptive parents. Full identities or partial identities may be disclosed. The openness may continue after the birth in a variety of ways. In many cases the adoptive parents and birth mother maintain contact by sending pictures and letters once or twice a year up to the child's eighteenth birthday. In some adoptions the adoptive parents, birth mother and the child maintain face-to-face contact as mutually desired, just as it may occur in an independent adoption. Some birth mothers prefer the other extreme and want no post-birth contact at all.

Many adoptive parents have a knee-jerk reaction against open adoption, often thinking it will "complicate" their lives, or undermine their role as parents. Although you as parents have the right to select the kind of adoption you prefer, you might want to ask yourself:

- If our child ever needs bone marrow, or something like a kidney transplant, who will we be contacting? Answer: the birth parent.
- We will be raising our child from birth with the knowledge that he or she was adopted, and that adoption was a loving act by his or her birth parents. Won't it be natural that at some point our child will want to meet this person? And won't that be easier if we stayed in touch prior to that?
- If the birth parents' rights have been terminated and the adoption is finalized, and we are our child's only legal parents, do we really need to feel worried and insecure about the continuing existence of a birth parent? (Most would agree that, absent safety concerns, the answer should be "no.")
- We have a lot of distant relatives who we see once or twice a year. They are part of our family, but have no right to interfere in our child-raising decisions. Is there a reason that a birth mother (or father) can't have a similar role?
- Can a child have too many people who love them?
- We believe the birth mother placed her child with us because she wanted us to be his or her permanent parents, and she only wants the best for us and our child, so is there any reason to fear her?

Although private agency adoptions have become quite open, those through public agencies still tend to be completely closed. This is often because most of the children's birth parents' rights were involuntarily terminated by court action due to inadequate or improper parenting, and because continued contact would not be in the child's best interests. Furthermore, the selection of the adoptive parents, and the placement of the child with them, was done completely by the agency. The birth parent had no role. Even in the small number of voluntary newborn adoptions which a public agency may handle, traditionally these adoptions remain closed as well.

Public and private agencies working together. A great development over the last thirty years or so is the increase of private adoption agencies becoming foster family agencies. This is in large part due to the county agencies getting overloaded handling the many children who needed homes, leaving not enough time or staff to recruit, assess, train, and match potential adoptive families with these children.

So, what has become the norm in most states, particularly in larger metropolitan areas, is that private agencies are licensed to do the pre-placement home study of the adoptive parents, including the required parenting and adoption training. When a prospective adoptive family has been certified as a foster family, the private agency may show photos and give information to the family about children in the foster care system who are moving towards a plan of adoption. At minimum this will be the children in the county system in which you live, but often includes children from any county in your state.

Not every child in foster care is headed toward adoption. To the contrary, by law the public agency must to try to reunify the child with his or her birth parents or extended family. The timetable for this varies. Reunification efforts are common for six months or a year, but can extend much longer, such as where the birth family is making some efforts, or extended family is located after a period of time.

However, when those efforts at reunification fail, the child is designated "available for adoption," which means that either the court has terminated parental rights, or it appears a member of the birth family will be unable to parent the child so freeing the child from parental custody and control is likely.

It would be nice from the adoptive parent perspective if the parental rights were always severed fully by the court before you even consider a child. There are two reasons why that does not always happen, however. One is the reality that the court system is busy, and will feel no need to bring a termination of parental rights action until there is actually an adoptive family selecting that child. Also, the court may not see a benefit to terminate parental rights until there is actually someone ready to assume those rights and duties. In a growing number of states, the court is expressly forbidden by law from terminating parental rights unless and until the child has been placed in a pre-adoptive home and is doing well there.

These children are of all ethnic groups and of varying ages. Some will need extraordinary parenting due to the difficult life situation endured prior to the adoption, or there might be actual emotional, physical or intellectual difficulties. Some children have no such specific difficulties but had to be removed from their parents due to neglect, parental substance abuse, domestic violence, et cetera.

Post-Placement Procedures. Private and public agencies usually handle post-placement procedures (i.e., after the child is placed with you) differently.

If you are adopting a newborn with a private agency, you are usually acquainted with the birth mother, having met her and spent time getting to know each other, so you will usually be in contact with her at the hospital. In a county adoption, this is very rare as usually there has never been any contact between you and the birth mother. County adoptions are almost always closed.

If you are adopting a newborn, the child will usually be placed directly with you from the hospital. Some states will delay the placement until the birth mother has signed her consent (sometimes called a *relinquishment* or *surrender* in agency adoptions), and others allow the child to go home with you prior to that happening (with you understanding the adoption is still at risk). The state-by-state review gives each state's laws regarding when the consent can be signed and if there is a revocation period. Some states have the exact same laws regarding consents whether the adoption is independent or agency, and others have different rules on when the consents are taken and when they become irrevocable.

Some agencies have the policy of not placing the child with you until the consent is irrevocable, placing the child in a temporary foster home, but more and more are placing immediately, as everyone recognizes the benefit of immediate bonding with the adoptive parents.

Whether you are adopting a newborn or a waiting child, there is post-placement supervision by the agency. The time varies by state and is discussed in the state-by-state review, but is usually about six months.

Adopting a waiting child might have a longer supervision period, depending on when the termination of parental rights order is issued.

When the supervision period is over, and all legal requirements have been met (the legal issues discussed in Chapter 12) your adoption can be set for the final court hearing. Some agencies do the final adoption paperwork for you and set the court hearing for you to appear on your own. Others suggest you retain an attorney for that minimal function, as all the work has been done and only the final paperwork and court appearance is needed. Chapter 12 discusses the final hearing.

Adoption Exchanges

An *adoption exchange* is an odd term, but what it refers to is the compilation of waiting children in a state or particular region, by an authorized group or governmental entity. Think of an exchange as a list of children in foster care for whom adoptive homes are sought.

Almost every county adoption agency has its own exchange or participates in regional exchange meetings. Some very large counties even have multiple exchanges. Each state has a statewide exchange. Some regional exchanges cover multiple states. Finally, there is the national adoption exchange (adoptuskids.org). Appendix A lists the national and regional exchanges, and the state-by-state review lists the state exchanges.

Exchanges were created to make sure no child gets lost in the system, and to allow him or her to be seen by people who might be interested in adopting. The goal, quite simply, is to find the children permanent homes. What is wonderful about the exchanges is you can look at them right now. You can go online and see actual waiting children. Be aware, however, that not all available children are viewable on the various exchange websites. Actually, only a small number are because most don't yet have court orders permitting them to be shown online. Many of the available children are too new to the system to be listed, so don't be discouraged if you take a quick view of some exchanges and don't see a child you hope to adopt. You are seeing only the tip of the proverbial iceberg.

To see the full list of waiting children, you need to view the private databases of the agency with which you are working. Since those are not viewable by the public online, court orders are not required for you—as an approved agency family—to learn about them. Some of the kids will be so new to the system they won't even be on the county's online system, and you will instead see them in old-fashioned photo books, or in a "Child Available" email sent out by a county social worker to private agencies. Children are added and removed every day.

But just who *are* these waiting children we've been talking about? The U.S. Department of Health and Human Services has provided the following information about children in the United States who are presently awaiting adoptive homes. The government is slow to provide statistics for each year, so these numbers are from 2015, but the percentages change little from year to year.

Age of children in foster care:

Under age 1:   7%
Ages 1-5:   32%
Ages 6-10:   23%
Ages 11-14:   17%
Ages 15 and over: 21%

More helpful, however, is the percentages of children who are specifically waiting for adoptive homes, meaning parental rights have already been terminated, or is is planned to do so:

Age of waiting children:

Under age 1:   4%
Ages 1-5:   40%
Ages 6-10:   28%
Ages 11-14:   16%
Ages 15 and over: 11%

Ethnicity of waiting children:

Caucasian: 43%
African-American: 24%
Hispanic: 21%
Native American: 2%
Asian: 1%
Unknown: 9%

What is the average delay between the termination of parental rights and adoption? (This shows how quickly children can be free for adoption):

Less than 1 month: 2%
1-5 months:29%
6-11 months: 35%
12-17 months: 17%
Over 18 months: 16%

What about the adoptive parents of waiting children? Who are they?

Married couple: 68%
Unmarried couple: 3%
Single female: 26%
Single male: 3%

Private vs public agency services. We've discussed how you can adopt a child from an adoption exchange via either a public agency or a private agency licensed as a foster family agency (this is true of almost all states). So, what is the difference?

- The county is usually free from the beginning, as are some private agencies. Some private agencies, however, will charge the home study fee, which may be reimbursed later when you adopt a waiting child.

- You will usually receive your parenting training by the agency with which you are working. In some regions, people tend to find the training at private agencies is better than what is offered at the county level, with less of a bureaucratic feeling, and less focus on how to help the child reunify with the birth family.

- The agency supervising the placement will usually be the entity that completed your home study, so even though the child was in the county foster care system, once he or she is placed in your care, you are under the primary supervision of the private agency you selected, not the county. However, some states still require a county social worker to visit your home and to speak with you and with the child every month until the adoption has been finalized. Many adoptive parents report a better experience working with a private agency.

- Here is the biggest difference: Large county agencies will usually be focused on only the kids in their own county exchange. So, if you are working with the county agency, you will only see that county's available children. Private agencies, however, are more inclined to use a larger data base and will usually, at minimum, use the statewide exchange. Some will also use the regional and national adoption exchanges. This means you will see more waiting children and thus have more opportunity to make a faster match with a compatible child.

A common misconception about the national adoption exchange, adoptuskids.org, is that this includes all waiting children from all the state and regional exchanges. If that were the case, why bother to check

101

individual exchanges? This, however, is completely wrong. The national exchange does not automatically include all the children across the country, only those specifically submitted to it. Many children are only on their local or state exchange. Many more are never listed on an exchange at all, because the child's county social worker has developed a good working relationship with one or more private agencies, and can make good matches through networking directly with those agencies, eliminating the need to list the child on an exchange.

So, what happens if David and Rebecca of Michigan have their home study through their county or private foster family agency, and they don't find the right child immediately on the local or statewide exchange, and on their own they find an available child on Maine's exchange? Or Florida's? Or in Tennessee, but on the national exchange, or wherever? Can they adopt that child?

It would be nice in a perfect world to say "yes." But the answer is "maybe." The issue is that although interstate adoptions (the child crossing state lines for the adoption) can occur, and should occur more than they do, the additional bureaucratic steps for the agencies make it less likely for public agency workers to devote much time or assistance in making potential interstate matches. And frankly, some states play well together and some don't. Despite the great work done by the exchanges, one area in which they can improve is conquering the bureaucratic entanglements the state governments have created through the Interstate Compact on the Placement of Children ("ICPC") for foster children. Although the ICPC is fairly automatic in newborn independent and private agency adoptions, this is not the case for waiting children, as they are entrenched as a foster child in the court system of their home county. It is just the sad reality of bureaucracy. So sometimes interstate adoptions proceed smoothly, and sometimes they don't. Every state's and every child's situation is different.

There are other considerations. If you and a child are three thousand miles apart, it is more difficult to have meetings to gradually get you all to the point of comfort and readiness for the child to move in with you. Or maybe the child has a bond with a particular school or counselor, or there are local relatives it would be beneficial for the child to stay in contact with. So there are many considerations.

Don't forget, however, the purposes of these exchanges is to make adoptions happen. So be aggressive. Each exchange has a contact person, sometimes listed for each child. Provide this information to your caseworker and ask him or her to call and find out more information for you to determine if this is a good fit and can happen logistically. In most cases, private agencies seem to be more likely than county agencies to get these adoptions going. This is not said in disrespect to the county agencies; the hard reality is that they are so busy trying to adequately serve the kids in their foster care system, kids they are legally obligated to put first (and rightfully so), that they don't have extra time to find placements for children in another state's system.

Adoption Subsidies. The good news keeps coming regarding adopting waiting children. Truly, the government does all it can to encourage people to give loving permanent homes to children, rather than have them grow up in foster care, and potentially be without a family when they turn eighteen.

An adoption subsidy is a monthly maintenance payment to the adoptive parents to help offset the expenses of raising a child. So not only does the family receive monthly assistance during the foster parenting period leading to adoption, they can then receive the adoption subsidy after the adoption is final. This payment is usually about the same as the government would have been paying foster parents. This is for waiting children who have been designated as special-needs, so not every waiting child qualifies, but many do just upon factors like age, being of a particular ethnicity, or being a member of a sibling group adopted together.

This is not an automatic benefit, and it is negotiated with each adoptive family, largely based upon the needs of the child. The adoptive parents' income does not play a role in federal subsidy, but some states have their own subsidy for children who are not federally qualified, and some states' laws do permit adoptive parent income to play a role in eligibility.

Another huge benefit is that a subsidy-qualified child is usually Medicaid-qualified, thus covering most medical costs. All these things are negotiated between adoptive parents and the agency before the adoption is finalized to make sure the child's needs will be met.

To see each state's maximum subsidy, visit nacac.org (North American Council for Adoptable Children). Here is a sampling of a few randomly selected states' maximum monthly subsidy:

New Jersey (for children 0-5 years): $738
Kansas (no age differentiation): $500
Mississippi (0-3 years): $325
New York (0-5 years): $497
California (0-4 years): $707

Only the subsidies for younger children is shown above. The subsidy may be higher for older children, however, often by about an additional one-third. The subsidy usually continues until the child becomes an adult at age eighteen, but in some circumstances can continue until age 21.

What about the costs of your adoption? Even if the county or private agency provided their services for free, you might have had to pay a small amount to an attorney to finalize the adoption in court, or had significant travel costs if the child was out-of-area. For special-needs children, you can be reimbursed as a one-time payment (usually $1,500-$2,000 in most states) for those costs.

Some states even have special programs to help fund college for children coming out of the foster-care system, and this can include children adopted from foster care, as well. The goal is to help them become contributing members of society, despite the fact the rocky beginning they experienced through no fault of their own.

In a nutshell, here are some of the benefits of adopting a waiting child (particularly if they are also designated a special-needs child) that do not exist in other types of adoption:

- Children are literally waiting to be adopted, and you can easily view them online, or in your agency's photo books.
- You can often have a child in your home in less than one year from when you started the process.
- These adoptions are usually free or very low cost, even including the home study and post-placement supervision.

- You are eligible for the full federal adoption tax credit of $13,570, even if you had no actual adoption expenses. This can eliminate a large amount of tax that you would otherwise owe. (Chapter 13 gives more information on the tax credit.)
- Eligibility for reimbursement for some adoption expenses. For most states this goes up to a one-time payment of $2,000, covering travel expenses, possible attorney for the finalization hearing, et cetera).
- Your child's automatic eligibility of Medicaid.
- Eligibility for a monthly subsidy until your child becomes an adult.

Compare adopting an American waiting child to an intercountry adoption (where basically every child is a waiting child from age 3-8 years of age, although China's children are usually quite young). In an intercountry adoption, the waiting children are very similar to those in our own foster care system. But in intercountry adoption, you get *none* of the above benefits. Instead you will likely incur costs of about $40,000, face massive bureaucracy, likely have to travel one or more times overseas, and will be bringing home a child who does not speak English and will have a huge adjustment to learning an entirely new culture. Pointing this out is not intended to be disrespectful of intercountry adoption as an option, but to open up people's eyes to the adoption of American waiting children.

For more helpful reading on adopting children from the foster care system and adoption exchanges, visit DaveThomasFoundation.org. (Dave Thomas is the founder of Wendy's, the popular hamburger chain, and himself an adoptee.) Their site offers this insightful thought: "75.3 million Americans have considered adoption. If just 1 in 700 of these adults adopted, every waiting child in foster care would have a permanent family."

Adopting a Newborn

Much of the above has focused on waiting children, but let's not forget that more voluntarily placed newborns (not via foster care) are placed for adoption via private agencies than any other method, even more than independent adoption in some states. So, let's end with a review of the different options you have in the "private adoption agency" category.

If you want to adopt a newborn via private agency adoption, of course the first thing you will do is check out agencies in your own region. That only makes sense. There is no reason to select an agency thousands of miles away if one just as good is within an hour's drive from your home. But what if you can't find an agency that can meet your needs within your region? (In the next chapter we will explore specific questions to assist you in finding a well-qualified agency.) Let's explore other options to agencies in your home state.

Working with out-of-state adoption agencies. Most adoptive parents will complete every aspect of the adoption in the state in which they live. They will hire an agency there, the birth mother will live and give birth there, and the adoption will be finalized there, in their local court. If you live in a state with great agencies from which to choose, good adoption laws making you feel secure, and a sufficient number of birth mothers in your region or state, why leave your own state?

Many adoptive parents aren't so lucky. What if you don't like what the local agencies have to offer? Or what if you want to work with them, but you don't meet their eligibility requirements? Perhaps there are few adoptive placements in your region or state. Maybe you are concerned that your state has laws which give birth parents an excessively long time to change their minds. Or could it be that your state is fine, but you want to expand your options to increase the likelihood of being picked for an adoptive placement quickly. There are many reasons to either do your adoption out of state, or work in both your home state and another state. You have two ways to do this: 1) an "interstate adoption" where your birth mother lives in another state but you finalize in your home state; or 2) a "non-resident adoption" where the birth mother gives birth in another state and you finalize your adoption under her state's laws and in her home state court.

Alison Foster Davis, legal director of Family Connections Christian Adoptions, a full-service California private adoption agency, has this to say about the many options available in interstate agency adoptions:

"A good agency will encourage you to do what works for your situation, whether that means finding an out-of-state agency to assist you with a match, finalizing in another state, or adopting from foster care within your state. Don't hesitate to ask your agency for recommendations of matching agencies inside or outside of your state; often your agency will have worked with several and can assist you with finding one that has the types of match you are seeking. Honest, open communication should flow naturally with the agency that is the right fit for you. Mutual trust and respect should be present in order to maximize your opportunity for a positive adoption experience."

Interstate Adoption. Let's say you've found a great agency but it is located in another state. No problem. You can hire the out-of-state agency to help you find a birth mother, offer counseling to her, help with her signing her relinquishment of parental rights, and arrange for the child to be physically placed in your care. Very shortly after birth, when the initial paperwork is done and you get interstate approval to bring the child across state lines (discussed in Chapter 12), you return home with your child. A local in-state agency that you've selected will have done the pre-placement home study for you, and will also do the post-placement supervision, including writing the final report to the court to complete the adoption. You complete the adoption in your local court, primarily under your home state's laws. (Sometimes the out-of-state's laws can apply, as discussed in Chapter 12.)

You might fear using two agencies would double the cost, but that is usually not true. As discussed in more detail in Chapter 6 and 9, many agencies will only charge for the services they perform. Accordingly, if they are dividing their duties, their fees should be proportionally less. Not every agency will work that way, but most will.

Non-resident adoption. How about if we take all the reasons why you might be considering an out-of-state agency from the section above, and add one thing? What if the state in which you hired the out-of-state agency allowed non-residents to adopt, assuming the baby is born there? Perhaps you might want to finalize the adoption under that state's laws. Why? Maybe your state allows a birth mother thirty days to change her mind and the out-of-state agency's laws only permit 72 hours? What if it typically takes a year or more after birth to finalized your adoption in your state, compared to the out-of-state agency's usual time of three months? There are many other legal comparisons to be made between each state regarding such issues as birth father's rights, permitted birth parent expenses paid by adoptive parents, the adoption being open or closed, et cetera.

States permitting agency non-resident adoption are: Alabama, Alaska, Arkansas, California, Colorado, Delaware, District of Columbia, Hawaii, Illinois, Indiana, Iowa, Kansas, Louisiana, Maine, Maryland, Massachusetts, Michigan, Missouri, New Hampshire, New Jersey, New Mexico, New York, North Dakota, Ohio, Oregon, Pennsylvania, South Carolina, Texas, Utah, Vermont, Virginia and Washington. You can learn more about each state's laws and the agencies and attorneys within that state in the state-by state review.

In a non-resident agency adoption you start with the exact same scenario as we discussed for interstate adoption. You selected an out-of-state agency to help match you with a birth mother and that agency continues to do virtually everything in the adoption. After creating the adoptive match, it provides counseling for the birth mother, assists with her relinquishment, arranges for the baby to be released into your care, and makes the arrangements for your adoption to be finalized in its local court. The agency in your home state will only need to do your pre-placement home study and post-placement supervision. Generally, only the laws of the birth state where the out-of-state agency is located will apply, so there is less chance of a conflict of laws as compared to an interstate adoption. These potential conflicts are discussed in Chapter 12.

CHAPTER 6

SELECTING THE RIGHT AGENCY

Just as selecting an attorney is the central element of an independent adoption, choosing the right agency is the key ingredient in the success of an agency adoption. Despite the importance of this decision, the vast majority of adoptive parents give much less thought to this decision than they should. In most cases they call a few agencies in their home city or region and select one from those few. You can choose to be like everyone else, *or* you can choose to maximize your chances of success.

Considering there are more than 1,200 private adoption agencies in the nation (this is not even counting the equally high number of public/county agencies), you are clearly cheating yourself if you don't thoroughly consider agencies beyond those in a small radius of your home. There are many supremely qualified agencies located all around the country. There are also many to be avoided that fall short of what a good agency should do for you.

Adoption agencies are no different than any other business. You will see the same differences in quality of service as with other professionals you've hired, some great, some barely competent. The good news is that you can easily find an excellent agency by following some basic steps. Here are those steps, and following them we will review each one in detail:

1. Select between private or public agency adoption.
2. Narrow your list of possible agencies.

3. Is the agency licensed?
4. Is the agency able to perform the specific duties you need?
5. Do you meet the requirements of the agency?
6. Fine-tune your list.
7. Specific questions to ask the agency.
8. Test the agency's knowledge.
9. Determine if their personality and approach to adoption matches yours.

Select Between Private or Public Agency Adoption

Chapter 5 illustrated how different private and public agency adoption are. If you are planning a public agency adoption, you are normally restricted to working with your local county adoption office. In other words, you can't "shop around" like you can when selecting a private agency. If you can't find your local county adoption office online or in your local Yellow Pages (search County of _____, Adoptions), you can call the state adoption office as listed in the state-by-state review in Chapter 15, and that office can give you the needed contact information.

Accordingly, the suggestions below for finding the best agency are mainly applicable if you are seeking to adopt via a private agency, and in particular, if you are seeking to adopt a newborn.

Although you would have no reason to retain an agency out of your home *state* when you are planning a waiting child adoption, you may consider one outside your home *county.* This varies state-by-state, but in most states agencies are licensed not just in the county where they have their main office, but perhaps in surrounding counties. So if, for example, you hear that a neighboring county has a private agency which is a foster family agency and that is your chosen type of adoption—and you hear their classes and staff are superior to a similar agency in your own county, some states will permit you to use the out-of-county agency. The agency itself can let you know if they can provide the services you want. The point in sharing this is to make sure you know you can usually expand your horizons—and with it, your options. So, don't be afraid to ask.

Narrow Your List of Possible Agencies

There are more than 1,200 licensed private adoption agencies around the nation, although not all of them do newborn adoptions. How do you narrow it down and choose one? Sounds daunting, but it's not. Obviously, you won't be looking at a thousand-plus adoption agencies. It's helpful to know they are out there, however.

You may be looking only for an agency in your home state, or wish to consider agencies of a particular other state. It is recommended you start locally and expand from there as needed. Who knows, the right agency might be only twenty miles away. For others, it might be a county away, in a neighboring state, or even the other side of the country. The answer is dependent upon the region and state in which you live, the type of adoption you choose, the kind of child you hope to adopt, and the services you will require.

The government-sponsored website, childwelfare.gov, lists every private adoption agency in the nation—more than 1,200. So, your problem is narrowing down this list, and deciding which ones to contact. Let's explore how to do this.

- Only consider agencies in your preferred geographical regions or states. Your selected regions or states from which to adopt will be unique to you and different from other adoptive parents. You might live in a well-populated region in a state with advantageous adoption laws and a good percentage of birth mothers. If so, you will likely select an agency in your home region and state. In some large metropolitan areas, there might be over twenty within a hundred-mile radius. Another adoptive family may live in a state with very poor adoption options, so they'll select several states they feel are best for them, and will consider agencies in those states. (To determine the right states for you, consider the many in-state and out-of-state options we discussed in Chapter 2, and the information provided in the state-by-state review in Chapter 15. It is within only these states that you need focus your search for the best agency.)

- Call adoption attorneys. You might think that most adoption attorneys are "in competition" with agencies, so they would not recommend any. In most cases, this isn't true. Most attorneys, even in states where independent adoption competes with agency adoption, work regularly with adoption agencies. Adoption is a small world and the good professionals in the same region usually know and associate with each other. Although you might not succeed in directly reaching the attorney him or herself, usually speaking to a staff person is sufficient as they will know which agencies the attorney commonly works with. Some might have a relationship with one particular agency causing them to unjustly favor one over others, that's okay, since you are hoping for a consensus, hearing one or more agency names several times, from different sources.

- Join or visit adoptive parent support groups. They are an ideal source of which are the best agencies (and perhaps some to stay away from). If you live in an area with a large enough population base, it is likely you have a local adoptive parent support group. These are valuable people for you to contact as they've completed the process you are just starting. They can talk to you about their experiences with local agencies. Not only can they tell you why they hired the one they did, but why they didn't hire the others. There are several ways to find adoptive parents support groups. One is the Child Welfare Information Gateway's site: childwelfare.gov. Click "State Resources" from the top bar then from the dropdown menu select "National Foster Care and Adoption Directory." Then select the state of interest to you, and under the heading "Support Groups" click the box for "Kinship, Foster Care and Adoption Support Groups," then click the "Go" button. Listed will be both private groups, as well as private adoption agencies that have support groups. You can also find *online* discussion groups at AdoptiveFamilies.com. In the second row of options on the menu bar you will see "Groups." After clicking on that, you will see many different online groups from which to choose. (Websites are constantly redesigned and updated, so the above "first click here, then click there" directions might not be accurate in the future. But if you explore the sites, you should find their listings of groups.) You can also call local adoption agencies and attorneys and inquire if they know of any adoptive parent support groups.

- Join *Resolve*, or attend one of their meetings. Resolve is a very established and respected national infertility organization with regional chapters throughout the country. Part of their focus on infertility includes adoption. Many of their members are in the process of, or have completed, an adoption, and can talk about agencies they used. To find a Resolve chapter near you, visit resolve.org. For more information about Resolve, please see Appendix B.

- Talk to other adoptive parents. The more you start talking about adoption, the more you will find that people you already know have adopted. Most of these families feel no need to volunteer personal information about their family being formed by adoption unless there is a reason to do so. In most cases, upon hearing you share that interest, they are happy to share their adoption experiences. There are millions of adoptive parents out there. You will find them everywhere. You can ask which adoption agency they used and how they would rate their services. Also, ask if they can put you in touch with other adoptive parents who might have information to share with you about their adoption experiences. You will find that adoptive parents tend to know a lot of other adoptive parents.

- Talk to people you know in the healthcare industry. Many adoption agencies work with doctors, counselors and hospitals regarding the care of the birth mothers they are working with. For this reason, some healthcare professionals may be able to tell you about agencies with whom they have had contact in prior adoption situations.

If you previously read Chapter 4 (Selecting the Right Attorney) you have likely noticed that some of the recommended steps in compiling a list of possible agencies are the same as when inquiring about adoption attorneys. If you are like many adoptive parents just starting the process—perhaps unsure at this point if you will be doing an independent or agency adoption—clearly it makes sense to concurrently inquire about *both* agencies and attorneys when you speak to the people and groups recommended above.

Don't forget that your inquiries about adoption agencies need to be in the region where the agency has its office. That means that if you are inquiring about a local agency, let's say in your hometown of Chicago, you would be contacting Chicago professionals and support groups to ask about them. But let's say you were considering an agency in another city and state, perhaps Los Angeles. You will need to inquire about it with its local entities.

Is the Agency Licensed?

What you are really asking here isn't so much if the agency is licensed, rather *is it an adoption agency at all*. In many states, if you start your search for an adoption agency by opening your local yellow pages, or searching on the internet, many of the ads you will see are for what you will assume are adoption agencies. They have names with sound like agencies, and they do adoptions, so what could they be but a licensed adoption agency? Right?

Wrong. In the majority of states, some of these entities are not agencies but *facilitators*. A facilitator is a person or business which helps arrange adoptions for a fee, but is not licensed as an agency or attorney. They can't do home studies. They can't witness consents/ relinquishments. They can't prepare legal documents or give you legal advice. They can't write a court report approving the adoption. What *do* they do? They find birth mothers to make adoptive matches. In other words, they are primarily paid baby finders (more accurately, paid "birth mother finders"). Is this a bad thing? Often yes, but maybe not always. Let's face it, finding a birth mother is an important part of most newborn adoptions. But make that, finding the *right* birth mother. And therein is part of the problem in dealing with facilitators.

A good agency or attorney is educated, trained and licensed to do their job. Furthermore, they are monitored by a state office, and if they don't perform their services correctly, they risk losing their licenses. To be a facilitator, however, most states simply require getting a business license. How easy is that? Go spend $25 or so for your license, make up a business name, and presto! You're in business. Now you can run your ads proclaiming "#1 in adoptions!" Or, perhaps, "Christian adoptive parents waiting for your baby!" (Sadly, you will often see a religious theme used as what sometimes appears to be a marketing tool, as the business rarely has any official tie to any religion.)

Many in the adoption profession hold facilitators in such low esteem is that their advertising rarely clearly says: "We are not a licensed adoption agency or attorney." Instead, their ads imply to adoptive parents, and especially to less sophisticated birth mothers, that they are an actual licensed agency, with the protections that brings. A good question to ask facilitators is, "If you are truly dedicated to the field of adoptions, why don't you become a licensed agency?" The answer in many cases is that either they would be deemed ineligible due to lack of qualifications, or they wish to continue to operate without the legal restrictions placed on legitimate licensed agencies. And a good question for you, if you are considering hiring a facilitator, is if the ads of the facilitator are incomplete and misleading, what makes you think that they will be completely forthright in other matters with you?

Another example of providing misleading information is in the advertisements many facilitators use. Most of them advertising out of the state in which they are located will not provide any information about their actual whereabouts. They will provide a toll free number and no address. Why? To entice birth mother and adoptive parent calls from all around the country to "get them on the phone and plant their hook," and only later reveal that they are located in a different state. By then, they likely hope they have convinced the person to work with them, when initially the birth mother or adoptive parent may have never made the call if it was known their office was so far away. The average facilitator charges large fees, often more than most agencies and attorneys, despite the fact agencies and attorneys provide more services.

Facilitators are not the only entities which omit important information like their actual whereabouts from their ads. Some legitimate agencies and attorneys have also been known to do this, and caution should be exercised with them when they do as well. The practice seems to be most used by facilitators, however.

Is the Agency Able To Do
the Specific Duties You Need?

Each adoption agency is licensed to perform particular functions, or chooses to limit itself. Some do domestic; others do intercountry. A small number do both. Some are licensed in multiple states while most are licensed in only one. Even within a state, some might be licensed only in one county, while others are statewide. (And we already spoke about those which are foster family agencies—but here we are focusing more on those not seeking a waiting child, rather a newborn or intercountry adoption.

Of those doing domestic adoptions, some might be licensed only to perform home studies. Others are additionally licensed to make adoptive placements. Among those who make placements, they are further distinguished by those that have outreach programs, networking for birth mothers to contact their agency to select adoptive parents. Other agencies are more passive, and do little to create adoptive matches, leaving that to you to do on your own or via an adoption attorney.

With this wide diversity in services, it is critical you find the right agency offering the services you need. If you are hoping to be matched up with a birth mother to adopt a newborn, you will want an agency that actively networks and places children for adoption in addition to doing home studies. If you will be using another source to find a birth mother, such as an attorney or your own networking efforts, you might only need an agency that does home studies. If you are planning an intercountry adoption, ask does the agency only perform home studies which are accepted for intercountry adoption? Or does it also have a program in the country from the specific country from which you plan to adopt? Because intercountry adoptions involve such diverse procedures than domestic agency adoption, they are separately discussed in Chapter 7.

Do You Meet the Requirements of the Agency?

So far, we've talked about you choosing an agency. The reality, however, is that they are also choosing *you*. Private adoption agencies can set their own guidelines regarding which adoptive parents they will work with.

Some agencies have a religious affiliation, usually obvious from their name, such as Jewish Family Services or Lutheran Child and Family Services. Some of these religious-affiliated agencies will welcome adoptive parents of all religious backgrounds, but most will only work with adoptive parents of their designated faith (although the birth mother is usually welcomed regardless of her religious affiliation). Others will set their own unique requirements regarding your age, the number of existing children you have, whether you are married or single, length of your marriage, existence and number of any prior marriages, if one spouse must be a full-time parent, and similar factors. Over the last fifteen to twenty years, private agencies have loosened up on many of their restrictions. As with society in general, some issues are now more accepted and mainstream, such as same-sex couples adopting.

Public agency adoptions are both more lenient and more restrictive. For example, as a government institution they can't exclude you based upon your religion, but they might be more restrictive in other areas.

The one thing both private and public agencies will have in common in their requirements is that you show you can provide a secure and loving home for a child. In this regard, the existence of any evidence of child abuse, criminal activity or consistent financial instability is grounds for denial with both private and public agencies.

Fine-Tune Your List

You've likely eliminated a large number of agencies on your list simply by determining they don't offer the services you want, or that you do not meet their eligibility requirements. You should still have a large list of possible agencies (and if you don't, maybe you should be expanding your list to include other regions in your state, or other states). How do we further eliminate the "wrong" agencies, and get the right one for you? Here are some recommended steps:

- Request each agency's written materials describing all their services, fees and requirements, or view them if available on their website. Besides receiving the information in writing or online (which is more definitive than information over the phone), it also gives you a chance to see the quality of the materials they present. An adoption agency will be preparing and processing many important documents for you. If they can't put together a professional-looking informational packet or website, that tells you something about the quality of their work and attention to detail. Carefully review their information. Does it give you all the information you need about them? Be cautious if the information is nothing but baby pictures and fluff. Creating your family is an important decision and warrants thorough information. Good agencies recognize this.

- When you first called the agency, did you get a good feeling from the initial person who answered the phone? Was he or she professional and friendly? Was it a person employed by the agency or an answering service? Remember, this will be the same person a potential birth mother will likely get on the phone in her initial call. If the receptionist is not warm and friendly, why would a birth mother be interested in staying on the line to speak to a social worker? That would mean fewer birth mothers to be considering you as adoptive parents through that office.

You will likely be immediately impressed, or not, with the materials you receive or see on their website, allowing you to quickly shorten your list. We still have a ways to go, however, to get down to the best agency for you.

Specific Questions to Ask the Agency

Some of the following questions may be answered by the written materials from the agencies, or their websites. If not, these are important questions to ask. Since most agencies offer periodic free seminars to learn more about their services, that would be an excellent, and free, chance to get your questions answered. Depending upon the type of adoption you are planning, not all the following questions may be required.

- *How many years has your agency been in business?* (You've already verified they are an actual licensed agency, as discussed earlier.) There is no real detriment if the agency you are calling has only been in business a few years, as long as they appear to be doing their job well. Generally, however, the stability of a long-established agency is impressive.

- *How many adoptions has your agency done in its existence?* An agency's length of existence is impressive, but only as it relates to how many adoptions it has done. You can't ask for much more than the combination of an established reputation combined with a significant number of completed adoptions.

- *How many adoptions do you complete each year? How about last year?* This is particularly important to you if you are hiring an agency to not just do your home study and assist with the birth mother's relinquishment, but to help match you with a birth mother. Some agencies might only complete a dozen a year, while others complete one hundred. (Generally, those doing in excess of fifty are usually found in high population areas.) A high number of adoptions each year is impressive. As you will see in the next few questions, however, that information by itself can be misleading.

- *How many adoptive parents do you work with at one time waiting to be matched by a birth mother? Is there a maximum number you work with at one time? How many do you have at this moment?* These questions are what really put things in perspective. If an agency completes one hundred adoptions annually, but has three hundred waiting families, that means only one in every three couples are being picked in a year. An agency completing twenty adoptions with twenty waiting adoptive families being shown to each birth mother may only be completing one-fifth as many adoptions, but they appear to be making placements three times faster.

- *What is the average wait of your clients for an adoptive placement? For what kind of placements? What is a soonest versus longest estimate for a placement based upon prior clients?* When you ask these questions, you need to be clear about the type of adoption you want. For example, if you want to adopt a Caucasian or African-

American newborn, then ask that specifically. It won't help you any to find out the average wait for a placement is fourteen months, and ninety percent of those were Hispanic toddlers. Obviously, that sounds like the perfect agency for those seeking a Hispanic toddler adoption, but not if that isn't your choice of placement.

- *Are most of your adoptions "open" or "closed?"* Although each state has different laws and customs regarding how open or closed an adoption may be, often this is an area where the agency asserts its discretion, as they may elect to make adoptions more closed than independent adoptions in the same state. Assuming you want to adopt a newborn, find out if you meet the birth mother in person. If so, at what point of the pregnancy? Do you share first names? Last names? Can you be at the hospital for the birth? Hold the baby? What about post-birth contact with the birth family? If so, will it be pictures and letters one or two times a year, or face-to-face get-togethers? There is no right or wrong answer here. Adoptions are like marriages. They can all be different and yet work wonderfully. You simply want to make sure that your view of the degree of openness or closeness matches the agency's expectations.

- *Who selects us as the child's adoptive parents, the agency or the birth mother?* Some continue to do adoptions as they were done fifty years ago, with no contact at all between the birth mother and adoptive parents. Overall, in the United States, this is becoming rarer and rarer in newborn placements. You might be one of the small number of adoptive parents who desire that degree of closeness, however.

- *Do some adoptive parents who hire you never get an adoptive placement, or have to wait several years? Do you find these adoptive parents have any ethnic, religious or other qualities in common?* You want to know if the agency is creating adoptive placements that match your goals, for people with the qualities you offer. For example, if you are a member of an ethnic group seeing to adopt a child of that same ethnic group, why retain an agency located in a geographical area where that ethnicity is not represented. The same holds true of issues like religion, as some states, such as Utah, have a disproportionate degree of Mormons, meaning less of other religions.

- *Do you have an outreach program to find birth mothers to select us as adoptive parents, or do you just help us do it ourselves?* Some agencies are active in networking and create many matches for their waiting adoptive parents. Others do little or none, focusing on preparing home studies for adoptive parents who have found their own birth mother, or who are adopting older children already freed for adoption. (Chapters 8 and 9 are dedicated to teaching you strategies to find a birth mother and proceed with a newborn adoption. It is helpful, however, if your agency is working toward this goal as well.)

- *What percentage of the birth mothers you find are in-state, as compared to being from another state?* You may not care if your birth mother lives in, or out of, your home state, as you just want to get picked. Other families want to stay in-state, perhaps worrying about travel costs, easy access to the birth mother pre-birth and at the hospital, and the laws of the state where the birth will occur. If you want a birth mother from a particular state, there is no reason to hire an agency who appears to find birth mothers from other states.

- *When birth mothers contact you, how are we and other adoptive parents you are working with shown to her, giving us a chance to be selected?* Few agencies use waiting lists where they would only be showing the longest waiting families to each birth mother. Still, agency procedures can differ. Some show all their waiting adoptive parents, while others only show a few adoptive parents, selected to match characteristics of the birth mother which the agency feels is important. (Other than cases where a birth mother has characteristics not desired by the adoptive parents—ethnicity, drug usage, open or closed adoption, et cetera—you want to make sure you will be shown often and without delay, with the birth mother given a broad choice in adoptive parents. Why do you want her to have a "broad choice," rather than just you and one or two other adoptive families? A couple reasons. One is that if the agency only shows a few adoptive parents each time, think of all the times you are *not* being shown. The birth mother perhaps destined to pick you never got to even see you. The other is that even when you are shown to her, you want her decision to be solid. The more adoptive families she has to choose from, the more likely she can be truly happy with her decision. If she had only two or three families from which to choose, she might be choosing the best family available, but without a diverse enough group to be truly excited about who she is selecting. This will be one of the toughest decisions of her life. She needs to be truly impressed and emotionally attracted to the family she chooses.)

- *What percentage of your clients find a birth mother through your efforts, as compared to your clients finding a birth mother on their own?* If one of the key things you hope to accomplish in hiring an agency is to have them help you find a birth mother, you will want to know how effective their efforts are. For example, an agency may complete forty adoptions a year, but if ninety percent of the adoptive parents found their own birth mother, it is not as impressive as an agency completing only twenty-five, all of which resulted from the agency's own birth mother networking efforts.

- *Does your fee include your networking efforts to help us get picked by a birth mother, or is it a separate fee?* If the agency is networking for birth mothers, leading them to contact the agency to in turn select one of the waiting adoptive families, a lot of money is being spent by the agency in that outreach effort. This might include yellow page advertising and internet promotion of their website geared to birthmothers, contributions of time and/or money to organizations which indirectly leads to referrals, et cetera. Just like with their other expenses, these costs are passed on to you as the client benefiting from those efforts. The question is if it is part of their standard fee, which includes their agency services, or a separate fee specifically designated for networking efforts. (Either payment option is fine, as long as you know what you are paying for. Just like with attorneys, you can often expect to pay several thousand dollars or more for an effective networking campaign.)

- *What about if we want to adopt a toddler, older child, or a child with special-needs? Do you work with other agencies and exchanges in other states to help make a placement?* Some agencies primarily focus on the children relinquished through them, but many will work with agencies from all around the nation, as well as registries, to find the right child for you. If you want a child in this category, it is really essential that the agency takes full advantage of the information-sharing between agencies and states, or your options will be limited.

- *If we adopt a toddler, older child or a child with special-needs, is there any special funding programs to assist us with future costs?* You want to find out if these children are available for an Adoption Subsidy Program, and/or other benefits which might be unique to your state, if that is important to you. If you are talking to a foster family agency, this is standard fare for them.

- *Can we be listed with attorneys or other private agencies while we are working with you, and proceed with whichever attorney or agency finds an adoptive placement first?* The goal of every adoption agency and attorney should be to help you adopt. To that end, if you wish to hire more than one agency to obtain your goal as quickly as possible, you need agencies and attorneys who will work within that philosophy. Most all will be agreeable. Some agencies, however, require you to only work with them. Although this limitation makes sense for public agencies, or a private agency planning a waiting child placement for you (both of which are doing their services for free and their time is wasted if you get a placement elsewhere), the limitation is not reasonable by attorneys or private agencies when planning a newborn/non-waiting child adoption.

- *Do we pay for your services as we work through the adoption, or do we pay it all in advance?* A few agencies charge their entire fee in advance, but this is quite rare. That's because their services are usually clearly divided, as it makes little sense to charge fees before each stage of service is reached. For example, all agencies will require a pre-placement home study. That's one fee. When an adoptive placement is made there will need to be services provided to the birth mother, such as counseling and assisting with her relinquishment. There will be a fee for that. Then there will be a post-placement home study, and a fee for that. Why would they charge that in advance when it is not known when, or if, that post-placement home study will even be needed. Furthermore, why charge some of these fees if another agency (perhaps out-of-state) or an attorney, is providing some of those services? With these facts in mind, you should be very cautious in working with an agency requiring full payment for the entire adoption in advance.

- *What are typical birth mother expenses we will be expected to pay?* Almost all states allow adoptive parents to help with the adoption and birth expenses, although some states make different rules for independent or agency adoption. Standard costs may include medical bills (if no Medicare), counseling and the birth mother's living costs while she is incapacitated due to the pregnancy. Some agencies have, or are affiliated with, unwed mothers' homes. This is often an inexpensive way to meet a birth mother's food and rent needs (often about half what an apartment would cost), but many birth mothers don't like living in a group setting and are used to living on their own. (Some birth mothers have few, or no, expenses—they have insurance and are employed, or live at home), while others may have significant expenses. If your birth mother will have any expenses, you want to know in advance what they are, and for how long. As a general rule, expenses for birth mother needing full assistance will range from $600 - $1,600 per month for food and rent. Much is dependent upon where the birth mother lives, does she have a roommate, et cetera. When you get into high living costs, however, it is a sign for potential caution. For example, if an agency improperly encourages birth mothers to work with them by offering them a luxury apartment at several times the rent of a typical apartment (which you are paying for), or similar gratuitous inducements, it borders on bribery. And bribery is not conducive to a successful adoption, or finding the right kind of birth mother. To learn more about permitted living expenses, see the state-by-state review and Chapter 12.)

- *Do you provide counseling for birth mothers?* Placing a child for adoption will be one of the most emotional moments of a birth mother's life. The more prepared she is, the more likely she can make the placement as planned. Counseling is one major tool to

124

help prepare her for the birth, and the emotions to follow. Both she, and you, deserve the benefits she will receive from pregnancy/adoption counseling. Some state laws require counseling, and some do not. If an agency feels counseling is not important, or in any way discourages birth mothers from receiving it, it indicates a lack of not only empathy, but a basic understanding of the emotions at work, and the making of a successful adoption.

By the time you have received answers to these questions, you will have a definite "yes" and "no" pile of agencies. However, we still need to whittle down your list at bit to find the best agency for you.

Test the Agency's Knowledge

Just as recommended in the independent adoption chapter that you "test" an attorney's knowledge, it is suggested that you do the same regarding agencies. The problem is that this is harder to do with an agency. This is because with an attorney, you have one person—the attorney—who will be doing all the work, and you know who to question. With an agency, however, there are different people involved. Perhaps one social worker will be doing your pre-placement home study. Another will be doing your post-placement home study. Yet another might be working with the birth mother, providing counseling and assisting with her relinquishment. It is possible none of these social workers deal with the procedural and legal side of the adoption. It could be the director, an in-house attorney, or a private practice attorney hired as needed for legal work.

Regardless, just as the agency will need to be aware of these issues when a birth mother calls and they begin processing the adoption, someone should be prepared to answer your questions about important issues such as interstate adoption requirements, permitted expenses for birth mothers, the Indian Child Welfare Act, birth father's rights, et cetera. If the social worker answering your questions says such issues are not in her or his area of responsibility, ask to speak to the person who *does* have that responsibility. Asking hypothetical questions about how problems are solved is not at all unreasonable as if they can't answer those questions now, how can they solve them when they occur? As with attorneys, you will quickly see some agencies really "know their business," while others struggle.

Here are some recommended questions:

- *I've heard about something called the Indian Child Welfare Act (ICWA). Can you explain what that is?* As we will discuss later in Chapter 12, this is a federal law (and some states have their own state ICWA laws as well), which says if a child is a member of an Indian tribe, or eligible to be a member, the tribe must be given notice and certain procedures followed. If the agency is unfamiliar with the Indian Child Welfare Act, or says it never applies in their state, beware. More and more adoptions are at least potentially touched by the Indian Child Welfare Act, such as where the birth mother has a small degree of tribal heritage which could make the child a member. Noncompliance with the Indian Child Welfare Act can potentially invalidate an adoption, a high cost to pay for an agency's ignorance.

- *We may do an interstate adoption. Can you explain to me how the Interstate Compact works?* As we will discuss in Chapter 12, more and more adoptions are interstate, where you live in a different state than the state in which the child is born. The Interstate Compact for the Placement of Children (ICPC) provides that prior to a child being transported across state lines by adoptive parents, certain procedures will apply, such as a pre-placement home study of the adoptive parents, and approval from by both states before the child can cross state lines. In many states, however, the Interstate Compact administrator is not involved as it is in independent adoptions, and approval is given directly agency to agency when a full agency adoption. This is fundamental knowledge every agency should have regarding their own state procedure.

- *What are the birth mother and birth father's rights? Can they change their minds, and if so, for how long?* These issues are the most basic and important of all, so the agency should know these issues frontwards and backwards regarding their own state.

- *Is there a federal tax credit for adoptive parents?* The agency should certainly know about the Federal Adoption Tax Credit. The amount of the credit, and income eligibility changes each year. For 2017, if the adoptive parents have a modified adjusted gross income of $203,540 or less, they are eligible for a tax credit of $13,570 per child adopted. The income can actually go up to $243,540, but the credit is proportionally reduced when income exceeds $203,540. (The Adoption Tax Credit is much better than a deduction; it is a dollar for dollar reduction of tax owed.) It is not reasonable to expect an adoption agency to know the detailed tax repercussions of adoption. That is for a professional tax advisor. However, they should know the existence and basics of the tax credit. (More on the federal adoption tax credit in Chapter 13.)

There is much more to an agency adoption than the above questions, but these questions are diverse enough to give you an idea of an agency's knowledge. Those particular questions may not even be applicable to your individual adoption, but it doesn't matter. The questions are an excellent indicator of what your agency knows, or doesn't know. If they are ignorant about these issues, the same is likely true regarding other important adoption issues, and you know to look elsewhere.

Determine if the Agency Staff's Personality and Approach to Adoption Matches Yours

Deciding if an agency's "personality" matches yours is more difficult than with an attorney. That's because with an attorney you will be working almost exclusively with one person. True, he or she will have a secretary or paralegal, but the attorney has the primary responsibility for everything. For better or worse, most agency adoptions are more of a "by committee" undertaking. As mentioned earlier, there might be different social workers for the pre- and post-placement home study, yet another one for birth mother counseling, and perhaps even an attorney hired by the agency for legal work of terminating parental rights and the final court hearing. Some small agencies may have one person do virtually all the work. All you can do is your best to get a feel for the staff's personality and approach to adoption. Just as with attorneys, or any profession, you will find some agencies which are great at their job and very personable, and some that come up short.

CHAPTER 7

INTERCOUNTRY ADOPTION

An intercountry adoption (also called international adoption) is one where you adopt a child who is not a U.S. citizen. Intercountry adoptions have long been a popular method of adoption, peaking in 2004. However, they are potentially much more complex than domestic adoptions. Intercountry adoptions require that you work with three sets of laws: 1) U.S. federal law; 2) the laws of the country from which you are adopting; and 3) the laws of your home state.

Furthermore, federal laws will be administered by three entities, all of which you must deal with: 1) the Department of Homeland Security; 2) the U.S. Citizen and Immigration Service (USCIS), formerly known as the Immigration and Naturalization Service (INS), which approves the child's immigration application; and 3) the Department of State, which issues the visa for the adopted child to enter the United States.

To give you the full picture of how intercountry adoption works, and how to find the right program and country for you, this chapter will:

- Provide an overview of intercountry adoption, including information about the children available to be adopted.
- Discuss the pros and cons compared to domestic adoption.
- Walk you through the entire process step-by-step.
- Give statistics regarding the most popular countries from which to adopt.

• Discuss keys to finding the best intercountry agency, which you will be learning is really finding the best *Adoption Service Provider,* also called a *Primary Provider*. The terms are used interchangeably.

Overview

It wasn't that long ago that intercountry adoption was a very popular method of adoption. A lot has changed over the last few years with the Intercountry Adoption Act of 2000 and the Intercountry Adoption Universal Accreditation Act, and the landscape of intercountry adoptions have become more complex, expensive and longer to process. Let's look at the numbers. Here are the total number of children who have come to the United States via intercountry adoption:

2016:   5,372
2015:   5,647
2014:   6,438
2013:   7,092
2012:   8,667
2011:   9,319
2010:   11,058
2009:   12,744
2008:   17,449
2007:   19,601
2006:   20,675
2005:   22,726
2004:   22,989

This demonstrates a drastic shift away from intercountry adoption. From almost 23,000 to 5,372. Why has it happened, and should this discourage you from intercountry adoption?

• Some countries which permitted adoption by Americans no longer permit it (such as Russia), or are phasing it out.

- Some countries now have better infrastructure to find homes for the healthy waiting children within their own country, and now primarily only place children for adoption that are older or with special needs. (For example, China, and Columbia now primarily only place special-needs children for intercountry placements.)

- Adopting parents look at the high cost of intercountry adoption, the length of time it takes, the required travel, and the likely characteristics of the child they would be successful in adopting, and determine they can find a child with similar characteristics in the United States via the adoption exchanges (discussed in Chapter 5), and do so at no cost, and without the issues of bringing a child from a foreign culture and who will not speak English, therefore going through a difficult transition period.

- The U.S. government has barred adoptions from some countries due to concerns that those countries do not have a stable government, have not developed an adequate infrastructure to process intercountry adoptions, or there is child trafficking and other unethical practices.

What countries were most Americans adopting children from in the peak period of intercountry adoption as compared to now, and in what numbers?

	2004	2016
China:	7,038	2,231
Russia:	5,862	0
Guatemala:	3,264	13
S. Korea:	1,713	260
Kazakhstan:	835	0
Ukraine:	794	303

As from these statistics released from the Department of State, it can be seen that most of the popular countries from which to adopt either now allow no adoptions by Americans at all, or they are drastically reduced.

Even China is one-third of what it was before. The countries now following China as most popular are way, way, down compared to 2004. The second most popular country in 2016 was the Democratic Republic of the Congo-Kinshasa with only 360 adoptions (not shown above due to the low number in 2004), followed by Ukraine with 303, South Korea (260) and Bulgaria (201). Compare this to 2004 when the second most popular country was Russia with 5,862 and Guatemala with 3,264. To see the 2016 statistics for every country from which American have adopted visit:

https://travel.state.gov/content/adoptionsabroad/en/about-us/statistics.html

Characteristics of the children adopted. For 2016, here are the statistics for the three most popular countries from which intercountry adoptions are occurring, showing the age of the child when adopted:

	China	Congo	Ukraine
Under one year:	0	0	0
1-2 years:	425	3	21
3-4 years:	925	111	17
5-12 years:	738	233	86
13-17 years:	143	6	143
18 years:	0	7	34
male children:	51%	58%	55%
female children:	49%	42%	45%

What jumps out first is that for those who seek a newborn, it can be seen that they no longer exist in intercountry adoption. Just look at the "under one year" totals. The average age of children adopted from these three countries is between three and twelve years.

What about health issues? This is a difficult area to quantify as "special-needs" means different things to different people. However, here is one neutral landmark: The U.S. Department of States reports that in 2005 China's available children were 95% in the "healthy" category. In 2016, more than 90% were in the special-needs category. That is a huge change and perhaps what most adoptive parents are expecting when they look into intercountry adoption.

Some people will look at these statistics and ask, *"So what?"* and go on to say, *"The purpose of intercountry adoption is to meet the needs of the neediest children around the world, not meet the needs of the adoptive parents. We are adopting these children because they* have *special needs, not in spite of it."*

And that is a very kind and heartfelt statement for those who feel that way. But not everyone looking into intercountry adoption is aware this is the new nature of intercountry adoption, or is willing to accept a child with unknown or undiagnosed physical or mental issues that could greatly increase parenting responsibilities from what they initially imagined.

Accordingly, the above information, and that to follow, is not to discourage anyone from pursuing intercountry adoption, rather to make sure those considering it know what to expect. (Earlier editions of this book spoke very highly of the advantages of intercountry adoption—but the reality is things have drastically changed and someone needs to bluntly tell you that.) If something good is to come of the tragic decline of intercountry adoption, it is the increased attention which will go toward the half-million children in the American foster care system, many of whom are eligible for adoption. The same heartfelt reasons compelling adoptive parents to consider waiting children around the world can find them in our own country.

Hague v. Non-Hague Adoptions

There are two types of intercountry adoptions: Hague and non-Hague (also referred to as "orphan" cases). The Hague Adoption Convention is similar to a treaty among nations to follow certain rules and procedures to protect not just the children being adopted, but also the birth and the adoptive parents. The United States ratified the treaty on April 1, 2008. The goals of The Hague Treaty are honorable and good, but some critics feel it has added cost and bureaucracy while not truly serving the children needing homes around the world, and that evidence of this is seen in the diminishing number of intercountry adoptions.

Even though the United States is a party to The Hague Convention, that does not mean that all intercountry adoptions by Americans follow the requirements of The Hague Convention. The Hague provisions only apply if *both* countries—the child's country (the "sending country") and the adoptive parents' country (the "receiving country")—are parties to The Hague Convention. So even though the United States is a "Hague country," if the child's country is not, that adoption is done under the non-Hague country rules. They are not tremendously different, but they are at least *somewhat* different.

Whether the adoption is Hague or non-Hague, however, effective July 14, 2014 (pursuant to the Intercountry Adoption Universal Accreditation Act) all intercountry adoptions must have an *Adoption Service Provider* (ASP). Adoption Service Providers fall into two categories: 1) Accredited Agency; and 2) Approved Person.

Furthermore, the home study process is now exactly the same for Hague and non-Hague adoptions. Home studies must be performed by an accredited agency or an Approved Person in the state where you as the adopting parents reside. (The Approved Person category is a bit confusing as an Approved Person can be either an accredited agency *or accredited attorney*—but only an agency in this category can do home studies.) If there is no accredited agency in your state, then an *un*accredited agency will be permitted to conduct the home study, but an accredited agency must then approve it.

What is an "accredited" adoption agency? This is an adoption agency that has received the required accreditation by the Council on Accreditation (COA) or the Colorado Department of Human Resources. To become an Accredited Agency or Approved Person, they must go through rigorous screening, training and oversight.

An Adoption Service Provider is authorized to provide six specific services:

1. Identify a child for adoption and arrange the adoption.
2. Secure the consent to adoption by the child's parents or a court order terminating parental rights.
3. Conduct a home study of the adoptive parents and provide background information on the child to the adoptive parents.

4. Make a determination of the child's best interests and the appropriateness of the adoptive placement.
5. Monitor the child's placement with the adoptive parents until final adoption.
6. Assume custody of the child if the original adoptive placement is disrupted.

Adoption Service Providers may be Accredited Agencies or Approved Persons. However, only an Accredited Agency or an Approved Person (who is a licensed agency) can conduct home studies. The difference between an Accredited Agency and Approved Person is that the former most be a non-profit agency, and the latter may be a for-profit agency or attorney.

Some states have many Adoption Service Providers, while others have none. It is because of the fact not all states have accredited agencies that it is permitted that adoptive parents can use an unaccredited agency to conduct their home study, but then have that home study reviewed and approved by an agency that is officially accredited.

To see the list of Accredited Agencies and Approved Persons for each state, go to the Department of State's website: adoption.state.gov, then click on "Hague Convention." As stated previously, you may retain an Adoption Services Provider which is outside your state, and they will supervise an agency within your state for your home study.

Hague Adoptions.

Presently 90 countries are members of The Hague Adoption Convention. To see all 90 countries, to go the website of the U.S. Department of State / Bureau of Consular Affairs: travel.state.gov, and follow the "intercountry adoption" option to the list.

Here's how a typical Hague adoption works:

• Select an Adoption Service Provider/Primary Provider to guide you and oversee the entire adoption (from your home study, to getting USCIS approval of your petitions, the process in the child's country, and Consular processing). The Adoption Service Provider will either have a program in the country from which you want to adopt or will be willing to seek certification to handle your case in that country. (Be aware that the Adoption Service Provider acting as your Primary Provider does not have to be located in your state of residence.)

- Your Primary Provider will advise you as to which Accredited Agency it wants to prepare your home study.

- You or your Primary Provider will complete a form called the *Application for Determination of Suitability to Adopt a Child from a Convention Country* (USCIS form I-800A) and send it together with your home study and other documents to United States Citizenship and Immigration Services (USCIS). USCIS will determine if you are eligible to adopt.

- After USCIS approves your I-800A, your Primary Provider will assist you in preparing your *dossier* (this is your home study and other forms required by the child's country). The Adoption Service Provider or Approved Person can prepare your *dossier* (your home study and other forms required by the child's country), translate the dossier, and have all documents authenticated (usually by *apostille*—similar to notarizing but more complicated and expensive), then send it to the child's country's Central Adoption Authority. This package of documents is called "Article 15."

- The Central Adoption Authority of the child's country will identify a specific child or children for you. The Central Authority can only match you with a child if the rights of the biological parents have been terminated. The Central Authority then prepares an "Article 16 report" to your Primary Provider for you to review. It includes a photo of the child, a social and family history and results of a medical examination. Your Adoption Service Provider will translate the Article 16 report for you and you will have 14 days to accept the referral (commonly called "the match). You can ask for additional medical information and testing if you wish.

- You travel to the child's country and meet the child. Sometimes two or three visits are required, but one or two is the norm. It is not unusual to have "in country" time of about 3 weeks if only one visit is required, but shorter visits if multiple visits. Most all intercountry adoption programs arrange everything for you while you are in the child's country. They recommend or book a hotel, have a translator and driver for you, and provide an attorney if one is needed for court. Usually your translator goes almost everywhere with you, and certainly to the orphanage to help you interact with the orphanage staff and child. Your "child time" is critical, as this is when you make the determination this is the right child for you, and you for him or her, and that you feel the information presented regarding emotional and physical health is accurate. Even with the greater security of a Hague adoption, it is not unheard of that some of the information provided about the child might be inaccurate (e.g. subjective assessments of the child's emotional or psychological state).

- Once you have accepted the referral of a child, your Adoption Service Provider will file the *Petition to Classify Convention Adoptee as an Immediate Relative* (USCIS form I-800). After USCIS provisionally approves your I-800, there is a "changing of the guard" and your case is transferred from USCIS to the National Visa Center in Portsmouth, New Hampshire. After a few days, the National Visa Center sends the file electronically to the U.S. Consulate in the child's country. The U.S. Consul there will "issue" Article 5 (the affirmation you have complied with the adoption process of the child's country) and Article 17 (affirmation the U.S. Consul believes the child meets the legal requirements to immigrate to the United States). At this time your 1-800 is formally approved.

- *Warning:* If you obtain custody of the child or finalize the adoption before the U.S. Consul issues Article 5, your case will be denied.

- You finalize your adoption, usually done in the child's country. Every country has different laws and procedures to finalize an adoption. You will want your Adoption Service Provider to fully educate you on your selected country's procedures prior to formalizing an adoption plan with that country. Sometimes this can all be done on your one and only visit overseas, while sometimes it is a completely separate visit, after meeting the child previously. Just as in the United States, the finalization of the adoption will be in court (or administrative hearing), and your Adoption Service Provider will normally arrange for a translator to be present, as well as needed parties, like an attorney.

- With your adoption now finalized overseas, you are legal parents of the child, but you still need to get your child home. The child is not yet a U.S. citizen, however, so the child's country will issue a passport, not the United States.

- When the adoption is granted overseas you will receive a final decree of adoption (a few countries grant guardianship—more on this later). You will also receive a post-adoption birth certificate for the child, naming you as parents (assuming your adoption was granted in the child's country and not only guardianship), and as mentioned above, the child's country will issue a passport for the child. Your Adoption Service Provider will now file for the child's visa and the U.S. consulate or embassy will set an appointment for consular processing.

- The child must first be examined by a physician in the child's country designated by the U.S. government (called a "panel physician"). In order to make an appointment with a panel physician, you must have your appointment letter from the U.S. embassy. The primary purpose of the panel physician exam is to be sure the child does not have a contagious disease or medical issue that will be a bar to visa issuance.

- When the U.S. embassy or consulate issues a visa, it will be an IH-3 visa if the child's adoption was finalized in the child's country, or an IH-4 visa if only a guardianship was granted (with permission for the adoption to be finalized in the United States). Children who are granted an IH-3 visa are U.S. citizens upon their arrival to the United States, and 6-8 weeks thereafter they will automatically receive their Certificate of Citizenship in the mail. Children who were granted an IH-4 visa will receive a permanent resident card. They will not be U.S. citizens until their adoption is finalized in court in the United States.

Non-Hague Adoptions.

Even though the United States is a Hague country, if the child's country (the "sending" country) is not a signatory to The Hague Convention (a "non-Hague country"), the provisions of The Hague do not apply. The adoption will be done basically as intercountry adoptions were done before the implementation of The Hague Treaty. However, as of July, 2014 and the Intercountry Adoption Universal Accreditation Act, some of the Hague regulations have spilled over into non-Hague adoptions. To see which countries are "Hague countries" and which are not, visit adoption.state.gov.

Let's explore a non-Hague adoption step-by-step:

- Start off by selecting an Adoption Service Provider/Primary Provider to guide you and oversee your entire adoption (from your home study, to USCIS approving your petitions, to the adoption itself in the child's country, to consular processing). The Adoption Service Provider will either have a program in the country from which you wish to adopt, or will be willing to handle your case in that country. The Adoption Service Provider who acts as your Primary Provider does not have to be in your state of residence.

- Your Primary Provider will advise regarding which accredited agency it wants to prepare your home study.

- You or your Primary Provider will complete a form called the *Application for Advance Processing of Orphan Petition* (USCIS form I-600A), and send it along with your home study and other documents to United States Citizenship and Immigration Services (USCIS). USCIS will then determine if you are eligible to adopt.

- After USCIS approves your I-600A, your Primary Provider will assist you to prepare your *dossier* (your home study and other documents required by the child's country), then translate the dossier and have it authenticated or *apostilled* (a process similar to notarization but more complicated and expensive), and send it to the appropriate governmental body in the child's country.

- Your Adoption Service Provider will notify you when they have found a child deemed appropriate for you. This means the child's country has reviewed your dossier and selected a child for you.

Since this is a non-Hague country, the country may have no central adoption authority making the placement determination (required by Hague countries). Instead, your Adoption Service Provider may be working with a regional authority or even a specific orphanage. There is no specified transmittal of information about the child, as in Hague adoptions, but you will want to make sure you receive as much information as you feel you need prior to commencing further in the adoption plan, such as traveling to the child's country to meet him or her. Some countries do not identify a specific child, rather approve you and you learn about specific children when you arrive and meet with the adoption authority of that country.

- You normally adopt the child in their home country. Most countries require one or both of the adoptive parents to travel to there to finalize the adoption, while a few nations allow the child to be transported to the U.S. for the adoption to occur here. Regardless, the adoptive parents will want to spend time with the child prior to the adoption being finalized to make sure the placement feels right to them, and to learn more about the child and verify prior information provided to them about him or her.

- You apply for the child to be deemed eligible for immigration to the U.S. Just because the child's country permits you to adopt a child there does not mean that child will be granted permission to enter the U.S. Only children who meet certain qualifications are eligible. Your Adoption Service Provider should be familiar with the regulations for non-Hague adoptees to be classified as an "orphan," and what it means for a biological parent to be "incapable of providing care." The Adoption Service Provider should prepare a short legal brief that is supported with evidence showing how the child satisfies the complex definition of "orphan," as the requirements for children eligible for intercountry adoption is more restrictive in non-Hague adoptions than in Hague adoptions. This "orphan" determination is made by the USCIS when the adoptive parents file a *Petition to Classify Orphan as Immediate Relative* (USCIS form I-600). Normally the I-600 is filed with the USCIS in the United States, but some U.S. embassies or consulates will allow it to be filed with them in the child's country. Included with the I-

600 will be required documents such as the child's birth certificate, court decree of adoption and proof of orphan status.

- When the USCIS has approved the I-600, the file is electronically sent to the National Visa Center in Portsmouth, New Hampshire. After a visa is designated for the adopted child, the file is electronically forwarded to the U.S. embassy or consulate in the child's country. A consular officer will conduct an investigation to verify that the child satisfies the definition of orphan, and in cases where the birth parent selected the adoptive parents, whether the birth parent is capable for providing for the child.

- As is discussed above for Hague adoptions, the child will need to be examined by a panel physician as part of the visa process, and the child's country will issue a passport for the child, as he or she is not yet a U.S. citizen.

All the above referenced forms, I-600A, I-600, I-800A and I-800, can be viewed and downloaded at adoption.state.gov as well as at adoption101.com.

Irene Steffas, a respected intercountry adoption attorney (who is also an Approved Person), comments:

"Whether your adoption is Hague or non-Hague, intercountry adoptions are not a cake walk. There are many uncertainties—the sending country may create barriers that did not exist when you began or the U.S. government authorities may determine that adoption in the country where your child is from is fraught with fraud, poor standards or even an unstable government. You and your Adoption Service Provider must be ready to fight if need be, and deal with the intercountry politics which often play a role."

She also commented on the decline in popularity of intercountry adoption:

"Yes, intercountry adoptions by Americans are declining, but one area on the rise is adoption by relatives. However, in many cases these adoptions are from countries which have done few—if any—

intercountry adoptions, so you need an Adoption Service Provider who is willing to be a trailblazer."

Citizenship

Children adopted via intercountry adoption can enter the United States under one of four possible visas types: IR-3, IH-3, IR-4 or IH-4. A child who enters with an IR-3 or IH-3 visa (issued if the child's adoption was finalized in court in the child's country) is a U.S. citizen as soon as he or she enters the United States. However, a child who enters with an IR-4 or IH-4 visa (issued if the intended parents were granted guardianship and the adoption is to be finalized in the United States) is admitted as a lawful permanent resident. Note that "IH" visas designate it was a Hague adoption. "IR" visas are for non-Hague.

Regardless of the visa type, the bottom line is this . . . the Citizenship Act of 2000 provides that a child is automatically granted U.S. citizenship upon their entry in the United States, provided:

1) The child is under the age of 18;
2) Resides in the United States in the custody of the American adoptive parent upon the child's immigration;
3) The child lawfully entered the U.S. (e.g. with a visa); and
4) The adoption was finalized overseas.

If the adoption was not finalized overseas, and the adoption is instead granted until their arrival in the United States, the child becomes a U.S. citizen upon the granting of the U.S. adoption. In such cases the adoptive parents must file a form (the N-600) to obtain the Certificate of Citizenship after the U.S. adoption is granted. If the child was adopted in the child's country by the adoptive parents, the USCIS will automatically mail you the child's Certificate of Citizenship.

Expected Wait for Referral.

In the most recent survey by *Adoptive Families* magazine of their subscribers, it was reported that slightly more than half the adoptive parents from both Ethiopia and S. Korea received their referrals for their child within one year (measured from when they were approved to adopt, meaning a completed home study and the completion of required paperwork). (Note that as this book was going to print, Ethiopia had shut down intercountry adoptions.) In China, for a "healthy" child the wait was approximately five years, and for special-needs children it was said to be "minimal," with no listed time period.

Pros and Cons

Domestic and intercountry adoptions have tremendous differences, both in the way the adoptions are completed, and the characteristics of the children being adopted. What is a "pro" for one family might be a "con" for another. Why might some people prefer intercountry adoption over domestic? There are several reasons:

- You do not want to adopt a newborn, and feel the waiting children available in the U.S. are not right for you.
- You may be worried that if you do a domestic newborn adoption, you may wait a long time for a birth mother to select you. You want a more definite timetable to have a child in your home, which may be more likely in intercountry adoption.
- You wish to adopt a child of a specific ethnic group and believe (rightly or wrongly) such a child might be difficult to adopt in your region, or via an adoption exchange regionally or nationally.
- You have humanitarian concerns for the children living overseas in orphanages who desperately need homes, and this is more compelling for you than the domestic scenario, with many adoptive parents vying for the babies available, or children in foster care. Be aware, however, as was discussed in Chapter 1, that adopting to "save a child" by itself is actually seen as an inadvisable reason to adopt.
- You may not be comfortable with the typical open nature of many domestic newborn adoptions. Not everyone feels at ease in working

closely with a birth mother and possibly having continued contact. This is may also be the case with even some waiting children who have existing connections prior to meeting you that will be beneficial to maintain. You may prefer to work with a foreign government which has already severed the parental rights to a child, and complete a closed adoption.

- You may have extreme anxiety about the fact most birth mothers in most domestic newborn adoptions have a certain time in which to change their minds, often even after the child has gone home with you, and you refuse to take that risk (even though the percentage of failed adoptions is quite low). Likewise, in some waiting child adoption, some children may be placed in your home before parental rights have been fully terminated.

- You like the idea of foreign travel and foreign culture, and/or have ties with a particular country from which you wish to adopt.

There are also potential disadvantages to intercountry adoption:

- Most countries require you to travel to the child's country (usually once or twice, sometimes three times). Although some countries bring the child to the U.S. via an escort, the norm for most countries is to require you to go to their country and finalize the adoption there. This travel is time consuming and expensive.

- You will be traveling to a country where you will most likely not speak their language, and where few people speak English.

- Winters in some countries popular for intercountry adoptions can be quite severe (such as all the Eastern European nations).

- Although many of the countries from which you can do intercountry adoptions are not third-world nations, they are still going to be quite a bit more primitive than you are used to.

- Depending upon the country you adopt from, your out-of-country time may range from two weeks to two months, usually with both adoptive parents present for some or all of the process. This can be difficult to coordinate with employment and may be expensive.

- Things can still go wrong just as in domestic adoption. Some adoptive parents complain they arrived in the foreign country only to find the child did not have the characteristics anticipated. Although full disclosure is the goal of The Hague Convention, some things, like the degree of a special-need, or social and cognitive abilities, is very subjective.

- You will be dependent upon a translator and guide, and in some cases a foreign attorney, to navigate the complicated legal system in the child's country. They will be speaking a foreign language and you are trusting them to accurately relay important information about court proceedings and orphanage information about the child.

- Health histories may not be complete, or guaranteed to be accurate. (For example, when a child is left at an orphanage with no information from a birth parent, or abandoned without identification, so no health history from birth mother or father.)

- Most children are raised in orphanages and many of these institutions lack the resources and staff to fully emotionally and physically nurture a child, meaning the longer a child stays there, the more likely he or she is to be negatively affected by their environment. Orphanages can range from excellent to terrible, with most falling in the middle. Some countries, however, have reputations for more nurturing orphanages.

- Even in the best orphanages, where children are loved and nurtured, the care can't equal the one-on-one attention and love of a traditional parent-child relationship, or even that offered in foster care, which is closer to a family environment. For this reason it is not unusual for some children to initially be slightly to moderately underweight and physically underdeveloped compared to other children their age raised in traditional families. The good news is that most of these children physically "catch up" quite soon.

- Children raised in orphanages are more likely to suffer from "attachment disorder," usually more severe the longer they stay in the orphanage. In basic terms, attachment disorder is when a child has difficulty bonding with you as parents due to never having a loving and trusting parent-child relationship previously. He or she has simply never learned through experience and observation that "it is natural to get love and give it back." Instead, if a child was neglected or abused, he or she can become distrustful of adults, hampering the ability to fully bond with you, no matter how loving you are. Not all children suffer from severe attachment disorder simply because they lived in an orphanage, however. Many adoptive parents report they see little or no sign of it once the child has adjusted to their new home. This can be due to the fact some orphanages are staffed by loving and dedicated people with nurturing one-on-one relationships with their children, and that each child is unique and affected differently by their surroundings. Not all countries use orphanages due to concerns over these issues. A small number of countries are like America and use foster homes, allowing them to try to duplicate a more traditional family and a smoother transition into an adoptive home.

• There is always the risk the country you are adopting from will change its requirements in the middle of your adoption, or even shut down entirely. Sometimes it is our government which has a "problem" with a particular country and declines to continue working with it (perhaps due to a fear of child selling). Whether it is the decision is our country or theirs, examples of presently closed doors in countries from which Americans previously frequently adopted are Russia, Guatemala and Ethiopia.

You can see there are both good and bad elements to an intercountry adoption, and that those elements are completely different from domestic adoption. Most adoptive parents instinctively know right from the beginning if domestic or intercountry adoption is right for them. Some of the negative issues can be avoided by carefully choosing the intercountry program you will work with. This means not just choosing the right Adoption Service Provider operating a top quality intercountry program, but the right country from which to adopt. ("Intercountry program" is a loose term to describe accredited Adoption Service Providers and Approved Persons.)

The good news, however, is that virtually all of the above detailed steps are the job of your Adoption Service Provider or Approved Person. So, your first job is to find the right one, knowing the "ins and outs" of working with the USCIS and foreign governmental officials. The program should also know the exact eligibility requirements of the country with which they are working and what, if anything, you would be required to do in the child's country to legally complete the adoption and bring the child home.

Fees can vary in intercountry adoptions as much as in domestic adoptions. Most programs charge between $15,000-$20,000. Adoptive parents must be very careful to find out what is covered in the program fee. Some programs do not cover the cost of your home study, your translator/guide overseas, car and driver while you are overseas, the translation and authentication of your dossier, or the orphanage donation. These services can each cost thousands of dollars. When you add the cost of travel and staying overseas and end up with a total cost, most intercountry adoptions total $30,000-$40,000.

Keys to Finding the Best Intercountry Program

As was discussed in Chapter 2, you are not limited to agencies and attorneys (Adoption Service Providers and Approved Persons) with intercountry programs in your home state. *You want to find the best program, not the closest.* A significant number of adoptive parents retain an intercountry program located in another county, or even another state. This opens a lot of doors. To find potential intercountry adoption programs, and learn about different countries and what they have to offer, you can do the following:

- Make sure the entity you hire is authenticated as an Adoption Service Provider or Approved Person. There are facilitators in intercountry adoption, just as in domestic, who can't provide the full services you need, so avoid them.
- Talk to everyone you know who has adopted. Adoptive parents share information with each other, and tend to have a wide informational net. They can either tell you about their own experiences with one or more intercountry programs, or tell you about other adoptive parents they know who can. Try to meet

people who have adopted from different countries to learn more about what the children and procedures are like from that country. Only you know what is most important to you. For some adoptive parents the key question is where do they go to adopt the youngest possible child. For others it is where do they find the healthiest and most nurtured children. Still others go to where there is the greatest need for homes for the children of that country.

- Call local agencies and attorneys, even if they only do domestic adoptions, and ask for recommendations. They can often point you to a good intercountry program.

- Join or visit adoptive parent groups. Some of those participating have done intercountry adoption. To find them, visit the websites of *Adoptive Families* magazine and the federal government's Child Welfare Information Gateway, provided in Appendix B.

- Join or visit Resolve and attend their adoption support groups. To learn more about Resolve, see Appendix B.

- Read *Adoptive Families* magazine and peruse their ads.

Once you have your list of potential intercountry programs, consider the following questions to help find the best agency or attorney:

- *Are you COA accredited as an Adoption Service Provider or Approved Person?*

- *With which country or countries do your work?* Some Adoption Service Providers (either accredited agencies or Approved Persons) work with multiple countries, while others specialize in just one country. You might want to be a bit cautious with programs that list a very large number of countries from which they do adoptions. Sometimes working with an excessive number of countries indicates the agency or attorney does not have their own staff in those countries, rather is subcontracting from another agency. (More on this below.)

- *Does your overseas staff work directly for you, or are they contracted through another Adoption Service Provider?* If they subcontract another agency's labor overseas, it is not necessarily a reason to stop working with them. However, you want to be cautious and inquire why, if they have a viable program in that country, they have not invested the time and money to hire their own staff there.

- *We are interested in hiring you as our Adoption Service Provider, but you are located in a different state than the one we live in. Will that cause any problems or extra costs?* Often the answer is "no." You will need a home study by an agency local to you, but that will be required regardless of the state where the intercountry program is located, so is not an extra cost. And unlike domestic interstate adoptions, where you either finalize the adoption in the child's state of birth or your home state, most all intercountry adoptions are finalized in the child's country, having little or nothing to do with the state in which you live, or where the agency or attorney is located. Even if you do not complete your adoption overseas, and instead have your child brought to the U.S., you will usually finalize the adoption in your home state.

- *How many adoptions has your program done with the country we want to adopt from this year? How about last year?* You want to see a record of reasonable success. But bigger is not always better.

- *What are the children like which that country has available for adoption (age, ethnicity, health, gender, etc.)?* You want to make sure before you start a program if the children available in a particular country meet your age and health goals.

- *What specific health tests are given to the child before we consider them for adoption so we are fully informed? HIV? Hepatitis B? Syphilis?* Some countries have good orphanages and this includes regular physical check ups, and checking for various health problems. Other countries do much less, and it will be up to you when you arrive to either have a private physician do it (which can be difficult if a child is in an orphanage), or wait until the *panel physician* does the exam as required by the U.S. embassy before your child enters America.

- *Are there children waiting for immediate placement? What is the average time to complete an adoption, measured from the very start of the process, to bringing a child home?* Although your first goal should be to find the right child, from the right country, you will want to know your timetable. Some countries have children waiting and you are invited over quickly. Other countries have more applications than tchildren, do a backlog exists.

- *What are the procedures to adopt from the country we will be working with? Do we go to the country to bring the child home or does an escort transport the child to us? How many visits do we make? Both of us, or just one? How long will each visit be?* Some adoptive parents look at their visits to the child's country as a great adventure. Others, whether because of limitations in how much time they can take off from their jobs, or difficulty in leaving home due to having an existing child to care for, or simply the costs of repeated trips overseas, have limits on how many times they can travel, how long they will stay there, and if one or both adoptive parents need to go each time.

- *What is the full program fee? Does it include the authentication and translation of our dossier? The home study? A translator, car and driver to meet us at the airport and bring us to all our official meetings? The translator and driver's food and lodging? Are we expected to give the orphanage a donation to help the remaining children there, and if so, how much? What about the translation of the child's country's court documents for our embassy overseas? The cost of a lawyer doing our child's re-adoption for us when we get back? If it's not included, what will those fees be? What are travel/hotel costs?* Intercountry adoption program fees can be very misleading. Knowing all the required elements of your intercountry adoption in advance will allow you to figure out the true total program fee. An intercountry program which looks like a bargain at $15,000 may soon become overly expensive when you more than double it for other costs.

- *Is the adoption completed and approved by the court in the child's country or are we only given guardianship?* Some countries will only grant guardianship, thus requiring you to adopt the child under your state law when you return home. This means more costs and additional bureaucracy.

- *Do you have get-togethers of adoptive parents who have already adopted, so we can meet them and their children? If not, can you give me the names of several families who used your program in the last year whom we can call to ask about their experiences?*

These questions, coupled with some of the general questions regarding attorneys and agencies provided in Chapters 4 and 6, should help you find an excellent program, whether in, or outside, your state.

Final Cautions

There are two final cautions that arise with children of intercountry adoption, both involving when the child is already present in the United States when you are given "the opportunity" to adopt them.

Many people think that if a child is a citizen of another country, but the child is physically present in the United States (legally or illegally), that the adoption would not need to follow The Hague Convention regulations. Their reasoning is the child is already in the U.S., so it is only a regular domestic adoption. These people are incorrect (unless the child held dual U.S. citizenship or entered the child as a legal permanent resident). For example, if a person brought a non-citizen U.S. citizen foreign-born child—even if freed for adoption—into the United States on their own, this would not excuse compliance with the required procedures of intercountry adoption.

A more common situation is the potential tragedy of Unregulated Custody Transfer, commonly referred to as "rehoming." This is when an intercountry adoption has occurred, but failed to such a degree that the adoptive parents no longer wish to raise the child. Perhaps there were behaviors or disabilities that they were not prepared to handle. The appropriate action in such a situation is for the family to work with their Adoption Service Provider or Approved Person to serve the child's best interests in finding a new placement. Before 2014, however, non-Hague adoptions did not require the intercountry adoptions to be administered by Adoption Service Providers, and some agencies or attorneys did not provide appropriate post-placement services, or the adoptive parents elected to reject those services.

What some families have done is "rehome" the child by directly placing the child with another person or family. In some cases, this can be done legally, as the initial adoptive parents are fully legal parents pursuant to the adoption, with full parental rights, thus permitted to place their child for adoption with another properly approved family. But some families are bypassing appropriate procedures in finding a new and appropriate family—instead literally finding an adoptive family via social media, or something akin to Craigslist—clearly putting the child at great risk, and alarming the child's original country of origin when learning of such actions. Many states have now adopted laws addressing rehoming.

Sometimes, yes, a child's initial placement does not work out and a second home must be found. It is critical, however, that the selection of a new adoptive (or foster) family be through a licensed agency, and the prospective family is thoroughly screened and trained for a child's special-needs, with post-placement supervision.

CHAPTER 8

STRATEGIES TO
FIND A BABY TO ADOPT

This chapter is dedicated to one thing: helping those who wish to adopt a newborn find a birth mother to choose them as the adoptive parents for the child she is expecting. According to the National Center of Health Statistics, there are more than three million unplanned pregnancies in the United States each year. Three *million*. Of these, more than a million will elect to terminate their pregnancies. About 130,000 will plan adoption. The others will parent the child or place with a relative. So the question is how do you find one of these 130,000 women, or one that was considering abortion but may consider adoption, and how do you get information about you in front of them so they will pick you?

In previous chapters, we've discussed one critical strategy: hiring an adoption attorney or agency whose services include showing you to birth mothers who contact their office to start adoption planning (or guiding your networking efforts). Often hiring the right adoption professional is enough in itself to result in creating your adoptive match.

But there are two important reasons why you will want to consider doing your own networking, either in addition to what your agency/attorney is doing, or in place of it. There are three basic reasons why adoptive parents network:

1. *Budgetary reasons.* You might not have the budget to pay the higher fees agencies and attorneys usually charge when you include networking/matching in their services. For example, although it varies by state, many agencies charge $4,000-$10,000 for their full range of services (pre-placement home study, birth mother counseling, relinquishment services, post-placement supervision and writing the final court report approving the adoption). But most don't include networking and matching services in that fee. So their fees are more likely to be in the $15,000-$30,000 range when including networking and matching with a birth mother. Attorneys' fees will likewise usually be higher when including networking. You definitely need an attorney or agency to screen any birth mothers you find and make sure there are no red flags, but that does not mean they can't screen birth mothers that *you* find. Almost all agencies and attorneys are thrilled when you have found a potential birth mother and they don't need to do it for you, and will be anxious to help you make sure it looks like a viable placement.

2. *Limitation by state law.* A very small number of states permit only agencies to be paid for assisting in finding birth mothers and matching adoptive parents, meaning attorneys in those few states can advise you regarding your networking efforts, but can't do them on their own. That means you are doing the networking, or additionally hiring an attorney or agency in another state to do so, where it is permitted.

3. *Increased success.* Let's say you've hired an attorney or agency and they are networking for you with the hope to create an adoptive match. Great, that maximizes your chances, but don't just sit and wait for a match. You still want—*you still need*—to network on your own. Remember, the more you do, and the better you do it, the higher your chances of success. Plus, you don't want just *any* adoptive placement, you want the right one for you—the right birth mother placing for the right reasons—so wouldn't it be nice to have a *choice* of adoptive placements? Not just one? If you want to achieve that, be prepared to use some originality and effort to obtain it. This book will provide the originality if you'll provide the effort. Deal?

So whichever of the two groups you fall into, the result is the same . . . *you need to be actively networking*. While your attorney and/or agency is doing their best to match you with a birth mother if their services include that, you are doing the same.

Remember, even if your attorney or agency is networking for you, they are doing it for many of their other clients as well. That means that when they are contacted by a birth mother seeking the right adoptive parents for her expected baby, she will be shown the many waiting families your adoption professional represents. So your chances might be one in ten, one in forty, whatever. But when you find a birth mother on your own, and then have your attorney or agency get involved to make sure it looks like an appropriate and safe placement, *you* are normally the only considered adoptive parents. After all, your hard work should pay off for *you*, not other waiting adoptive parents.

You will want to attack your quest to adopt with the same double intensity you did for other important aspects of your life: such as getting an academic degree; finding the right job; planning your wedding, choosing your dream house; battling infertility.

Before listing these networking strategies, let remember one thing:

It only takes one.

What does that mean? It means that it only takes one of your photo-resume letters, or other means of outreach, to reach one birth mother. And if she is the right one, you have your match. Oftentimes adoptive parents are quick to disparage certain methods, saying, "Too many people already do that," or "If I send my photo-resume letter to doctors, they will just throw it away."

You may be right. Of the letters you send out, the calls you make, the people you talk to, ninety-nine percent of that effort may be wasted. Actually, let's be brutally honest. Ninety-nine percent *will* be wasted. Doctors will toss away your photo-resume letters without a glance, as will most healthcare professionals when given to them in the traditional way. Even your friends, without the right approach, will not know what to do with them.

So what? You only care about that one successful letter that got through.

It only takes one.

But to find that *one*, you need to get in the game, and use every opportunity to get yourself out there, waiting to be discovered by a birth mother. And more than that, you've got to do everything in the most effective manner, using both established and original techniques.

Prepare a Photo-Resume Letter

The photo-resume is the foundation of your search for a birth mother. For a birth mother to seriously consider you, she will want to initially see what you look like, and read what your life is like. This is the heart of a photo-resume letter. Because we are going to use it for so many things, and because most photo-resumes are poorly prepared, it's important to learn how to create of the best possible letter. It is the essence of your quest. A typical photo-resume letter will have a photo (or several) of you, and a letter describing what your life is like, giving a birth mother a chance to visualize what a child's life will be like with you. Every adoption professional will tell you that you need a photo-resume, but rarely do they give you the best advice on how to prepare it. Let's look at what makes a great one.

Your photo. Nothing is more important than your picture. You could have the most eloquent letter accompanying it, *but if the birth mother does not find the photo attractive, she won't even bother reading the letter*. That's just reality. Take it from someone who has literally sat next to hundreds of birth mothers and watched them go through a stack of photo-resume letters.

First let's talk about what is meant by the photo being "attractive." Some people will say, "But we don't look like models. We aren't gorgeous people." Or maybe, "I'm overweight." "We're too old." And so on. The reality is that about everyone is insecure about their appearance.

The reality, however, is that adoptive parents come from all walks of life, duplicating the general population that birth mothers come from. They will be skinny or obese, tall or short, black, brown or white,

Christian, Jewish or agnostic, college educated with a fancy job or a high school graduate working in manual labor. You get the idea.

Here's the key thing to make you relax and stop worrying if you feel you will not be "attractive" to a birth mother. Rarely does a birth mother elect adoptive parents based upon physical attractiveness or professional job status. True, they want their child to be raised in a financially secure home and be presented with options in life, but that exists with most middle-income families.

Here is the reality of who birth mothers choose as adoptive parents:

They select adoptive parents they can *identify* with,
and with whom they feel comfortable.

Comments frequently heard from birth mothers when explaining why they selected one family over a stack of others are:

- "The adoptive mom reminds me of my favorite aunt."
- "They look like they love to laugh."
- "I can tell they really love each other."
- "They like to do the same kind of things I do."
- "They look like they'd make great parents."

What isn't heard from birth mothers in choosing adoptive parents are such comments as:

- "She's the most beautiful woman I've ever seen!"
- "Wow, the adoptive dad has impressive muscles!"
- "I bet they're millionaires!"
- "With all those college degrees, they must be geniuses!"

Okay, that's a bit silly, but you get the point. The bottom line is when most birth mothers look at photo-resume letters, they will either get a spark, or they won't. A good example is when you are young and single, and you're walking across a college campus, or in the mall, and your eyes and mind are open to finding someone special. Maybe your head would be turned by a few people, but the rest go by unnoticed. Even you might be unable to explain why one person caught your eye and you hoped to engage them in conversation, and others didn't. In fact, the ones who attracted you had little in common; they were all different. It was just a gut feeling. And the odds are they weren't the physically most attractive people of all the people you walked by. It was other things that drew you to them.

The reality is that everyone is interested, and attracted to, different types of people. Even we don't know why we are so attracted to someone. Just look how different all your friends' spouses are from each other. Everyone finds different things attractive in people. For some, it is finding someone who is their complete opposite. Or it may be someone who is just like themselves. Birth mothers are no different. And because birth mothers come from all walks of life, as do adoptive parents, there is someone for everybody. An obese adopting parent couple may worry their obesity may disinterest many birth mothers. This may be true for skinny birth mothers, but they may be just the kind of couple an obese birth mother identifies with and will select. The same is true for the skinny-as-a-stick birth parents, for the "computer geeks," for athletes, et cetera. You get the idea. In fact, often being too attractive is a negative, as birth mothers feel no connection emotionally, and may even resent them for their beauty.

Now that we've (hopefully) tossed away your insecurities, let's discuss preparing your photo for your photo-resume letter:

- Take an accurate picture. Making yourself look like a fashion model, then walking in the door for your meeting with a birth mother looking completely different, serves no purpose. If you are not who she thought you would be, the meeting will likely go for naught. Just as bad, another birth mother who would have picked you if you looked "normal" didn't do so, because she wasn't interested in someone looking like a fashion diva.

- Don't hire a professional photographer. Instead, have a friend with some decent camera skills take the photo with a good quality camera, or use a timer. Why? Studio photos tend to look artificial, plus they look like you are trying too hard. But the biggest reason for not using a professional photographer is that you want to emphasize the personal aspect of your presentation. You want it to smell of *home* and *family*, not slick commercialism. You want the picture to be a casual one, emphasizing the fact you will be a fun and loving family.

- Some adoptive parents use just one photo of themselves, while others use five or six and make a collage. Neither is better than the other, but if a single picture is used it must be a great picture. Collages are definitely advantageous when the adoptive parents already have one or more children. It can be difficult to get a perfect picture with all of you, and a collage lets you mix and match to give an accurate view of your family. If you do elect to use a collage, don't use multiple pictures of the same thing: you standing in front of the fireplace; you standing in front of your house; you standing in front of your fountain in the backyard. Instead, use the collage to show a full view of your family: A picture of both of you; a picture of your extended family (so a birth mother can see beaming future grandparents, aunts and uncles et cetera, at a family event), one or both of you doing one of your favorite activities, such as hiking in the mountains or doing a craft or construction project. By the time she sees all the pictures, a birth mother should feel she really knows you.

- Smile! So many photo-resumes exist with the wife showing her glowing smile, and next to her is a husband with a toothless version of a smile. For some reason, even the happiest and most motivated husbands have a tough time showing a nice, friendly smile. A birth mother will assume if he can't smile to be picked for adoption, he never smiles.

- Inside or outside? Outside photos are best. Inside pictures are usually filled with distraction, the backgrounds containing the edge of a doorway, the corner of a painting, et cetera. If you are outside you can select a bright and beautiful background. This might be the beach, the mountains, a local park with beautiful flowering shrubs, a local restaurant with a gorgeous Mexican tile fountain, an historic building, etc. One caution with outside pictures, though. Avoid looking into bright sunlight. You don't want to be squinting in your pictures, and you definitely don't want your eyes hidden behind sunglasses. (Whether inside or outside, avoid using holiday pictures. For example, a photo of you standing in front of a Christmas tree is nice for December, but untimely when a birth mother sees it in July.)

- Wearing casual clothes is preferable to something formal like a suit and tie. This is not an Easter picture to give to your parents. This is to show a birth mother what you are like. Successful but casual clothes, like a polo shirt and slacks for men, is perfect. For women, a casual dress or pants is fine.

- Make sure your faces are easily recognizable. For example, you might have a great picture of you on vacation standing in front of a volcano in Hawaii, but if you are so tiny that your bodies are an inch tall in the picture, with your face a fraction of that, no one can see what you look like. Instead, either have your faces fill the picture, or go with a full-body shot (sitting on a bench, standing arm-in-arm, et cetera, with your faces close clearly visible).

- Choosing the right picture is the key. How do you do it? Start by taking *lots* of pictures. Don't just go through your existing pictures and use one of those. If you are already thinking of using some old photo you have, you are on the wrong mental path for success. For the best photo, most adoptive parents will need to take pictures specifically for their photo-resume letter. Because it is hard to create the photo which best personifies you, and because so much is riding on it, you should be taking *at least* 100 photos. If you are like most everyone you have a digital camera, so photos are free. Why limit how many you take? Take a dozen in one location in one pose, then another dozen in another pose. Then off to yet another location. Maybe some with pets, some without. Try a few clothing changes. Play "model for a day." Don't be shy about showing affection in your picture. Arms around each other, or hands held, emphasizes your affection for each other. (If you are a single person your main picture will be of you alone, but a collage is the perfect chance to show the significant others in your life. This visual demonstration of the support of family and friends is important for birth mothers to see.)

- The odds are, even after taking all these pictures, you will only find a few which satisfy you. Actually, it is not uncommon for adoptive parents to not like any of the pictures and use the first round of photos as a learning experience, and do better the next time around. Perhaps you notice you were squinting in the sun, framed the pictures poorly, the background was not attractive, et cetera. In your second go-round you can correct any such mistakes. In addition to the fact that your photo is the most important part of you being selected by a birth mother, it is also the least expensive part of the process. Even if you repeated the process three straight weekends to come up with the perfect picture, what would the cost be? A few hours of your time?

- If you are using just one picture, the size is usually 3 X 5 or 4 X 6. You can scan the picture into the letter, use a color copier, or have prints made and staple one to each letter. Any of these three options are acceptable. If you are using a collage approach, most of the photos will likely be a bit smaller, and will almost certainly be scanned or copied onto the resume letter, as stapling multiple photos would be too time-consuming and not very visually appealing. A warning: if you are attaching a photo to letter rather than creating it on a computer, don't paperclip it. Pictures have a habit of becoming separated from letters, and when they get reattached, your face might be on someone else's letter. A staple or glue gun is usually best—don't use glue sticks as they seem to lose their adhesiveness quickly.

- If you create the photo-resume on your computer and print it, or use a color copier, it is critical to use top quality equipment. Nothing is worse than blurred or distorted photos. Before paying your local copy store to make a large quantity of your letter, have them print one and check out the quality.

- If you already have a child, or children, feature them in your photos. This may sound obvious, but some adoption "strategists" advise you to hide the fact you have children, and present yourselves as childless. Their reasoning is that some birth mothers are less likely to select you if you already have one or more children. While there is some truth to this statement, to hide the existence of your children is not a good strategy. You want to honestly represent yourselves to a birth mother. Either she will like you for who you are, or she won't. (Hiding the existence of your existing children is doubly ridiculous as at some point the birth mother will know you have children. So what is gained by hiding the fact initially? And the birth mother who may have liked the fact that the adoptive parents had children didn't consider them because she thought they were childless. So not only is this dishonesty unfair and offensive to birth mothers, but it actually potentially hurts your chances of success. (So think twice about an adoption attorney or agency who recommends that.)

The resume letter. The ideal resume letter should be long enough to describe yourselves, but not so long as to start boring the reader. Remember, the photo-resume letter is just a first look at you. It is not expected to tell a birth mother every fact about you. It is to have a birth mother say, "I like what I see and I want to learn more." Let's talk about what to include and what to leave out.

- How do you start out your letter? Common is the salutation, "Dear Birth Mother." But don't do that. It is so impersonal that it strikes the wrong tone right from the start. But decide for yourself. When you get mail addressed "Dear Homeowner," is it greeted with enthusiasm and anticipation? No, clearly not. Instead, start out with "Dear Friend," "Hi," "Hello," or a similar greeting. Actually, there is no need to even have a salutation at all. Why not just start out your letter getting right to the point: "We are Carol and Mike and we are hoping to adopt."

- Your names. Depending upon the custom in your state, and on the advice of your agency or attorney, you will list either only your first names, or your last name as well. (If you are going to use your photo-resume on the internet or for wide networking, it is suggested you omit your last name and share it only when comfortable with whomever responds to your photo-resume. (Networking via the internet is discussed later in this chapter.) You might want the photo-resumes your attorney or agency personally gives out to have your last name as well (as some birth mother like to imagine their child with that last name).

- Just as with your picture, you want to show a birth mother that a child will be loved in your home, and that you have a life filled with activities of interest. For one couple it might be quiet activities: reading the Sunday paper in bed together with a box of donuts; Friday nights spent renting old movies and popping popcorn. Others might be active and like hiking, scuba diving and skiing. Just like we discussed above about appearances, birth mothers are all different in what attracts them to certain adoptive parents. Some birth mothers will identify with quiet couples, while others are into active people and sports. Or music. Whatever. The point is, you don't need to be anything but yourself, as there is no perfect description in the eyes of most birth mothers, beyond wanting a loving and secure home for their child.

- Talk about your jobs, or if one of you will be a stay-at-home parent, but keep job information brief. For example, writing that you have been a 4th grade teacher for five years is sufficient. You don't need to add that you were voted teacher of the year and are the only teacher in your district with a PhD in childhood psychology. This is not to say that a birth mother is not interested in those impressive facts, but save them for later, and not risk boring her when initially reading mny resumes.

- Your hobbies and interests are what define you in many ways, and what a birth mother will identify with. Either she has the same hobbies, or dreamed of doing them but never had the opportunity, and wants her child to have the chance to experience them. You can't list too many hobbies, as long as they are genuine interests. Such activities might be scrap-booking, gourmet cooking, church, aerobics, movies, softball, tennis, reading, and countless more. Just be honest and describe yourselves.

- Where you live is important to birth mothers. You may choose to list the city and state, or just the general area. Some birth mothers like the idea of doing the adoption in the same state where she lives, so will prefer in-state couples, while others might visualize a family on a distant coast as the best place to for a child to be raised. When you mention where you live, talk about why you like it: "We go to Cub games every weekend and love the museums the city has to offer;" "We like the mountains so we can hike in the summer and ski in the winter," or "We really enjoy our house in the suburbs. We have a lot of kids on our street and a great park just around the corner."

- Your pets are part of your family so don't forget to mention them. When describing dogs, particularly large breeds, it is a good idea to mention their gentleness and experience around children. Or, leave them out of the photo and just talk about them.

- Your letter should be typed, not handwritten, in an easy-to-read font. The length, including the photos, should be *one page maximum, or one double-sided page*. The last thing you want is for a birth mother to get a short, well-written letter from every other couple, and yours is a long rambling treatise. She is likely to put yours on the bottom to be read last, and find someone she falls in love with before she gets to it. Some people go with an 11 X 17 inch page, which then folds into a four-page 8.5 X 11 presentation. This is alright as well—not that you need that much space—and sometimes it's actually a burden to fill it with quality photos and information.

- The paper you use is important. This is not a job resume. You aren't going to use plain, boring paper. Your target audience of this letter is female, and young females at that. You want your letter to be *pretty*. Either choose a nice color, or perhaps stationary with a pretty border. Alternatively, you might dress it up with some stamped images, or punch holes and intertwine a ribbon. How many photo-resumes you plan to print will help you decide how much handiwork will need to go into each letter. Remember, you are showing the birth mother receiving it that you care about what you are doing and have invested time and emotion into it. She doesn't think about the fact you had to print 500 or 2,000 or whatever. She just sees the one in her hands.

- There is no need to volunteer something potentially negative in the letter. For example, you may be concerned that you have several prior marriages, a bankruptcy many years ago, you are in a non-mainstream religion, or one or both of you are older than you look. In most all states, a birth mother is entitled to know these facts prior to consenting to the adoption (and most birth mothers are very open-minded about such information), so you know she needs to be told these things. The question is whether you put it in your photo-resume letter, which is perhaps seen by her when she is alone, and no one is present to give extra information or immediately answer a question. (This situation is different from the wrongness of initially omitting that you have existing children. Having one or more children is something you should be proud of and be shouting from the rooftops.) A fact which some might see as negative is different as a birth mother might unfairly dismiss you when a little more knowledge might keep her interested. As long as you, or your adoption attorney or agency—whomever is the first person to speak to a birth mother about you—tells her in the initial call about those "negative" facts, that should not offend anyone's ethics. This slight delay in sharing the information is appropriate as it would be hard to describe some things in a letter without being unfair to yourself, and so much easier to mention verbally. Upon knowing the extra information, she can decide for herself if she wants to take the next step and meet you or not.)

- Be yourselves. There is no need to strike a false chord in your letter. If you are funny, great, be funny. Some couples make funny "Top Ten" lists why they'd make great parents, or what they love about each other. If you are a quiet, thoughtful couple, that's fine too, and your letter should reflect that in its style and tone. Birth mothers come in all sizes and personalities, just like you.

- Don't dwell on your infertility or personal heartbreak in trying to conceive a child. Birth mothers are facing their own personal crisis with the pregnancy and don't want to read letters from people sharing theirs. Mentioning you are adopting due to infertility is fine, but don't try to gain a birth mother's sympathy. Remember, every other adoptive family is adopting for the same reason. Keep your letter positive and uplifting and fun to read.

- Mentioning, or not mentioning, your religion is a difficult decision. A birth mother is entitled to know it, but do you want to put it in your letter? For Christian adoptive parents, there is usually no downside to mentioning it. In fact, in most cases it will be beneficial. For adoptive parents who have no religious affiliation, writing "we have no religion" strikes a potentially negative chord. And what if you are of a religion, such as Seventh Day Adventist or Mormon, which some birth mothers know little about? Perhaps reading that would cause a birth mother to unfairly dismiss you from consideration. Instead, if you, or your attorney or agency, immediately tells her about your religion when she expresses an interest in you, immediately followed by giving her some information about it, she is much more likely to be open-minded and consider you.

- Your letter must have a contact phone number. It can be your number, or that of your attorney or agency. If you are networking with your photo-resume letter outside of your region, it was previously common to get a toll free number, and most attorneys and agencies have one for that purpose. Nowadays, however, most all birth mothers have cell phones where dialing a local call is the same as a call out of state. The old "long distance" concerns are rarely an issue. As mentioned before, however, it is best to not put your home landline number in the photo-resume. If you want to use your own number, rather than your attorney or agency's, consider a temporary extra phone line or extra cell phone, one you can discard when your networking is over.

- Each letter should be hand-signed so it looks personal, not mass-produced. After the letter has been printed, sign your first names as the bottom of each letter, not before it is copied.

- A sample photo-resume letter is provided in Appendix C.

Okay, you've got your photo-resume letter. If it's not a major effort, you are doing it wrong. To repeat: the photo-resume letter is the heart of your networking. Even if you find her through another way—such as your attorney or agency directly handing it to a birth mother—your photo-resume is still the first thing she will see about you.

Now the question is how many copies to make. The answer will depend upon how you use it. If your attorney or agency is networking for you, they will want some copies—from dozens to hundreds—depending upon how they plan to use them. To maximize the exposure you will get from them, however, the largest distribution of the letters should be through your own networking efforts, supplementing your attorney or agency's efforts.

We will start with the most basic strategies, and advance to some lesser-known techniques. It is not necessary to do all of them. You will likely find that some methods appeal to you more than others. The more you do, however, the wider your outreach and the better your chances of quickly finding the right birth mother. (In the next chapter, we will continue with strategies for success).

Traditional Networking

There is no limit to how broad your networking attempts will be through *traditional networking* with your photo-resume letter. Traditional networking involves compiling lists of people in the health care industry, who may come into contact with a woman with an unplanned pregnancy, and give them your photo-resume letter, perhaps leading that birth mother to you. This will include obstetricians, gynecologists, family practice doctors (as many women start their pregnancy care with a general practitioner before transferring to an OB/GYN), counselors and psychologists (as unplanned pregnancies lead many to counseling to deal with their decisions), college health centers, hospitals and abortion/pregnancy planning clinics. It is usually a waste of time to send them to high school counselors (unless you have a personal connection there) as high-schoolers are minors and the school staff will rarely bring "strangers" into a student's life. Rather, they will direct her to an adoption agency or attorney directly.

You can elect to send these out to local professionals in the above categories in your region, throughout your state, or in other states. A small traditional networking campaign would be 500 letters. A good campaign would be at least 1,000 letters.

Three reasons commonly heard from adoptive parents why they don't do general networking:

1. *My letter will just get thrown away.* True, most of them will be discarded. But remember, it only takes one letter reaching one

birth mother to make the entire campaign a success. The more letters you send, the better your odds of success.

2. *Everyone sends out letters to healthcare professionals, so even if my letter is kept by the doctor or counselor receiving it, it will just be lost in the mass of other letters.* Actually, the vast majority of adoptive parents *don't* do traditional networking. Either they don't know about it, or they convince themselves it will be a waste of time. And even among those who do it, not everyone is networking in the same regions as you. Not to mention, many are sending out very poor photo-resume letters.

3. *I don't know how to compile a list of names and addresses to send the letters to.* You can compile a list by doing a Google search (ex. "Obstetricians, gynecologists, Dallas, Texas) if that is the region you choose. But that's a lot of work to find them, then print the information on address labels (which is exactly why most people don't make the effort). But do you know you can buy the information online? (More on this option later.).

Although most of your letters will go out by mail, always deliver those you can in person, such as in your local region. For example, let's say you take the time to go to your local college's health services offices and offer your letter to the receptionist. Meeting you in person, and liking you, makes her your ally. You may be the only person who has done that, or if not, you are likely only one of a few. Isn't she more likely to keep it in a drawer and in the back of her mind than some letter that came in the mail, which is much more likely to end up in the trash can?

Yes, this takes a lot of courage. That's why so few people do it. The most successful adoptive parents want success the most and leave their egos at the door.

Cover letter. If you are mailing the photo-resume, whether it be to a doctor or whomever, include a cover letter. It can be mass-produced so there is no extra time going into it, just make sure it is attractive (e.g. nice paper, nicely printed and formatted). This can be as simple as:

Hi,

We are hoping to adopt and are sending you our photo-resume letter in the hope you will pass it along if you hear of a woman facing an unplanned pregnancy who would like to learn about us.

Thanks!

Ben and Alyssa

When you create your cover letters, you could even print two "cover letters" to a page, and cut them horizontally or vertically, to reduce copying costs and give the recipient a simpler, smaller packet to review. See Appendix D for a sample.

Non-Traditional Networking

The healthcare industry is the obvious place to start for networking. It is not the only place, however. A much less known category in which to network, but one the author has found to be very successful, is hair and nail salons. These are female-dominated industries, and discussing other people's business seems to be the order of the day when getting a haircut, or your nails done. A customer's best friend's pregnancy would not be an uncommon topic of conversation. Getting your photo-resume letter into the right hands can in turn get it to birth mothers.

There are other reasons why including beauticians in your networking campaign is a good idea. One is that there are a lot of them. If a mid-sized city has ten obstetricians and gynecologists, don't be surprised if it has ten or twenty times as many hair and nail salons. This allows you to focus on a particular geographical area and not run out of appropriate recipients. Another reason is that even among adoptive parents who do elect to network, many don't think to include people in the category. This makes them an under-used group of people, and few have received photo-resume letters.

If you are networking in your own region, you may want to personally deliver some or all of your photo-resume letters. In a hair salon, for example, you'd give one to each person working in the store (hopefully catching some not working at the moment), taking a minute to tell them how you hope they will help you: simply keep the letter on hand until they hear of an unplanned pregnancy situation, then to pass it along. If they like you, most will be excited to do it and be part of the creation of your family, more so than a physician's office where you have no relationship with that office. And yes, some will tell you they don't want the letters and don't think they can help. That's okay. (Focus more on salons that cut women's hair, rather than generic *Supercuts* type places.)

Besides personally delivering them, you can also purchase mailing lists of hair and nail salons, just as with healthcare professionals, as discussed earlier. If you are mailing the letters, as mentioned above, use a cover letter. See sample in Appendix D.

Let's discuss what to do if you want to widely network but can't imagine researching addresses online and re-typing all that address information. That might make sense for fifty or so local entities, but not for a campaign of 500 or 1,000 or 2,000.

You can do a Google search for "buy mailing lists" and find dozens of companies that have mailing lists in every category in every region. So you can ask how many there are for each, such as "how many OB/GYNs in Oklahoma?" And so on. Prices vary widely. Some tips to save money is to go with the option "single use only" and "one recipient per location" (so if there are five OB/GYNs in one office, you might feel only one is sufficient).

Some of these companies will offer to print them on peel-off labels, usually coming 30 to a page (measuring approximately 1 X 2 inches each), so they are ready for you to put on an envelope). Or you can buy the information and print them on sheets of labels yourself (assuming you have some computer skills to format the information). One suggestion if you do this is to buy clear labels rather than white ones. The clear ones tend to diminish the fact it is a label and looks less like a mass-mailing. One company, Avery, offers 1,500 clear labels, 30 to a page (product number 5660) for about $65.

Here's a checklist for traditional and non-traditional networking:

1. Prepare your photo-resume letters.
2. Copy the number of photo-resume letters you will need.

3. Prepare a cover letter.
4. Copy the cover letters you will need.
5. Buy a mailing list of healthcare professionals, and other groups you think will be helpful, in the region you wish to network (perhaps buying them on pre-printed mailing labels (or have the ability to create them yourself on your computer from the data provided). Or create your own list from online and Yellow Page research. (The drawback to Yellow Pages is that zip codes are rarely provided.)
6. Buy #10 business sized envelopes.
7. Buy return address mailing labels (you can find these online for about $7 per 500).
8. Mail (or as you can—hand deliver) one cover letter with each one photo-resume letter, to each professional on your list. (If you are personally delivering them, it is optional to include a cover letter.)

Personal Networking

Traditional networking can be effective, and it is recommended you do it. Admittedly, however, the author's favorite kind of networking is called *personal networking*. It requires no purchase of mailing lists, no huge mailings of a thousand or so letters, and no direct mailings to healthcare professionals where the risk is higher your letter will be tossed.

The heart of personal networking is to ask people you know to *personally* give their healthcare professionals, or other helpful individuals, your photo-resume letter. This is their family doctor, their OB/GYN, their hair salon, their nail salon, their minister/rabbi, their friends who work in the healthcare industry. The biggest advantage to this method is that because they (the doctor or other selected recipients) are getting it personally from someone they have a relationship with (their patient or customer), so they are much more likely to take it seriously and keep it. By sending one packet of five photo-resumes to the people on your list, you are perhaps getting your photo-resume *personally delivered* by someone who knows the recipient.

Here's how you mount an effective personal networking campaign:

1. *Make a list of friends and family.* This means a *big* list. You are not just listing your best friends; you are listing *everyone you know.* This means your friends from work, from your college days, your neighbors, people you exercise or work out with, who go to your place of worship, et cetera. You get the idea. Start with your Christmas or Hanukkah list and try to triple it. Try to compile a list of at least a hundred people if you can. For some, based upon where they work, this is easy. For others it is impossible. Just do your best. Some brave souls will open their church directory and presto, they've got two hundred names. You may be thinking that, sure, friends will help, but why would mere acquaintances do so? Keep reading, and you will see why they will likely participate, and how effective this can be.

2. *Write a "Dear Friends" cover letter.* Unlike the cover letter used for healthcare professionals or hair/nail salons, this cover letter takes a different approach. It will be a short, typed letter stating you are hoping to adopt, and ask for the help of your friends and acquaintances by doing several *specific* things. You will ask them that the next time they go to their family doctor, *personally* give him or her your photo-resume letter, and mention they know you. The next time they go to their gynecologist or obstetrician, *personally* give him or her your photo-resume letter, and mention they know you. The same with their minister or rabbi, hair stylist, nail salon, et cetera. A sample "Dear Friends" cover letter is provided in Appendix E.

3. *Mail each person on your networking list five copies of your photo-resume letter (with a traditional networking cover letter— provided in Appendix D—stapled to each one), with a single cover letter to your friend, paper-clipped to the top of the stack, explaining why you are enclosing the letters, and what to do with them.* Now, your friends, who'd like to help you adopt but don't know how without specific guidance, know exactly what to do. So the next time they go to their family doctor, they bring along a letter. Their next OB/GYN appointment, they bring a letter. The next time they go to church, they bring a letter. If they can think of friends in other healthcare fields working with pregnant

women, such as counselors, they give him or her a letter. (Personal networking is primarily a local means of networking, as most of the people you know will live in the region where you live and work. But don't forget about friends and family out of state. Send them a packet as well.)

4. *Be confident your letters will be handed out as you are hoping.* Here is a question for you. If you received a letter like this from an acquaintance, maybe not a best friend, but someone you know and thought well of, wouldn't you enjoy the chance of helping— and maybe being the person who created the link which lead to the creation of their family? Most women are thrilled to do this. True, most husbands getting the letters won't run out to hand them out, but most of the wives, a definite yes. As always, it's women who get things done!

5. *Let the numbers work for you.* If you have one hundred people on your list, and each one gives out the five photo-resume letters you sent them, you have now perhaps reached 500 key people. And a high percentage are likely to keep the letter, because they personally got it from someone they know.

Personal networking is *a must* in an effective adoption campaign. You may be shy about telling others you hope to adopt, but you are encouraged to get past that. Your friends and relatives likely know many people who have adopted and are very comfortable with the subject. In fact, you will be amazed how may calls you will get from acquaintances receiving your letter who have personal experience with adoption they never had reason to share before, not knowing your interest in adoption.

Here is a checklist for personal networking:

1. Prepare your photo-resume letters
2. Prepare a "Dear Friends" cover letter for your friends who will receive them (Appendix E).
3. Prepare (if not already done for traditional networking) a traditional networking cover letter (Appendix D) and staple one cover letter to each of the photo-resume letters.

4. Paperclip one "Dear Friends" cover letter on top of a stack of five photo-resume letters explaining to your friend what you want done with the five photo-resumes (each of which already has a traditional cover letter stapled to it).
5. Buy large 9 X 12 inch envelopes so you won't have to fold the photo-resume letters.
6. Mail, or hand-deliver, your packet to each person on your list containing one cover letter and five photo-resume letters.

Here is a comment to the naysayers. Some will say,

"This is a waste of time. We've been telling our friends for years we hope to adopt, and nothing has happened."

And they are right. It is almost a waste of time. But just telling them is not what we are doing. Let's say someone told you they wanted to adopt and "Keep your eyes open for us!" Seriously, what can someone do with that information? Nothing. People need to be *guided and empowered* through specific instruction. That's what personal networking does. And remember, what's our motto?

It only takes one letter to make the campaign successful.

Advertising. Placing a classified ad in local newspapers has been a popular way to reach birth mothers for decades, less so since the internet has taken over for the print media. About half the states permit adoption ads (the state-by-state review tells you which states permit adoption advertising by non-adoption agencies, and which don't, although the laws on the subject tend to be a bit fuzzy). The author has never been a big fan of newspaper advertising, but to be fair, some adoption professionals have used the method with decent results.

Usually an advertisement, or "announcement" if that sounds better, is a small ad placed in the personals or classified section of a newspaper. Some consider doing Craigslist posts. Even when it is permitted in a state, the individual newspaper may have its own requirements, such as a letter from your attorney or agency to be sure an adoption listing is lawful.

If you elect to place an ad, as with all types of networking, you might elect to only do it locally, or go into other states. The newspapers can range from being major papers with huge circulations to small town weeklies. Although most will be "general circulation" newspapers, the newspapers of college, special interest and religiously-oriented entities are possibilities too. Those who employ advertising as one of their prime networking methods usually advertise in several dozen papers, and expect to do so for several months.

Typical ads/posts might be:

ADOPTION. LOVING COUPLE IN OREGON HOPES TO ADOPT INFANT. MEDICAL BILLS PAID. (500) 555-5555.

ADOPTION NOT ABORTION. WE ARE A CHRISTIAN COUPLE HOPING TO ADOPT. CAN HELP WITH LIVING AND MEDICAL COSTS. CONFIDENTIAL. CALL COLLECT: 1 (500) 555-5555.

PREGNANT? WE HOPE TO ADOPT AND CAN OFFER A LOVING HOME AND A WONDERFUL LIFE IN THE COUNTRY. WE HAVE A COMPLETED HOME STUDY. WE CAN COME TO MEET YOU. 1 (555) 555-5555.

OPEN ADOPTION. WE ARE HOPING TO ADOPT A CHILD FROM A BIRTH MOTHER WHO WOULD LIKE TO STAY A PART OF OUR LIVES. WE LIVE IN (NAME YOUR STATE) AND CAN PAY YOUR LIVING, MEDICAL, LEGAL AND COUNSELING COSTS. CALL US AND GET TO KNOW US AND LET'S SEE IF WE CAN PLAN A LOVING ADOPTION TOGETHER! (555) 555-5555.

For those adoption professionals who endorse it, newspaper advertising has been popular over the years for one simple reason. It's easy. You can reach a decent number of people by simply creating an ad, rather than compiling mailing lists and stuffing envelopes.

The primary disadvantage of newspaper advertising is its impersonal nature and lack of any control over who sees the ads. Compare it to a networking campaign, where you are directing your photo-resume letters toward people in the healthcare industry, or specific people like beauticians. But your ad or internet post can be seen by anyone, including people who are not even pregnant and think they see an opportunity to manipulate someone. The chance of attempted fraud, and calls from people who are not even pregnant, is much higher.

If you feel advertising is an outreach method you wish to employ, it is strongly recommended you have an adoption attorney or agency to receive any calls, and have them heavily screen any callers before passing them through to any contact with you. Good adoption situations can come out of adoption advertisements, but extra caution is needed at the early stages to be sure you are working with a legitimate person sincere about adoption planning. As a general rule, however, this method trails both traditional and personal networking in likely success. It's the easy and lazier way to network, and to an overly broad audience.

The internet. The internet has become our new Yellow Pages and educational resource rolled into one. For this reason, some birth mothers, just like some adoptive parents, will make going online their first step toward adoption.

There is also a tragic result of the popularity of internet advertisements. A small number of adoption agencies, attorneys and facilitators have "taken over" most of the high-profile advertising spots. When you go to some of the biggest internet sites, and you see the banners at the top and prime space advertising—or you do a Google search and see the paid placements at the top of the page—the cost can run into the hundreds of thousands of dollars annually. Think how much those agencies, attorneys now need to charge to make up for that huge cash outlay. This greatly drives up the cost of the adoption, with some of these entities charging double or triple the norm. Of course, there are many agencies and attorneys who don't use this method of outreach, or who use it in great moderation. There is some animosity behind the scenes of the adoption world, however, toward these agencies and attorneys who are seen to be driving up the cost of adoption.

There is no denying the outreach of the internet, however, in reaching birth mothers, whether it is by an adoption professional or an adoptive parent networking on their own. Most adoptive parents benefit indirectly, if they are using an attorney or agency who has an internet presence, as those ads attract birth mothers who can in turn select them as adoptive parents.

The other way to be exposed to birth mothers who go online is to work with one or more of the services which showcase adoptive parent photo-resume letters. They charge you a fee, of course, usually from $100 to $300 per month. No recommendation is made here for any specific company. You can find them by googling terms like "adoption advertising."

A better way to perhaps find a potentially good one is to google terms like you think a birth mother would use if she were searching and see what listings come up. Use your imagination, but these might include the obvious like "adoption," "adoption lawyers," "adoption agencies," "place a baby for adoption." Of course, this will also lead you to agencies, attorneys and facilitators. You will also likely find some showcase sites for adoptive parents to directly present their photo-resume. With a little digging into these sites, you will find out how to have your photo-resume letter listed and what the cost is. Adoptive parents report mixed results from their success using such sites. Some find a birth mother. Some spend their money with no result. Almost all, however, seem to report quite a few false starts from calls from birth mothers who were not serious or legitimate, but this is true for any type of general outreach, such as the internet.

Creating your own website. A better option, if you are a computer savvy person, is to create your own website. You can go to sites like GoDaddy.com or HostGator.com and search for available URLs (website names) and buy one for about $13 a year. When you consider all the extensions (not just ".com" or ".org" but ".us" and literally dozens more, you can get almost any name you want. Let's say you go with: JerriLynneandDavyWantToAdopt.com.

You can also build a website on sites like Go Daddy/HostGator, either using their own software, designed to be easy for non-computer people, or create a WordPress site, for more advanced users. They can "host" your site, so it is visible online, for a small monthly fee.

Now you can directly promote your site via Google. Learn about their Adwords program at adwords.google.com where you can be one of those people or businesses listing their URL in the top three spots. You choose the words you want to be found under when people search online. Most importantly, you can also set the specific region, so you can select just your city or county.

This advertising is expensive and you pay each time someone clicks on your ad. You authorize up to a certain cost per click. The more popular the word, the more it will cost you. Don't be surprised if you want to be in the top three for a popular word like "adoption" that it may cost you a lot, perhaps $15 every click, and it's just your tough luck if the wrong people or lookiloos click on it a hundred times with no benefit to you. But at least it is a more controlled environment that paying one of those listing services, where you are side-by-side being shown by countless other couples. Less popular search terms, such as "adoption information" will be less expensive as less people are bidding on them. You can select less popular search words than obvious ones like "adoption" that will not be as costly. Consider any terms you would use if you were a pregnant woman considering adoption. For example, you don't have to be an attorney select a search term like "independent adoption attorneys." This will get far fewer hits than a term like "adoption," but will likely cost much less.

Adwords has phone support and you will need it. You will want to ask about excluding certain search terms (called "negative" search words) where you don't want your ad to be shown or the money will be wasted. For example, if you select the word "adoption" and elect a broad display option, someone searching for "dog adoption" will have your ad come up. An Adwords representative, and a lot of reading on your part about how it all works, will help you limit your ad to the audience you want. You can also set your budget per day or month.

If you select this option make sure it is easy for birth mothers to reach you, so have an email and phone number clearly visible, and always be available at that number. A birth mother who calls is unlikely to leave a voice mail and may just move on to the next family and bond with them before she ever gets back to you.

As stated before, you need to be cautious when "putting yourself out there" like this, so omitting last names is wise, as well as using a phone number you can discard when your networking campaign is over. Sadly, any outreach like this is subject to the wrong people finding you, so you have to be on the lookout for fraud and scam adoption situations. Those are discussed in multiple parts of this book, as well as how to spot them. If you get a call from an agency, attorney or facilitator who says they saw your ad and have a birth mother for you, hang up. *Yes, hang up!* If they have to troll the internet to find adoptive parents for birth mothers they are supposedly working with, something is clearly wrong. If they are legitimate, wouldn't they clearly have their own waiting families to show? The reality is these people tend to be the dregs of the adoption world, if not outright frauds.

Facebook. Posting your photo-resume is potentially a great way to get the word out, and you can ask Friends to forward it to their Friends as well. Be aware this does not take the place of your personal networking where you mailed them 5 copies of your photo-resume. Posting on Facebook does *not* put a copy of your photo-resume in their hands. So, the Facebook posting is easy, yes, but don't kid yourself it has anything close to the same effectiveness. Still, it is so simple, consider it.

Adoption "Business Cards." Think how often you stumble across someone's business card, perhaps left in a restaurant, or on the seat of a cab, et cetera. Often it is for a realtor or mortgage broker, or other professions where people sometimes have to be aggressive to get noticed. Clearly, they leave their cards everywhere to be found. Sometimes adoptive parents do the same thing. A typical adoption business card (the same size as a regular business card) might have your picture, with the caption, "Hoping to adopt!" in large letters next to it. On the other side might be a very short bio, providing a small photo, your first names, some bare bones information, and a contact phone number. An example may be:

We are Glen and Carrie. Our dream is to start our family through adoption. We are both teachers. We can help with pregnancy-related costs. Please call to learn more about us! 1-800-555-1234.

You then give a card to each person you interact with each day, or leave them in public places where they are likely to be found. Like with other non-personal outreach networking, it is recommended you don't use your home phone number or give your last name.

By googling "cheap business cards," you can find them for about $10 for 500 color business cards. Another very small investment that can pay rewards.

Legality of advertising. We've talked a lot about networking via the internet (ads, Facebook, Craigslist, et cetera) and newspapers, but let's talk about the legality of advertising. This is complicated because what is "advertising"? Is it advertising when you are not selling something? Or are you just are giving notice you want to adopt?

Every state has laws governing adoption advertising, but often they are not very clear about if it only applies to those offering a service for a fee (like an agency, attorney or facilitator) or to someone like you who wants to share your desire to adopt. For this reason, it is important you speak to your attorney or agency about your advertising plans and see what you can do and where and how you can do it. Don't rely on the fact that you see adoption ads on the internet in your state and assume that means it is legal. It could well be that that entity is just violating the law. (Yes, it is true that it seems most of the adoption advertising laws are ignored, and violations not prosecuted, but why take a chance? Best to obey the law and not worry about a future problem.)

Facilitators. A facilitator is a person or business that is not an attorney or an agency, rather and entity which finds birth mothers, usually for a fee. Usually for a *large* fee. Many, in fact, charge as much or more than agencies or attorneys, despite the fact they can provide only a small portion of the needed services. As a general rule, the author cautions adoptive parents against using facilitators as they can't perform any of the functions attorneys or agencies can. They can't give legal advice, do legal work or make court appearances. They can't do home studies, place children in an adoptive home or write court reports. Some states make facilitating an adoption for a fee a crime, while most states have no legislation on the issue. Some states expressly permit them but with limitations. Those caveats being said, however, if you are aware of what a facilitator is, and still want to use one to help you find a birth mother, it is an additional option for you.

Just like attorneys and agencies, facilitators find birth mothers in many different ways. Many facilitators rely heavily on large yellow page ads and the internet. Some birth mothers will decline to work with a facilitator when they learn their true nature as a non-agency or attorney (although it is tough for anyone, especially young birth mothers, to know their true status as facilitators, as facilitators usually employ names which sound like agencies). Other birth mothers, however, may prefer a facilitator as they wish to go outside of what they may see as normal, more legitimate, adoption channels to make an adoptive placement. Of course, that may be the very reason to avoid such a birth mother.

Despite the questionable issue of the high fees facilitators charge in relation to their limited services, the bottom line is that some do produce results. Because they are largely unlicensed and often untrained, however, unlike attorneys and agencies, they are less able to effectively determine a good from a bad adoption. For this reason, it is particularly important when working with a facilitator that you have an experienced attorney or agency to screen any birth mothers located by the facilitator, and help you make sure you have a viable adoption.

Complicating the issue is that unlike attorneys and agencies, there is no formal data base for facilitators in most states. This is because it is a largely unregulated industry, without the strict licensing laws affecting attorneys and agencies. The simplest way to determine if the entity you are considering is a facilitator or not is to just ask if they are a licensed agency, and if so, in what state. If the answer is no, they usually fall into the general category of facilitator. To verify what they tell you, you can call the state social services office (provided in the state-by-state review) for the state in which they are located and ask the agency licensing office if they are a listed agency.

How do you spot a good facilitator from a bad one? This is a difficult question. For example, with an attorney, a prospective client could call the state bar and inquire about any disciplinary actions against the attorney, and learn where they went to law school and how long they'd been in practice. With an agency you can call the state social services office and verify their status and ask about how long they've been in business. Such questions about facilitators to a similar independent government office are generally impossible. The best advice in this area is to read the suggestions for selecting a good attorney in Chapter 4 and ask the same questions. In addition, here are some specific recommendations if you are determined to hire a facilitator:

1. Ask for the full contract you will be expected to sign in advance of arranging a meeting or paying any initial fees. Have your attorney look it over to be sure it seems appropriate.

2. Don't pay a large portion of your fee in advance. This is also recommended when hiring an attorney or agency, so it will most certainly be recommended regarding facilitators. Pay for services as you go through the process. Why pay their entire fee, or a significant portion of it, before you even know if they can indeed find you a birth mother, and if they do, if you will want to work with that birth mother?

3. Ask what methods they use to find birth mothers and make sure you agree with the methods used.

4. Ask what region or states the birth mothers typically come from. This may not matter to you, but if you only want a local birth mother in your home state, that is unlikely to happen if they rely solely on national internet advertising, leading to most placements being out of state.

5. Ask the attorney or agency you will be working with if they agree to work with facilitators. Some work regularly with facilitators and have a good relationship. Others may view them as *infantpreneurs* using questionable taste in networking techniques and a reputation for arranging risky and expensive adoptions, and will decline to work with them.

6. Ask the facilitator for a list of past adoptive parent clients. Don't accept referrals to adoptive parents simply "matched up" with a birth mother, or who just received a baby but the adoption is not finalized. Those are adoptions "in progress" where things can still go wrong. You want to insist to speak to recent adoptive parents who have *completed* their adoptions in court. And ask for a significant number of referrals, not just three or four. Even the worst professional in any business will please *some* of their

clients. You want to be sure they please *most* of them. Make sure they are recent ones too. Most facilitators boast of helping with a very large number of adoptive placements every year. If this is true, there should be no problem giving you a large number of referrals.

When you speak to their prior adoptive parent clients, ask:

1. How long did you wait to be selected by your birth mother?
2. What was she like? (See if the typical birth mother located by the facilitator is of the ethnic group you hope to adopt from, has a health and drug history you feel is appropriate, et cetera). Remember that you are talking about the birth mother of the child the adoptive parents adopted, so you want to be respectful in your questions, but thorough enough you feel confident in the information you obtain.
3. Did you have any false leads prior to the placement that worked?
4. What were the fees you paid the facilitator?
5. Where there any fees you didn't expect?
6. Did you get the chance to meet the birth mother before the birth? Before you had to pay substantial fees to the facilitator?
7. Were you given complete birth mother (and birth father, if available) health histories?
8. Did the facilitator cooperate with your attorney or agency?
9. Did they force you to use a particular attorney or agency or let you select the one you wanted?

There may be some good facilitators performing a valid service, for a fee commensurate with the limited services they are able to provide. Unfortunately for the adoption field as a whole, however, many are seen as profiteers with little adoption training, and adoptive parents have little recourse when the adoption is handled improperly.

So there you have it, a wide selection of networking techniques and strategies to help match you with a birth mother. Let's review what we have so far:

- You are going to not only select a skilled adoption attorney or agency, but one whose services includes networking for birth mothers, helping to lead to an adoptive match, or alternatively advise you on your own networking campaign.

- You are not going to sit and wait to see when, or if, your attorney or agency will be successful in creating an adoptive match. You are going to mount your own networking campaign.

- You are going to put great effort into the best photo-resume letter you can do, and duplicate it as needed to effectively network.

- You are going to choose not one, but several, networking strategies, and one of them must be personal networking, specifically as outlined in this chapter.

- You are going to vow not to take the easy way. Earlier it was said few adoptive parents mount a full personal and traditional networking campaign. Now you can see why. They decide it is easier to just pay someone (like an internet birth mother-finding site) or a facilitator, and convince themselves it is "just as good, and easier too." The difference in these options that are less demanding of your time is they are not as likely to reach a quality birth mother, as is found when reaching her more directly (via her doctor, friends, et cetera), who are telling her about you or handing her your photo-resume or adoption business card.

Do you think we are done strategizing? Not a chance! An additional way leading to a fast, newborn adoption is in the next chapter, *The Power of Three*.

But wait . . . what if you are one of those adoptive parents who think there is just no way you could do *any* of these things. It is just not in your makeup to mail photo-resumes to your friends, drop them off in clinics, post on Facebook, et cetera.

Don't worry. That's okay. You don't *have* to do these things. But be aware that if you are relying only on your attorney or agency's efforts, your chances of success, especially quick success, go down significantly. The good news is the next chapter, the Power of Three, is a way you can balance the scales.

Remember too that if you are open to adopting a waiting child rather than a newborn, you don't need to do *any* of these things. Those children are literally waiting for someone like you. To learn more about that option, please read Chapter 5 and learn about adoption exchanges, and the many children available there.

CHAPTER 9

THE POWER OF THREE

The routine way to do a newborn adoption is to select an adoption attorney or agency, and wait for them to tell you that you've been selected by a birth mother. That's the norm across America. It's just the way it has always been done. There is certainly nothing wrong with that, particularly if you maximize your odds of success by hiring a great attorney or agency, and are diligent in your networking.

Even when doing everything right, however, you might still find that you wait longer than you want for your adoptive match to occur, or not get selected at all. Part of the reason for this is that no matter how active you are in your adoption efforts, the bottom line is that you still have to wait for a birth mother to pick you for the process to begin.

Adoption is a game of "hurry up and wait." You diligently hire the right professional, energetically prepare your photo-resume letter, get your networking efforts going, but then the reality is that you sit and wait to be picked. You might be lucky and get picked in the fraction of the time you expected. It happens. But for every adoptive parent who gets picked in only a month or two, there is someone else at the other extreme, perhaps waiting years and years. This can be true even for adoptive parents in the same geographical area, with the same personal characteristics and lifestyle, to present to birth mothers. It's much like dating in that the process is not always fair. Why does one person find the perfect spouse at age twenty-five, and another person, equal in every way, never finds that special partner? Adoption has the same dynamics. Thus, the issue becomes beating the odds, and doing so quickly.

This is how you do it. As we've discussed, the key element of being matched with a birth mother is to hire an attorney or agency that includes birth mother networking in their services. But who says you only have to hire one? Yes, that's the tradition?

Forget tradition.

You are hereby encouraged to adopt *The Power of Three* and hire *three* attorneys and/or agencies. That's right, three, not one. And It is recommended you will hire them all *simultaneously,* not wait to hire someone new only if you become disappointed with how long the process might be taking with the first one you hire.

Here is your first thought upon hearing this advice:

"I can't afford that!"

Wrong. You are probably assuming that hiring three adoption professionals will triple the cost. To the contrary, although it will increase the cost of your adoption, it will not even double it. Here's why. You are not hiring three adoption professionals to do the *entire* adoption for you. Instead, you are hiring them to perform the initial stage of their services: advise you of adoption laws and procedures in their region or state, and to show you to birth mothers contacting their office to select adoptive parents (so, of course, you are only selecting those that do their own networking). As we discussed in Chapters 4 and 6 regarding selecting the right attorney or agency, those with the fairest payment schedules charge as they work through the different stages of the adoption. Only a portion of that will be due initially, until you are matched with a birth mother.

So you pay each of the selected professional their initial fee, then when one of them comes up with an adoptive match you wish to accept, what do you do?

*You kindly thank the other two for their services
and let them know their services are no longer needed.*

The only fees you have thereafter will be for the attorney or agency who created your adoptive match. (If you are doing an interstate adoption, you will still need one attorney/agency in each state.)

So how do you put such a plan into action? Think back to when we discussed finding the best attorney and/or agency, looking in both your home region and other states you wanted to consider. Likely you found several well-qualified attorneys and agencies and had a hard time narrowing it down to just one, particularly if you did a broad search in more than one state. Now you don't need to limit yourself to just one.

Not every attorney or agency is right for this strategy, however. Some will have fee structures which require an unreasonably large percentage of their fee up front. These attorneys or agencies are not for you. You also need to be honest with whomever you are hiring that you plan to take this approach of hiring several adoption professionals and continue only with the one who first helps create a good adoptive match. There are some adoption professionals who do not like this multi-professional strategy, and will insist on being the only entity involved in your adoption. Fine, that attorney or agency is not right for you. You should be the center of the process, not them.

The vast majority will be happy to work with other adoption professionals, knowing you will proceed only with the one creating your adoptive match. In fact, you are creating a healthy unspoken competition between the entities you hired. This can only be to your benefit. Each wants to look good and produce results. Each wants to do the entire adoption and earn their fee. It's simply human nature. They know you are going to be telling people, *"I hired one attorney, Joe Smith, and an agency, XYZ Family Services, both in our home state, and an attorney out-of-state, Jane Doe. . . and it was Joe who came through for us first."*

The key question for you when employing this strategy is whether to focus your efforts in one region, or to spread out into other states. As you know from Chapter 2, there are fifteen different types of adoption available to you. If you are like most adoptive parents, several options seemed attractive. In fact, it was likely tough for you to choose between doing everything in-state, doing an interstate adoption, an identified adoption, or a non-resident adoption. Now you don't need to choose just one. You can open the door to several types, and see which comes through for you first.

Here is some specific advice. Let's say you live in a large metropolitan area (Los Angeles, Seattle, et cetera). in a state with good adoption laws, good adoption attorneys and agencies from which to choose and a significant number of birth mothers making placements within the state. With all that going for you, you might prefer an in-state adoption using only local professionals. Therefore, you might want to hire all three of your professionals in your state, but it's important to spread them out over different parts of the state, often at least one hundred miles apart. This is particularly true when the attorney or agency's referral sources are primarily local, like neighborhood doctors, hospitals and clinics.

If you are open to an interstate or non-resident adoption, this opens up unlimited doors for you, as you are not considering just attorneys and agencies in one state, but several. Perhaps the entire nation. Now you can really analyze the state-by-state review and determine which states appear attractive when them, and consider a non-resident or interstate adoption.

Often the best utilization of The Power of Three strategy is to mix attorneys and agencies, selecting one of one type and two of the other. Depending upon your state, either attorneys or agencies will be the primary way in which adoptive matches are created. Also, even if your local agencies do not create as many adoptive matches as attorneys, if your state requires a pre-placement home study from a private agency (as compared to some states which only require a post-placement home study), why not use the agency for the double duty of the required home study, and also trying to create an adoptive match?

Due to the fact laws and procedures vary so much from state to state, it is impossible to provide one perfect strategy for everyone. However, by the time you have finished this book, and spoken to some local professionals, you will find that the routes best for you will become immediately clear. It is just up to you to act on them.

Here are some sample scenarios, and how to perhaps best use The Power of Three:

- *You live in a state with unfair adoption laws and few or no adoption options.* Hire all three attorneys or agencies in states permitting non-resident adoption, and do virtually everything in the state of birth. (You will still need a local agency for your home study, so you might want to consider that as one of the three).

- *You might be moving to another state and hesitant to hire local attorneys or agencies.* If your present state permits non-residents to adopt, and the adoption laws are fair, there is no detriment to hiring local attorneys or agencies as they can continue to fully serve you if you move. However, if your present state does not allow non-residents to adopt, you should consider adoption professionals in states allowing non-resident adoption, so they can assist you regardless of where you live. Alternatively, the adoption professionals you hired before you moved can continue to network for a birth mother, and do the adoption as an interstate adoption, to be finalized in your new home state.

- *You live in Connecticut, Georgia, Illinois, Maryland, Minnesota, New Jersey or New York which bar attorneys from finding birth mothers to create adoptive matches, or doing so for a fee.* Hire a skilled adoption attorney in your home state, but hire two out-of-state attorneys or agencies who can network as part of their services to you. Or, you can retain an in-state agency, which unlike attorneys *can* network under the states' laws, to meet your in-state needs, *if* you feel the agency and their in-house attorney can meet your legal needs as well as an independent attorney.

- *You live in a region with good adoption attorneys and/or agencies, and with fair adoption laws, so you'd like to finalize the adoption in your home state, but there appear to be few birth mother matches created locally.* Hire a local attorney or agency to handle the in-state work and court finalization, but concurrently hire two out-of-state attorneys or agencies experienced in creating adoptive matches. You can then do an interstate adoption from virtually any state, where the child will be born, but you will be completing it in your home state.

- *You just want a child as soon as possible and don't care if you adopt a newborn or older child, via domestic or intercountry adoption.* If this is you, you can stop all your networking and thoughts of hiring multiple attorneys. Those waiting children are indeed, *waiting* for you to select that option, either through the county's public agency or a private agency licensed as a foster family agency and using the adoption exchanges. Why spend your efforts on another option if a waiting child is for you? It's free and the children are waiting.

Well, you can't say you don't have options! You might even complain you have too many. That's a nice problem to have. Best of all, The Power of Three strategy triples your chances of success, and opens the door to hundreds of supremely qualified attorneys and more than a thousand agencies throughout the nation. The only limits you have are those you choose to set on yourself. Yes, it does add cost, and that will eliminate if from consideration for some adoptive parents, as adoption is already expensive, but as stated already, the Power of Three does not triple or even double adoption costs, but it will increase the overall cost depending upon the initial fees including networking, but before the adoptive match, of the adoption professionals you select.

This Power of Three plan of attack is ideal for those adoptive parents who can't bring themselves to do networking or any personal outreach and recognize they need to put more effort into an attorney or agency creating the match. But this option is not limited to those adoptive parents. It is also for those who are active in networking, but want to do even more to maximize their chances of quick success.

CHAPTER 10

RED FLAGS TO A RISKY ADOPTION

Here is some important wisdom: *The surest way to avoid a failed adoption is to never start a risky one.* Just because you are selected by a birth mother doesn't mean that you will want to accept the placement and work with her. You want to make sure she is the right person for you, doing it for the right reasons. Hard as it may be to believe, sometimes that means passing on an adoption opportunity.

How do you spot a risky adoption? It is not mystical at all. No fortuneteller is required. Looking at specific characteristics of the birth family and the motivations for adoption will give you the answer. That, and your gut instincts—the same instincts which safely guide you through life—will separate the "right" from the "wrong" placements.

The Birth Mother's Age

Many people wrongly assume that most adoptions are started by high school girls facing unplanned pregnancies. Although there is a high number of unplanned pregnancies in the high school years, fewer of these pregnancies result in adoption than those of older women, usually aged 18 to 26. What happens to all those high school pregnancies? Most of these young women will terminate their pregnancies, or raise the children themselves.

Generally speaking, the younger the birth mother is (as well as the birth father), the riskier the adoption is. There are several reasons for this. The biggest one is the lack of life experience and maturity that a young girl will have, as compared to someone older. A young birth mother doesn't yet know what it means to face the obligations of parenthood and life as an adult. All her needs have been met by her family.

An older birth mother, however, has faced issues such as having to earn money for rent, what it feels like to be hungry because your paycheck wasn't as much as needed, coming home from work tired and having no energy to do anything, much less care for a child as a single parent.

Also, a young birth mother is subjected to the peer pressure of her equally young and inexperienced friends who think it would be "fun" to have a baby, or who perhaps are young single moms themselves and want their friend to share the experience.

The biggest reason working with young birth mothers is risky is simply the narcissistic nature of most teenagers. Most care about themselves, and their life at this moment in time, and little else. This may sound simplistic, but talk to any parent of the vast majority of teenagers, or a psychologist, and you will be convinced it is true. An example we can all associate with is the first time someone breaks your heart, the girl or guy who you were sure—let's say at age sixteen—was the person you wanted to spend your life with, and your heart aches when you lose them.

At the moment of that break-up, you believe that pain you are feeling will never heal, and your life is over. As adults, we all know that feeling will pass, and we will grow up to fall in love again. But when you were sixteen you would have done *anything* to make that pain go away if you had it within your power.

So, let's compare this to adoption. Imagine you are a very young birth mother giving birth for the first time. You face more emotions than you ever thought possible, and the pain of losing your child is unimaginable, despite common sense and parents telling you that you are too young to parent. You know adoption is the right thing, but it hurts to say goodbye to the child you just gave birth to. It hurts way more than you thought it would. More than you thought possible.

What do you do if you are that young birth mother if the law grants you the right to change your mind? Unlike with failed love, you *do* have the power to eliminate your pain. So do you eliminate your pain by stopping the adoption? Some will, and that is the danger of young birth mothers. Of course, any birth mother can change her mind, teenager or adult, but the younger she is, the chances are higher that she will be unable to deny her emotions.

Does this mean you should never work with a birth mother under a certain age? And if so, what is that age? Fourteen? Sixteen? Eighteen? No, it does not mean that. The author has worked with birth mothers as young as twelve (sad to say) and have seen those adoptions work out fine. So what is the answer?

The key is not focusing specifically on a numerical age, rather the birth mother's maturity. Although, generally speaking, the older a person, the more mature he or she is. This is not always the case, however. There might be cases where a fifteen-year old birth mother is more mature, and therefore more likely to make the placement, than some twenty-year olds. Her maturity is going to depend on many factors: her life experiences, or lack of them, to date; how she was raised; her degree of intestinal fortitude, and similar factors. The only way to determine this is to personally get to know the birth mother, and encourage her to receive professional counseling (discussed momentarily) to help prepare her for the emotions ahead. All these issues apply equally regarding the birth father's age and maturity (but the reality is fewer of them elect to be involved).

The Influence of Family and Friends

We are all influenced by those around us, particularly the people most important to us. Our family. Our friends. For this reason, if a birth mother is surrounded by negativity, where her closest friends and family members are trying to dissuade her about placing her child for adoption, it creates a significant risk. Remember that her family and friends are only doing what they feel is right for her and themselves. Don't take it personally, as rarely does it have anything to do with you as the adoptive parents. It is simply their hope that she will keep the child in the family.

Sadly, often it is clear to an impartial person that the birth parent should not be listening to this negative advice, as anyone could see the future for the birth mother and child would be bleak. But the reality of the world is that there are millions of people in the United States, and hundreds of millions around the world, who live in similar, or worse, situations than she does. They face poverty, lack of education, single parenthood and other challenges, yet they survive. We have to understand that not every decision has to make sense to us. Some families and friends will just be against adoption, despite all the reasons to the contrary.

So what do you do when see she is getting negative input? One important consideration is the birth mother's age. If she is young she is much more likely to give in to family pressure. This is particularly true if she is a minor living with her parents. In most states, a birth mother under age eighteen does not need parental consent to place a child for adoption (see the state-by-state review), but she is dependent upon them for everything. She would be hesitant, as would any of us, to alienate those she is dependent upon. Also, if her family says they will take care of the baby and do all the work required, the birth mother is more inclined to say "Yes, why not?"

Situations involving negative input from family members is entirely different when a birth mother is an adult and no longer lives at home, and is not financially dependent upon them. A disagreement over the pregnancy and how to deal with it is likely not the first time she has had disagreements with her family about how she should live her life. Since she is already on her own she is much less likely to be controlled by their desires. So the negative input from others is still a concern, but less so than with more mature birth mothers. If her parents do not live locally, she may not even share the fact she is pregnant, preferring to not admit the unplanned pregnancy to her parents.

Luckily, few adoptions involve a great deal of anti-adoption sentiment by a birth mother's family and friends. Most want what is best for her and know raising a child under difficult circumstances will cause both her and the child to suffer. That is why it is a significant concern when that support does not exist. It is not unusual for a birth mother to have one or two people against the adoption, but if this is just a small percentage of the people impacting her life, you can feel good about the fact she is receiving emotional support from most of her key people.

The Due Date

Birth mothers can start adoption at any time in the pregnancy. Some will call an adoption attorney or agency the minute they discover they are pregnant, perhaps only two months along. Others ignore the fact they are pregnant, wait until the last minute, and finally contact someone when they give birth. This brings up a question: Is there a good or bad time to start adoption planning?

The answer is yes, there are times when adoption planning should be avoided, or at least delayed. Starting an adoption with birth mother early in her pregnancy, such as in the first trimester, has several risks. Let's look at the practical reasons first. There is a 15% chance that a pregnancy will be miscarried during the first trimester. Do you want to incur the financial and emotional costs of an adoption only to have it result in a miscarriage? You may have already gone through that heartbreak as part of the reasons which brought you to adoption. The last thing you want to do is go through it again, even indirectly via adoption, if it can be avoided.

The other reason is that when a birth mother is so early in her pregnancy, it is generally too soon for her to make a complete emotional commitment to adoption. She can *intellectually* determine it is the best decision for herself and the baby. *Emotionally*, however, she can't anticipate how she will feel about the pregnancy until she *feels* pregnant. Until she is far enough along to feel a baby inside her, and perhaps even start "showing" enough for people around her to remark on the pregnancy, she can't truly emotionally come to grips with the pregnancy. So what happens if she made a commitment to you as adoptive parents when only two months pregnant, then by the eighth month is asking herself how she got herself into this situation, and wants a way out without hurting you? The likely answer is a failed adoption.

This doesn't mean you can't start an adoption with a birth mother two or three months along, but it does mean you acknowledge extra risk in doing so. The safest course is to work with birth mothers who are at least halfway through their pregnancy. Even better, in their last trimester. If a birth mother contacts your attorney or agency and she is too early to intelligently start adoption planning, the smart professional won't immediately match her up with adoptive parents, nor will he or she turn the birth mother away. Instead, your agency or attorney should begin to work with her, perhaps start counseling and get her started on paperwork which will later be necessary in the adoption (health history forms, et cetera.). This allows the birth mother to feel she is accomplishing something and know she has a plan in place, yet slows down the start of the adoption. Soon, a month or two will have passed and she is far enough along to start adoption planning by meeting you.

There is usually no such thing as starting "too late." Some birth mothers will even wait until they are at the hospital and they have already given birth. They may have been in emotional denial about the pregnancy, been embarrassed, or simply not known who to call.

There are good and bad elements to last minute adoptions. On the "bad" side, there is little time for some important things to happen:

- Is there time for the birth mother and adoptive parents to get to know each other and bond sufficiently to give the birth mother the needed confidence in the placement?
- Is there time to find the birth father to see if he will cooperate?
- Is there time to complete health histories and contact doctors about the pregnancy?
- Is there time for counseling?

But in other ways, last minute "after-birth" placements can sometimes be the most secure. Why? Because, the birth mother has gone through the one emotional moment most adoptive parents fear the most—the birth— and is saying she wants to do an adoption. That's the big moment every adoptive parent fears . . . how will she react to the birth? And in these "last minute" cases, she has already made it through those emotions when she initiates adoption planning. Many adoptive professionals feel these placements are actually the most secure.

Health History

Your agency or attorney should have the birth mother (and birth father if he is available) complete detailed health history forms. Adoptive parents should be given this information prior to even meeting a birth mother. This is because some health issues, such as extensive drug usage during the pregnancy or extended family members with congenital health problems or psychological disabilities, could be so severe that those issue may influence your desire to even start the adoption. Even if there are no such serious conditions in the birth family, you will want to know as much information as possible to share with your future pediatrician.

Knowing as much about your child's biological history is tremendously important. Think of the questions you or your child's pediatrician will be asking over the years. Is anyone in the family is allergic to a particular medicine or certain environmentals? (Perhaps meaning no dogs or cats in the house when you bring the baby home if a strong allergy to cats, for example.) Do people in your family start needing eye glasses at a particular age? Does diabetes run in the family so we should alter the child's diet from a young age? Is there a history of asthma, cancer . . . You get the idea. The more your pediatrician knows the more carefully he or she can monitor certain issues that might otherwise not be promptly caught.

You need and deserve complete written health histories. If you are adopting a not-yet-born baby, the health history you receive will likely be provided exclusively from the birth mother (and sometimes the birth father) based upon their family knowledge, and any relatives they contact for more information. If you are adopting an older child, you should additionally have the child's existing medical records.

It is unreasonable to expect an adopted child to have a perfect health history? Yes. You can't reasonably expect a perfect health history. Every family—likely yours included—has a grandparent who had a heart attack, an aunt who battled obesity, an uncle with diabetes, a second-cousin, Rebecca, who is just a tad mentally "off." Such things are just part of life. We take them for granted in our own families, but sometimes adoptive parents are overly fearful when they learn of them in a birth parent's medical history.

Those problems don't make everyone in *your* genetic circle unadoptable, so why think of other people that way? However, if there are potential health concerns of a major nature, you owe it to yourselves and the child to be sure you are prepared for the challenges that might lie ahead.

Adoptive parents often ask if the child they plan to adopt is born with a medical problem which they did not anticipate and feel they can't handle, do they have to complete the adoption? This question might sound hard-hearted and cruel, but it is a fair question. The answer is "no." You are not the legal parents until the adoption is granted by a court. This means, as tragic as it would be, that adoptive parents normally have the right to stop a placement should they feel they need to do so. Although this may sound wrong, remember that birth mothers have the same right to change *their* mind after the birth, so to some extent it is fair, as each can back away from the other. Happily, it is almost unheard of for adoptive parents to have a baby placed with them, then have something occur to stop the placement. A very, very small number may be stopped at the hospital by the adoptive parents, due to an unforeseen birth circumstance, such as evidence of substantial drug usage that was not anticipated.

In addition to the completion of birth parent history forms, an important part of obtaining health information is via the birth mother's doctor. It is common for the birth mother to sign an *Authorization to Release Medical Information*. This form waives the doctor-patient privilege and allows the medical office to release records and information about the pregnancy and fetus to the attorney or agency, or directly to the adoptive parents. In many open adoptions, the adoptive parents are accompanying the birth mother to some of her doctor appointments, so they are right there next to her to hear what is said, ask questions to the doctor, and stay up to date. This may seem to make the need of an information release form unnecessary, but there may be instances where the adoptive parents do not accompany the birth mother to the doctor, or want to discuss information not addressed at the medical appointment. This helps reduce any surprises about the baby's situation.

In many cases, the birth father is unfindable so his health history is unavailable. This is due to the fact that a significant number of adoption situations arise out of one-night stands and casual relationships, meaning last names and contact information were not exchanged. Or, perhaps he is known but he does not wish to be contacted, perhaps being fearful of child support obligations if the birth mother were to keep the baby, and he ignores efforts to contact him. The result of these common situations is that sometimes there is no birth father health history available, besides the cursory information the birth mother will know, such as his ethnicity and general appearance.

The same issues exist in intercountry adoption, but even more so, as sometimes there is little or no information about *either* birth parent.

Drug or Alcohol Usage

Sadly, drugs have been commonplace in our culture for decades, so they are a reality we have to deal with in adoption as well. Does this mean that all birth mothers use drugs? No. Does it mean *most* birth mothers use drugs? Again, no. But it is a potential issue. There is no way to definitively state the percentage of birth mothers who use drugs, but it is fair to say it is a not a majority, but is a sizable enough percentage that you may face the issue. (This is referring to voluntary newborn adoptions, not county adoptions where the child was taken from the birth parents due to drug usage or other problems. In those cases, drug usage is higher.)

Naturally, you want a drug-free pregnancy. Every adoptive parent does. But does that mean you should decline a birth mother who has selected you if she used drugs or alcohol during the pregnancy? Obviously, you can decline such placements, but you may be passing on what might be an excellent adoption without the risks that you believe exist.

First of all, you need to decide where you draw the line in drug and alcohol usage, and that requires that you educate yourself. In addition to the assistance of your family doctor and gynecologist, and your attorney or agency, an excellent resource to learn more about the potential effects of drugs on a fetus is the Organization of Teratology Information Specialists (OTIS). They have access to studies on all types of fetal drug exposure and the potential consequences and can answer hypothetical questions, such as, "If a woman used crystal methamphetamine a few times in the first trimester, then stopped, but smoked marijuana twice a week in the last trimester to help stop nausea, what is the likelihood that could affect the baby, and if so, how?"

No one can give you a guaranteed, definitive answer, but they can tell you what is known from research. OTIS's website is MotherToBaby.org. Their toll free number is (866) 626-6847 or you can even text message them at 855-999-3525. Learning this little-known resource alone is worth the price of this book. OTIS is a great source of information, easy and free to access. Few people seem to know about it, however.

You will be surprised that some drugs do not "cross the placenta," meaning they usually don't directly affect the fetus. So this may eliminate many fears about some scary-sounding drugs. What about drugs that *do* affect the child? Every adoptive parent will view the situation with a different comfort level.

Would you consider working with a birth mother who only smoked marijuana a few times early in the pregnancy, then stopped when she learned she was pregnant? Most adoptive parents would accept that placement with no hesitation. What if the drug was crystal methamphetamine, but again only a few times early in the pregnancy? At this point, perhaps some adoptive parents are backing away, while most all are still on board. But what if it was consistent usage of methamphetamine throughout the pregnancy, and she tested positive for drugs at birth? Or daily alcohol? Now most adoptive parents are abandoning ship right and left, leaving only a few families interested in the placement. These are personal decisions for adoptive parents and everyone's feelings and interpretation of available research will vary.

Whatever you decide, it is important to make your decisions based upon actual research, not knee-jerk reactions. Here's an example:

Let's say you are presented with a birth mother who consumed a glass of wine every day throughout the pregnancy. And let's also say she smoked one or two packs of cigarettes a day throughout the pregnancy too.

You are probably ready to bail on this adoption already. You are thinking of such things as fetal alcohol syndrome and the carcinogens from the tobacco. Yes, those are valid concerns, but here is a question for you:

Ask everyone you know who is in their 50s or older if their mothers smoked several packs of cigarettes a day, and had alcohol on a daily basis when their mothers were pregnant with them. In fact, ask yourself about *your* mother's pregnancy if you are in this age range. Or your mother's mother.

Can you see where this is headed? The answer will be that a large number of you will answer "yes" to both alcohol and tobacco. No one knew any better back then, so many women drank wine every night, perhaps cocktails on the weekend, and smoked while pregnant. Now ask yourself, are all those people who just answered "yes," fetal alcohol syndrome suffering individuals? Are they in terrible health due to their mothers smoking? Probably the answer is no, and your friends in that age group are normal people, not a generation of unadoptable men and women.

Don't misunderstand . . . you are not being encouraged to ignore issues like drugs and alcohol. They are indeed important and you need to talk to your family doctor, your obstetrician/gynecologist, et cetera. What you are being encouraged to do is to not pass on a placement due to what might be incorrect assumptions on your part, perhaps losing a placement which was actually the best one you could have asked for.

The birth mother's honesty. Many worry that a birth mother may lie on important issues like her health history and drug usage. This is true; they could lie. Many adoptive professionals will actually tell you that in their experience, it is adoptive parents who are more likely to lie about something in their background than birth mothers. Luckily, once we've eliminated the scam adoption situations (which you've learned how to spot earlier in this book) most birth mothers are honest. The reason is that most of them are planning adoption for one simple reason: they want a wonderful life for their child. They are hardly fulfilling that goal if they lie about important health facts, hurting the child later by having hidden that information. After all, she could have terminated the pregnancy—in some ways an easier option for her—but instead she went through a 40-week pregnancy, the painful and potentially life-threatening experience of childbirth, just to give that child to you. Such sacrifices do not normally gel with lying.

Still, there will always be some birth mothers who do lie, and if so, usually it will be about an issue causing them embarrassment, like drug or alcohol usage, because they want you to like and respect them. This is where your attorney or agency's approach is critical. If he or she is very non-judgmental with the birth mother, and from the very beginning makes clear to her that there are adoptive families waiting out there regardless of whether there was previous drug usage or not, the birth mother is much more likely to be honest.

Drug testing. Fears over a birth mother using drugs may lead you to request drug testing. This is a possible option, but has disadvantages. For example, if you are working on having the kind of open, trusting relationship many newborn adoptions start with, and she tells you she has never used drugs, and you reply, "Of course we believe you, but take a monthly drug test anyway," her opinion of you is likely damaged. She may agree to what you want and not complain, but a bit of the unequivocal trust she needs to see in you to be her child's parents is perhaps gone. A good example might be if your spouse required you before marriage to take a polygraph test, fearing you were lying about things in your past, like past partners. You might agree to do so, but you'd be deeply hurt over the request and your relationship may suffer.

Another reason drug testing is not as beneficial as you might think is that they are not infallible. Certain drugs only show up for certain periods of time after usage (some only days, and some longer). Blood tests generally show positive results longer than urine tests, so if you elect drug testing, doing so by blood is usually more reliable, but it is also more intrusive for the birth mother to have to give. If a birth mother is a savvy drug user, however, she likely knows exactly how long a particular drug will be in her system, and know when she'd be clean for a test.

Of course, the reverse could be true as well. It's conceivable that a birth mother inclined to take drugs could be dissuaded from doing so if she knows she'll soon be tested. This is not very persuasive, however, because if she used and then tested positive, and you declined to work with her anymore, she'd just find another adoptive family. So there goes the dissuasion theory; there's no real penalty for her if that's her true inclination.

Be aware that even without you asking, hospitals in most states do drug tests at birth, and if she has signed an information release as is the norm, you will have access to that information. The same is true of some doctors in prenatal care. So the issue may be resolved for you without you having to do anything, or make a choice on the issue.

Rather than rely on drug tests, many adoption professionals believe the best route is to decline to work with a birth mother you don't believe in, and work with one you trust. And if you trust her, you are not demanding drug tests. That may sound absurdly simple, and is not foolproof, but then neither are the above "safeguards" of drug testing. Each option has its pros and cons. But selecting the right birth mother, then showing faith and trust in her, generally offers the most "pros" and the least "cons." At this point, the birth mother is just an imaginary person in your mind, but when she is a real life, nice person, scared and wanting to do the right thing, many or all or your fears are likely to disappear.

Goals and Future Plans

A birth mother who has future goals and plans is more likely to place than one who doesn't. Those that have no interest in getting a job, pursuing an education, improving her lifestyle, et cetera, is more likely to look at the baby right after birth and think that the baby will fill the void and make her life complete.

Compare this to a birth mother who has dreams and goals, and can recognize that raising a child at this time, under these circumstances, will hurt or delay the goals she has for her future. This latter type of birth mother is more aware of the child's future as well, and how those future opportunities and lifestyle will be diminished if she were to try to parent under her present difficult circumstances.

Feelings of the Birth Father

This book consistently discusses birth mothers, but doesn't mention birth fathers nearly as often. This is no disrespect to birth fathers, rather a reflection of the reality that very few of them elect to get involved in adoption planning. Every adoption has a birth father, however, whether they are findable or not, and that makes them potentially an important part of the adoption.

When the birth father is unknown or can't be found, or is findable but has no interest in the pregnancy, this is probably one of many factors leading many birth mothers to consider adoption. A pregnancy is viewed completely differently, however, when it results from a caring relationship with a loving partner. If he wants to raise the baby, either alone or with her, this is potentially a major disruption in the adoption on two fronts. One is that he could seek to object to the adoption on legal grounds (discussed in Chapter 12). The other is that, even if he has no plans to object in court, if he prefers that she keep the baby, he may try to influence her to change her mind. If their relationship is, or was, a solid one, this will make his feelings a significant influence upon her. The bottom line is if she loves the birth father and fears she will lose him if she makes an adoptive placement against his wishes, she will likely choose him over you.

Luckily for adoptive parents, a very small percentage of non-marital birth fathers elect to object to adoption planning. Most of the pregnancies these birth fathers were involved in leading to adoption were one-night stands, casual encounters or terminated relationships. This makes both the birth mother and birth father unlikely to want to be linked to each other for life through the child, and is one more reason for adoption.

Regardless of the birth father's initial feelings when he is first contacted, usually the surest way to get him to cooperate in adoption planning is to treat him with respect. Acknowledging that he is an important part of the child's creation, asking him for a personal and health history, and extending a similar offer as to the birth mother regarding sending pictures and updating letters about the child (if he is interested and you are open to that), are important courtesies. This is particularly true with birth fathers who are initially unsure if they want to parent the baby or not, and are confused. Sometimes, just like a birth mother, they need time and counseling to see the benefits of adoption and see it as a loving, unselfish act. Some wrongly initially see adoption as abandoning their duties as a man. The more understanding they have about the true nature of adoption, and its unselfish nature in putting a child first, the less likely any anti-adoption sentiments will persist.

Legal Risks

An important consideration in starting any adoption is if there will be any legal risks. To some degree, every adoption has risk, such as the chance the birth mother will change her mind. But here we are talking about avoidable issues. For example, does it appear a legal challenge will be filed in the adoption? This could be by an objecting birth father, an Indian tribe's intervention pursuant to the Indian Child Welfare Act, or other problem. (There are several potential trouble spots in every adoption and these issues are discussed in Chapter 12).

It is critical is to analyze every possible complication based upon the unique facts in your adoption. You may elect to proceed despite the possibility of a known problem, but if you do, you want to know the full extent of the risk. Will you have to go to court? How long will the court action take? How much will it cost? How likely are you to win? Have you considered the effect on you and the child if you bond, then have to give up custody after protracted litigation? Fortunately, litigated adoptions are rare. One reason for this, however, is that many adoptions destined to be litigated are passed on before the birth, before getting to that point.

Motivation for Adoption

There are many reasons for a birth mother to start an adoption. In a nutshell, the "good" reasons are a combination of either not wanting to parent a child, or recognizing she is not ready to be a mom, usually combined with factors like insufficient income, inadequate employment, having one or more other existing children to raise, the goals of college or a career, or lack of an appropriate relationship with the birth father. We need to be on the lookout, however, for the "wrong" reasons.

Sometimes a birth mother will either consciously or subconsciously start adoption planning as a way to spur the birth father into action. Perhaps he greeted her disclosure of the pregnancy with apathy, and he is a man she hoped—and still hopes—to have a relationship with. She may think adoption will get his attention and nudge him into action, to mature and solidify their relationship. The only way to determine if this is her motivation is to get to know her and learn more about her feelings and changing emotions toward the birth father. Some giveaways can be that the birth mother and father had a long relationship, or are only very recently broken up. Usually it is fairly clear when she is not "over him."

Another improper motivation is if she is placating someone important to her, doing the adoption to get their approval, when it is really not what she wants. This could be the birth father who is telling her he will continue being her boyfriend, but not if she keeps the baby, or her parents who are perhaps already raising one or more of her children (and know this one will soon become their responsibility as well). In these situations, the birth mother is trying to please *them*. But if it's not what *she* really wants and feels in her heart is the right thing, she is likely to change her mind when the baby is born and her true emotions come out.

One of the greatest concerns regarding improper motivation is monetary. It is understandable that a birth mother needs a safe and comfortable place to live, and food to eat, both during the pregnancy and while she recovers. For this reason, most all states permit adoptive parents to provide pregnancy-related assistance, such as rent and food costs. There are two areas of concern, however, in these financial arrangements. Some birth mothers will want improper financial benefits, literally wanting to be "paid" for her baby. Not only is this illegal, but demonstrates a birth mother placing a child for the wrong reasons and who is trouble in every way. These situations are easy to spot and avoid. (See Chapter 12 regarding permitted financial assistance, and the state-by-state review.)

Questionable financial situations that are more difficult to spot are those where the birth mother is seeking assistance in categories that are legally permitted, but are grossly excessive. For example, a birth mother may need to rent an apartment. Accordingly, a standard apartment, likely one she could afford on her own when she starts working again after the pregnancy, is reasonable. Some birth mothers may insist on an apartment which might be double or triple what they would normally stay in, and she could not afford to live in afterward. With this kind of birth mother, you will usually see other pregnancy-related costs be enhanced as well, such as food, maternity clothing and transportation. Even if these expenses could be considered lawful as they fall within appropriate categories for pregnancy-related expenses, it is clear the birth mother is seeking to grossly escalate her lifestyle at your expense. (For example, most birth moms might spend approximately $350 for maternity clothes, so a birth mom who estimates $1,200 for clothes is a red flag.) When this becomes the motivation for adoption—turning a pregnancy into a temporary luxury—she is a risky birth mother and her true motivations are suspect.

Will She Accept Counseling?

Counseling is often an important part of success in adoption. The problem is, however, that most birth mothers feel they don't need counseling, so don't embrace it when offered. (Although a few states make counseling mandatory, in most cases it is optional.) Birth mothers will often say they know what they want, and don't need counseling on the subject. It could be they are correct, but they could also be wrong.

What they typically don't understand, due to their young age and inexperience, is that while their decision toward adoption seems obvious to them now, things can change dramatically at, and shortly after, the birth. The emotions of going through giving birth—likely for the first time—and seeing the baby, plus the effect of hormonal changes due to the pregnancy and child's birth (you've likely heard of "baby blues" and postpartum depression—which can be very real things), not to mention the reality that she may never see her child again, can hit her like an emotional sledgehammer.

The goal of counseling is two-fold. First, it is to help her explore her options and let her reaffirm to herself that adoption is the best option for her and the baby. Second, it is to prepare her for the likely emotions of birth and separation, so she knows to expect them. Counseling can serve as "pause button." If she is feeling more emotional pain than she anticipated post-birth and is thinking the only way to stop that pain is to stop the adoption, she can remind herself that her counselor discussed these very emotions, and that her pain means she is a normal, loving human being, not that she is making a mistake. Rather than give in to those temporary emotions, she is more likely to look back to the decisions she made when she was more analytical.

Pressure to Go Forward

Earlier we discussed the dangers of pressure on a birth mother, such as by relatives who feel she is not ready to parent. Now let's talk about pressure on *you*. It is possible that your photo-resume will fall into the hands of an adoption facilitator (or even an agency or attorney) who is less than ethical and will aggressively contact you (one more reason to put your attorney or agency's number on your photo-resume letter, not your own, so they can screen bad calls out). These adoption businesses of questionable integrity may have seen your photo-resume letter online, or received it indirectly from your networking.

Many of these entities have few or no waiting adoptive parent clients, but advertise for birth mothers. When they find one, they show any available photo-resume letters (yours), then call you to say you've "been picked" by a birth mother they are working with. It likely does not surprise you to hear that this revelation is immediately followed by the need for you to send money to them, or the birth mother, to "secure the placement." If you hesitate, they will say that they will have to call another family, one "the birth mother can count on."

It is best to ignore such calls. If they were a reputable entity, they would have adoptive parent clients and would show their photo-resume, rather than troll the internet for adoptive parents they don't even know. Rejecting these unsolicited calls makes perfect sense, doesn't it? Yet every year, families are scammed by such situations. Sometimes the birth mother may not even exist.

But if after hearing these cautions you still want to look into the situation, do so with these safeguards:

- Have your attorney or agency talk to the birth mother and make sure it appears to be an appropriate placement, with no legal impediments to success.

- Have your attorney or agency talk to the entity who found the birth mother and is requesting a fee to inquire about their legitimacy, fees and any information they have on the birth parents.

- Receive a full health history for the birth mother (and if he's available and willing, the birth father).

- Have her sign an Authorization to Release Medical Information so you can speak to her doctor to confirm the pregnancy and inquire about her medical condition.

- In most states (laws vary) it is wise to have your attorney or agency speak to the birth father to be sure he will not be opposing the adoption.

- Speak to the birth mother initially by phone, make sure she likes you and you feel confident in her. If the initial calls go well, arrange to quickly meet her in her region, or pay to have her come to you, so you can meet face-to-face to be sure the placement feels right.

- If your attorney or agency is in the same region where you will be meeting the birth mother, have him or her meet with the birth mother face-to-face as well to give you additional feedback.

- Only pay the intermediary when you are confident and ready to go forward with the placement, meaning most or all of the above steps have been done. Also, ask yourself, why this business is calling you, a stranger to them, rather than making a placement with one of their own existing families. These types of questionable entities, even if they are a licensed agency or attorney, usually state they "can't keep up with so many birth mothers calling." The reality, however, with many such businesses is that the word is out on them, and they can't attract clients, so must stoop to being adoption version of an ambulance chaser. Don't forget the advice from Chapters 4 and 6 regarding how to inquire about the legitimacy of an attorney or agency. Many of them will apply to situations like these.

The scam calls are easy to distinguish because the facilitator/attorney/ agency will usually not let you or your attorney or agency speak to the birth mother or see important documents like health histories, until you have sent in a substantial fee. They treat birth mothers as a product to be sold, owned by them. Do yourself a favor and don't give these entities a minute of your time.

As you can see, there are many red flags to a risky adoption. Does this mean you never do an adoption with a red flag? No, it does not. It would be nice if every adoption were perfect, but the fact is that many aren't. Birth mothers' lives are rarely neat and perfect. If they were, they wouldn't be doing an adoption. They'd be raising the child themselves, or have a family member do so.

Accordingly, that does not mean you pass on an adoption if one aspect of it is not perfect. The pros and cons in each adoption must be weighed and analyzed, by both you and your adoption professional. Some red flags, such as a birth mother "selling" her baby, are so significant that the one such factor alone is enough to send you running away.

Other factors, however, are less significant and you might only want to pass on the adoption if there are multiple cautions. For example, let's say that a birth mother presents you with an excellent adoption situation but refuses to go to counseling, saying she "does not need it" (a common refrain). If she appears emotionally stable and her health history indicates no psychological disabilities, most adoptive parents would still do the adoption, and hope that they and their adoption professional can prepare her for the birth experience or later convince her to receive counseling.

What if that same birth mother declining counseling also reports that her parents are divorced, and her mother supports the adoption but her father doesn't. You are disappointed her father is against the adoption, but unless the birth mother is young and living with him, making her dependent upon him, you are still likely going forward with the adoption. We have two red flags at this point, but likely not significant ones.

But now let's add a relationship with the birth father which you fear is not over, with emotions still flowing between them, with reconciliation a possibility. Or perhaps the additional caution is high projected costs, or a possible legal problem such as the Indian Child Welfare Act (discussed in Chapter 12). Any one of those concerns might be enough to push you to declining the placement. This is where the guidance of your adoption professional will be tremendously helpful. Likely he or she has met hundreds of birth mothers and has a good feel for what to expect. That, combined with your own gut instinct, usually results in a good decision and a successful adoption.

CHAPTER 11

WORKING WITH
THE DOCTOR AND HOSPITAL

Adoptive parents often have a great deal of anxiety about being fully informed about their future child's health. This is understandable. When you are planning to adopt a not-yet-born baby, it is the birth parent's health history, and that of their extended families, which is sought. We've previously addressed the fact that this is accomplished by having birth parents complete detailed health histories.

But what about the records and information about: the fetus; the birth mother while pregnant; and the baby at birth? You naturally want all this information to be as sure as possible that there are no medical situations which could affect your ability and desire to go forward with the adoption, such as an unanticipated major medical problem.

Access to Medical Records

If you are like most adoptive parents, you understandably want to do more than look at health histories and review her medical file (even assuming it could be deciphered by a non-doctor). The reality is you want to call the doctor or his or her staff and ask pre-birth questions like, "Is the baby okay?" "Does the ultrasound look normal?" "Is there anything we should know, or problems we should be prepared for?"

There are two ways to make this happen. Every birth mother should be asked to sign an *Authorization to Disclose Medical Information*. This form waives the doctor-patient privilege and allows the doctor's office to speak to those named on the form. Usually the form will list you and either the agency or attorney as authorized recipients of information. If it is a closed adoption and everything will be done through an adoption agency, they will usually be the ones having the direct contact and will forward the information to you.

If you live in a state where it is the norm to have an open pre-birth relationship, and you live close enough to make it feasible, it is not unusual for you to actually accompany the birth mother to several of her doctor appointments. This is great for both you and her. For you it is wonderful to share in the pre-natal care, get to know the doctor and personally ask questions, and have special moments like seeing the fetus in an ultrasound, or hearing his or her heartbeat. From a birth mother's perspective, these moments are also important. The chance for her to see your emotion at these times helps reassure her how much you want to be parents, and how excited you are about the baby. It can help forestall any subconscious doubts that you will not love the baby like your own.

Post-birth, the hospital is given the *Authorization to Disclose Medical Information* form, allowing you to have full access to medical information for both the birth mother and the baby. This applies to not only verbally asking questions, but having a copy of the birth records sent to the child's pediatrician whom you've selected.

The Hospital

While the child is at the hospital, most states allow you to have contact with the baby, including both holding and feeding, with the birth mother's permission. You can also have contact with the birth mother while she's in the hospital. In fact, in many open adoptions, the adoptive mother, sometimes the adoptive father as well, is asked by the birth mother to be her labor coach. Not only will sharing in the birth of your child be a wonderful moment for you, who better than you to take part in the birth in the eyes of the birth mother. Of course, some birth mothers are more physically modest and private and prefer that you wait outside the room until the birth is complete, and those feelings are to be respected.

When you interact with your birth mother at the hospital, it is important that she sees you care about *her* as a person, not just as a means to get a baby. That means spending time with her, not just the baby. It is also a great time, if she has elected to see the baby, to take pictures of all of you together. This is a great way to one day show your child it took all of you, loving him or her, to create your family. It also shows your birth mother that you value and appreciate her, and that you will be sharing that picture and her critical role in your child's birth with your child as he or she grows up. Don't forget common courtesies, like flowers in her room.

Some birth mothers fear seeing the baby after the birth will be too difficult for them, and naturally those feelings should be respected. We never want to make a birth mother do something she is not comfortable with, whether it is encouraging no contact, or to have contact. The reality is that it is her legal right to do as she wishes. Most birth mothers want to see the child they created, and to have time for a personal goodbye, and this is understandable. Many birth mothers refer to the time with the baby at the hospital as "her time," noting you have a lifetime thereafter. These options should be addressed in her pre-birth emotional counseling.

Insurance and Medical Costs

Virtually every state allows you to pay your birth mother's medical costs, although some states require that it be paid through an agency or attorney, or obtain court approval first. It's nice, however, if you can avoid medical costs. It may surprise you, but it is very common in adoption that the adoptive parents don't have to pay *any* medical costs. Some birth mothers have insurance through their job. Others may be covered by their parents' policy, if she meets certain age and residency requirements. Regardless of which situation it might be, the coverage might be an HMO (health maintenance organization) with one hundred percent coverage, or a PPO (preferred provider organization) with only eighty percent. Still, paying only twenty percent is much better than one hundred percent. Both HMO and PPO plans vary.

Her insurance eligibility should not be affected in any way due to the fact the baby is being placed for adoption, other than the fact that coverage will usually not extend into nursery or pediatric care after you have taken custody. Of course, usually your health insurance coverage will pick up coverage from this point, leaving you with no uninsured period. You will want to discuss this with your health insurance provider in advance. Sometimes though, even when both you and the birth mother have insurance, there will be an interim period when neither insurer feels they should provide coverage. This is an issue your adoption professional can look into before the birth to avoid any surprises.

What about if she has no insurance? Can she use yours? The answer is no. This is because each policy holder is a determined risk by the insurer, and while they agreed to insure you, they did not agree to insure someone whose health history they know nothing about. You are the insured, not the birth mother, even if the baby is to be placed with you. That doesn't mean you are looking at paying medical bills, however.

Medicaid

Not all birth mothers will have private health insurance. In fact, most won't. That doesn't mean you are destined to pay medical bills, however. That is because most birth mothers, either due to the being unemployed, or employed but with a low income, are usually eligible for their state's version of Medicaid. Many birth mothers will already be on such a program when they start adoption planning, and if they aren't, you can often assist them to apply. Usually the only requirements are to show that she is a resident of a particular county and state, is pregnant, and has a sufficiently low income with few assets. Just as with insurance, the fact she is placing the child for adoption should not affect her eligibility. Usually Medicaid coverage will cover 100% of her medical costs, although not all doctors and hospitals will accept the coverage, as frequently the payment is less than paid through private insurance. Your attorney or agency will usually know the Medicaid doctors in your area, however.

What if the birth mother has no insurance and is not eligible for Medicaid? This is rare, but perhaps she makes too much money at her job to qualify for Medicaid, but insurance is not offered by her employer. Well, this means you are probably paying medical bills, so you will want to know what they will be in advance. You will usually be paying a doctor for both prenatal care and to deliver the baby, and separately the hospital for using their facility. Sometimes other doctors are required, such as an anesthesiologist if she is having a caesarean birth, or an epidural. Also, a pediatrician will charge for examining the baby at the hospital.

Doctors usually charge a flat fee for both pre-natal care and the delivery. Usually there is one set fee for vaginal deliveries and a higher one for caesarean births. Some doctors, if they know a patient has no insurance, will offer you a pre-pay discount if you pay in advance. Many hospitals are the same way. They often have a special discount rate if you pay before the patient (the birth mother) is discharged. Sometimes these discounts are huge, particularly with hospitals, often as much as fifty percent. Apparently their reasoning is that when someone comes in for medical care and has no insurance, the hospital may never receive any payment, so they'll gladly accept a lesser payment if it is timely.

Luckily, however, to repeat, virtually all birth mothers can qualify for Medicaid if they don't have private insurance.

Releasing the Baby from the Hospital

Each state has different procedures regarding releasing the baby to you from the hospital. This can also differ based on whether you are planning an independent or agency adoption. Even within the same state, individual hospitals may have different policies. As a general rule, however, in most independent and private agency adoptions the child will be released directly to you, usually requiring the written permission of the birth mother, or in some states, a judge's order. Either way, it will be the job of your attorney or agency to meet these requirements. But you and the birth mother should know them in advance so everyone is prepared for them, and be comfortable with the procedures.

In some states, in private agency adoptions, rather than permit an immediate placement with you, the child is placed in a foster home for a few days, until the child is legally free for adoption. Rarely does it exceed a few days.

The state-by-state review in Chapter 15 provides the typical hospital release procedure for both independent and agency adoption in each state.

CHAPTER 12

LEGAL ISSUES: STEP-BY-STEP

There are many legal steps on the road to a completed adoption. Some of them are routine steps. Others involve issues you hope to avoid that typically only arise in difficult or contested adoptions. The best way to avoid those issues, however, is to know about them from the start. That allows you to have a chance to solve the problem before becoming too involved emotionally or financially in an adoption, or avoid the adoption entirely. Let's look at the routine procedural steps in every adoption, as well as the legal issues which can come up along the way, in the order you are likely to encounter them.

The Petition for Adoption

Every adoption requires court approval to be granted. The start of the process to obtain approval is to file a *Petition for Adoption*. In most cases this is filed shortly after the child is placed in your custody. Some states will require that the birth mother first sign her consent, and others will allow that it be signed and filed later. In some agency adoptions, particularly public adoption agencies, the child may need to be in your home for a prescribed period before the Petition can be filed, often six months.

The Petition for Adoption will normally identify you as the adoptive parents and establish the court has jurisdiction to handle your case (based upon your residence, where the baby was born, et cetera). It will also usually name the birth mother and father (if known), the date and place of the child's birth, the name of the child on the initial birth certificate and how you would like it to be changed after the adoption is granted, and list what agency, social worker or state adoption office will be doing your home study.

Who prepares and files your Petition for Adoption? In an independent adoption, it will be your attorney. In an agency adoption, it will usually be either an attorney you have hired, or one on staff for the agency. The first issue is where you will file your Petition for Adoption. In most cases you will file it in the county and state in which you live. In fact, usually you have no choice and can only file in your local court. Some states, however, allow non-residents to adopt in their state, and permit you to file it in the county and state of the child's birth, the location of the placing adoption agency, or sometimes even the birth mother's residence. The state-by-state review identifies states permitting non-resident adoption.

Your Petition for Adoption, once filed, will be assigned a case number by the court and a file will be opened. Adoption files are normally confidential, so the only parties permitted access besides court personnel are you, your attorney, and the home study agency.

The Birth Mother's Consent to Adoption

As an adoptive parent, one of your primary concerns in your adoption is when will the birth mother sign her consent to adoption, and when does it become permanent and irrevocable. Every state is different, not only regarding what they call the consent, but also when it can be signed, who must act as a witness, and when it becomes permanent. The form used for a birth mother to give up her parental rights might be called a *consent*, a *relinquishment*, a *surrender* or a *voluntary termination of parental rights*.

Most states impose a waiting time after the birth before a consent can be signed. Many states make this period seventy-two hours, while others require a longer time. Some shorter. Each state will also designate a specific person who can witness the consent. This is usually a social worker, notary or sometimes a judge or an attorney. Even within a state, the laws regarding when a consent can be signed and before whom can vary between independent and agency adoption. Please refer to the state-by-state review in Chapter 15 to see the specific procedures in the states of interest to you.

You might wonder, if you live in different states, do you execute a consent under the birth state's laws, or those of the state where you live? The answer depends upon the states involved. Some states will accept the consent to adoption as prescribed under the laws of the state where the birth occurred. Other states require that your home state's consent forms and procedures be used, even if the birth occurred in another state. It is important that any *conflict of laws* issue has been waived by the birth mother in writing in interstate adoptions.

Usually, the consent to adoption is done under the laws of the state where the adoption is to be finalized. So if the adoptive parents live in Virginia and adopt a baby in California, if they plan to finalize the adoption in their home state of Virginia, then Virginia consents will be signed by the birth mother, even though she is in California. But if the adoptive parents are planning a non-resident adoption to adopt under California law, then California consents will be used.

Some states require birth mothers to have their own attorney and advise them of their rights. Others require counseling or meetings with a social worker. The goal is the same: to protect a birth mother and make sure she knows her rights and options. In a very small number of states, if the birth mother is under eighteen, she must have the consent of a parent, or a court-appointed individual (usually called a guardian ad litem), to give up her parental rights. In the vast majority of states, however, birth mothers under eighteen do not require the consent of a parent or other person.

Can the Birth Mother Revoke Her Consent?

Every adoptive parent's worst nightmare is that their birth mother will place the child for adoption, then change her mind. Although some states make her signed consent irrevocable the moment it is signed, most give her a prescribed time in which to revoke the consent. This might be twenty-four hours, seventy-two hours, ten days or even a month or more.

Some states make this right to revoke the consent automatic, imposing no burden upon the birth mother, other than to perhaps fill out a form. Other states require a court hearing and require a birth mother to prove the child's best interests would be served by being with her rather than with you.

Once the revocation period is over, the birth mother has basically lost the right to change her mind and you can feel fairly secure. The principal exception would be cases where the birth mother can prove that fraud or duress was used to obtain her consent. Such a showing could invalidate a birth mother's consent after the usual revocation period has passed. Such situations are extremely rare, however, for the simple reason adoptive parents and the adoption professionals they work with are smart enough—not to mention ethical—to not to use fraud or duress.

Fraud, by the way, is usually considered a significant deception, not simply a small misunderstanding. For example, situations involving sufficient fraud to perhaps invalidate a consent would be such situations as the post-birth discovery that the adoptive parents had a criminal history that they tried to hide, not something insignificant like the birth mother thought your eyes were blue when in fact they are green. Fortunately, it is almost unheard of for a birth mother to challenge an adoption on grounds of fraud, even more so for such a request to be granted.

Because each state is different regarding how long a birth mother has to change her mind and revoke her consent to adoption, and any burden she is required to prove, the state-by-state review provides each state's unique laws.

When the Birth Mother Does Not Consent

If the birth mother refuses to sign a consent, and wants to stop the adoption, normally she has the automatic right to stop the process and reclaim her baby. There are some circumstances, however, where an adoption can proceed without the birth mother's consent.

Every state has some kind of provision to involuntarily terminate parental rights when called for to protect a child's best interests. One such legal ground is *abandonment*. Typically, if a birth parent fails to fulfill her parental responsibilities, specifically not having any contact with the child, and/or providing financial support, a court can terminate their rights and allow those who have been caring for the child to adopt. The required length of time to constitute abandonment differs, but is usually six months or one year. Abandonment situations are rare in independent or private agency adoptions, and are more common in the adoption of older children via public agency adoptions.

The Rights of the Birth Father

When a pregnancy results from an established, caring relationship, even outside of marriage, the mother and father of the expected baby usually elect to keep the baby. Adoptions, however, rarely come from these situations. Instead, they are usually the result of one-night stands, short relationships, or relationships which soured with news of the pregnancy, leading to the birth father to distance himself (often fearful of 18 years of child support and parental obligations). For this reason, many birth fathers welcome the news of adoption and elect to cooperate.

Determining the rights of birth fathers, and if a signed consent is required—as compared to merely giving notice—can be a complicated legal issue. This is because not only does each state have different laws regarding birth fathers' rights in adoption, but each state will also distinguish between different categories of birth fathers.

Escalated Fathers' Rights. Some birth fathers will have escalated rights due to a special relationship with the birth mother or the child. This usually includes a man who is married to the birth mother, or who has lived with or supported the child prior to the adoption. He may also earn escalated rights if he is named on the birth certificate in many states. Usually for an adoption to proceed with a birth father in this category you will need to obtain his consent. If he refuses to give it, you may be unable to adopt the child, unless a situation such as abandonment exists.

Sometimes this creates tragic results. For example, a birth mother may honestly tell you of fleeing her spouse due to his physical abuse of her. That birth father will be subject to both criminal and civil penalties for that behavior, but it will be almost impossible for you to use that as grounds to adopt his biological child without his consent.

Alleged or Putative Fathers. Most birth fathers do not fall into the escalated categories above. As you may likely assume, most birth fathers in adoptive placements are one-night stands, casual encounters, or perhaps he had been dating the birth mother for some time but has no desire to take responsibility for a child. There is no marriage, he's never had the child in his custody or supported the child, and he's not named on the birth certificate.

Most states label this category of birth fathers as "putative" or "alleged." The overwhelming majority of men in this category not only support adoption, but are thrilled about it, as it will end their anxiety over potential child support obligations if the birth mother were to keep the child. We must be cautious, however, with the few birth fathers who may seek to challenge the adoption against the desires of the birth mother.

States fall into two general categories in determining the rights of these types of birth fathers. Some states have *birth father registries* where he has a set time to register and be entitled to notice, and others are called "notice" states, as they put the burden on you as the adoptive parents and require your attorney or agency to give written notice any possible birth father, without the easy of just checking a registry. Some states merge the two and have a hybrid of sorts. If is a much more complicated subject than birth mother's rights, which are fairly simple by comparison.

Whether a state is a "registry" or a "notice" state, usually the birth father will have a set time in which to object, and if he doesn't, his rights can be terminated in a fairly simple court proceeding. Many states even allow alleged/putative birth fathers to waive their rights *before* the baby is born, usually by signing a simple form, and a court can usually terminate their rights shortly after the birth.

In "notice" states, sometimes the birth father can't be found to give him the required notice. He may have moved and not given the birth mother his new address, or their relationship was so short that phone numbers and addresses were never exchanged. He could even be hiding out of fear of his potential obligations and court proceedings. In these situations, your attorney or agency will usually need to show due diligence was used in trying to find him. This might include a property records check, a phone book/online search and a Motor Vehicles Bureau inquiry. Some states will require publishing the notice of paternity and adoption in a local newspaper, usually buried in the back with the other legal notices.

If he can't be found with due diligence, typically the court can sever his rights and the adoption proceed without difficulty. Sometimes a birth mother will not even know the birth father's last name. In those cases, search efforts are usually impossible (you can't do a search for "John in Cleveland"), so his rights are terminated as an "unknown father."

What if an alleged/putative father receives his notice and is one of the few who wishes to object and seek custody? Each state will define his rights differently, but most will require a judge to examine his behavior and lifestyle and ask questions like: "Did he take responsibility for the pregnancy and help the birth mother with her expenses and other needs during the pregnancy?" "Can he emotionally and financially care for a child?" "Would the child's best interests be served by being with him . . . or would the baby be better off with the adoptive parents?" Accordingly, if the birth father acted "like a man should" with a baby on the way, he may be tough to defeat in court. If he avoided responsibility, requiring you to step in and fulfill the birth mother's needs, and his lifestyle is not compatible with parenthood, he is more likely to lose. (Remember, here we are talking about putative fathers, those with weaker rights. If he falls into the escalated rights category discussed above, a higher legal burden to terminate his parental rights will usually apply.)

As a general rule, a good philosophy to have is that if you are *sure* there will be an objection from the birth father, it is safest to not even start the adoption, unless your attorney tells you the law is so stacked against him that he can't win. "Slam dunks" are rare in the legal world, however, and the high emotional and financial cost of a court trial, with no guarantee of winning, would wisely lead many adoptive parents to not go forward.

Here's what makes the decision so tough, however. Sometimes, you may be unsure how a birth father will react, making your decision difficult. For example, the birth father's feelings may vacillate, or he may sound off about objecting, but you believe he has no intent to follow through. In those cases, you may wish to proceed, but you want to be sure the law will be on your side if litigation ends up being required. It is a reality that many men *say* they will object, but never show up in court to do so, meaning you normally win by default. Sometimes it is easy to see "serious" birth fathers who will actually follow through and object. For example, they hire an attorney before the birth. He is serious about objecting. But another birth father may have failed in every option he had to act responsibly in the pregnancy and flaked out each time (no financial contribution, no emotional support, et cetera), which increases the likelihood he will actually do nothing about objecting in court. Deciding when to pass on the adoption, and when to call the birth father's bluff, is an area where your attorney or agency's guidance is critical. They have likely dealt with birth fathers in similar situations literally hundreds of times.

Not all states are "notice" states, however. A "registry" state is completely different in that it usually puts the burden on the birth father, not the adoptive parents. Men in these states typically must voluntarily register themselves as the possible father of child born, or due to be born, in order to later seek to establish any rights. Their failure to do so will normally result in the termination of their rights when a designated period has passed, often 30 days. A court hearing will still be required to terminate his rights, but often all that must be established is his failure to register.

Unknown "John Doe" Birth Fathers. What about if a birth mother has relations with more than one person and is not sure who is the birth father? Do you have to do blood tests to see which one is the actual birth father? Normally, no. In most cases you give notice to each possible birth father, or see if they listed themselves in the state birth father registry, and see if any of them plans to object. If one or more does, then paternity testing will be required as obviously only that father would have the right to object. If all are agreeable, however, or apathetic and do nothing, your attorney or agency will simply terminate the rights of every possible father without DNA testing to determine actual parentage.

The state-by-state review provides information about birth father's rights in each state. In some states, the laws in this area are either too complex, or too vague, in which case they are not included.

Interstate Compact for the Placement of Children

It is becoming more and more common for adoptions to be interstate, meaning the child is born or is living in one state, and you as adoptive parents live in a different state. Whenever a child is brought across state lines for purposes of adoption, a special law applies called the Interstate Compact for the Placement of Children (the ICPC). Basically, it says that before a child can be brought across state lines, both the "sending state" (where the child was born or is living) and the "receiving state" (where you live) must give their approval in writing. Violating the ICPC can put your adoption at risk. Some states even make violation a criminal offense.

The ICPC applies to both independent and agency adoptions. It normally is not applicable to intercountry adoptive placements, however. To obtain Interstate Compact approval, your attorney or agency will initially contact the sending state's Interstate Compact Administrator. Each state has this special office, usually a division of the state's Department of Social Services. There are specific uniform guidelines about what documents must be provided, but some states add additional requirements or view some requirements more stringently than other states. At a minimum, you will be required to provide your pre-placement home study, the birth mother's health history (and the birth father if it is available, if not the birth mother can provide what she knows about him), the birth mother's consent, medical records on the baby/child, and about a dozen additional forms detailing the planned placement and outlining who will have financial and medical responsibility for the child.

If you live in a state where independent adoptions do not require a pre-placement home study, this is the one situation where you will be required to have one. Depending upon your state, you will obtain it through a private adoption agency, a social worker, or a state adoption office.

It commonly takes about one week post-birth for the attorney or agency in the sending state to obtain the birth mother's consent and all the other documents, and get the sending state's Interstate Compact Administrator's approval. At that point, the documents are forwarded to the sending state for its Interstate Compact Administrator's approval. Usually each ICPC office will only take one day to give its consent once receiving the packet. It is almost automatic that the required approval will be given, but the bureaucracy and detailed knowledge to obtain it can be daunting to anyone not an adoption professional. Some states allow the documents to be filed electronically (via email) which speeds up the process quite a bit, rather than using air-couriers like FedEx. If the adoption is a private adoption agency adoption at both the sending and receiving states—called "agency to agency" it's possible in some states that the agencies themselves can give ICPC approval, rather than the state's ICPC Administrator. The required documents and timetable are the same, however.

The Indian Child Welfare Act

The Indian Child Welfare Act (ICWA), is a federal law taking precedent over state law. Passed into law by Congress in 1978, it was intended to protect Indian culture and keep Indian children from being removed from existing Indian families and placed into non-Indian foster or adoptive homes. The intent of the law is an honorable one, but sadly the language of the law is so vague and far-reaching it has become difficult to apply. Complicating the issue is that some states have enacted their own state ICWA legislation, which may be slightly different than the federal law. We will discuss only the federal ICWA.

The ICWA provides that if a child is a member of an American Indian tribe, or is the biological child of a member and is eligible for membership, then written notice of the planned adoption must be given to the potential tribes (and other governmental entities and parties), giving the tribe the right to object and allowing Indian adoptive parents to be considered. It also requires a court hearing to find "good cause" to place the child with a non-Indian family (such factors as the desires of the birth parents, lack of the Indian birth parent having a true cultural connection with the tribe, et cetera), and for a judge to witness the birth parent's consent. Also under the ICWA, a birth parent has a longer time in which to withdraw their consent, as the ICWA grants them until the adoption is finalized, which might be six months or more after birth, whereas traditional state law might make it irrevocable much faster. Obviously, this scenario adds potential risk to you.

On the one hand, very few adoptions are actually affected by the ICWA, as most birth parents are not Native American (Eskimo tribes are also applicable). On the other, many adoptions are impacted. How can both those contradictory statements be true? Here's how. Many of the young mothers or fathers placing a child for adoption, when asked about their family background as part of a normal adoption health and social family history, will state they may have a small amount of Indian heritage. In this sense, many adoptions can be affected, as any possible tribes must be given notice to inquire about membership. To find the location of any named tribe, your attorney or agency will usually contact either the Bureau of Indian Affairs, or review the *Tribal Leaders List*. (The Bureau of Indian Affairs is a federal government office with its headquarters in Washington, D.C., with regional offices all over the nation.) It is then up to any contacted tribe to write back and state if membership exists or not, determining if the ICWA applies.

Even if it is verified that the child you plan to adopt has some Indian blood does not mean the ICWA applies to your adoption. Every tribe has different rules regarding tribal eligibility. Many require a minimum of twenty-five percent Indian blood, while some use other factors and can accept less. Some tribes have closed membership, perhaps so as to not dilute their existing tribal benefits among a larger group, and will decline membership even for someone who otherwise might be eligible.

So in many cases you will have to give ICWA notice, but when the replies come back that the child is not eligible for membership, then it is a "normal" adoption again and governed by regular state law. In most states this ICWA inquiry can be made pre-birth, with the hope it will be resolved before the birth so as to not delay the adoption. But sometimes it drags on post-birth, delaying the taking of the consent to adoption until it is known which laws and procedures to follow.

Most ICWA inquires tend to come back with "the birth parent is not a member, or eligible for membership in our tribe" letters, meaning you can do your adoption under traditional state law. However, if your adoption is one of the few that is determined the ICWA applies, the next inquiry is if the birth parent or child is living or domiciled on the tribal reservation. If the answer is yes, it increases the tribe's rights, as clearly the child has a significant connection to the tribe, and their interest is understandably greater. In these cases, which are very rare, the tribe has the right to block the adoption and have a tribal court hear matters related to the child.

In the few cases where the ICWA does end up applying, however, normally the birth parent is not living or domiciled on a reservation. In these cases, the tribe has a less significant connection to the birth parent and child, and the tribe's rights are not as strong as a result.

Some good news is that many tribes are not oppositional, even if the law allows them to be. Many tribes are supportive of adoption, even when you as the planned adoptive parents are non-Indian. The usual thinking is: "If this is what the birth parent wants, we will respect their decision about whom they've selected as adoptive parents." This is especially true in the many cases where the birth parent has had virtually no connection in her or his life to the tribe, never visiting the reservation or embracing tribal customs, et cetera.

It is only a small number of tribes that actively seek to disrupt voluntary adoptions. In these cases, however, great caution must be used to do everything correctly. In some cases, such as where a tribe has indicated it will object and the birth parent was living on the tribal reservation, maximizing tribal rights, good judgment may dictate not even starting that adoption.

Birth Mother Financial Assistance

Some adoptions involve almost no financial assistance to the birth mother. She lives at home or has a job, and has insurance or Medicaid. She doesn't need, or is too proud to accept, financial help. Often the assistance might be limited to counseling and maternity clothes. The author has done approximately 1,000 adoptions and in about half those adoptions, the birth mother needed less than a total of $1,000 in assistance for the entire pre- and post-birth assistance.

However, some adoptions will involve more substantial financial assistance. Usually this is due to the birth mother being unemployed, or maybe she and the birth father were living together and the pregnancy led to their breakup and now she is homeless. Regardless of the reason, some birth mothers will need your assistance. And think about it . . . a woman would not be going to the extreme in placing her child for adoption unless her life was in true disarray. Many birth mothers are in a terrible place in their lives when they go through adoption planning. Whether their own decisions led to the situation, or just bad luck, it is common in adoption. The point is you can't expect someone to select an extreme option like adoption if their lives were nice and perfect. If their lives were ideal, they'd keep the baby. So some degree of anarchy in a birth mother's life must be almost expected as part of what led her to the decision of adoption.

In the author's experience, about half of all birth mothers, or just slightly more than half, do need financial assistance over a minimal amount. Most of them are already living inexpensively (compared to your monthly expenses) and have monthly expenses of about $600-$1,600 depending on where in the country they live. Sometimes, birth mothers have partial income, such as from a public assistance program, which would then lower the monthly amount expected from you.

For those needing assistance, it usually totals about four to five months, with most of it pre-birth and some in the post-birth period.

Almost every state permits you to assist the birth mother with pregnancy-related assistance. Unlike surrogacy, where some states allow an actual payment for the service of being a surrogate, adoption laws forbids such remuneration. Most states will permit you to help with such basics as medical care, rent, food, utilities, maternity clothes, counseling and transportation needs. (See your state's limits in the state-by-state review.) A small number of states will require a judge's approval prior to the payment, while most do not, perhaps requiring an accounting of all prior expenses to be submitted prior to the granting of the adoption.

Any assistance you provide is basically a gift. This means if she changes her mind and stops the adoption, you can't demand your money back. Neither can you write up a contract that says you will pay her rent in exchange for a baby. That's buying and selling a baby. It is usually wisest to make any pregnancy-related assistance through your agency or attorney. That way, not only does that give the agency or attorney a chance to confirm the payment is legal and appropriate, but it establishes a degree of financial formality with the birth mother.

Regarding the emotional side of adoption, the closer you are with her, the better. In financial areas, however, it can not only make both you and her feel uncomfortable, it can lead to potential conflict. Let's say, for example, she requests assistance with a particular item and you know it falls outside of the permitted pregnancy-related assistance categories. It is much better for the birth mother to be told "no" by your agency or attorney (whom she will view as just doing their job), rather than by you (which she might interpret as being cheap or uncaring).

Some states have specific periods both before and after birth when assistance is allowed. Most, however, use general language like "the pregnancy-related period," which creates some flexibility. In most cases, living assistance starts, if needed at all, several months before the birth, and continues until about six weeks post-birth. As was discussed in Chapter 10, you should be cautious in working with a birth mother if her expenses seem inappropriately high, perhaps seeking to greatly escalate her lifestyle at your expense, even if the assistance is technically legal and falling into permitted pregnancy-related categories.

CHAPTER 13

FINALIZING THE ADOPTION AND POST BIRTH ISSUES

Normally, going to court causes anxiety. It's rare that we go to court for a "good" reason. In the case of adoptions, however, we go only with joy. This is because most adoptive parents only have to go to court one time, and it's when everything is done and the adoption is ready to be finalized.

The Court Finalization Hearing

When the birth mother's consent has become irrevocable, the birth father has consented (or waived his rights or otherwise had his rights terminated), any other legal obstacles have been satisfied and your final court report from your agency or social worker is complete, your attorney or agency will schedule a court hearing for you to finalize the adoption. (Even in agency adoptions an attorney is normally used for the final hearing.) In almost every state each adoptive parent must be present, as well as the baby (and the attorney, unless you are doing it without legal representation). The hearing is closed to the general public, although you can invite guests who can be present. Unlike most court hearings, which are quite formal, adoption finalizations tend to be casual and relaxed. In fact, most judges spend as much time posing for pictures with the adoptive family and the baby than in conducting the legal proceeding.

Usually the hearings start with you being "sworn in." Then you confirm your identity, your desire to adopt the baby, and your willingness to raise the child as your own, with the duties and obligations which accompany that, including the right of inheritance. The judge will then confirm that he or she read the final report from your agency or social worker in which you are recommended as adoptive parents. He or she will then sign and issue what is called a *Decree of Adoption* or *Order of Adoption*, granting the adoption and making you, officially and permanently, parents. This, along with other required documents, will have been prepared and submitted in advance to the court.

The time to get into court to finalize varies tremendously by state, from a few weeks to a year. Each state's usual waiting time after placement is given in the state-by-state review.

The Amended Birth Certificate

The original birth certificate (naming the biological mother as the child's mother, and with the child's name listed as she elected) will become sealed and technically no longer exist almost immediately after your adoption is finalized. A new, amended birth certificate will then be issued, listing you as the child's new and only parents. This new birth certificate will not name you as *adoptive* parents, rather just as parents, as if you gave birth yourselves.

It will also name the child as you've elected, in the event the birth mother put another first or last name. This new birth certificate will usually take several months to arrive from your state's Birth Registrar or Bureau of Vital Statistics. In the meantime, you can use the *Decree of Adoption* to show your legal status as parents. In the future, when you do the many things parents do, such as registering your child for your local soccer league, little league, and so on, you will only need to show your child's birth certificate, as would any parent. The Decree will not be needed, except in a few legal areas, as discussed below.

Obtaining a Social Security Card

When your child's amended birth certificate arrives you can obtain such items as a Social Security card and passport. Some birth mothers will have started the Social Security card process in the hospital, or you might be adopting an older child where one already exists. In those cases, you can show the Decree of Adoption and the new birth certificate and have the Social Security office change the name of parents and child, and keep the existing Social Security number. Or, you have the option of getting a new Social Security number for your child. This second option is usually selected, especially in the case of newborns. Changing the number guards against misuse by others in possession of the child's Social Security number that existed prior to the adoption. This is an issue to discuss with your attorney or agency and see what is best for your child, and if any benefits exist which could be lost in changing the Social Security number (re older children).

In most newborn adoptions, however, the hospitals do not have the birth mothers complete Social Security card applications when adoption is being planned, leaving it to be done by you when the adoption is complete. The Social Security Administration has vacillated regarding how adoptive parents can get a new Social Security card. Previously they could issue one immediately after the finalization hearing, and require only the original birth certificate and the Decree of Adoption. It was not necessary to wait for your amended birth certificate. More recently, however, they have been requiring the Decree of Adoption. This policy seems to vary state to state and office to office.

Taxes, Tax Credits and Dependents

You have the right to name your child as a dependent on your tax forms as soon as you have lawful physically custody. You don't need to wait until the adoption is granted. You will not have a Social Security card number at this early point, most likely, so the Internal Revenue Service can issue a *Temporary Tax Identification Number* (ATIN) for your child, to be used in place of a Social Security number on your return. You can obtain an ATIN with IRS form W-7A.

You are additionally eligible for a federal Adoption Tax Credit as an adoptive parent, and it's substantial. It may even pay for your entire adoption. For adoptions finalized in 2017, if your modified adjusted gross income is $203,540 or less, you are eligible for a $13,570 tax credit per adopted child. (It's per child, so this means a $27,140 tax credit for adopting two children, such as siblings or twins.) Your income can actually go up to $243,540, but the tax credit decreases proportionally when the income exceeds $203,540. Congress adjusts the tax credit for inflation each year and recently made it permanent.

Be aware that a *credit* is much better than a mere *deduction*. An example of a deduction would be the interest payment on your home mortgage. The interest is deducted from your gross income, reducing the net income on which you pay taxes. A credit is a dollar for dollar elimination of taxes owed, like giving you back up to $13,570. If you can't use the full credit in the year in which you adopt because you don't have that much tax liability, it can be carried over for up to five years until fully used.

In both domestic and intercountry adoptions, the credit is only for actual expenses you incurred. These adoption expenses can include: attorney fees, agency fees, court costs, travel expenses and any expenses directly related and necessary for the adoption.

Here are some examples. If your adoption only cost $5,500, you could only claim a tax credit of that amount. If you adopted a single child and your expenses were $18,000, you could claim the full $13,570 credit, but would not be able to claim it for the amount in excess. A limitation is if you have a special employer adoption program that reimburses you for some of your adoption expenses. You can't "double up" and claim those expenses if your employer is paying them for you.

The tax credit also exists in special-needs adoptions. There is one huge difference, however. This book has detailed many virtues in adopting a waiting child and here is one more. If the child is designated as "special needs" (your agency can tell you if they have been or not) the $13,570 credit stays the same, *but you don't need to show that you actually incurred any expenses.* So if your special-needs adoption cost $0 (since almost everything is provided free, or you paid but were reimbursed), you are still eligible for the $13,570 tax credit.

(At the time this book was going to print, the 2018 federal tax credit amount was still being determined by Congress. Although Congress made the tax credit permanent in 2013, there are still annual efforts to curtail its benefits by some members of Congress. If you would like to see the tax credit continue, consider sharing your thoughts with your Congressional representatives in both the Senate and the House of Representatives.)

Use IRS form 8839 "Qualified Adoption Expenses" to claim the credit. It is a little complicated when you take the credit. In a domestic (not intercountry) adoption, you claim the adoption tax credit in the year after you incurred the expenses. However, if you finalize the adoption in the same year you incurred the expenses, you claim the adoption tax credit in that year. If you incur expenses in the year after the adoption is finalized, you may take the tax credit in the year you incurred the expenses.

Intercountry adoptions are a little different. In those, you take the credit only after the adoption is finalized.

Tax issues are complicated, so every adoptive parent should consult a tax professional. You might find that your state even has an additional state adoption tax credit, or other tax benefit. Several states do.

Post-Birth Agreements

As discussed in more detail earlier, some adoptions are open. Many states provide that the birth mother or father can put an agreement with the adoptive parents in writing, and file the document with the court. These agreements might call for the annual sending of pictures or letters, phone calls or personal contact. These contracts are generally binding, unless their enforcement would no longer serve the best interests of the child.

Even in states where the agreements are specifically permitted, it is interesting that many birth and adoptive parents elect not to use them. Many seem to feel, upon getting to know and trusting each other, that no such formal contract is required. They seem to view this as some might a pre-marital agreement, feeling it taints their relationship. In adoption, however, a birth parent is very dependent upon adoptive parents keeping their promises, so you should never feel insulted if a birth mother indicates she'd like your promises in writing. After all, she's given you her promise in writing (the consent to adoption) that the child is yours forever. Receiving a promise in return is not asking too much. Even in states that don't have laws specifically permitting post-birth adoption agreements, they may be deemed enforceable, so you want to make sure that any promises you are asked to make are those you feel comfortable with.

Last Will and Testament

Once your child is adopted, he or she is your heir, just as if born to you. Accordingly, completing your adoption is an excellent time to update your will, or to write one if you don't yet have one. Separate from financial issues, however, is the welfare of your child if you and your spouse were to both die. You will want to consider who shall be the child's guardian, and who would manage your estate to best provide for your child's future.

CHAPTER 15

SURROGACY &
ASSISTED REPRODUCTIVE
TECHNOLOGY

This is a book on adoption. To adequately discuss the issues of surrogacy and assisted reproduction would take a book in itself, and indeed, many books exist on the subject. Accordingly, this chapter is to just give you a basic primer of how surrogacy works (the different types available, and some basic pros and cons) as well as options that exist in assisted reproductive technology. This brief overview might help you compare it to adoption if you are considering it as one of your family building options.

Traditional Surrogacy

In traditional or "true" surrogacy, the surrogate is artificially inseminated, and she carries the child to term. It is her own egg that is fertilized, so she is the biological mother of the child. The sperm is that of the intended father (let's think of him as the adoptive father) or a sperm donor. In many states, after she releases the child to the intended parents (you), a stepparent adoption occurs, as the intended/adoptive father is the biological father, and his wife is the adopting parent. In other states, a court adjudication of parentage might be issued prior to the birth, or parentage might be addressed after the birth through an administrative process. At this point any parental rights of the surrogate would end. Although this method was initially popular, with the advancement of new medical procedures, few surrogacies are now of the traditional variety. With traditional surrogacy, there is much greater legal risk if the surrogate were to change her mind and want to keep the child because she is the biological parent.

Gestational Surrogacy

In gestational surrogacy, the surrogate is implanted with an embryo via in vitro fertilization. The embryo is composed of the fertilized egg of the intended mother or egg donor. The egg is fertilized by the sperm of the intended father or a sperm donor. In a gestational surrogacy, the surrogate is not genetically related to the child she is carrying.

In most states, her rights as the birthing mother (and her husband's rights if applicable) are usually terminated in the fifth to eight month of the pregnancy via a court adjudication of parentage. This gives rights to the intended parents upon the birth of the child, based upon the contract terms and the decisions reached by the parties prior to the pregnancy taking place. However, some states only provide for a post-birth parentage proceeding. The vast majority of surrogacies are of this type (gestational rather than traditional).

Non-Surrogate Assisted Reproductive Technology

Sometimes you are medically able to carry a child to term so you don't need a surrogate, but you need a viable egg and/or sperm from a donor. Some options include:

- *Intrauterine insemination (also known as artificial insemination).* The sperm of your partner, or a donor, is prepared and inserted into your uterus through a catheter. (Usually taking fertility drugs accompanies these efforts to increase the likelihood of pregnancy.)

- *In vitro fertilization (IVF).* Your eggs are extracted and fertilized with the sperm of your partner, or a donor. Once embryos are developed one (or more) are implanted in your uterus.

- *Donor eggs.* The eggs from another woman are fertilized by the sperm of your partner or a donor. The embryo is transferred into your uterus.

- *Donor embryos.* Embryos are provided to you by a man and woman who have unused cryopreserved embryos. The embryo is implanted into your uterus.

- *Gamete Intrafallopian Transfer (GIFT).* Your eggs are collected and mixed with the sperm of your partner or a donor in a lab and placed in your fallopian tubes in the hope fertilization will occur.

- *Zygote Intrafallopian Transfer (ZIFT).* This is like in vitro fertilization, but the embryo is inserted into your fallopian tubes rather than your uterus. (Fertilization of the egg can be confirmed prior to placing the egg into your fallopian tubes, allowing fewer eggs to be implanted than in GIFT, thus reducing the chance of multiple births.)

In all states, it is critical when using donor egg or sperm to obtain a proper donor agreement or release to ensure that the donor has no parental rights or responsibilities. Colleen Marea Quinn, a Virginia attorney who specializes in both adoption and assisted reproductive technology, and the immediate past-president of the American Academy of Adoption Attorneys, advises:

"There have been numerous cases where the parties did not have such an agreement and either the donor came back and successfully asserted parental rights or the intended parent came back and successfully obtained child support from the donor. So having a proper agreement or release in place that is enforceable under the law of the applicable state is very important to properly securing legal parentage."

The Role of the Attorney

Just as attorneys are deemed advisable in adoption, it is the same in surrogacy or assisted reproduction. In surrogacy, attorneys, fertility clinics and surrogacy programs typically coordinate to ensure that the potential surrogate receives both medical and mental health screening and counseling. This helps to ensure that the potential surrogate is emotionally able to fulfill the role as surrogate, and that her pregnancy history is appropriate. Full medical background information is critical to obtain in a traditional surrogacy (since it is her egg), but also in gestational surrogacy to be sure she can safely carry a child to term. Contracts will be required to define the duties of the carrier/surrogate and the intended parents, will address compensation issues and insurance coverage, and prescribe what happens if things don't go as planned (such as a miscarriage, and many other issues). If she is married, the spouse of the carrier/surrogate will have rights in most states, and so typically the spouse is also a party to the contract and parentage procedures.

Issues also arise in assisted reproduction regarding "ownership" of eggs/sperm/gametes/zygotes. When using a donated egg, sperm or embryos, attorneys should be used to draft and negotiate proper donor agreements and releases. The Adoption Academy of Adoption Attorneys (AAAA) has a division of attorneys who have extensive experience in Assisted Reproductive Technology, the *American Academy of Assisted Reproductive Technology Attorneys* (AAARTA) and they can be found at adoptionattorneys.org, or directly at adoptionattorneys.org/aaarta-page/home. Most are listed as adoption attorneys as well in the biographies listed in the state-by-state review in Chapter 15.

Costs

Surrogacy is normally more expensive than adoption, sometimes a lot more. There are two reasons for this. One is the medical cost involved in the surrogacy. The other is the cost of the surrogate. Unlike adoption, where a birth mother can't receive any gain (other than pregnancy related costs like food and rent), a surrogate can legally be paid a fee in most states.

In a traditional surrogacy, the medical fees involved in the insemination, the surrogacy program fees, and the surrogate's costs will usually total from $45,000 to $70,000. A gestational surrogacy will usually cost an additional $6,000 to $25,000 for the medical fees involved in the in vitro fertilization. If a compassionate or altruistic surrogate or gestational carrier (one that is not expecting to be paid a fee and often is a relative or close friend) is used, then overall costs can be much less.

Risks and Issues

Just as in adoption, surrogacy involves risks. A surrogate might fail to become pregnant, meaning the medical costs are for naught. Her contracted fee, and that of the program which is overseeing the surrogacy, will be reduced, but some compensation will be required. If the pregnancy is initially successful but there is a miscarriage, she might be owed a larger portion of her fee, or her full fee. The same is true regarding the program overseeing the surrogacy.

There are also legal risks. In a traditional surrogacy, since the surrogate is the biological mother, she may seek to void the contract and seek to maintain her parental rights. Her rights will be particularly strong in states where there is no specific authorization for surrogacy contracts. Even in gestational surrogacy, where she has no biological connection with the child, she might seek to establish custody or visitation. In these cases the courts are most likely to uphold the initial intent of the parties as set down in the contract, usually benefiting the intended/adoptive parents. For this reason, gestational surrogacy is seen as having fewer legal risks than traditional surrogacy.

There are some problematic issues that can arise in surrogacy. One term you will see in surrogacy contracts is "selective reduction." This means if the pregnancy is determined to be multiple births (not uncommon with fertility drugs and the in vitro fertilization process, but becoming less common due to evolving recommendations and guidelines by the American Society of Reproductive Medicine) the intended/adoptive parents may have the legal right in their contract to terminate the viability of the other births.

"Selective reduction or termination" also might arise when the expected baby is seen to have a serious medical problem, such as Down Syndrome, giving the intended parents the right to terminate the pregnancy. The rights and desires of the surrogate and the intended parents must be fully explored and resolved prior to contract drafting and then must be addressed in their contract.

Summary

There are positive and negative aspects to family building by using a gestational carrier as opposed to adoption. For families using gestational surrogacy, there is more control over the chosen genetics of the child, the pre-natal care taken by the carrier (especially since the carrier agrees to abstain from non-prescription drugs, alcohol and tobacco, and to closely adhere to doctor's orders), the involvement of the intended parents in the pregnancy, and the certainty of the placement of the child with the intended parents.

In adoption, there is not as much control or choice over the child's genetics, the pre-natal care, the level of involvement by the adoptive parents during the pregnancy or the placing parent's decision to stay committed to the adoption plan and place the child for adoption. However, while using a gestational carrier may have some advantages over pursuing adoption, using a gestational carrier generally is much more expensive than adoption and there is no guarantee that the gestational carrier will get pregnant.

This has been a very limited overview of assisted reproduction. Whether pursuing adoption or assisted reproduction—or both—be certain to consult with an experienced legal professional.

CHAPTER 15

STATE-BY-STATE REVIEW

Each state has different laws and procedures. You will want to review the laws for your home state, and all states in which you are considering working. Provided is information about each state's unique adoption laws and procedures, a listing of American Academy of Adoption Attorney members and their biographies, as well as contact information for the state's adoption office and adoption exchange (waiting children).

State Adoption Office Information

The following is listed for every state:

- The website for the state office overseeing adoption within the state.
- The website for the state adoption exchange. (In some cases the URL for the state adoption exchange is so lengthy it does not make sense to list it as it is easier to find it via a link on the state adoption office website, so for some states that has been recommended.) Please also see Appendix A for national and regional exchanges.)

Summary of State Laws and Procedures

Many key legal issues are explored individually for each state. The information was compiled via independent research of state statutes and data provided by attorneys practicing within each state. Be aware that laws can change, be interpreted differently, or applied by individual judges or authorities in different ways. Consultation with an attorney or licensed agency is necessary before initiating an adoption. The following information is provided for each state and the District of Columbia, allowing you to see the pros and cons of each state, and determine which states might be right for you:

- Are both independent and agency adoptions permitted?
- Is a pre-placement home study required for an independent adoption?
- Who does the home study in an independent adoption?
- What is the typical cost of a home study?
- Who can file a Petition for Adoption within the state? Is it only residents, or can non-residents do so? (The latter is indicated when the legal summary indicates the Petition can be filed within the state if the baby is born there, the birth mother lives there, or the agency supervising the placement is located there.)
- How open are most newborn adoptions?
- Are the adoptive parents permitted to help with the birth mother's pregnancy-related assistance, and if so, for what specific items?
- Can adoptive parents advertise for a birth mother?
- When does the birth mother sign her consent?
- Who must witness the consent?
- How soon after birth may the birth mother sign the consent?
- Does she have a set period in which to withdraw her consent, and if so, for how long and with what legal burden?
- Is the consent process different for independent and agency adoptions?
- If the birth mother is a minor does she need the consent of a parent or a guardian ad litem to consent to an adoption? (This

information will only be listed if it is required, so its absence means there is no such requirement.)

- What are the birth father's rights? Is there a putative birth father registry or is separate notice required? Only putative fathers (typically this means non-marital but will vary by state) are discussed as this is the most common type of birth father in adoption and their rights vary tremendously state-by-state. Men who are married to the birth mother (or who have otherwise escalated their rights, such as where they were living with and supporting an existing child) generally have rights equal to the birth mother, meaning their consent is normally required. In that case usually the same procedures outlined for birth mothers also apply to birth fathers. (It will also usually apply to putative fathers as well, if they elect to consent to the adoption.)
- How quickly is the baby released from the hospital to the adoptive parents, and what documents or procedures are required? Is an intermediary needed?
- How long does it take after the baby's placement before the final hearing is set to finalize the adoption?
- Must the adoptive parents and the child appear in court for the final hearing granting the adoption?

Adoption Attorneys

Only attorneys who are members of the American Academy of Adoption Attorneys (over 300 members nationwide, discussed in Chapter 3) are listed. To see the attorney's photographs, you may wish to visit the American Academy of Adoption Attorney's website: www.adoptionattorneys.org.

Some attorneys' biographies are shorter than others, perhaps indicating the attorney did not receive or reply to the questionnaire, or did not complete it fully. If an attorney completed a biography for a previous edition of this book, but did not return one for the current edition, the some or all of the information the attorney provided for the earlier edition has been used.

Private Adoption Agencies

To view a listing of private adoption agencies for each state (including their address, telephone number, website and email address) please visit childwelfare.gov.

*　　*　　*　　*　　*

ALABAMA

Official State Adoption Website:
http://dhr.alabama.gov/services/Adoption/Intro_Adoption.aspx

State Adoption Exchange or Related Website:
http://www.adoptuskids.org/states/al/index.aspx

State laws and procedures:

General Information. Alabama permits both independent and agency adoption. Advertising is permitted but it is best to check with an Alabama attorney for limitations. To file a Petition for Adoption within Alabama either the adoptive parents must reside there, or the child to be adopted must be born there (so non-resident adoption is possible). Normally, adoptions are finalized three-four months after the child is placed with the adoptive parents.

Independent Adoption. A pre-placement home study of the adoptive parents is normally required before a child may be placed in their home, although a court has the authority in some circumstances to allow a child to be placed before the home study is completed. The home study may be conducted by a licensed adoption agency or an individual licensed by the state as a Private Independent Practitioner (usually a licensed social worker). The home study fees are approximately $1,500.

The birth mother and the adoptive parents are not required by law to meet and share identities, although most elect to do so voluntarily. The adoptive parents are permitted to assist the birth mother with pregnancy-related expenses, such as medical, legal and living costs. The child may be placed with the adoptive parents directly upon his or her release from the hospital. Most hospitals have a special form for the birth mother to sign allowing the child's release to the adoptive parents.

The birth mother may sign her consent to the adoption before or after the birth. If signed before the birth it must be signed before a probate judge. If signed after the birth it may be witnessed by a probate judge or a notary public (a notary is the norm). Most birth mothers sign their consents before, or within a few days after, the birth. If the birth mother is under the age of 19 she must be appointed a guardian ad litem before she signs her consent, to be sure she understands her rights. This individual is usually an attorney whose fees, usually paid by the adoptive parents, average $1,000-$1,500.

There is a five-day period after the consent is signed, or the birth occurs, whichever is later, in which the birth mother has the automatic right to withdraw her consent. After the five days have elapsed, but within 14 days of the signing or the birth (whichever occurs first), the consent can only be withdrawn by the birth mother proving to a court the child's best interests would be served by being removed from the adoptive parents. After the 14-day period has elapsed, the consent can only be withdrawn upon proof of fraud, duress or legal mistake.

Alabama has a putative birth father registry. Putative birth fathers are required to register no later than 30 days post-birth or their consent is implied. The identity of men listed with the registry can only be released by court order. Many counties additionally require notice to a putative birth father if known by the birth mother, even if he does not file with the registry. If the putative birth father objects, the court will look at his behavior during the pregnancy and see if he abandoned his responsibilities toward the mother/fetus and if the best interests of the child will be served by adoption.

Agency Adoption. There is no difference regarding the process in which a birth mother signs her consent to adoption in an independent or agency adoption. The information provided above regarding independent adoption (e.g. when it can be signed, before whom, legal burden to seek to withdraw a signed consent, requirement for guardian ad litem) is identical regarding agency adoption.

Some agencies within Alabama agree to do identified adoptions. Some agencies will also agree to make immediate hospital "at risk" placements.

American Academy of Adoption Attorney members:

David Broome; 155 Monroe St., P.O. Box 1944, Mobile, AL 36633
Tel: (251) 432-9933 ● d.broome@adoptionattorneys.org
A graduate of the University of Alabama School of Law, he has been practicing law since 1977. He accepts contested cases and handles assisted reproduction matters. He is a fellow in the American Academy of Matrimonial Lawyers, the International Academy of Family Lawyers, and is board certified in family law advocacy by the National Board of Trial Advocacy. He is an adoptee.

Bryant "Drew" Whitmire, Jr.; 215 Richard Arrington Jr. Blvd. N, #501, Birmingham, AL 35203;
Tel: (205) 324-6631 ● dwhitm@bellsouth.net
A graduate of the University of Alabama School of Law, he has been practicing law since 1972. He estimates he completed 160 adoptions last year (75 independent; 75 agency; 10 intercountry readopts). His clients locate their own birth mother. He accepts contested cases.

ALASKA

Official State Adoption Website:
http://dhss.alaska.gov/ocs/Pages/adoptions/default.aspx

State Adoption Exchange: Use above state website

State laws and procedures:

General Information. Alaska permits both independent and agency adoption. The permissibility of advertising is not addressed in state laws, so it is generally presumed it is permitted. To file a Petition for Adoption within Alaska either the adopting parents, or the child being adopted, must reside there (typically defined as being born there in a newborn adoption), or the agency having custody must be located there (so non-resident adoption is possible). Normally, adoptions are finalized approximately seven months after the child is placed in the adoptive parents' custody, as the final hearing cannot occur until the child has been placed for six months. The adoptive parents and the child being adopted are required to appear at the final court hearing, but some judges approve that this may be done telephonically.

Independent Adoption. A pre-placement home study of the adoptive parents is required before a child may be placed in their home. The pre- and post-placement home study usually ranges in cost from $750-$1,750, and each post-placement visit is $200-$400.is done by a licensed social worker at a usual fee of approximately $750.

The birth mother and adoptive parents are not required by law to meet and share identities, although some do so voluntarily. The adoptive parents are permitted to assist the birth mother with pregnancy-related medical, legal and living expenses, but some judges are very conservative with what they consider appropriate and not excessive. The child may be placed with the adoptive parents directly upon his or her release from the hospital, although each hospital has its own forms and policies.

The birth mother signs a consent to adoption, called a Relinquishment of Parental Rights, which can be witnessed by either a notary public or judge, and can be signed any time after birth. Once signed, she has ten days thereafter with the automatic right to withdraw it. After the initial ten days have elapsed, she can only withdraw it by proving to a court that the child's best interests would be served by being removed from the adoptive parents. Once the adoption is finalized by a judge, the consent becomes irrevocable. (Be aware that Alaska has a high percentage of Native Americans/Alaskan Natives who might fall under the Indian Child Welfare Act, changing these procedures and laws.)

Alaska has no putative birth father registry. Notice must be given to putative fathers unless they can't be found. The notice is a 30-day notice of the final adoption hearing. Mere proof of his paternity is often enough to block an adoption, if that is the birth father's desire. If the birth father was actually known and could have been identified but was not given notice, he may have up to two years, even after finalization of the adoption, to contest the adoption.

Agency Adoption. The information provided above regarding independent adoption is identical regarding agency adoption with the exception of the birth mother's consent. In an agency adoption, she signs a *relinquishment*. Once signed, she has ten days with the automatic right to withdraw it. Once the ten days have elapsed, it is irrevocable. The relinquishment must be witnessed by a judge.

Some agencies within Alaska agree to do identified and "at risk" adoptions

ARIZONA

Official State Adoption Website:
https://dcs.az.gov/services/foster-care-and-adoption

State Adoption Exchange or Related Website:
https://www.azdes.gov/dcyf/adoption/meet.asp

State laws and procedures:

General Information. Arizona permits both independent and agency adoption. Advertising is permitted. To file a Petition for Adoption in Arizona the adoptive parents must be residents of the state, generally for at least 90 days. Most adoptions can be finalized approximately three months from the filing of the Petition of Adoption if the child is under age three. The adoptive parents and the child being adopted are required to appear at the final court hearing.

Independent Adoption. A pre-placement home study of the adoptive parents, resulting in "certification" of the adoptive parents, is usually required before a child is placed in the adoptive parents' home. In some cases where there is no certification, a placement with the adoptive parents may be made, provided a petition for temporary custody order is filed within 5 days of the placement (and then a hearing must be held within 10 days). The home study may be conducted by the state adoption office or a licensed private agency. The cost of the home study varies. Once the home study is completed it must be filed with the juvenile court, allowing the adoptive parents to be certified as adoptive parents, after which time the adoptive placement can occur. If the adoptive parents were unable to complete a pre-placement home study, they may request a court to issue a temporary custody order, allowing them to have immediate custody of the child and complete their home study after the placement.

The birth mother and adoptive parents are not required by law to meet and share identities, although most do so voluntarily. The adoptive parents are permitted to assist the birth mother with pregnancy-related expenses, but the payment of her living expenses requires advance court approval if the total expenses are in excess of $1,000. The child may be placed with the adoptive parents directly upon release from the hospital, but some hospitals require that the release be made directly to the attorney or agency handling the adoption.

The birth mother may sign her consent to the adoption no sooner than 72 hours after the birth. It must be witnessed by a notary public or two witnesses over the age of 18. Most consents are signed three to four days after the baby's birth. Once the consent to adoption is signed it is irrevocable, unless the birth mother can prove it was signed based upon fraud, duress or undue influence.

Arizona has a putative birth father registry but notice is required to any known father even if he does not register with the registry. Putative birth fathers must be given notice if identified by the birth mother, or if they are listed with the birth father registry (birth fathers must file with the putative father registry within 30 days of the child's birth). Alternatively, notice can be served on a putative father prior to the birth, and in such cases he has 30 days to file a paternity action. Failure to file a paternity action within 30 days, and serve the birth mother notice, results in the putative father having no legal right to bring a court action and his consent is not required.

Agency Adoption. There is no difference regarding the process in which a birth mother signs her consent to adoption in an independent or agency adoption. The information provided above regarding independent adoption (e.g. when it can be signed, before whom, legal burden to withdraw a signed consent) is identical regarding agency adoption.

Some agencies within Arizona agree to do identified adoptions. Some agencies will also agree to make hospital "at risk" placements.

American Academy of Adoption Attorney members:

Kristy B. Blackwell; 1490 S. Price Rd. #208, Chandler, AZ 85286
Tel: (408) 420-2900 ● stuartandblackwell.com ● kbb@stuartandblackwell.com
A graduate of ASU College of Law, she has been practicing law since 2004. She estimates she has completed hundreds of adoptions in her career and presently completes over 50 annually. She completes all types of adoptions (independent, agency, international re-adoptions, adult, stepparent and other relative adoptions). She assists in creating adoptive matches. She accepts contested adoption cases.

Brent D. Ellsworth; 4445 E. Holmes Ave. #106, Mesa, AZ 85206
Tel: (408) 654-3668 ● b.ellsworth@adoptionattorneys.org

Philip (Jay) McCarthy; 508 N. Humphreys St., Flagstaff, AZ 86001
Tel: (928) 779-4252 ● mccarthyweston.com ●
j.mccarthy@adoptionattorneys.org
A graduate of the Creighton Law School, he has been practicing law since 1980. He estimates he has completed more than 600 adoptions in his career, and

completes 80 annually: 75% independent; 25% agency. He assists in creating adoptive matches.

Rita A. Meiser; 7012 No. 18th St., Phoenix, AZ 85020
Tel: (602) 650-2473 ● www.meiserlaw.com ● r.meiser@adoptionattorneys.org
A graduate of the University of Arizona School of Law, she has been practicing adoption law since 1978. She is an adoptive parent, and works in all areas of adoption, including: private, agency, and foster adoption. She assists in creating adoptive matches.

Abigail J. Mills; 1221 E. Osborn Rd. #105, Phoenix, AZ 85014
Tel: (602) 277-7000 ● azbarristers.com ● a.mills@adoptionattorneys.org

Kathryn A. Pidgeon; 4742 North 24th St. #300, Phoenix, AZ 85016
Tel: (602) 522-8700 ● adoptaz.com ● kpidgeon@adoptaz.com
A graduate of the University of Miami, she has been practicing law since 1989. She estimates she completes approximately 130 adoptions annually: 25% independent; 75% agency. She assists in creating adoptive matches.

Heather M. Strickland; 3180 E. Grant Rd., Tucson, AZ 85716
Tel: (520) 327-6041 ● arizonaadoptionlaw.com ●
h.strickland@adoptionattorneys.org

Daniel I. Ziskin; P.O. Box 7447, Phoenix, AZ 85011
Tel: (602) 234-2280 ● dan@adoptz.com
A graduate of the Arizona State University School of Law, he has been practicing law since 1975. He estimates he has completed about 2,000 adoptions since 1983, and completes 35 annually, most of them independent. He assists in creating adoptive matches. He accepts contested adoption cases. He is an adoptive parent. He has handled assisted reproductive technology matters since 1995 and succeeded in obtaining hundreds of birth orders making the intended parents the parents of children born through surrogacy.

ARKANSAS

Official State Adoption Website: http://www.adoptarkansas.org/Arkansas Heart Gallery

State Adoption Exchange: Use above state website

State laws and procedures:

General Information. Arkansas permits both independent and agency adoption. Advertising is permitted but some newspapers place restrictions on whom may place ads. To file a Petition for Adoption within Arkansas either the adopting parents, or the birth mother, must be residents of the state. (If jurisdiction is based solely upon the birth mother's residency, however, she must have resided in Arkansas for at least four months pre-birth.) This makes non-resident adoption possible. If it is an agency adoption the Petition can also be filed there if the adoption agency having custody of the child is located in Arkansas. Normally, adoptions are finalized approximately 6-14 days after the child's placement with the adoptive parents, one of the fastest times in the nation. The adopting parents are required to appear in court for the final hearing.

Independent Adoption. A pre-placement home study of the adoptive parents is required before a child is placed in their home. The home study can be done by a licensed adoption agency or a licensed certified social worker. The average cost is $800-2,500. No post-placement supervision is required (except in some interstate adoption cases where it is the adoptive parents' out of state agency making the requirement).

The birth mother and the adoptive parents are not required by law to meet and share identities, although most do so. The adoptive parents are permitted to assist the birth mother with pregnancy-related medical, legal and living expenses. The child may be placed with the adoptive parents directly upon his or her discharge from the hospital, but only upon the hospital receiving a copy of the consent to adoption, and the birth mother signing a release of the child to the designated adoptive parent.

The birth mother may sign her consent any time after the birth. It is witnessed by a judge or notary public. If the birth mother is under the age of 18 she must be appointed a guardian ad litem prior to her signing of the consent to be sure she understands her rights. Once the consent is signed the birth mother has ten days to revoke the consent via affidavit with the court with no legal burden. She can shorten this period to five days if she elects.

Arkansas has a putative birth father registry. Notice is only given to birth fathers who file with the registry prior to the filing of the Petition for Adoption. Putative birth fathers who register must additionally show they established a significant relationship with the child, such as a personal, custodial or financial relationship.

Agency Adoption. There is no difference regarding the process in which a birth mother can sign her consent to adoption in an independent or agency adoption. The information provided above regarding independent adoption (e.g. when the consent can be signed, legal burden to withdraw a signed consent) is identical regarding agency adoption. One additional option, however, is that a birth mother can sign a pre-birth relinquishment in an agency adoption, giving the power of consent to the agency. This form is witnessed by a notary. The same five or ten-day revocation period applies. Court hearings are usually set immediately after the revocation period has expired, which is why finalizations can occur as soon as they do in Arkansas.

Some agencies agree to do identified adoptions. Some agencies also agree to make immediate hospital "at risk" placements.

American Academy of Adoption Attorney members:

Sandra Bradshaw; P.O. Box 249, Crossett, AR 71635
Tel: (870) 305-4700 ● s.bradshaw@adoptionattorneys.org
A graduate of the University of Mississippi School of Law, she has been practicing law since 1992.

Eugene T. Kelley; 303 West Walnut Street, Rogers, AR 72757
Tel: (479) 636-1051 ● kelleyadoptionlegalservices.com ●
e.kelley@adoptionattorneys.org
A graduate of the University of Arkansas School of Law, he has been practicing law since 1968. He has completed more than 1,000 adoptions in his career. He received the Congressional Angel in Adoption Award in 2005. He assists in creating adoptive matches. He practices law with his daughter, Jodie J. Kelley, and his son, Glenn E. Kelley. His firm also handles contested adoptions.

Kaye H. McLeod; 210 Linwood Court, Little Rock, AR 72205
Tel: (501) 663-6224 ● k.mcleod@adoptionattorneys.org
A graduate of the University of Arkansas School of Law, she has been practicing law since 1981. She estimates she has completed more than 1,600 adoptions in her career, and completes 60 annually: 90% independent; 5% agency; 5% intercountry. She received the Congressional Angel in Adoption Award in 2002.

Keith H. Morrison; 1 E. Center St. #310, Fayetteville, AR 72701
Tel: (479) 521-5820 ● h.morrison@adoptionattorneys.org

CALIFORNIA

Official State Adoption Website: http://www.childsworld.ca.gov/PG1301.htm

State Adoption Exchange or Related Website:
http://www.cakidsconnection.org

State laws and procedures:

General Information. California permits both independent and agency adoption. The majority of California's infant adoptions are completed via independent adoption but the private agency process is very similar. Advertising is permitted only by licensed adoption agencies. To file a Petition for Adoption in California the adopting parents must reside there or the baby must be born there (making non-resident adoption available). Normally, adoptions are finalized 7 to 10 months after the placement of the child with the adoptive parents. The adopting parents and child being adopted are required to appear in court for the final hearing, although a court may waive their appearance for good cause.

Independent Adoption. A pre-placement home study of the adoptive parents is not required before a child is placed in their home. It may be done voluntarily, however, and if so is done by a licensed private adoption agency, and it is called an Independent Adoption Pre-Assessment. The post-placement home study may be conducted by the California Department of Social Services (CDSS) or a county adoption agency designated by CDSS to perform independent adoption services for that county. The state fee for the home study is $4,500. (However, if an Independent Adoption Pre-Assessment was completed prior to the minor's placement, the fee is reduced to $1,550.)

The birth mother is required by law to personally select the adoptive parents with full sharing of identities. Although it is not required by law that they meet in person, this is done in virtually all adoptions. The adoptive parents are permitted to assist the birth mother with pregnancy-related legal, medical, counseling and living expenses. The child may be placed with the adoptive parents directly from the hospital upon the birth mother's signature upon a standard hospital form entitled the Health Facility Minor Release.

The birth mother must receive advice and information, called an Advisement of Rights, from a licensed social worker approved by CDSS as an Adoption Services Provider (often referred to as an ASP), or a licensed adoption agency acting as an ASP, at least ten days before she signs her consent to adoption. The consent form is called the Adoption Placement Agreement, which is also signed by the adoptive parents, and outlines the rights and duties of each party. It may only be signed after the birth mother's medical discharge from the hospital. (An additional required consent form is called the Statement of Understanding.) The Adoption Services Provider then sends the birth mother's consent and related documents to the CDSS (or its designated county entity) which will assign an adoption caseworker who will oversee the remainder of the adoption.

The Adoption Placement Agreement is normally signed hours or days after the hospital discharge. However, it is not an effective forfeiture of rights by the birth mother until one of two events occur, whichever occurs first: 1) The birth mother can sign a Waiver of Right to Revoke Consent in the presence of CDSS or designated county agency any time after signing the Adoption Placement Agreement, or a simpler option is to have it witnessed by the ASP, which is permitted if the birth mother was represented by independent counsel (in either case the Waiver of Right to Revoke Consent becomes irrevocable the next business day); or 2) if the birth mother does not elect to sign a Waiver of Right to Revoke Consent, her consent to adoption becomes permanent and irrevocable on the 31st day after the signing of the Adoption Placement Agreement.

California does not have a putative birth father registry. "Alleged" birth fathers (which generally means men not married to the birth mother, not listed on the birth certificate, and who have never had the child in his home and held out as his own child), must be given notice of alleged paternity and adoption, unless he can't be located with due diligence. If an alleged father objects in court, he must prove he acted responsibly to meet the birth mother's needs, and also that he objected promptly to the adoption. If he can establish both those things, he must be proven "unfit" to terminate his rights. If he can't prove he did both these things, the adoptive parents must only prove the child's best interests are served by being with them, rather than the birth father. If he did do both those things, the adoptive parents must prove he is unfit. Alleged birth fathers wishing to cooperate may sign either a *Waiver of Notice* or *Denial of Paternity* before the birth, witnessed by a notary, and it can be filed with the court post-birth and result in the termination of his parental rights.

Agency Adoption. The process for agency adoptions is very similar to independent, although a pre-placement home study is required of the adoptive parents before placement. The birth mother signs a two-form consent, one being the Statement of Understanding and the other being a *relinquishment* (rather than the Adoption Placement Agreement used in independent adoption). The birth mother has the option to have her relinquishment "held" by the agency before it becomes effective, as written into the Statement of Understanding (for example, 15 days, 20 days or until the birth father's rights are terminated). If she makes no such special notation, however, it becomes irrevocable upon the California Department of Social Services (CDSS) receiving and "acknowledging" it. The agency can't send the relinquishment to CDSS until the end of the next business day following the signing of the relinquishment. It commonly takes about ten days for CDSS to receive and acknowledge a relinquishment, but if CDSS takes longer, the relinquishment automatically becomes irrevocable ten days after being sent by the agency. The faster way for the relinquishment to become irrevocable is if the birth mother elected to sign a Waiver of Right to Revoke Consent. Just as with independent adoption, she must be represented by independent counsel, and it becomes irrevocable at the end of the next business day after signing. Thus, the Waiver makes the CDSS date of acknowledgement immaterial.

Virtually all agencies agree to do identified adoptions. Most will also make "at risk" placements directly to the adoptive parents from the hospital.

American Academy of Adoption Attorney members (also visit Academy of California Adoption Lawyers at acal.org):

Timothy J. Blied; 400 N. Tustin Avenue, #209, Santa Ana, CA 92705
Tel: (949) 863-0200 ● sbsmlaw.com ● t.blied@adoptionattorneys.org
A graduate of the Pepperdine University School of Law, he has been practicing law since 1979. He is an adoptive parent.

Kristine E. Colburn; 3033 Fifth Ave. # 430, San Diego, CA 92103
Tel: (619) 231-2085 ● stockscolburn.com ● kcolburn@stockscolburn.com
A graduate of Thomas Jefferson School of Law, she has been practicing law since 1993. She estimates she has completed 250 adoptions in her career and completes 20 annually, most independent. She assists in creating adoptive matches.

D. Durand Cook; 10170 Culver Boulevard, Culver City, CA 90232
Tel: (323) 655-2601 ● adoption-option.com ● d.cook@adoptionattorneys.org
A graduate of California Western School of Law, he has been practicing law since 1970. He estimates he has completed more than 5,000 adoptions in his career and presently completes 65 annually, most independent. He assists in creating adoptive matches.

Douglas Donnelly; 1332 Santa Barbara St, Santa Barbara, CA 93101
Tel: (805) 962-0988 ● Adoptionlawfirm.com ●
d.donnelly@adoptionattorneys.org
A graduate of the Loyola University School of Law in Los Angeles, he has been practicing law since 1977. He estimates he has completed more than 3,000 adoptions in his career, and completes 50 annually: 90% independent; 10% agency. He assists in creating adoptive matches. He accepts contested adoption cases. He is an adoptive parent and past president of the Academy of California Adoption Lawyers.

Randall B. Hicks; 11801 Pierce Street #200, Riverside, CA 92505
Tel: (951) 787-8300 ● randallhicks.com ● randy@randallhicks.com
A graduate of Pepperdine University School of Law, he has been practicing law since 1986. He also has offices in San Diego, Orange and Los Angeles Counties. He estimates he has completed more than 1,000 adoptions in his career: independent, intercountry, stepparent, adult). Now, however, he focuses on stepparent adoption. He is the author of several "how to" adoption books. (He was a member of the American Academy of Adoption Attorneys from 1992-2016 but withdrew due to an inability to attend required annual meetings, but still holds the organization in high regard so includes members' biographies in this book.) He is a member of the Academy of California Adoption Lawyers. (ACAL.org)

Allen Hultquist; 28581 Old Town Front St. #212, Temecula, CA 92590 ● Tel: (951) 302-7777 ● a.hultquist@adoptionattorneys.org
A graduate of the Western State University College of Law of San Diego, he has been practicing law since 1981. He estimates he has completed 1,500 adoptions in his career and completes 45 annually: 90% independent; 10% agency. He assists in creating adoptive matches.

Karen R. Lane; 100 Wilshire Bl. #2075, Santa Monica, CA 90401
Tel: (310) 393-9802 ● klane-adopt.com ● k.lane@adoptionattorneys.org
She has been practicing law since 1979.

Steven Lazarus; 4640 Admiralty Way #500, Marina Del Ray, CA 90292 •
Tel: (310) 496-5758 • lazlawfirm.com •
slazarus@lazlawfirm.com
A graduate of Pepperdine University School of Law, he has been practicing law
since 1988.

Celeste E. Liversidge; 140 S. Lake Ave. #348, Pasadena, CA 91101
Tel: (626) 229-0600 • adoptionlawgroup.com •
c.liversidge@adoptionattorneys.org

Shannon M. Matteson; 3033 Fifth Ave. #430, San Diego, CA 92103
Tel: (925) 297-4626 • stockscolburn.com •
s.matteson@adoptionattorneys.org

David J. Radis; 1801 Century Park East, 24th Fl, Los Angeles, CA 90067
Tel: (310) 552-0536 • radis-adopt.com • d.radis@adoptionattorneys.org
A graduate of the Southwestern School of Law, he has been practicing law since
1974. He estimates he has completed more than 3,000 adoptions in his career
and completes 45 annually: 50% independent, 50% agency. He assists in
creating adoptive matches.

Karin Stoeckenius; 201 First St. #200, Petaluma, CA 94952
Tel: (415) 643-4523 • adamsromer.com •
k.stoeckenius@adoptionattorneys.org

Robert R. Walmsley; 25 East Anapamu St. 2nd Fl. Santa Barbara, CA 93101
Tel: (805) 845-7701 • jarrettewalmsley.com •
r.walmsley@adoptionattorneys.org
A graduate of Whittier College School of Law, he has been practicing law since
1987.

Felice A. Webster; 1920 Hillhurst Ave. #402, Los Angeles, CA 90027 • Tel:
(323) 664-5600 • felicewebster.com •
f.webster@adoptionattorneys.org
A graduate of Loyola Law School, she has been practicing law since 1974. She
estimates she completes 50 adoptions annually (independent, agency, foster
parent, stepparent, adult).

Nanci R. Worcester; 1216 High Street #C, Auburn, CA 95603
Tel: (530) 888-1311 ● adoption-center.com ●
n.worcester@adoptionattorneys.org
A graduate of Southwestern School of Law, she has been practicing law since 1981. She estimates she has completed more than 2,000 adoptions in her career and completes 50 annually: 90% independent; 10% agency. She assists in creating adoptive matches. She is an adoptive parent.

Holly Wotherspoon; 201 1st Street. #200, Petaluma, CA 94952
Tel: (415) 643-4523 ● adamsromer.com ●
h.wotherspoon@adoptionattorneys.org

Ted Youmans; 505 S. Villa Real Dr. #112, Anaheim Hills, CA 92807
Tel: (714) 408-2900 ● familybuilding.com ●
t.youmans@adoptionattorneys.org
A graduate of Whittier School of Law, he has been practicing since 1987. He has been involved in over 3,000 adoptions in his career. His firm does every type of adoption (approximately 80% independent; 20% agency). He assists in creating adoptive matches. He is an adoptive parent.

.

COLORADO

Official State Adoption Website: http://www.COFosterandAdopt.org

State Adoption Exchange or Related Website: http://www.adoptex.org/

State laws and procedures:

General Information. Colorado permits only agency adoption, although "direct" adoption is permitted where the child is placed with a close family relative (known as "kinship adoption") or when the child has been in the adoptive parents' care for one year or longer, in limited circumstances. Advertising laws regarding adoption are ambiguous but it is generally permitted. To file a Petition for Adoption within Colorado the adopting parents are not required to reside there, as long as the child-placing agency is located there (allowing non-resident adoption). In interstate adoptions, Colorado ICPC charges a $170.00 fee. Normally, adoptions are finalized six months after the placement of the child with the adoptive parents.

A pre-placement home study of the adopting parents is required before a child can be placed in their home. The home study may be performed by the county Department of Human Services (but usually only if the child is a ward of the state) or most often a licensed adoption agency. The cost for pre- and post-birth home study services is usually about $2,500 when done by private agencies.

Although birth mothers and adoptive parents are not required by law to meet in person, many elect to do so voluntarily. Adopting parents are permitted to assist with pregnancy-related expenses. The child is typically released directly from the hospital to the custody of the adoption agency, which will usually elect to immediately place the child with the adoptive parents. Identified adoptions are common.

There are two methods to terminate a birth mother's parental rights. The traditional method is, rather than sign a consent to adoption, she files a Petition for Relinquishment with the court any time after the birth. It need only be witnessed by a notary public. A court hearing is then scheduled, usually within several weeks. At the hearing, the birth mother confirms to the court that she has received agency relinquishment counseling, her decision is voluntary and knowing, and it is determined the relinquishment will serve the child's best interests. Once the court has entered the Order of Relinquishment, it can only be revoked within 90 days, if proven it was obtained by fraud or duress.

The other method is where a birth mother files an Expedited Petition for Relinquishment, which allows the court to order her parental rights relinquished without the necessity of a court hearing. This cannot be filed until at least four days have elapsed after birth, and the child must be under one year of age. Upon filing, the court is permitted to terminate the birth mother's rights in no more than seven business days. Most, but not all, Colorado courts accept Expedited Petitions.

Colorado does not have a putative birth father registry. Notice must be given to both presumed and putative fathers, unless their identity is unknown, then notice must be by publication. Once notice is given, a presumed father has 35 days after receiving notice in which to object. For putative fathers, once notice is given, he has 21 days from the date of the notice, or the date the relinquishment was filed, whichever occurred later, in which to file a reply objecting to his parental rights being terminated and to file a paternity action. If a presumed or putative father elects to object, his rights can only be terminated if proven he failed to establish a substantial and positive relationship with the child, did not promptly take substantial responsibility, is unfit, or cannot personally assume legal and physical custody of the child, taking into account the child's needs.

Most agencies within Colorado agree to do identified adoptions. Most agencies also agree to make immediate hospital "at risk" placements directly from the hospital before an Order of Relinquishment is entered by the court.

American Academy of Adoption Attorney members:

Timothy Eirich; 12596 W. Bayaud Ave. #390, Lakewood, CO 80228
Tel: (303) 679-8266 ● grobeirich.com ● tim@grobeirich.com
A graduate of the Loyola University Chicago School of Law, he has been practicing law since 2004. He estimates he has completed more than 500 adoptions in his career and his firm is involved in more than 150 adoptions annually: 30% independent, 60% agency, 10% international. He assists in creating adoptive matches. He handles contested adoptions, agency adoptions, adoption subsidy negotiations, foster parent adoptions, stepparent adoptions, custodial adoptions, kinship adoptions, second parent adoptions, adoption dissolutions, and adult adoptions.

Virginia "Ginny" L. Frank; 1434 Spruce #100, Boulder, CO 80302
Tel: (303) 756-4673 ● virginialfrank.com ● v.frank@adoptionattorneys.org
A graduate of Oklahoma City University School of Law, she has been practicing law since 1992. She estimates she has completed 4,000 adoptions in her career and presently completes more than 200 annually, including independent, agency, interstate, and re-adoptions. She also handles assisted reproductive technology matters.

Seth A. Grob; 12596 W. Bayaud Ave. #390, Lakewood, CO 80228
Tel: (303) 679-8266 ● grobeirich.com ● seth@grobeirich.com
A graduate of the University of California at Los Angeles School of Law, he has been practicing law since 1991. He estimates he has completed more than 2,000 adoptions in his career and his firm is involved in more than 150 adoptions annually: 30% independent; 60% agency; 10% international. He does not assist in creating adoptive matches. He handles agency, foster parent, stepparent, kinship, second parent, adult and custodial adoptions, as well as adoption subsidy negotiations and contested adoption matters. He also handles assisted reproductive technology cases. In 2008, the American Academy of Adoption Attorneys awarded him the "Amy M. Silberberg Award" in recognition of his unique contributions to the adoption of special needs children. In 2006, the Congressional Coalition on Adoption Institute awarded him the Angel in Adoption Award.

Daniel A. West; 405 S. Cascade Ave. #302, Colorado Springs, CO 80903 ● Tel: (719) 473-4444 ● beltzandwest.com ●
d.west@adoptionattorneys.org

CONNECTICUT

Official State Adoption Website:
http://www.ctfosteradopt.com/fosteradopt/site/default.asp

State Adoption Exchange or Related Website:
http://www.adoptuskids.org/states/ct/index.aspx

State laws and procedures:

Connecticut only permits agency adoption. However, identified adoptions are permitted, where the birth mother was located outside the agency, as long as the attorney or intermediary did not receive a fee for locating the birth mother. Accordingly, all adoptions within Connecticut are agency adoptions. Advertising is permitted. To file a Petition for Adoption within Connecticut the adopting parents must reside there. Normally, adoptions are finalized 6 to 12 months after the placement of the child with the adoptive parents. The adoptive parents are required to appear in court for the final hearing.

A pre-placement home study of the adopting parents is required before a child can be placed in their home. The home study may be performed by a licensed adoption agency or the Department of Children Services. The Department of Children Services charges no fee for their home study services, but their services are usually limited to children being adopted who are wards of the state. The fees of private agencies for the pre-placement home study is usually about $2,000 and post-placement supervision an additional $1,000-$2,000. For agencies which are assisting in matching with a birth mother leading to an adoptive placement (referred to as "placement fees"), typical agency fees total about $25,000.

Birth mothers and adoptive parents are not required by law to meet in person, although some elect to do so voluntarily. Normally, full identities are not disclosed. Adopting parents are permitted to assist with pregnancy-related expenses, such as medical, legal and living costs, although any assistance must be paid through the agency and not directly to the birth mother. Assistance living expenses cannot exceed $1,500 without special court approval. The child may not be released directly to the adoptive parents from the hospital. Instead, the child is released to the custody of the adoption agency. In some cases the agency will elect to immediately place the child with the adoptive parents as an "at risk" placement before the child is permanently free for adoption.

The consent to adoption process is made by the birth mother, or the agency, filing a voluntary Petition to Terminate Parental Rights with the court. This petition to voluntarily terminate parental rights may not be signed by the birth mother until at least 48 hours have elapsed after the birth and must be witnessed by a notary public. A hearing is set to terminate parental rights based upon the signed consent, usually 40 days after birth. Prior to this hearing the birth mother has the automatic right to revoke her consent. After the hearing and the court's termination of parental rights, the consent is irrevocable.

If the birth mother is under the age of 18 a guardian ad litem, usually an attorney, shall be appointed prior to her signing of the consent to termination of parental rights to be sure she understands her legal rights. The consent may also not be signed until the birth mother has received mandatory counseling. The consent cannot be withdrawn once the court has approved the consent and resulting termination of parental rights, except upon proof of fraud or coercion.

Connecticut does not have a putative birth father registry. Notice must be given to any putative father, and if he can't be located, then notice by publication is required. If he elects to object the adoption can't proceed without his consent absent a finding of grounds, such as abandonment.

American Academy of Adoption Attorney members:

Donald B. Sherer; 1010 Summer Street, #101, Stamford, CT 06905 • Tel: (203) 327-2084 • d.sherer@adoptionattorneys.org

DELAWARE

Official State Adoption Website: http://kids.delaware.gov/fs/adoption.shtml

State Adoption Exchange: Use above state website.

State laws and procedures:

General Information. All non-familial adoptions much be processed through a Delaware license agency. Independent adoption is prohibited. Advertising is only permitted by adoption agencies. Delaware residents may finalize in the state court system, and non-residents may finalize in Delaware if the termination proceedings occurred in the Delaware court system. Adoptions are normally finalized six months to one year after the birth or the placement of the child with the adoptive parents. The adopting parents and the child are generally not required to appear in court for the final hearing.

A pre-placement home study of the adopting parents is required before a child may be placed in their home. The home study must be conducted by a licensed adoption agency. The fee varies for pre- and post-placement services but they typically range from$1,500 to $3,500. If the agency is also providing networking/matching services their fees will usually be significantly higher. The birth mother and adoptive parents are not required by law to meet in person and share identities, although some elect to do so voluntarily. Adopting parents are permitted to assist with pregnancy-related expenses, such as medical, legal and living costs, provided they are paid through the agency and not directly by the adoptive parents to the birth mother.

The child may not be released directly to the adoptive parents from the hospital. Instead, the child is released to the custody of the adoption agency. In some cases the agency will elect to immediately place the child with the adoptive parents as an "at risk" placement where the child is not yet permanently free for adoption.

The birth mother may sign her consent to adoption any time after the birth. (A birth father may sign before the birth.) The consent to adoption must be presented by, and signed in the presence of, certain individuals permitted to take consents under Delaware law, including a staff member of a Delaware licensed agency, a judge or court approved individual, agency representative, or an attorney not representing the adoptive parents or adoption agency. The consent is signed and filed with the court, in conjunction with a voluntary Petition for Termination of Parental Rights. A birth mother has the right to revoke her consent to adoption within 14 days of signing her consent with no legal burden. After the 14 days it is irrevocable, except upon proof of fraud or duress.

Delaware has a putative birth father registry. A birth father must register either before the birth, or within 30 days after the birth, to be entitled to notice of an action to terminate his rights. Despite the law, must courts still require personal service or notice by publication, even for birth fathers who have not registered with the birth father registry.

Identified adoptions are common and most agencies will agree to make them. Many agencies will also agree to make immediate hospital "at risk" placements.

American Academy of Adoption Attorney members:

Deborah E. Spivack; 800 King St, 1st Floor, Wilmington, DE, 19801
Tel: (215) 763-5550 ● familybuildinglaw.net ●
d.spivack@adoptionattorneys.org
A graduate of the Widener, University School of Law, she has been practicing law since 1993. She estimates she has completed more than 1,000 adoptions in her career and presently completes 80-100 (agency, independent, foreign re-adoption and intra family/stepparent). She is an adoptive parent. She is an adoptive parent and received the 2105 Congressional Coalition of Adoption Angel Award. She has offices in New Jersey, Pennsylvania and Delaware.

DISTRICT OF COLUMBIA

Official State Adoption Website:
http://cfsa.dc.gov/service/greatest-gift-forever-family

State Adoption Exchange or Related Website:
http://www.adoptionstogether.org/Events/Heart-Gallery/

State laws and procedures:

General Information. The District of Columbia permits both independent and agency adoption. Advertising is permitted. To file a Petition for Adoption in the District of Columbia the adoptive parents must have resided there for one year, or the child must be born there (making non-resident adoption possible). If it is an agency adoption the Petition may also be filed there if the adoption agency having custody of the child is located there (making non-resident adoption possible). Usually, adoptions are finalized approximately six to eight months after the child's placement with the adoptive parents. The adoptive parents and the child are normally required to appear in court for the final hearing.

Independent Adoption. A pre-placement home study is not required of the adoptive parents before a child may be placed in their home, if both the adoptive and birth parents reside the District of Columbia. The post-placement home study may be conducted by the state adoption office or a licensed adoption agency. The cost varies. Attorneys are not permitted to "match" birth mothers and adoptive parents.

The adoptive parents and the birth mother are not required by law to meet in person and share identities, although many do so voluntarily. The adoptive parents are permitted to assist the birth mother with pregnancy-related medical and legal expenses. Living expense assistance is not permitted. The child may be released from the hospital upon his or her discharge directly to the adoptive parents, although each hospital has different policies. Some hospitals will accept a release form while others require a court order.

The birth mother may sign her consent any time after the birth. It may be witnessed by a person authorized to take acknowledgments, such as a notary public, or in some cases an adoption agency representative or representative of the Mayor of the District of Columbia. Absent proof of fraud or undue influence, the consent is generally considered irrevocable upon filing it with the court, assuming the child has been placed in the custody of the adoptive parents.

The District of Columbia does not have a putative birth father registry. Notice must be given, unless the birth father can't be located.

Agency Adoption.   All aspects of agency adoption are the same with the following exceptions. A pre-placement home study is required in an agency adoption. Living expenses can be paid for reasonable and necessary pregnancy-related expenses. A birth mother may sign her consent to the adoption, called a relinquishment in an agency adoption, any time following the birth. She must also have received counseling prior to the signing of the relinquishment. Once the relinquishment is signed, there is a 14-day period in which the birth mother may automatically withdraw her consent by written request. After the 14 days have elapsed, the relinquishment can only be withdrawn upon proving to a court that fraud or undue influence was used. Once the adoption is finalized the relinquishment is basically irrevocable.

Many adoption agencies within the District of Columbia do identified adoptions. Many will also agree to make "at risk" placements of the child with the adoptive parents directly from the hospital before relinquishments are irrevocable.

American Academy of Adoption Attorney members:

Maria T. Bates; 1050 Connecticut Ave. NW, Washington, DC
Tel: (202) 567-0077 ● familyplanninglaw.com ●
m.bates@adoptionattorneys.org

Susan L. Crockin; 2100 M. St. #107-356, Washington, DC 20037
Tel: (617) 332-7070 ● crockinlaw.com ● s.crockin@adoptionattorneys.org

Mark McDermott; 910 17th Street NW, #800, Washington, DC 20006
Tel: (202) 331-1440 ● mtm-law.com ● mcdermott@mtm-law.com
A graduate of the Indiana University School of Law, he has been practicing law since 1974. He estimates he has completed 1,700 adoptions in his career and completes 60 annually: 65% independent; 10% agency; 25% international. He does not assist in creating adoptive matches. He is an adoptive parent and a past-president of the American Academy of Adoption Attorneys.

Please be aware that many attorneys located in neighboring states, particularly Virginia and Maryland, also practice in the District of Columbia. You may wish to see more information about them in their state listings.

FLORIDA

Official State Adoption Website: http://www.adoptflorida.org/

State Adoption Exchange: Use above state website

State laws and procedures:

General Information. Florida permits both independent and agency adoption. Advertising is permitted but only by a Florida-licensed attorney or agency. To file a Petition for Adoption within Florida the adoptive parents must reside there or the child must be born there (making non-resident adoption possible). Normally, adoptions are finalized three to four months after the child's placement with the adoptive parents. The adoptive parents are required to appear in court for the final hearing in some regions, but many judges are willing to excuse their appearance in person and let them appear telephonically.

Independent Adoption. A pre-placement home study of the adoptive parents is required before a child may be placed in their home. The home study may be conducted by a licensed private adoption agency, licensed social worker or the state adoption office if no agency is available in that region. The cost varies.

The adoptive parents and birth mother are not required by law to meet in person and share identities, although most elect to do so. The adoptive parents are permitted to assist the birth mother with pregnancy-related (including living) expenses, although they may not continue beyond six weeks after the birth. Court approval is required for all expenses, but this is done at the conclusion of the adoption, except that prior court approval is required for disbursement of expenses exceeding the statutory cap of $5,000. The child may be released from the hospital directly to the adoptive parents, usually by means of a release form to the attorney who in turns places the child with the adoptive parents.

When the child being adopted is under the age of six months, the birth mother may sign her consent 48 hours after the birth or the day she is medically discharged from the hospital, whichever is sooner. It must be witnessed by two witnesses and a notary public. Most birth mothers sign their consents two days after birth. Once signed, the consent is irrevocable unless proven it was obtained by fraud or duress. However, if the child being adopted was over the age of six months at the time the birth mother signs her consent, there is a three-day revocation period.

Florida has a putative father registry, where any man may register a claim of paternity at any time prior to the date a petition for termination of parental rights is filed, and confirm his willingness and intent to support the child. For those wishing to assent to the adoption, any man can sign an Affidavit of Non-Paternity, either before or after the birth of the child, or sign a consent after the birth.

Agency Adoption. There is no difference regarding the process in which a birth mother signs her consent to adoption in an independent or agency adoption. The information provided above regarding independent adoption (e.g. when it can be signed, before whom, legal burden to seek to withdraw a signed consent) is identical regarding agency adoption.

Some agencies within Florida agree to do identified adoptions, as well as agree to make immediate hospital "at risk" placements.

American Academy of Adoption Attorney members:

Ginger S. Allen; 16831 N.E. 6th Ave. N. Miami Beach, FL 33162
Tel: (305) 653-2474 ● adoptionflorida.org ●
g.allen@adoptionattorneys.org
A graduate of St. Thomas University School of Law, she has been practicing law since 1995.

Christine E. Arendas; 1516 E. Colonial Dr. #202, Orlando, FL 32803
Tel: (407) 894-1525 ● asflf.com ● c.arendas@adoptionattorneys.org

Danelle Dykes Barksdale; 418 W. Platt Street, Tampa, FL 33606
Tel: (813) 258-3355 ● floridaadoptionattorney.com ●
d.barksdale@adoptionattorneys.org

Maria T. Bates; 970 Lake Carillon Dr. #300, St. Petersburg, FL 33716 ● Tel:
(727) 265-5438 ● familyplanninglaw.com ● m.bates@adoptionattorneys.org

Martha A. Curtis; 418 W. Platt St. Tampa, FL 33606
Tel: (813) 258-3355 ● floridaadoptionattorney.com ●
m.curtis@aaarta.org
A graduate of the University of Florida College of Law, she has been practicing
law since 1978 and handling adoption cases since 2001. She estimates she has
completed several hundred adoptions in her career and presently completes 30-
40 adoptions annually (independent, agency, interstate, Hague-accredited
agency intercountry, grandparent, relative, stepparent, finalization of foreign
adoptions, and recognition of finalized foreign adoptions). She also has handled
assisted reproductive technology cases since 2001 (including gestational
surrogacy, traditional surrogacy, preplanned adoption, egg donation, sperm
donation and embryo donation).
Cheryl Eisen-Yeary; 202 N. Swinton Ave., Delray Beach, FL 33444
Tel: (561) 789-0030 ● eisenlawoffice.com ●
c.yeary@adoptionattorneys.org

Madonna M. Finney; 2252 Killearn Center Blvd. #101, Tallahassee, FL
32309;
Tel: (850) 577-3077 ● madonnafinney.com ●
m.finney@adoptionattorneys.org
A graduate of the University of Florida School of Law, she has been practicing
law since 1988. She estimates she has completed 300 adoptions in her career and
completes 40 annually: 95% independent; 5% agency. She assists in creating
adoptive matches. She is vice-president of the Florida Adoption Council and is
a past president of the Florida Association of Adoption Lawyers.

Scott Hamilton; 2400 Manatee Ave. West, Bradenton, FL 34205
Tel: (941) 748-0550 ● phpchtd.com ● s.hamilton@adoptionattorneys.org

Robison R. Harrell; 3 Clifford Drive Shaliman, FL 32579
Tel: (850) 651-5225 ● adoptioncenter.org ● r.harrell@adoptionattorneys.org
A graduate of the Florida State University School of Law, he has been practicing
law since 1970.

Michelle Hausmann; 2423 Quantum Blvd, Boynton Beach, FL 33426
Tel: (561) 732-7030 ● hausmannandhickman.com ●
m.hausmann@adoptionattorneys.org
A graduate of the Nova University School of Law, she has been practicing law since 1990.

Amy U. Hickman; 2423 Quantum Blvd., Boynton Beach, FL 33426
Tel: (561) 732-7030 ● hausmannandhickman.com ●
a.hickman@adoptionattorneys.org
A graduate of the University of Florida School of Law, she has been practicing law since 1989.

Ellen M. Kaplan; 9900 West Sample Rd. 3rd Fl., Coral Springs, FL 33065
Tel: (954) 341-1309 ● ellenkaplanadoptions.com ●
e.kaplan@adoptionattorneys.org

Brian Kelly; 3821 Atlantic Bl, P.O. Box 10007, Jacksonville, FL 32247
Tel: (904) 348-6400 ● adoption-USA.com ●
b.kelly@adoptionattorneys.org
A graduate of the University of Florida School of Law, he has been practicing law since 1983.

Anthony Marchese; 308 E. Oak Ave., 2nd Fl., Tampa, FL 33602
Tel: (813) 229-5528 ● anthonymarchese.com ●
a.marchese@adoptionattorneys.org

Nicole Ward Moore; 1604 S. Bumby Avenue, Orlando, FL 32806
Tel: (407) 898-8015 ● floridaadoptionattorney.com ●
Nicole@jtatelaw.com
A graduate of the University of Florida Levin School of Law, she has been practicing law since 2005. She completes 40-50 adoptions annually. She handles agency adoptions, contested adoptions, stepparent adoptions, adult adoptions, and relative adoptions. (Offices also in Tampa, Merritt Island, and Naples.)

Mary Ann Scherer; 2001 E. Commercial Bl, Ft. Lauderdale, FL 33308
Tel: (954) 564-6900 ● adoptionflorida.com ●
m.scherer@adoptionattorneys.org

Elizabeth F. Schwartz; 3050 Biscayne Blvd. Suite 600, Miami, FL 33137

Tel: (305) 674-9222 ● elizabethschwartz.com● liz@elizabethschwartz.com
A graduate of University of Miami School of Law, she has been practicing law since 1997. She estimates she completes 60 adoptions annually: 70% independent and 30% agency. She assists in creating adoptive matches. She also handles second parent and stepparent adoptions as well as assisted reproduction matters.

Peggy Clarie Senentz; 1101 Pasadena Ave. South #3, South Pasadena, FL 33707 ● Tel: (727) 345-0041 ● myfladoptions.com ●
info@myflaadoptions.com
A graduate of Barry University School of Law, she has been practicing law since 2004. She assists in creating adoptive matches. She accepts contested adoption cases. She handles assisted reproductive technology matters. She is Florida Bar Board Certified in Adoption Law.

Michael A. Shorstein; 3821 Atlantic Blvd, P.O. Box 10007, Jacksonville, FL 32247 ● Tel: (904) 348-6400 ● adoption-usa.com ●
m.shorstein@adoptionattorneys.org
A graduate of Florida State University School of Law, he has been practicing law since 1986.

Susan L. Stockham; 4017 Swift Road, Sarasota, FL 34231
Tel: (941) 924-4949 ● stockhamlaw.com ● susan@stockhamlaw.com
A graduate of the University of Florida School of Law, she has been practicing law since 1981. She estimates she has completed over 2,000 adoptions in her career and completes 60 annually: 50% independent, 50% agency. She also handles second parent partner adoption, grandparent, stepparent, and foster care adoptions as well as assisted reproduction cases. She assists in creating adoptive matches. She is a past president of the Florida Adoption Council and an adoptive mom of four sons.

Jeanne Trudeau Tate; 418 W. Platt St. Tampa, FL 33606
Tel: (813) 258-3355 ● floridaadoptionattorney.com ●
j.tate@adoptionattorneys.org
A graduate of the University of Florida School of Law, she has been practicing law since 1982. She also has offices in Orlando, Naples and Merritt Island. She and her firm handle more than 200 adoptions annually. She is a board certified adoption attorney, specializes in contested, interstate, relative, military and special needs adoptions. Jeanne has been recognized by Congress as an Angel in Adoption

GEORGIA

Official State Adoption Website: http://dfcs.dhs.georgia.gov/adoption

State Adoption Exchange or Related Website:
http://itsmyturnnow.dhs.ga.gov/WebForms/MeetChildren.aspx

State laws and procedures:

General Information. Georgia permits both independent and agency adoption. Attorneys are not permitted to locate birth mothers for adoptive parents to start adoption planning for a fee. Advertising is not permitted, except by licensed adoption agencies. To file a Petition for Adoption in Georgia the adoptive parents must reside there for six months. Normally, adoptions are finalized within four months of the placement of the child and filing of the Petition for Adoption. The adoptive parents and the child are required to appear at the final court hearing.

Independent Adoption. A pre-placement home study of the adoptive parents is required of the adoptive parents before a child is placed in their home. The post-placement court report may be conducted by a licensed private adoption agency or other court appointed individual. The fee varies.

The adoptive parents and birth mother are not required by law to meet in person and share identities, although many do so voluntarily. The adoptive parents are permitted to assist the birth mother with medical and legal expenses only (but at the time of publication of this book a 2017 legislative bill was pending to permit living expenses). The child may be placed with the adoptive parents immediately upon discharge from the hospital, usually through the attorney by means of a "Third Party Discharge" form.

The birth mother may sign her consent (called a surrender) any time after the birth. It must be witnessed by a notary public and an additional witness. Most consents are signed within several days of the birth. There is a ten-day period after the signing of the consent in which the birth mother has the automatic right to withdraw her consent. After the ten-day period has expired the consent is irrevocable, except upon proof of fraud or duress.

Georgia has a putative birth father registry. A putative father must be given notice if his identity is known, or if he has filed with the registry. Upon notice, he has 30 days to file his objection (a Petition to Legitimate the Child) or his rights will be terminated.

Agency Adoption. There is no difference regarding the process in which a birth mother signs her surrender in an independent or agency adoption, although agencies must wait until at least 24 hours after birth and have an agency representative act as an additional witness.

Many agencies within Georgia agree to do identified adoptions. Many agencies agree to make immediate hospital "at risk" placements.

American Academy of Adoption Attorney members:

Lila Newberry Bradley; 60 Lenox Pointe, NE, Atlanta, GA 30324
Tel: (404) 442-6969 ● gababylaw.com ● lila@gababylaw.com
She handles assisted reproductive technology matters and accepts contested adoption cases.

Ruth F. Claiborne; 60 Lenox Pointe, NE, Atlanta, GA 30324
Tel: (404) 442-6969 ● gababylaw.com ●
r.claiborne@adoptionattorneys.org
A graduate of the University of California Hastings College of Law, she has been practicing law since 1976.

Rhonda L. Fishbein; One Glenlake Pkwy., #700, Atlanta, GA 30328
Tel: (770) 437-8582 ● rfishbeinadoption-law.com ●
r.fishbein@adoptionattorneys.org
A graduate of Benjamin N. Cardozo School of Law, she has been practicing law since 1982. She estimates she has completed approximately 2,500 adoptions in her career and completes 100 adoptions annually. She is an adoptive parent and the former founder and director of a licensed adoption agency.

Jessica Gordon; 2265 Roswell Rd. #100, Marietta, GA 30062
Tel: (678) 304-8525 ● gordon.legal ● j.gordon@adoptionattorneys.org

Jerrold W. Hester; St. Simons Island Office, 507 Ocean Blvd. #304, St. Simmons Island, GA 31522
Tel: (770) 446-3645 ● hesteroutman.com ● j.hester@adoptionattorneys.org
A graduate of the University of Georgia School of Law, he has been practicing law since 1975. He has completed more than 2,000 adoptions in his career and completes about 60 annually. He was the recipient of the Congressional Angel in Adoption Award in 2002.

Sherriann H. Hicks; 368 South Perry St., Lawrenceville, GA 30046
Tel: (404) 786-7365 ● thehickslawgroup.com ● shhicks@bellsouth.net
A graduate of the University of Memphis School of Law, she has been practicing law since 1995. She is a past president of the Georgia Council of Adoption Lawyers and a former president of the Gwinnett County Bar Association.

Richard Horder; 1230 Peachtree St. NE #3600, Atlanta, GA 30309
Tel: (404) 812-0843 ● r.horder@adoptionattorneys.org
A graduate of the University of Florida School of Law, he has been practicing law since 1971. He is an adoptive parent.

Barbara E. Katz; 3128 Clairmont Rd. NE, Atlanta, GA 30329
Tel: (404) 298-5050 ● bekatzlaw.com ● barbara@bekatzlaw.com
A graduate of the City University of New York School of Law, she has been practicing law since 1992. She handles ICPC, relative, stepparent, independent and agency adoptions for traditional and alternative families, including single parents and same sex couples. She also handles all matters involving assisted reproductive technology law. She does not assist in creating adoptive matches. She is a member of the Georgia Council of Adoption Lawyers.

Sherry V. Neal; P.O. Box 5207, Atlanta, GA 31107
Tel: (678) 596-3207 ● nealandwright.com ● sherry@nealandwright.com
A graduate of the University of Georgia School of Law, she has been practicing law since 1999. She is the founder and a past president of the Georgia Council of Adoption Lawyers. She handles ICPC, relative, stepparent, independent and agency adoptions. She does not assist in creating adoptive matches.

James B. Outman; P.O. Box 942075, Atlanta, GA 31141
Tel: (404) 317-3044 ● hesteroutman.com ● j.outman@adoptionattorneys.org
A graduate of the Georgetown University School of Law, he has been practicing law since 1971.

Josie Redwine; 2440 Sandy Plains Rd. #7, Marietta, GA 30066
Tel: (770) 579-6070 ● redwineadoption.com ●
j.redwine@adoptionattorneys.org
A graduate of the Georgia State University School of Law, she has been practicing law since 1996.

Irene Steffas; 4343 Shallowford Rd, Bldg. H #1, Marietta, GA 30062
Tel: (770) 642-6075 ● hagueadoptions.com ● isteffas@steffaslaw.com
A graduate of South Texas College of Law, she has been practicing law since 1984. She represents clients in complex intercountry adoptions, estimating that she completes approximately 30 adoptions annually, including Hague and non-Hague (orphan) intercountry adoptions, as well as independent and agency. She is an accredited Approved Person for intercountry adoptions. She is an adoptive parent and was a recipient of the 2007 Angel in Adoption Award from the Congressional Coalition on Adoption.

Lori M. Surmay; P.O. Box 98403, Atlanta, GA 30359
Tel: (678) 883-8893 ● atlbabylaw.com ● lori@atlbabylaw.com
A graduate of the University of Georgia School of Law, she has been practicing law since 1992. She handles all types of adoptions, including both independent and agency placements and ICPC cases. She assists in creating adoptive matches. Around 50% of her practice involves assisted reproductive technology matters. She received the Congressional Angel in Adoption award in 2007.

William E. Turnipseed; 233 Peachtree St., 2700 Harris Tower, Atlanta, GA 30303 ● Tel: (404) 614-3511 ● savellwilliams.com ● w.turnipseed@adoptionattorneys.org
A graduate of the University of South Carolina Law School in 1974, he has been handling adoption cases for more than 30 years. He completes 10-20 adoptions annually. He is a member of the Georgia Council of Adoption Lawyers.

HAWAII

Official Adoption Website: http://humanservices.hawaii.gov/ssd/home/child-welfare-services/foster-and-adoptive-care/

State Adoption Exchange: Use above state website

State laws and procedures:

General Information. Hawaii permits both independent and agency adoption. Advertising is permitted by law, but most Hawaii newspapers refuse to accept advertising by adoptive parents. To file a Petition for Adoption in Hawaii either the adopting parents must reside there, or the child to be adopted must have been born there or reside there (making non-resident adoption possible). If it is an agency adoption the Petition for Adoption can additionally be filed in Hawaii if the agency having custody of the child is located there. Normally, adoptions are finalized two to six months after the placement of the child with the adoptive parents, but is sometimes longer. At least one of the adopting parents and the child are required to appear at the final hearing, but some judges waive the court appearance.

Independent Adoption. A pre-placement home study of the adoptive parents is not required before a child may be placed in their home, although some judges will require one (but one is always required for interstate adoptions). In fact, there is no statutory requirement for even a post-placement home study, although judges have discretion to require one and often do. If a home study is required, it may be conducted by any person or organization approved by the court, usually a licensed social worker. The fee for the home study is typically $2,000.

The birth mother and adoptive parents are not required by law to meet in person and share identities, although most elect to do so voluntarily. The adopting parents are permitted by law to assist with the birth mother's pregnancy-related medical, legal and living expenses. The child may be released from the hospital directly to the adoptive parents, usually by the birth mother signing a hospital form authorizing the release.

The birth mother may sign her consent to the adoption any time after the birth. It may be witnessed by a notary or a judge. Once the consent is signed and the child has been placed with the adoptive parents, the consent can only be withdrawn if the best interests of the child would be served by being removed from the adoptive parents. Once the adoption is finalized by the court, there is a one-year period where the adoption can be "set aside" and the consent revoked if fraud or duress is proved.

Hawaii does not have a birth father registry but does require notice to birth fathers. This notice to putative birth fathers is usually by personal notice or publication. If he has not objected at, or prior to, the noticed hearing to terminate his rights, his rights are terminated. If he elects to object, the court will consider the best interests of the child and rule accordingly.

Agency Adoption. There is no difference regarding the process in which a birth mother signs her consent to adoption in an independent or agency adoption. The information provided above regarding independent adoption consent (e.g. when it can be signed, before whom, legal burden to seek to withdraw a signed consent) is identical regarding agency adoption. However, in an agency adoption a pre-placement home study is required as well as two post-placement visits and a final report.

Many agencies in Hawaii agree to do identified adoptions, as well as make immediate "at risk" placements before consents are irrevocable.

American Academy of Adoption Attorney members:

Laurie A. Loomis; 1001 Bishop Street, #2850, Honolulu, HI 96813
Tel: (808) 524-5066 ● l.loomis@adoptionattorneys.org
A graduate of the Catholic University School of Law, she has been practicing law since 1985.

IDAHO

Official State Adoption Website:
http://healthandwelfare.idaho.gov/Children/AdoptionFosterCareHome/Adoptio n/tabid/1911/Default.aspx

State Adoption Exchange or Related Website:
http://www.icwrtc.org/PRIDE/pre-service-foster-and-adoptive-parent-training-pride

State laws and procedures:

General Information. Idaho permits both independent and agency adoption.

Advertising is not permitted. To file a Petition for Adoption in Idaho the adoptive parents must reside there, usually for a minimum of six months prior to filing the Petition for Adoption. Normally, independent adoptions are finalized approximately three months after the placement of the child with the adoptive parents, while agency adoptions take seven months. The adopting parents and the child are required to appear in court for the final hearing.

Independent Adoption. A pre-placement home study of the adopting parents is required before a child can be placed in their home. The home study is usually performed by a licensed private adoption agency or licensed social worker approved to perform home studies. The fee averages $600 to $1,200. No post-placement supervision is required in independent adoption.

The adoptive parents and birth mother are not required by law to meet in person and share identities, although it is often done voluntarily. The adopting parents are permitted to assist the birth mother with medical and legal expenses related to the pregnancy. Living expense assistance is permitted up to $500 without court approval, and up to $2,000 with court approval. Expenses in excess of $2,000 require showing the court that extraordinary circumstances exist. The child may be released to the adoptive parents directly from the hospital upon discharge, although the forms and procedures among hospitals varies. Some hospitals require the attorney to be present at the discharge.

The birth mother may sign her consent to the adoption any time after the birth, and it must be witnessed by a judge. Most judges will require at least 48 hours to pass after birth before the signing of the consent. The consent is irrevocable upon signing. Most consents are signed several days after the birth.

Idaho has a putative birth father registry. A putative birth father must file a paternity action and register that he has done so before termination proceedings are commenced or the natural mother has signed her consent, or he loses his opportunity to object.

Agency Adoption. There is no difference regarding the process in which a birth mother signs her consent to adoption in an independent or agency adoption. The information provided above regarding independent adoption (e.g. when it can be signed, before whom, legal burden to seek to withdraw a signed consent) is identical regarding agency adoption. Agencies, however, will require post-placement supervision while this is not required in independent adoption.

Most agencies within Idaho agree to do identified adoptions. Most agencies will also agree to make immediate hospital "at risk" placements.

American Academy of Adoption Attorney members:

Alfred E. Barrus; P.O. Box 487, Burley, ID 83318
Tel: (208) 678-1155 • a.barrus@adoptionattorneys.org
A graduate of the University of Idaho School of Law, he has been practicing law since 1974. He is an adoptive parent.

Bart D. Browning; 1419 W. Washington, Boise, ID 83702
Tel: (208) 429-0905 • maybrowning.com •
b.browning@adoptionattorneys.org
A graduate of BYU School of Law, he has been practicing law since 1985. He estimates he has completed more 1,000 adoptions in his career. He is an adoptive parent.

Wiley R. Dennert; 490 Memorial Dr., P.O. Box 51630, Idaho Falls, ID 83405
• Tel: (208) 522-3001 • nhptlaw.com • w.dennert@adoptionattorneys.org

David J. Hardy; 565 Terra Vista Dr., Rexburg, ID 83440
Tel: (801) 557-6412 • d.hardy@adoptionattorneys.org

Jeffrey T. Sheehan; 702 W. Idaho Street, Suite 1100, Boise, ID 83702 • Tel: (208) 287-4429 • idahofamilylaw.com •
j.sheehan@adoptionattorneys.org

ILLINOIS

Official State Adoption Website: www.illinois.gov/dcfs

State Adoption Exchange: Use above state website

State laws and procedures:

General Information. Illinois permits both independent and agency adoption. It is difficult to distinguish the percentage of independent and agency adoptions in Illinois as the vast majority of newborn adoptions are "identified" adoptions, where both attorneys and agencies have a united role. Advertising is permitted, but only by individuals (adoptive parents) from any state, and only by agencies and attorneys located in Illinois. Out-of-state agencies/attorneys/facilitators cannot advertise. To file a Petition for Adoption within Illinois the adopting parents must reside there, usually for a minimum of six months prior to the filing of the Petition for Adoption. If it is an agency adoption, the Petition for Adoption can additionally be filed within Illinois if the adoption agency having custody of the child is located there (making non-resident adoption possible). Illinois residents adopting from another state are required to have a pre-placement home study. Normally, adoptions are finalized six months after the placement of the child with the adoptive parents. The adoptive parents and the child are required to appear in court for one hearing, but counties differ on whether that appearance must be at an initial, or a final hearing.

Independent Adoption. A pre-placement home study of the adoptive parents is normally not required before a child may be placed in their home (unless it is an interstate adoption). The post-placement home study may be conducted by the state adoption office, county social services agency, a licensed private adoption agency or other court approved individual. The fee varies.

Attorneys cannot be paid for creating adoptive matches, meaning they can assist in birth mother matching, but not for compensation. The adoptive parents and the birth mother are not required by law to meet in person, although it is done voluntarily in most cases. The adopting parents are permitted to assist the birth mother with her pregnancy-related expenses, including living costs incurred 120 days before the due date and up to 60 days after the child's birth. Advance court approval is required if the total amount exceeds $1,000. The child may be placed directly with the adopting parents immediately upon hospital discharge, although a court order giving temporary legal custody to the adopting parents is sometimes required. Other hospitals may require a short-term guardianship appointment.

The birth mother may sign a traditional consent or designated consent to the adoption no sooner than 72 hours after the birth. It must be witnessed by a judge, licensed adoption agency, or other individual authorized by the court to act as a witness. Once signed, the consent is irrevocable. A designated consent (a consent naming specific adoptive parents), however, is voidable if the adoptive parents do not proceed to file a Petition for Adoption within 60 days or do not finalize the adoption.

Illinois has a putative birth father registry. Any putative birth father, either identified by the birth mother, or who has registered within 30 days after the birth, must be given notice. A putative father may sign his consent pre-birth, but it is revocable for 72 hours after birth. A putative or legal father may also sign a notarized waiver before or after birth if he denies paternity, or chooses to neither admit not deny paternity, and that waiver is normally irrevocable.

Agency Adoption. There are few differences regarding the process in which a birth mother signs her consent to adoption in an agency adoption. The information provided above regarding independent adoption is similar regarding agency adoption, except for the following. A pre-placement home study is required. An agency may pay for the birth mother's living expenses without advance court approval. Also, the birth mother may sign her consent to adoption, called a surrender, after a minimum of 72 hours have elapsed after the birth. It may be witnessed by a representative of the adoption agency and a notary public. Once signed, the surrender is irrevocable, except upon proof of fraud or duress. Also, the agency can facilitate a birth mother's living expenses without court approval.

Some agencies within Illinois agree to handle identified adoptions. Many agencies also agree to make "at risk" placements.

American Academy of Adoption Attorney members:

Shelley B. Ballard; 180 N. LaSalle St. #3700, Chicago, IL 60601
Tel: (312) 981-9272 ● sballardlaw.com ● sb@sballardlaw.com

A graduate of Northwestern University School of Law, she has been practicing law since 1987. She estimates she has completed over 3,000 adoptions in her career and completes 100-150 annually, including agency, private, foster care, relative, reproductive technology-related, adult and intercountry. She also accepts contested adoptions. She is a Guardian ad Litem for children in the Cook County Adoption court and is an Adjunct Professor at Loyola Law School teaching an Adoption Seminar. She occasionally assists in creating adoptive matches. She is an adoptive parent.

Kirsten Crouse Bays; 1513 University Dr., Charleston, IL 61920
Tel: (217) 345-6099 ● illinoisadoption.attorney ●
k.bays@adoptionattorneys.org
A graduate of the Washington University School of Law in St. Louis, she has been practicing law since 1994.

Ellyn J. Bullock; 100 N. Chestnut St. #230, Champaign, IL 61820
Tel: (217) 351-6156 ● solbergbullock.com ● e.bullock@adoptionattorneys.org
A graduate of the University of Illinois at Urbana-Champaign, she has been practicing law since 1994. She estimates she has completed approximately 2,000 adoptions in her career and completes 150 annually: 10% independent; 20% agency; 5% international; 50% special needs; 15% related. She assists in creating adoptive matches. She is an adoptive parent.

Deborah Crouse Cobb; 515 West Main St., Colinsville, IL 62234
Tel: (618) 344-6300 ● illinoisadoption.attorney ●
d.cobb@adoptionattorneys.org
A graduate of the Washington University School of Law in St. Louis, she has
been practicing law since 1984.

Nidhi Desai; 221 N. LaSalle St. #1136, Chicago, IL 60601
Tel: (312) 673-5312 ● familybuildinglaw.com ●
n.desai@adoptionattorneys.org

Genie Miller Gillespie; 105 W. Madison St. #1101, Chicago, IL 60602 ● Tel:
(312) 332-6339 ● illinoisadoptionlawyer.com ●
gmg@illinoisadoptionlawyer.com
A graduate of Columbus School of Law at the Catholic University of America,
she began practicing law in 1993. She estimates she has completed
approximately 2,000 adoptions in her career and presently completes 200
adoptions annually, including private, agency, interstate, relative/stepparent,
foster care, adult, intercountry and contested adoptions. She does not assist in
creating adoptive matches. She also handles assisted reproductive technology
matters. In 2016, she was named an Angel in Adoption by the Congressional
Coalition on Adoption Institute.

Michelle M. Hughes; 221 N. LaSalle St., #2020, Chicago, IL 60601
Tel: (312) 857-7287 ● m.hughes@adoptionattorney.org
A graduate of the University of Chicago School of Law, she has been practicing
law since 1989. She estimates she has completed more than 3,000 adoptions in
her career and completes 100 annually: 15% independent; 80% agency; 5%
international. She assists in creating adoptive matches. She is an adoptive parent
and adoption educator with an emphasis on transracial adoption.

Kimberly Kuhlengel-Jones; 1070 N. Mill St. P.O. Box 186, Nashville, IL
62263
Tel: (618) 327-3093 ● k.kuhlengel-jones@adoptionattorneys.org
A graduate of the Southern Illinois University School of Law at Carbondale, she
has been practicing law since 1995.

Sheila Maloney; 633 Rogers Street, #102, Downers Grove, IL 60515
Tel: (630) 512-8400 ● sheilamaloneylaw.com ●
s.maloney@adoptionattorneys.org

A graduate of the John Marshall School of Law, she has been practicing law since 1986. She estimates she has completed more than 3,500 adoptions in her career and completes 100 annually: 15% independent; 75% agency; 10% international. She does not assist with creating adoptive matches. She is an adoptive parent. Areas of practice include assisted reproduction, egg donation, contested adoptions, grandparent representation, interstate (ICPC) adoption, LGBT adoption, adoption mediation, and ICWA adoption.

Sean Martin McCumber; 1749 S. Naperville Rd. #106, Wheaton, IL 60189 ● Tel: (630) 665-7676 ● stglawfirm.com ● s.mccumber@adoptionattorneys.org
A graduate of the University of Illinois, he has been practicing since 1998. He estimates he completes approximately 40 adoptions annually: 80% private; 20% agency. He does not assist in creating adoptive matches. Areas of practice include assisted reproduction, egg donation, contested adoptions, grandparent representation, interstate (ICPC) adoption, LGBT adoption, adoption mediation, and ICWA adoption. He is an adoptive parent of three.

Kathleen Morrison; 70 W. Madison St. #1101, Chicago, IL 60602
Tel: (312) 977-4477 ● chicagoadoptionattorney.com ● k.morrison@adoptionattorneys.org
A graduate of the John Marshall School of Law, she has been practicing law since 1976. She estimates she has completed 7,500 adoptions in her career and completes 400 annually: 25% independent; 45% agency; 30% international. She does not assist in creating adoptive matches.

Robert R. Parker; 411 Hamilton Blvd. #1900, Peoria, IL 61602
Tel: (309) 673-0069 ● parkerandparkerattorneys.com ● rparker@mtco.com
A graduate of St. Louis University School of Law, he has been practicing since 2009. He estimates he completes approximately 80 adoptions annually: 35% independent and 65% agency. He does not assist in creating adoptive matches. He accepts and emphasizes contested adoption cases.

Denise J. Patton; 4760 Fairfax Avenue, Palatine, IL 60067
Tel: (847) 925-9072 ● growyourfamily.net ● d.patton@adoptionattorneys.org
A graduate of DePaul University College of Law, she has been practicing since 1996. She estimates she has completed close to 2,000 adoptions in her career and completes over 100 annually: 50% agency; 25% related; 5% independent; 20% international. She does not create adoptive matches. She is an adoptive parent. She is the 2016-17 Chair of the Chicago Bar Association's Adoption Law Committee.

Sally Wildman; 200 N. LaSalle St. #2750, Northbrook, IL 60601
Tel: (312) 726-9214 ● swildmanlaw.com ●
s.wildman@adoptionattorneys.org
A graduate of DePaul University School of Law, she has been practicing law
since 1985. Currently, Ms. Wildman represents adoptive parents in all types of
adoption. She has served as the chairperson for the American Bar Association
Adoption Committee.

INDIANA

Official State Adoption Website: http://www.in.gov/dcs/2730.htm

State Adoption Exchange: Use above state website

State laws and procedures:

General Information. Indiana permits both independent and agency adoption.
Advertising is permitted. To file a Petition for Adoption within Indiana the
adopting parents must reside within the state, except if the child is designated as
hard-to-place, then out-of-state residents may adopt in-state. Normally,
adoptions are finalized three months to one year after the placement of the child
with the adoptive parents. The adoptive parents are required to appear in court
for the final hearing.

Independent Adoption. A pre-placement home study of the adoptive parents is
required before a child can be placed in their home. The post-placement home
study may be done by the state adoption office or a licensed private adoption
agency. The fee varies.

    Adoptive parents and birth mothers are not required to meet in person and
share identifying information, although it is sometimes done voluntarily. The
adoptive parents are permitted to assist the birth mother with pregnancy-related
expenses, but the maximum total which can be paid is $3,000 whether the
adoption will occur in, or out of, Indiana. The child may be placed directly with
the adoptive parents from the hospital, although generally a court order is
required.

    The birth mother may sign her consent to the adoption any time after the
birth. It must be witnessed by a judge or a notary public. Most consents are
signed within several days of the birth. Once the consent is signed it may be

withdrawn with 30 days only by proving the child's best interests would be served by being removed from the adoptive parents, or that fraud or duress existed. However, if the birth mother elects to appear in court to confirm her consent, the consent becomes irrevocable immediately at the time of the court appearance. This appearance may usually be made by telephone.

Indiana has a putative birth father registry. Failure of a putative father to register during the pregnancy, or the latter of the filing of the Petition for Adoption or 30 days following the birth, constitutes an irrevocable implied consent to adoption, relieving any requirement to notice.

Agency Adoption. There is no difference regarding the process in which a birth mother signs her consent to adoption in an independent or agency adoption. The information provided above regarding independent adoption is identical regarding agency adoption.

Some agencies in Indiana agree to do identified adoptions. Some agencies will also agree to make immediate hospital "at risk" placements.

American Academy of Adoption Attorney members:

Allyson R. Breeden; 20 NW 1st St. 9th Fl, P.O. Box 916, Evansville, IN 47706
● Tel: (812) 424-7575 ● zsws.com ● abreeden@zsws.com
A graduate of the Indiana University McKinney School of Law, she has been practicing law since 2001. She estimates she has completed over 150 adoptions in her career and presently completes about 50 adoptions per year. Her adoption practice includes independent, agency, foster parent, stepparent, and grandparent adoptions. She assists in creating adoptive matches and will accept contested adoption cases and assisted reproductive technology matters.

Rebecca S. Bruce; 108 N. Liberty Street, Suite A, Muncie, IN 47305
Tel: (765) 286-1776 ● adoptindiana.org ●
r.bruce@adoptionattorneys.org
A graduate of the Indiana University School of Law, she has been practicing law since 1998. She completes 100 adoptions annually: 35% independent; 60% agency; 5% international. She assists in creating adoptive matches.

Donald W. Francis Jr.; 1505 W. Arlington Rd., Bloomington, IN 47404 ● Tel: (812) 336-8300 ● fbdlawfirm.com ● d.francis@adoptionattorneys.org

John Q. Herrin; 3815 River Crossing Pkwy. #100, Indianapolis, IN 46240 ●
Tel: (317) 566-2174 ● indianaadoptionlawyer.com ●
j.herrin@adoptionattorneys.org

Timothy J. Hubert; 20 NW First St., 9th floor; P.O. Box 916, Evansville, IN
47706 ● Tel: (812) 424-7575 ● zsws.com ● t.hubert@adoptionattorneys.org

Joel D. Kirsh; 2930 E. 96th Street, Indianapolis, IN 46240
Tel: (317) 575-5555 ● indianaadoption.com ● joel@kirsh.com
A graduate of the Indiana University School of Law at Indianapolis, he has been
practicing law since 1984. He estimates he has completed more than 3,500
newborn adoptions in his career and completes 75 annually: 95% independent;
5% agency. He additionally estimates he has completed more than 1,500
"relative" adoptions including step-parent, grandparent, adult and international
re-adoptions in his career. His practice is limited to adoptions and assisted
reproductive technology law. He practices with his brother, Steve Kirsh, and his
nephew, Grant Kirsh.

Steven M. Kirsh; 2930 E. 96th Street, Indianapolis, IN 46240
Tel: (317) 575-5555 ● indianaadoption.com ● steve@kirsh.com
A graduate of the Indiana University School of Law, he has been practicing law
since 1979. He estimates he has completed more than 3,500 newborn adoptions
in his career and completes 75 annually: 95% independent; 5% agency. He is a
past president of the American Academy of Adoption Attorneys and the 2005
recipient of the Congressional Angels in Adoption Award. He practices with his
brother, Joel Kirsh, and his son, Grant Kirsh. The Indiana General Assembly
issued a proclamation recognizing him for his efforts in bringing about changes
to Indiana's adoption laws.

Nathan A. Leach; 3815 River Crossing Pkwy. #100, Indianapolis, IN 46240 ●
Tel: (317) 566-2174 ● indianaadoptionlawyer.com ●
n.leach@adoptionattorneys.org

Keith M. Wallace; 401 SE 6th Street, Suite 202, Evansville, IN 47713
Tel: (812) 479-9900 ● ftia.org ● kwallace@ftia.org
A graduate of the Valparaiso University School of Law, he has been practicing
law since 1983.

IOWA

Official State Adoption Website:
http://dhs.iowa.gov/foster-care-and-adoption

State Adoption Exchange or Related Website: http://www.iakids.org

State laws and procedures:

General Information. Iowa permits both independent and agency adoption. Advertising is permitted. To file a Petition for Adoption within Iowa either the adoptive parents must reside there or the child is born and resides there (making non-resident adoption possible). Normally, adoptions are finalized seven months after the placement of the child with the adoptive parents. The adopting parents and the child are required to appear in court for the final hearing, although some courts may waive the requirement for out-of-state residents and allow them to appear with their attorney by telephone.

Independent Adoption. A pre-placement home study of the adoptive parents is required before a child can be placed in their home. The home study is performed by a certified adoption investigator (a person certified by the state to perform home studies) or a licensed adoption agency. The fee varies from approximately $1,500 to $4,000. The post-placement evaluation is $1,500-$3,500.

 The adoptive parents and birth mother are not required by law to meet in person and share identities, although in most cases it is done voluntarily. The adoptive parents are permitted to assist the birth mother with pregnancy-related medical, legal and living expenses, although if she is receiving welfare, she may be required to reimburse the welfare office the amount she received from the adoptive parents. The birth mother must also be offered three hours of counseling, although she may waive it. The baby may be placed directly with the adoptive parents from the hospital, although some hospitals require a court order. Occasionally a short-term foster home placement is made until the birth mother's consent is irrevocable.

 Normally, the juvenile court will appoint a custodian for the child, who will witness the birth mother signing her consent to adoption, called a Release of Custody. The birth mother cannot sign the Release of Custody until at least 72 hours after the birth. Once signed, there is a 96-hour period in which the birth mother has the automatic right to withdraw it. A termination of parental rights hearing is then scheduled after the expiration of the 96-hour period. After the 96-hour period, but before the termination of parental rights hearing, the birth mother can withdraw her consent if she can show good cause to do so, usually proof of fraud or duress. After the court order terminating parental rights, the consent is irrevocable.

Iowa has a putative birth father registry. A putative father may file a Declaration of Paternity with the Department of Vital Statistics. Those who do, or who can be identified by the birth mother as a possible birth father, are entitled to notice. The notice will be of a termination of parental rights hearing.

Agency Adoption. There is no difference regarding the process in which a birth mother signs her consent to adoption in an independent or agency adoption. The information provided above regarding independent adoption (e.g. when it can be signed, before whom, legal burden to seek to withdraw a signed relinquishment) is identical regarding agency adoption.

Some agencies within Iowa agree to do identified adoptions. Few agencies agree to make immediate hospital "at risk" placements.

American Academy of Adoption Attorney members:

Maxine M. Buckmeier; 600 Fourth St. #304: P.O. Box 634, Sioux City, IA 51102 ● Tel: (712) 233-3660 ● m.buckmeier@adoptionattorneys.org

David A. Grooters; 103 E. State St. #800, Mason City, IA 50401
Tel: (641) 423-4264 ● iowaadoptionattorney.com ●
d.grooters@adoptionattorneys.org

Lori L. Klockau; 402 S. Linn Street, Iowa City, IA 52240
Tel: (319) 338-7968 ● lklockau@bkfamilylaw.com
A graduate of the Iowa University School of Law, she has been practicing law since 1991. She has completed more than 1,000 adoptions in her career and presently completes 25 a year (independent, agency, intercountry, adult, stepparent). She assists in creating adoptive matches and accepts contested adoption cases, as well as handles assisted reproductive technology matters. She has served as the chairperson for Adoption Committee of the American Bar Association.

Kenneth Nelson; 3112 Brockway Rd., P.O. Box 1020, Waterloo, IA 50704 ●
Tel: (319) 291-6161 ● nlfiowa.com ●
k.nelson@adoptionattorneys.org

KANSAS

Official State Adoption Website:
http://www.dcf.ks.gov/services/PPS/Pages/AdoptionServices.aspx

State Adoption Exchange: Use above state website

State laws and procedures:

General Information. Kansas permits both independent and agency adoption. Advertising is permitted if done by a licensed adoption agency, although many newspapers will accept an advertisement from adoptive parents if accompanied by a letter from an attorney. To file a Petition for Adoption within Kansas either the adoptive parents must reside there or the child is born there and the birth mother resides there (making non-resident adoption possible). If it is an agency adoption the Petition for Adoption can also be filed there if the adoption agency having custody of the child is located there. Normally, independent adoptions are finalized three weeks to three months after the child's placement with the adoptive parents; one to three months for agency adoptions. The adopting parents are required to appear in court for the final hearing, but some judges will waive this requirement.

Independent Adoption. A pre-placement home study of the adoptive parents is required before a child can be placed in their home, although the court has discretion to waive this requirement. The home study may be conducted by a licensed clinical social worker or licensed private adoption agency. Most home study fees total approximately $1,000. In independent adoption there is no post-placement supervision required (except in interstate placements which require a post-placement report).

Adoptive parents and birth mothers are not required by law to meet in person and share identities, although it is sometimes done voluntarily. The adoptive parents are permitted to assist with pregnancy-related expenses, such as medical, legal and living costs. The child may be released from the hospital directly to the adoptive parents, but hospitals procedures vary. Many hospitals will require a power of attorney signed by the birth mother, or a court order granting the adoptive parents temporary custody.

The consent to adoption may be signed no sooner than 12 hours after the birth. It may be witnessed by a judge or a notary public. Most consents are signed from 12 hours to only several days after the birth. If the birth mother is under the age of 18 she must have her own attorney prior to signing the consent to adoption. Once signed, the consent is irrevocable, except by clear and convincing evidence it was not freely and voluntarily given.

Kansas does not have a putative birth father registry. Notice must be given to putative fathers, unless due diligence shows they can't be found. The time of notice before the hearing to terminate parental rights will vary, but is usually 10 to 30 days. If he objects, it must be shown he is unfit, abandoned the child, raped of the birth mother, or failed to support the birth mother during the last six months of the pregnancy.

Agency Adoption. There is no difference regarding the process in which a birth mother signs her consent to adoption in an independent or agency adoption, although agencies call the consent a *relinquishment.* The information provided above regarding independent adoption (e.g. when it can be signed, before whom, legal burden to seek to withdraw a signed consent) is identical regarding agency adoption. Unlike independent adoption, however, where there is no post-placement supervision required, most agencies will require at least one post-placement visit.

Some agencies within Kansas agree to do identified adoptions. Some agencies will agree to make immediate hospital "at risk" placements.

American Academy of Adoption Attorney members:

Martin W. Bauer; 100 N. Broadway #500, Wichita, KS 67202
Tel: (316) 265-9311 ● m.bauer@adoptionattorneys.org

Jill Bremyer; P.O. Box 443, McPherson, KS 67460
Tel: (620) 755-6904 ● kansasadoptionlaw.com ●
jill.bremyer@icloud.com
A graduate of the Washburn University School of Law, she has been practicing law since 1980. Her practice is dedicated to family formation law including adoption and artificial reproductive techniques.

Allan A. Hazlett; 1608 SW Mulvane St., Topeka, KS 66604
Tel: (785) 232-2011 ● unkanfam@aol.com ●
a.hazlett@adoptionattorneys.org
A graduate of the University of Kansas Law School, he has been practicing law since 1967. He is a past president of the American Academy of Adoption Attorneys. He completes between 30 and 50 adoptions each year, with approximately 75% independent adoptions and 25% with agencies. He assists in

creating adoptive matches and he accepts contested adoption cases. He is an adjunct at Washburn Law School in adoption law.

Kevin Kenney; 7301 Mission Road, #243, Prairie Village, KS 66208
Tel: (913) 671- 8008 ● kevinwkenney.com ●
k.kenney@adoptionattorneys.org

Richard A. Macias; 901 North Broadway, Wichita, KS 67214-3531
Tel: (316) 265-5245 ● r.macias@adoptionattorneys.org

Megan Monsour; 100 N. Broadway #500, Wichita, KS 67202
Tel: (316) 265-9311 ● martinpringle.com ●
m.monsour@adoptionattorneys.org

KENTUCKY

Official State Adoption Website: http://adopt.ky.gov/Pages/index.aspx

State Adoption Exchange or Related Website:
http://adopt.ky.gov/learnMore/Pages/snap.aspx

State laws and procedures:

General Information. Kentucky permits both independent and agency adoption. Advertising is not permitted. To file a Petition for Adoption within Kentucky the adopting parents must reside there. Normally, adoptions are finalized three to four months after the placement of the child. At least one of the adoptive parents is required to appear in court for the final hearing.

Independent Adoption. A pre-placement home study of the adoptive parents is required before a child can be placed in their home. The home study is conducted by either the state adoption office (Cabinet for Health and Family Services) or a licensed agency. The fee, in the form of a "filing fee," is $200 if done by the Cabinet. The Cabinet will not start the pre-placement home study until a specific child has been born, and will only conduct the home study if the adoptive parents' income does not exceed 200% of the poverty level. Those in excess of that amount, which will be most adoptive parents, must have their home study done by a private agency. Typical fees range from $1,700 - $2,500.

The adopting parents and the birth mother are not required to meet in person and share identities, although some do so voluntarily. The adoptive parents are permitted to assist the birth mother with pregnancy-related expenses, such as medical, legal and living costs, all of which must be approved by the Cabinet or the court. The child may be released directly from the hospital to the adoptive parents if they have a preapproved home study from a Kentucky licensed adoption agency and/or a temporary custody order from the court. Each hospital has different forms and procedures regarding the child's release and some will not release the child to the adoptive parents if they reside out of state and are planning an interstate adoption absent a court order.

The birth mother may assent to the adoption in one of two ways, either by signing a *Voluntary and Informed Consent*, or by filing a voluntary *Petition to Terminate Parental Rights* with the court. The former is less complicated, although it does not become irrevocable until 20 days after state approval of the adoption placement. The latter option is more secure, as it is irrevocable upon the judge signing the order terminating the birth mother's rights. If the birth mother is a minor, a guardian ad litem is appointed for her. Neither the *Voluntary and Informed Consent* nor the voluntary *Petition to Terminate Parental Rights* can be signed and filed until at least 72 hours after birth.

Depending upon the county, the hearing on the *Petition to Terminate Parental Rights* may be scheduled immediately after this 72-hour period or within 30 days, and if the birth mother appears with her attorney, and a guardian ad litem is appointed for the child, the court can often issue its order terminating her rights, if the adoption placement has been approved by the Cabinet for Health and Family Services.

Kentucky does not have a putative birth father registry. Notice is only given to a man married to the birth mother, named on the birth certificate, lived with her during the pregnancy, paid her medical bills, or was identified by her affidavit. Men in these categories will be given 20 days notice in which to file their objection. If he is not known or identified, he has 60 days in which to assert rights.

Agency Adoption. There is no difference regarding the process in which a birth mother indicates her consent to adoption in an independent or agency adoption, except that the simpler *Voluntary and Informed Consent* method (out of court) is unavailable in agency adoptions. Otherwise, the information provided above regarding independent adoption (e.g. when it can be signed, before whom, legal burden to seek to withdraw a signed consent, etc.) is identical regarding agency adoption.

Although adoption agencies in Kentucky sometimes arrange "open" adoptions, identified adoptions (where the adoptive parents and birth parents initially became acquainted outside the agency) are not permitted. Some agencies agree to make hospital "at risk" placements.

American Academy of Adoption Attorney members:

Carolyn S. Arnett; 2518 Frankfort Avenue, Louisville KY 40206
Tel: (502) 585-4368 ● carolynarnett.com ● ckarnett1@gmail.com
A graduate of the University of Louisville School of Law, she has been practicing law since 1984. She completes 50 adoptions annually, 100% of them independent. She assists in creating adoptive matches.

Mitchell A. Charney; 9301 Dayflower Street, Prospect, KY 40059
Tel: (502) 589-4440 ● m.charney@adoptionattorneys.org
A graduate of the University of Louisville School of Law, he has been practicing law since 1970. He estimates he has completed more than 500 adoptions in his career and completes 11 annually: 60% independent; 35% agency; 5% international. He assists in creating adoptive matches.

Jennifer R. Dusing; 6900 Houston Rd. #43, Florence, KY 41042
Tel: (859) 578-6600 ● rbcdlaw.com ● j.dusing@adoptionattorneys.org
A graduate of the University of Kentucky College of Law, she has been practicing law since 2005. She estimates she has handled close to 300 adoptions in her career and handles 25 annually. Her adoption practice includes experience with interstate compact placements, international adoption re-finalizations, relative adoptions, adoptions from foster care, private agency adoptions, and Kentucky independent adoptions. She is an adoptive parent.

Gregory K. Northcutt; P.O. Box 996, Calvert City, KY 42029
Tel: (270) 5714 ● g.northcutt@adoptionattorneys.org

Waverley Townes; 401 W. Main Street, #1900, Louisville, KY 40202
Tel: (502) 589-4404 ● mtlawky.com ● wtownes@mstwlegal.com
A graduate of the University of Kentucky School of Law, he has been practicing law since 1969. He has completed more than 1,100 adoptions in his career and completes approximately 40 annually: 35% independent and 65% agency. He accepts contested cases and assists in creating adoptive matches. He also handles assisted reproductive technology matters. In 2016 he received the Judge Richard A. Revell Family Practitioner of the Year Award.

LOUISIANA

Official State Adoption Website:
http://www.dss.state.la.us/index.cfm?md=pagebuilder&tmp=home&nid=185&
pnid=184&pid=375

State Adoption Exchange or Related Website:
http://www.adoptuskids.org/states/la/index.aspx

State laws and procedures:

General Information. Louisiana permits both independent and agency adoption. Advertising is permitted by licensed adoption agencies, social workers and attorneys (with bar approval). To file a Petition for Adoption within Louisiana the adoptive parents must reside there, or the birth parent relinquishing custody must be domiciled for at least eight months in Louisiana and surrender the child. Normally, independent adoptions are finalized shortly after the child has been in the adoptive home for 12 months; agency adoptions after six months in the home. The adoptive parents are required to appear in court for the final hearing.

Independent Adoption. A pre-placement home study of the adoptive parents is required before the child can be placed in their home, unless a court specifically approves a direct placement without a home study. Upon completion of a pre-placement home study, the adoptive parents receive a *Certification for Adoption.* The home study may be conducted by a licensed private adoption agency, licensed social worker, psychologist or psychiatrist. The individual or agency which conducts the home study also issues the *Certification for Adoption.* The cost of the pre- and post-placement home study services typically varies from $1,000 to $1,500.

The birth mother and adoptive parents are not required to meet in person. The adoptive parents are permitted to assist the birth mother with pregnancy-related medical, legal and living expenses. The child may be released directly from the hospital to the adoptive parents, but some will require releasing the child to the attorney handling the adoption. Hospitals vary widely on this policy.

The birth mother may sign her consent to adoption, called a *surrender*, no sooner than five days after the birth. She must have her own attorney to advise her. The surrender must be witnessed by a notary and two witnesses, as well as her attorney. If the birth mother is under the age of eighteen, she must also have her parent, or a guardian (called a *tutor*) sign the surrender as well. Once signed, the surrender is irrevocable, but for proof of fraud or duress.

Louisiana has a putative birth father registry. Notice must be given to any putative fathers who either list themselves with the registry, or who can be identified by the birth mother. If the birth mother signs a pre-birth *Notice of Intent to Surrender*, notice can be given to the putative father pre-birth, and if he does not object within 15 days from the date of notice (even if pre-birth) his consent to the adoption will not be required. Alternately, he can be given notice after birth, when the birth mother has signed her surrender, and he is given 15 days from the date of that notice to object.

Agency Adoption. There is no difference regarding the process in which a birth mother signs her consent to adoption in an independent or agency adoption, except that a birth mother need not have her own attorney, and instead the witnessing attorney can be the agency's attorney. The surrender can be signed as soon as three days after the birth of the child. The legal burden to seek to withdraw a surrender as provided above for independent adoption is identical regarding agency adoption.

Some agencies agree to do identified adoptions. Some agencies will also agree to make immediate hospital "at risk" placements.

American Academy of Adoption Attorney members:

Steven R. Baker; 401 Edwards St. #2010, Shreveport, LA 71101
Tel: (318) 588-8000 ● warrenbaker-law.com ● s.baker@adoptionattorneys.org

Suzanne Ecuyer Bayle; 1515 Poydras St. #1420, New Orleans, LA 70471 ●
Tel: (504) 524-3781 ● s.bayle@adoptionattorneys.org

Terri Hoover-Odom; 500 N. 7th Street, West Monroe, LA 71294;
Tel: (318) 387-8811 ● centerforadoption.com ●
t.odom@adoptionattoorneys.org
A graduate of the Loyola University School of Law at New Orleans, she has been practicing law since 1986.

Bernadette R. Lee; 1515 Poydras St. #1420, New Orleans, LA 70112 ● Tel: (504) 524-3781 ● b.lee@adoptionattorneys.org

Edith H. Morris; 1515 Poydras Street, #1870, New Orleans, LA 70112
Tel: (504) 524-3781 ● e.morris@adoptionattorneys.org
A graduate of Loyola University School of Law, she has been practicing law
since 1985.

Noel E. Vargas II; 146 N. Telemachus St. P.O. Box 792209, New Orleans, LA
70179 ● Tel: (504) 488-0200 ● nevjradoptlaw.com ●
n.vargas@adoptionattorneys.org
A graduate of the Loyola University School of Law, he began practicing in
1978. He estimates he completes 65 adoptions per year: 75% independent and
25% agency. He assists in creating adoptive matches. He handles all aspects of
adoption, including contested adoption.

Albert "Jay" F. Widmer Jr.; Two Lakeway Ctr., 3850 N. Causeway Blvd.
#630, Metairie, LA 70002 ● Tel: (504) 779-0022 ● afwidmerjr.com ●
a.widmer@adoptionattorneys.org

Jennifer Guillot Womble; 4828 Evangeline St., Metairie, LA 70001
Tel: (504) 231-4751 ● jenniferguillotwomble.com ●
j.womble@adoptionattorneys.org

MAINE

Official State Adoption Website:
http://www.maine.gov/dhhs/ocfs/cw/adoption/index.shtml

State Adoption Exchange or Related Website:
http://www.adoptuskids.org/?r=1

State laws and procedures:

General Information. Maine permits both independent and agency adoption.
Advertising is permitted by adoption agencies licensed in Maine. To file a
Petition for Adoption within Maine the adoptive parents, or the child to be
adopted, must reside there (making non-resident adoption possible). If it is an
agency adoption, the Petition for Adoption may also be filed in Maine if the
adoption agency having custody of the child is located there. Normally,
independent adoptions are finalized one to twelve months after the placement of
the child with the adoptive parents (varies greatly by county and if the birth father

was reachable to consent or if his rights must be terminated). Agency adoptions are typically finalized six-eight months after placement. The adoptive parents are required to appear in court for the final hearing, although some courts may waive this requirement and allow them to appear by phone.

Independent Adoption. A pre-placement home study of the adoptive parents is not required before a child can be placed in their home. The post-placement home study is performed by a licensed private adoption agency. The fee varies but is typically $2,000-7,000.

The birth parents and adoptive parents are not required to meet and share identities, although it is sometimes done voluntarily. Adoptive parents may assist the birth mother by paying pregnancy-related medical, legal and living expenses. The child can be released to the adoptive parents directly from the hospital, usually upon the birth mother's signature on a Power of Attorney and/or hospital release forms.

The consent to adoption may be signed any time after the birth. It must be witnessed by a probate judge and cannot be taken before the Petition for Adoption has been filed. The consent may be withdrawn only within three days of signing the consent. After the three-day period has elapsed, the consent can only be withdrawn upon proof of fraud or duress.

Maine does not have a putative birth father registry. Putative fathers must be given notice post-birth, then they have 20 days in which to file their objection/paternity action. If they can't be located, notice by publication is required, which then allows a 35-day period from the first day of publication.

Agency Adoption. There is little difference regarding the process in which a birth mother signs her consent to adoption in an independent or agency adoption, although the consent form employed by adoption agencies is called a *Surrender and Release*. Also, a pre-placement home study is required. The remaining information provided above regarding independent adoption (e.g. when the consent can be signed, before whom, legal burden to seek to withdraw a signed consent) is identical regarding agency adoption.

Some agencies within Maine do identified adoptions. Few agree to do immediate hospital "at risk" adoptions.

American Academy of Adoption Attorney members:

Christopher Berry; 28 State Street, Gorham, ME 04038
Tel: (207) 839-7004 ● cjberrylaw.com ● c.berry@adoptionattorneys.org
A graduate of William and Mary School of Law, he has been practicing law since 2004. He estimates he has completed over 1,000 adoptions in his career and presently completes about 150 annually: 67% state placements; 33% independent. He accepts contested adoption cases.

Abigail King Diggins; P.O. Box 7950, Portland, ME 04112
Tel: (207) 772-2800 ● leblancyoung.com ● a.diggins@adoptionattorneys.org

MARYLAND

Official State Adoption Website: http://dhr.maryland.gov/adoption/

State Adoption Exchange or Related Website:
http://www.adoptuskids.org/states/md/index.aspx

State laws and procedures:

General Information. Maryland allows both independent and agency adoption. Advertising is permitted. Intermediaries, other than licensed adoption agencies, are not permitted to receive compensation for locating a birth mother to create an adoptive match for adoptive parents. Adoptive parents can file their Petition for Adoption in Maryland if they reside there or if the baby was born there (making non-resident adoption possible). Adoptions are usually finalized 3 to 6 months after the filing of the Petition for Adoption. The adoptive parents and the child to be adopted are required to appear at the final court hearing, although a court may waive the requirement for good cause.

Independent Adoption. Adoptive parents are not required to have a pre-placement home study completed before a child is placed in their home if both adoptive and birth parents reside in the state. Maryland requires a temporary custody order to be issued in all independent adoptions. After the child's placement with the adoptive parents, the home study may be performed by a licensed adoption agency, court investigator, social worker or county social services department. The fee for the home study varies from free to approximately $2,300 based upon who performs the home study, and the county in which the adoptive parents live.

The birth parents and adoptive parents are not required to meet and share identities, but many elect to do so. Adoptive parents may assist the birth mother by paying her pregnancy-related medical and legal expenses, and living expenses is she obtains a letter from her doctor stating she is unable to support herself due to a pregnancy-related issue. The child may be placed with the adoptive parents directly from the hospital, but a court order granting the adoptive parents temporary legal custody is required.

The birth mother may sign her consent to the adoption any time after the birth. A witness is required, but the statutes do not appear to specify if it must be a judge, social worker, or similar person. Most consents are signed one to four days after the birth. The birth mother has the automatic right to withdraw the consent for a period of 30 days after signing. Once the 30-day period has passed her consent is irrevocable absent proof of fraud or.

Maryland does not have a putative birth father registry. Notice must be given and if he can't be found notice by publication is required. Putative father's rights are normally severed if they do not object within 30 days of notice.

Agency Adoption. There is no difference regarding the process in which a birth mother signs her consent to adoption in an independent or agency adoption except that a pre-placement home study is required, and that the child must be in the adoptive parents' care for six months prior to finalization. The other information provided above regarding independent adoption (e.g. when the consent can be signed, before whom, legal burden to seek to withdraw a signed consent) is identical regarding agency adoption. Some agencies agree to do identified adoptions. Some agencies also agree to do immediate hospital "at risk" placements.

American Academy of Adoption Attorney members:

Jeffrey E. Badger; P.O. Box 259, Salisbury, MD 21803
Tel: (410) 749-2356 ● longbadger.com ● j.badger@adoptionattorneys.org
A graduate of the Washington & Lee University School of Law, he has been practicing law since 1980. He has represented adoptive parents and birth parents in approximately 750 adoptions. He is an adoptive parent.

Jennifer Fairfax; 827 Woodside Parkway, Silver Spring, MD 20910
Tel: (301) 221-9651 ● jenniferfairfax.com ●
j.fairfax@adoptionattorneys.org

A graduate of University of Baltimore, she has been practicing law since 1996. She estimates she completes 75 adoptions annually: 75% private, 20% agency, 5% international. She does not assist in creating adoptive matches. She has been the past Vice President of the American Academy of Adoption Attorneys. She is also licensed in Virginia and the District of Columbia.

John R. Greene; 802 Landmark Dr. #111, Glen Burnie, MD 21061
Tel: (410) 878-7230 ● familiesthruadoption.com ●
j.greene@adoptionattorneys.org
A graduate of the New York University School of Law, he has been practicing law since 1976. He estimates he has completed 600 adoptions in his career and completes 75 annually: 50% independent; 30% agency; 20% international. He assists in creating adoptive matches.

Sherry L. Leichman; 51 Monroe Street, #1901, Rockville, MD 20850 ● Tel: (301) 545-1840 leichmansnyderlaw.com ●
s.leichman@adoptionlawyer.org

Harvey Schweitzer; 4520 East-West Hwy, #700, Bethesda, MD 20814 ● Tel: (301) 469-3382 ● schweitzerlaw.net ● lawharvey@gmail.com
A graduate of UCLA school of law, he practices in both Maryland and the District of Columbia. He handles many areas of adoption matters, including foster parent adoptions and post-adoption contact issues.

Margaret "Peggy" Swain; P.O. Box 219, Riderwood, MD 21139; 301 W. Pennsylvania Ave., Towson, MD 21204
Tel: (443) 857-3350 ● m.swain@adoptionattorneys.org
A graduate of the University of Baltimore School of Law, she has been practicing law since 1987. She estimates she has completed approximately 400 adoptions in her. She is a Trustee of the American Academy of Adoption Attorneys. She independently represents birth parents as well as adoptive parents. She does not create adoptive matches.

Peter J. Wiernicki; 11140 Rockville Pike, #620, Rockville, MD 20852 ● Tel: (301) 230-2446 ● p.wiernicki@adoptionattorneys.org
A graduate of the University of Baltimore School of Law, he has been practicing law since 1986. He is also licensed to practice law in Virginia and the District of Columbia.

Please be aware that some attorneys located in neighboring states, particularly Virginia and the District of Columbia, also practice in Maryland. You may wish to see more information about them in the Maryland state listings.

MASSACHUSETTS

Official State Adoption Website:
http://www.mass.gov/eohhs/gov/departments/dcf/adoption/

State Adoption Exchange or Related Website:
http://www.mareinc.org/index.html

State laws and procedures:

General Information. Massachusetts permits only agency adoption, unless the child is a blood relative. Accordingly, most all of Massachusetts' infant adoptions are completed via agency adoption. Advertising is permitted only by licensed adoption agencies. To file a Petition for Adoption within Massachusetts either the adoptive parents, or the child, must reside there (making non-resident adoption possible). Massachusetts law enforces open adoption agreements. Normally, adoptions are finalized seven to twelve months after the placement of the child with the adoptive parents. The adoptive parents and the child are required to appear in court for the final hearing.

A pre-placement home study of the adoptive parents is required before a child can be placed in their home. The home study must be performed by a licensed adoption agency. The fee varies among private agencies for pre- and post-placement home study services from $2,500 to over $12,000, depending upon the services rendered.

It is not required that the birth mother and adoptive parents meet in person and share identities, although it is done voluntarily in many cases. Many agencies do identified adoptions, where meetings between the parties occur and identities are usually shared. The adoptive parents are permitted to assist with pregnancy-related medical, legal and living expenses. The child may be released directly from the hospital to the adoptive placement as an "at risk" placement if the agency authorizes the release.

The consent to adoption, called a *surrender*, may be signed no sooner than the fourth day after birth. It must be witnessed by a notary and two witnesses. The surrender is irrevocable upon signing, but for proof of fraud and duress.

Massachusetts has a putative birth father registry, but it seems to be deemed ineffective by the courts, at least in its present form. Accordingly, all putative fathers are given notice, or if they can't be found then give notice by publication, of an action to terminate their rights. The birth father must file an objection in court prior to a specified date in the notice, usually approximately two months later. At that hearing the child's best interests and the birth father's fitness will be considered.

American Academy of Adoption Attorney members:

Herbert D. Friedman; 92 State Street, 7th floor, Boston, MA 02109
Tel: (617) 723-7700 ● massadopt.com ●
h.friedman@adoptionattorneys.org

Karen K. Greenberg; 195 Worcester Street, Wellesley Hills, MA 02481 ● Tel: (781) 237-0033 ● kongreen.com ● kkg@kongreen.com
A graduate of the Suffolk University School of Law, she has been practicing law since 1983. She does not assist in creating adoptive matches because Massachusetts' only allows licensed agencies to place. She currently concentrates on contested/problematic adoptions, including contested guardianship matters, appeals and problematic assisted reproduction situations. She is an adoptive parent, past president of the American Academy of Adoption Attorneys, and was awarded the Congressional Angel in Adoption award in 2008. She has published several articles and wrote Gestational and Surrogacy Agreements for the, *LexisNexis Practice Guide* (2016), *Inside the Minds of Lawyers, Navigating Adoption and Surrogacy Laws* (Aspatore Books, 2014).

Jeffrey M. Kaye; 302 Broadway, Methuen, MA 01844
Tel: (978) 682-4413 ● j.kaye@adoptionattorneys.org

Lisa J. Marino; 288 Walnut St., Newton, MA 02460
Tel: (617) 964-8090 ● wmblawfirm.com ● marino@wmblawfirm.com
A graduate of Suffolk University Law School, she has been practicing law since 1991. She specializes in family law, including adoption and assisted reproductive technology (ART) law. She is a fellow of the American Academy of Assisted Reproductive Technology Attorneys (AAARTA), and was awarded the Congressional Angel in Adoption in 2016. She is an adoptive mother to two daughters.

MICHIGAN

Official State Adoption Website: http://www.michigan.gov/dhs/0,1607,7-124-5452_7116---,00.html

State Adoption Exchange or Related Website: http://www.mare.org

State laws and procedures:

General Information. Michigan permits both independent and agency adoptions. Advertising is permitted by adoptive parents, but not necessarily by third parties. To file a Petition for Adoption in Michigan, either the adoptive parents or one of the birth parents must reside there, or the child to be adopted must be physically present there (making non-resident adoptions possible). Normally, adoptions are finalized about six months after placement with the adoptive parents for children one year and over; for children under one year, three to four months after placement.

Independent Adoption. A pre-placement home study of the adoptive parents is required before a child can be placed in their home. The home study must be performed by a licensed child-placing agency. The fee usually ranges from $2,000 to $3,500. Post-placement supervision agency fees are typically $300 per report. Only one such visit and report is usually required if the child is under one year of age.

It is not required by law for the birth mother and adoptive parents to meet in person and share identities, but it is usually done. The adoptive parents are permitted to assist the birth mother with medical and living expenses if of a reasonable amount and supported by receipts. Living costs assistance can only start upon commencement of the adoption plan and continue for six weeks after birth. The child may be released directly to the adoptive parents from the hospital with the birth mother's signature on a special *Temporary Placement* form.

The consent to adoption can be signed in two ways: in court or out of court. If in court, it is usually scheduled anywhere from three days to three months later, depending upon the county. It is witnessed by the judge and the birth mother usually has her own attorney but she can waive having one. The consent is irrevocable upon signing. If the consent is taken out of court, it can't be signed until 72 hours have elapsed after birth. It must be witnessed by the birth mother's attorney and a social worker or employee from a child-placing adoption agency. When signed out of court, the birth mother has five business days in which to seek to withdraw the consent, but this is only granted if proven the withdrawal would serve the best interests of the child.

Michigan has something similar to a putative birth father registry, where putative fathers can file a *Notice of Intent to Claim Paternity,* giving him the right to notice. Notice must also be given to any putative fathers if known to the birth mother. If a putative birth father elects to object and seek custody in court, the court will examine if he attempted to assume parental responsibilities as a threshold inquiry, and then consider the best interests of the child in determining whether to terminate parental rights.

Agency Adoption. There is no difference regarding the process in which a birth mother signs her consent to adoption in an independent or agency adoption, with the exception that in most cases in an agency adoption the birth mother relinquishes her child directly to the agency, rather than making a direct placement to the adoptive parents. Either form of consent is irrevocable upon signing in court.

Most agencies in Michigan agree to do identified adoptions. Many will do immediate "at risk" placements with the adoptive parents before the irrevocable consents are taken if the adoptive parents are properly licensed.

American Academy of Adoption Attorney members:

Kenneth A. Rathert; 137 N. Park St., Kalamazoo, MI 49007
Tel: (269) 349-6808 ● rathertlaw.com ● k.rathert@adoptionattorneys.org
A graduate of the Valparaiso University School of Law, he has been practicing law since 1976. He estimates he has completed over 1,000 adoptions in his career. He does not assist in creating adoptive matches. He accepts contested cases. He is a member of the Adoption Subcommittee to the Michigan State Bar.

MINNESOTA

Official State Adoption Website: http://mn.gov/dhs/people-we-serve/children-and-families/services/adoption/index.jsp

State Adoption Exchange or Related Website: https://www.mnadopt.org/

State laws and procedures:

General Information. Minnesota permits both independent (technically called "direct placement" in Minnesota) and agency adoption. Advertising is permitted. Attorneys are not permitted to locate birth mothers for adoptive parents. To file a Petition for Adoption within Minnesota the adoptive parents must reside there for a minimum of one year, although a court may waive this requirement. Normally, adoptions are completed no sooner than three months after the child's placement with the adoptive parents. The adoptive parents and the child are required to appear in court for the final hearing.

Independent ("direct placement") Adoption. A pre-placement home study of the adoptive parents is required before a child can be placed in their home, although in emergency situations exceptions may be permitted. The home study must be conducted by a licensed private adoption agency. The fee for pre- and post-placement services varies but is usually $2,200 to $7,500.

It is not required for the adoptive parents and birth mother to meet in person and share identities, although most elect to do so voluntarily. The adoptive parents are permitted to assist with the birth mother's pregnancy-related expenses. The child may be released directly from the hospital to the adoptive parents. Normally, however, the child's release must be by court order, through an adoption agency, or the birth mother must be discharged with the child then personally place the child with the adoptive parents outside the hospital.

The consent may be signed no sooner than 72 hours after the birth. It may be witnessed by a judge or a licensed adoption agency if that agency provided counseling services to her. If the birth mother did not receive counseling, her consent must be witnessed by a judge. Birth mothers must be offered an independent attorney at the adoptive parents' expense. If the birth mother is a minor, her legal custodian must (usually this is one of her parents) also sign a consent, and if her legal custodian refuses, a guardian ad litem can be appointed to do so. Most consents are signed within one to two weeks after the birth. Once the consent is signed, the birth mother has the automatic right to withdraw the consent for a period of ten business days. Once the ten days have elapsed, the consent may only be withdrawn upon proof of fraud.

Minnesota has a putative birth father registry. A putative birth father can file anytime up to 30 days after birth. If he fails to register, he is not entitled to notice. If he does register, he must be given notice of his right to initiate a paternity action within 30 days of receiving the notice and he must file a statement of intent to retain parental rights with the court. If he does not do so, he has waived his right to object, unless he can show good cause for his failure to do so.

Agency Adoption. There is no difference regarding the process in which a birth mother signs her consent to adoption in an independent or agency adoption (e.g. when the consent can be signed, before whom, legal burden to seek to withdraw a signed consent) is identical regarding agency adoption, except there is no right to her own attorney at the adoptive parents' expense.

Some agencies in Minnesota agree to do identified adoptions, as well as make "at risk" placements before consents are irrevocable.

American Academy of Adoption Attorney members:

Gary A. Debele; 121 S. 8th Street, #1100, Minneapolis, MN 55402
Tel: (612) 335-4288 ● innovativefamilylaw.com ●
g.debele@innovativefamilylaw.com
A graduate of the University of Minnesota School of Law, he has been practicing law since 1987. He estimates he has completed 400 adoptions in his career and completes 35 annually: 85% independent; 10% agency; 5% international. He does not assist in creating adoptive matches. He is an adoptive parent.

Jody O. DeSmidt; 121 S. 8th Street, #1100, Minneapolis, MN 55402
Tel: (612) 335-4284 ● innovativefamilylaw.com ●
j.desmidt@innovativefamilylaw.com
A graduate of the William Mitchell College of Law, she has been practicing law since 1982. She estimates she has completed over 900 adoptions in her career and completes 20 annually: 75% independent; 20% agency; 5% international. She does not assist in creating adoptive matches. She accepts contested adoption cases. Her practice includes assisted reproductive technology law.

Stacia W. Driver; P.O. Box 80846, Minneapolis, MN 55408
Tel: (612) 335-4295 ● wbdlaw.com ● s.driver@adoptionattorneys.org

Mark D. Fiddler; 6800 France Ave. S. #190, Minneapolis, MN 55435 ● Tel:
(612) 822-4095 ● fiddler-law.com ● m.fiddler@adoptionattorneys.org

Jessica J. W. Maher; 121 S. 8th St, #1100, Minneapolis, MN 55402
Tel: (612) 335-4291 ● j.maher@adoptionattorneys.org

Brittany Shively; 111 3rd Ave. S. #360, Minneapolis, MN 55401
Tel: (612) 332-7772 ● adoptionlaw-mn.com ●
b.shively@adoptionattorneys.org

Judith Vincent; 111 3rd Ave. S. #360, Minneapolis, MN 55401
Tel: (612) 332-7772 ● adoptionlaw-mn.com ●
j.vincent@adoptionlaw-mn.com
A graduate of the University of Minnesota School of Law, she has been
practicing law since 1978. She estimates she has completed more than 2,500
adoptions in her career and completes 60-90 annually: 85% independent; 10%
agency; 5% other. She does not assist in creating adoptive matches. She is an
adoptive parent.

Wright S. Walling; P.O. Box 80846, Minneapolis, MN 55408
Tel: (612) 340-1150 ● wbdlaw.com ● w.walling@adoptionattorneys.org

MISSISSIPPI

Official State Adoption Website:
http://www.mdhs.state.ms.us/fcs_adoptall.htmlexternal link

State Adoption Exchange or Related Website: http://www.mdhs.state.ms.us/

State laws and procedures:

General Information. Mississippi permits both independent and agency
adoption. Advertising is permitted. To file a Petition for Adoption in Mississippi
either the adoptive parents must be residents or the adoption agency having
custody of the child must be located there (making non-resident adoption
possible in some agency adoptions). Normally, adoptions are finalized

approximately three-six months after the placement of the child with the adoptive parents. The adoptive parents and the child to be adopted are normally required to appear in court for the final hearing.

Independent Adoption. A pre-placement home study of the adoptive parents is required before a child is placed in their home. The home study must be done by a licensed social worker working for an adoption agency.

It is not required by law that the adoptive parents and birth mother meet in person and share identities, although many do so voluntarily. The adoptive parents are permitted by law to assist the birth mother with pregnancy-related medical, legal and living expenses. The child may be released directly to the adoptive parents from the hospital, usually through an attorney.

The consent to adoption cannot be signed sooner than 72 hours after the birth. A judge must validate the signed consent and this is usually done within days of the consent being signed by the birth mother. There are no state statutory laws governing the possible withdrawal of a consent to adoption, but case law indicates that once the consent is signed it is irrevocable, except for proof of fraud or duress. The state statute also does not mention who, if anyone, must act as a witness to the signing of the consent. As a practical matter, however, all consents are normally witnessed by a notary public.

Mississippi does not have a putative birth father registry. Putative birth fathers are given personal notice, or by publication if they can't be located, of the action to terminate their parental rights. The putative father's identity is unknown, the court determines what, if any, notice is required.

Agency Adoption. There is no difference regarding the process in which a birth mother signs her consent to adoption in an independent or agency adoption, except that both a pre- and post-placement home study are routinely done, usually at a cost of about $1,500-2,500. The other information provided above regarding independent adoption (e.g. when the consent can be signed, before whom, legal burden to seek to withdraw a signed consent) is identical regarding agency adoption.

Some agencies in the state agree to do identified adoptions, as well as make immediate "at risk" placements before consents are signed.

American Academy of Adoption Attorney members:

Wes Daughdrill; 141 Township Ave. #300, P.O. Box 6005, Ridgeland, MS 39158 ● Tel: (601) 360-9030 ● youngwells.com ● w.daughdrill@adoptionattorneys.org
A graduate of the University of Mississippi School of Law, he has been practicing law since 1993.

Dan J. Davis; 352 N. Spring Street: P.O. Box 7262, Tupelo, MS 38802 ● Tel: (662) 841-1090 ● dandavisattorney.com ● d.davis@adoptionattorneys.org
A graduate of University of Iowa, he has been practicing law since 1989. He estimates he completes 50 adoptions annually: 60% independent; 30% agency; 10% international. He does not assist in creating adoptive matches.

MISSOURI

Official State Adoption Website: http://www.dss.mo.gov/cd/adopt.htm

State Adoption Exchange or Related Website:
http://www.adoptex.org/site/PageServer?pagename=locations_mo_programs

State laws and procedures:

General Information. Missouri permits both independent and agency adoption. Advertising is permitted. To file a Petition for Adoption within Missouri either the adoptive parents, the birth mother, or the child to be adopted, must reside there (making non-resident adoption possible). Normally, adoptions are finalized approximately six months after the placement of the child with the adoptive parents. The adoptive parents and the child are usually, but not always, required to appear in court for the final hearing.

Independent Adoption. A pre-placement home study of the adoptive parents is required before a child is placed in the adoptive home. It may be conducted by a licensed adoption agency or licensed social worker. The fees vary but typical pre- and post-placement home study fees total $1,000 to $5,000.

Adoptive parents and birth mothers are not required by law to meet in person or share identities, although it is done voluntarily in most cases. The adoptive parents are permitted to assist with pregnancy-related medical, living, counseling and legal expenses. The child may be released directly from the hospital to the adoptive parents, although hospital policies vary. Some hospitals accept a Power of Attorney form while others require a court order called an *Order of Transfer of Custody.*

The consent to adoption of the birth mother can be signed no sooner than 48 hours after the birth. It must be witnessed by a notary or two witnesses. Most consents are signed within several days of the birth. The consent is irrevocable upon signing. It may only be withdrawn upon proof of fraud, coercion or duress.

Missouri has a putative birth father registry. Putative birth fathers must register no later than 15 days after the birth. There is no independent requirement that birth mothers identify putative fathers. A birth father who fails to either register within 15 days, be acknowledged on the birth certificate, or file a paternity action, is typically found to have waived his right to withhold his consent to the adoption.

Agency Adoption. There is no difference regarding the process in which a birth mother signs her consent to adoption in an independent or agency adoption. The information provided above regarding independent adoption (e.g. when the consent can be signed, before whom, legal burden to seek to withdraw a signed consent) is identical regarding agency adoption.

Some agencies in Missouri agree to do identified adoptions. Some agencies also agree to make immediate hospital "at risk" placements with the adoptive parents before the consents are irrevocable.

American Academy of Adoption Attorney members:

Mary Beck; 2775 W. Shag Bark, Columbia, MO 65203
Tel: (573) 446-7554 ● marybecklaw.com ● mary@marybecklaw.com
A graduate of the Missouri University School of Law, she has been practicing law since 1988. She estimates she completes approximately 70 annually: 50% independent; 50% agency. She does not assist in creating adoptive matches. She is active in writing adoption legislation in Missouri, and other states.
Michael Belfonte; 1125 Grand Blvd., #1301, Kansas City, MO 64106 ● Tel: (816) 842-3580 ● michaelbelfonte.com ● m.belfonte@adoptionattorneys.org

Cindy A Bentch; 2775 W. Shag Bark Ct., Columbia, MO 65203
Tel: (573) 569-2344 ● marybecklaw.com ● cindy@marybecklaw.com
A graduate of the University of Virginia School of Law, she began practicing in 1994. She estimates she completes approximately 70 adoptions annually: 50% independent; 50% agency. She does not assist in creating adoptive matches. She is active in the Mennonite Tender Touch Prison Program assisting incarcerated

woman place their newborns pending prison release and/or for adoption and guardianship.

Daniel M. Buescher; 104 S. McKinley #B, Union, MO 63084
Tel: (636) 390-2202 ● abglawfirm.com ● d.buescher@adoptionattorneys.org
A graduate of Washington University, he has been practicing law since 1964. He estimates he completes 40 adoptions annually: 60% independent; 39% agency; 1% international. He assists in creating adoptive matches.

Jayne M. Glaser; 222 S. Central #708, Clayton, MO 63105
Tel: (314) 726-6242 ● keefebrodie.com ● j.glaser@adoptionattorneys.org

Sarah S. Johnston; 401 W 89th St., Kansas City, MO 64114
Tel: (816) 363-5466 ● wbbhj.com ● s.johnston@adoptionattorneys.org

Catherine W. Keefe; 222 S. Central Ave., #708, Clayton, MO 63105
Tel: (314) 726-6242 ● c.keefe@adoptionattorneys.org
A graduate of the St. Louis University School of Law, she has been practicing law since 1986. She estimates she has completed more than 500 adoptions in her career, and last year completed approximately 37 (15 independent; 12 agency; 10 intercountry). Approximately 30% of her practice consists of adoptions (typically 50% independent; 30% agency; 20% intercountry), and of these 75% are newborn placements, 25% are toddlers or above. She reports all of her clients locate their own birth mother.

Harold V. O'Rourke; 222 S. Central Ave., #202, Clayton, MO 63105
Tel: (314) 863-8484 ● lawsmo.com ● h.orourke@adoptionattorneys.org

Karen Rosenberg; 4520 Main St. #700, Kansas City, MO 64111
Tel: (816) 756-5800 ● krigelandkrigel.com ●
k.rosenberg@adoptionattorneys.org
A graduate of the University of Missouri-Columbia School of Law, she has been practicing since 1985. She is also licensed in Kansas.

Allan F. Stewart; 222 S. Central St. #202, St. Louis, MO 63105
Tel: (314) 863-8484 ● lawsmo.com ● a.stewart@adoptionattorneys.org
A graduate of the St. Louis University School of Law, he has been practicing law since 1973.

Kay A. Van Pelt; 1524 E. Primrose Suite A , Springfield, MO 65804

Tel: (417) 886-9080 ● www.vanpeltlaw.com ●
k.vanpelt@adoptionattorneys.org
A graduate of the University of Missouri at Columbia School of Law, she has
been practicing law since 1983.

Rachel J. White; P.O. Box 358, Rolla, MO 65402
Tel: (573) 426-3346 ● r.white@adoptionattorneys.org

Joanna Beck Wilkinson; 232 N. Kingshighway Blvd. #1109, St. Louis, MO
63108 ● Tel: (314) 962-0292 ● marybecklaw.com ●
joanna@marybecklaw.com
A graduate of the University of Minnesota School of Law, she began practicing
in 2008. She estimates she completes approximately 70 adoptions annually: 50%
independent, 50% agency. She does not assist in creating adoptive matches. She
specializes in technology in law office practice and assisted reproductive
technology law.

Elizabeth Karsian Wilson; 401 Locust St., #406, Columbia, MO 65205 ● Tel:
(573) 443-3134 ● www.owwlaw.com ● e.wilson@adoptionattorneys.org
A graduate of the University of Missouri School of Law at Columbia, she has
been practicing law since 1975.

Please be aware that many attorneys located in neighboring states, particularly
Kansas and Illinois, also practice in Missouri.

MONTANA

Official State Adoption Website:
http://www.dphhs.mt.gov/cfsd/adoption/adoptioninmontana.shtml

State Adoption Exchange: Use above state website.

State laws and procedures:

General Information. Montana permits both independent (called "direct
placement") and agency adoption. Advertising is not permitted. To file a Petition
for Adoption within Montana the adoptive parents must be residents of the state.
Normally, adoptions are finalized approximately six months after the child's

placement with the adoptive parents. The adoptive parents and the child are required to appear in court for the final hearing.

Independent Adoption. A pre-placement home study of the adoptive parents is required. The home study may be conducted by a licensed adoption agency or licensed social worker. The fee for the pre-and post-placement home study ranges from $1,000 - $2,000.

It is required by law that the adoptive parents and birth mother share identities, and virtually all elect to meet each other in person. The adoptive parents are allowed by law to assist the birth mother with pregnancy-related expenses, including living expenses. The child can be released to the adoptive parents directly from the hospital.

The consent, called a *relinquishment of parental rights and consent to adoption*, may be signed no sooner than 72 hours after the birth. It may be witnessed by a notary or representative of the court or a licensed adoption agency. It is later filed with the court and a request to a judge is made to enter an *Order Terminating Parental Rights*. Prior to the order being issued, the birth mother may seek to withdraw her consent only if she can prove fraud or duress in the signing of the consent. Once the order is issued the consent is irrevocable.

Montana has a putative birth father registry.

Agency Adoption. There is no difference regarding the process in which a birth mother signs her consent to adoption in an independent or agency adoption. The information provided above regarding independent adoption (e.g. when the consent can be signed and before whom) is identical regarding agency adoption.

Some agencies in Montana agree to do identified adoptions. Some agencies also agree to make immediate hospital "at risk" placements with the adoptive parents before the consents are irrevocable.

American Academy of Adoption Attorney members:

Dennis E. Lind; 201 W. Main Street #201, Missoula, MT 59802
Tel: (406) 728-0810 ● d.lind@adoptionattorneys.org

NEBRASKA

Official State Adoption Website:
http://dhhs.ne.gov/children_family_services/Pages/adoption.aspx

State Adoption Exchange or Related Website:
http://nfapa.org/welcome.html

State laws and procedures:

General Information. Nebraska permits both independent and agency adoption. Advertising is permitted. To file a Petition for Adoption within Nebraska the adoptive parents must reside there. Normally, adoptions are finalized approximately seven months after the child's placement with the adoptive parents. The adoptive parents and the child are required to appear in court for the final hearing.

Independent Adoption. A pre-placement home study of the adoptive parents is required before a child can be placed in their home. The home study may be performed by a licensed adoption agency or the Nebraska Department of Social Services (which serves only certain counties in an independent adoption). The agency fees for pre- and post-placement home study services usually range from $1,500 to 2,500.

It is not required by law for the birth mother and adoptive parents to meet in person or share identities, although some elect to do so voluntarily. There are no statutes governing permitted expenses, just case law. The normal practice is to allow adoptive parents to assist the birth mother with pregnancy-related medical and legal expenses. Living expenses are normally not permitted unless there is a significant safety issue for the birth mother and fetus (such as homelessness, or the inability to pay a heating bill in winter, et cetera), to eliminate any possible appearance of improper influence by the adoptive parents. The child may be released to the adoptive parents directly from the hospital, although many hospitals will only arrange the release through an attorney or agency.

Prior to signing a consent to adoption, the birth mother must have independent representation, and be offered three hours of counseling (although she can waive it), at the adoptive parents' expense. The consent can be signed no sooner than 48 hours after the birth. It must be witnessed by a notary and one witness. There are no state statutes governing the withdrawal of a consent to adoption, but case law indicates they are irrevocable, and can only be withdrawn by proof to the court fraud or duress was used, or the child's best interests would be served by being removed from the adoptive parents. Once the adoption is finalized the consent becomes irrevocable.

Nebraska has a putative birth father registry. The birth mother must sign an affidavit identifying all possible putative fathers, who must then be given notice by certified mail or personal service. If he can't be located, notice by publication can be used. He then has 5 business days from his receipt of notice, or the birth, whichever is later, to file an objection to adoption with the registry. If he does, he has an additional 30 days to file a paternity action. If he fails to do so his rights will no longer be recognized.

Nebraska has laws governing the enforceability of post-adoption contact agreements, should adoptive and birth parents elect to have one.

Agency Adoption. There is no difference regarding the process in which a birth mother signs her consent to adoption in an independent or agency adoption, with the exception that the consent is called a *relinquishment* and is irrevocable once it is signed and the agency has accepted it.

Some agencies in Nebraska agree to do identified adoptions. Some agencies also agree to make immediate hospital "at risk" placements with the adoptive parents before the consents are irrevocable.

American Academy of Adoption Attorney members:

Susan Kubert Sapp; 233 South 13th Street, #1900, Lincoln, NE 68508 ● Tel: (402) 474-6900 ● clinewilliams.com ● s.sapp@adoptionattorneys.org
Susan Sapp has completed hundreds of adoptions since 1989. She is a trial attorney and adoptions make up about 25% of her practice. She also has offices in Omaha and in western Nebraska (Scotts Bluff).

Kelly N. Tollefsen; 8540 Executive Woods Dr. #100, Lincoln, NE 68512 ● Tel: (402) 802-7514 ● kellytollefsenlaw.com ●
k.tollefsen@adoptionattorneys.org
A graduate of the University of Nebraska College of Law, she has been practicing law since 2000.

Please be aware that some attorneys located in neighboring states, particularly Iowa and South Dakota, also practice in Nebraska.

NEVADA

Official State Adoption Website:
http://dcfs.nv.gov/Programs/CWS/Adoption/

State Adoption Exchange or Related Website: http://www.adoptex.org

State laws and procedures:

General Information. Nevada permits both independent and agency adoption. Advertising is not permitted. To file a Petition for Adoption within Nevada the adopting parents must reside there, or the child must be born there (meaning non-resident adoption is permitted). The Petition for Adoption can be filed only after the child has been in the home for 30 days. Normally, adoptions are finalized approximately seven months after the child's placement with the adoptive parents. The adopting parents and the child are required to appear in court at the final hearing, except for non-residents, in which case the final appearance can usually be made telephonically.

Independent Adoption. A pre-placement home study of the adoptive parents is required before a child can be placed in their home. The home study must be conducted by a licensed adoption agency. The fee is usually about $2,500. Post-placement supervision by the agency is also about $2,500.

It is not required by law that adoptive parents and birth mothers meet in person, although it is usually done voluntarily. It is required that full identities be shared. The adoptive parents are permitted to assist the birth mother with pregnancy-related expenses. The child may be released directly from the hospital to the adoptive parents.

The consent to adoption can be signed no sooner than 72 hours after the birth. It must be witnessed by two witnesses, one of whom must be a social worker, and it must be notarized. The consent is irrevocable once signed, except upon proof of fraud or duress.

Nevada does not have a putative birth father registry. Putative fathers must be given notice of an action to terminate their parental rights. If he can't be found, notice by publication will be required, and twenty days thereafter the hearing can occur. The primary issues of interest to the court are the best interests of the child and a parenting fault (e.g. abandonment) in the determination to terminate a putative father's rights, usually based on abandonment. If a putative father wishes to assent to the adoption, he may sign a consent even prior to the birth.

Agency Adoption. There is no difference regarding the process in which a birth mother signs her consent to adoption in an independent or agency adoption. The information provided above regarding independent adoption (e.g. when it can be signed, before whom, legal burden to seek to withdraw a signed consent) is identical regarding agency adoption.

American Academy of Adoption Attorney members:

Virginia "Ginny" L. Frank; 200 Ridge Street, Suite 75, Reno, NV 89501
Tel: (303) 918-6707 ●virginialfrank.com ● v.frank@adoptionattorneys.org
A graduate of Oklahoma City University School of Law, she has been practicing law since 1992. She estimates she has completed 4,000 adoptions in her career and presently completes more than 200 annually, including independent, agency, interstate, and re-adoptions. She also handles assisted reproductive technology matters.

Heather E. Kemp; 7435 W. Azure Road, #110, Las Vegas, NV 89130 ● Tel: (702) 258-1183 ● kemp-attorneys.com ● heather@kemp-attorneys.com

Israel "Ishi" Kunin; 3551 E. Bonanza Rd., #110, Las Vegas, NV 89110 ● Tel: (702) 438-8060 ● kuninlawgroup.com ●
ishi@kuninlawgroup.com
A graduate of the Cal-Western School of Law, she has been practicing law since 1980. She estimates she has completed 500 adoptions in her career and completes 50 annually. She does not assist in creating adoptive matches. She handles independent, foster care, relative, stepparent and adult adoptions.

Shoshana Kunin-Leavitt; 3551 E. Bonanza Rd. #110, Las Vegas, NV 89110 ● Tel: (702) 438-8060 ● kuninlawgroup.com ●
shoshana@kuninlawgroup.com

Todd L. Moody; 10080 W. Alta Drive, #200, Las Vegas, NV 89145
Tel: (702) 385-2500 ● hutchlegal.com ●
t.moodyd@adoptionattorneys.org

Eric A. Stovall; 10000 W. Charleston, Howard Hughes Plaza #140, Las Vegas, NV 89135 ● Tel: (775) 337-1444 ● nevadaadoptionlawyer.com ●
e.stovall@adoptionattorneys.org
A graduate of the Nevada School of Law, he has been practicing law since 1987. He estimates he has completed more than 1,250 adoptions in his career and

completes 100 annually: 60% independent; 40% agency. He does not assist in creating adoptive matches. He accepts contested adoption cases. He is the 2018 president of the American Academy of Adoption Attorneys.

NEW HAMPSHIRE

Official State Adoption Website: http://www.dhhs.nh.gov/dcyf/adoption/

State Adoption Exchange or Related Website:
http://www.dhhs.nh.gov/dcyf/adoption/

State laws and procedures:

General Information. New Hampshire permits both independent and agency adoption. Advertising is permitted by agencies or directly by adoptive parents. To file a Petition for Adoption in New Hampshire either the adoptive parents, or the child to be adopted, must be residents of the state (making non-resident adoption possible). If it is an agency adoption the Petition for Adoption may also be filed there if the agency having custody of the child is located in New Hampshire. Normally, adoptions can't be finalized sooner than six months after the child's placement with the adoptive parents, and the hearing is usually within weeks thereafter. The adoptive parents are required to appear in court for the interlocutory hearing.

Independent Adoption. A pre-placement home study of the adoptive parents is required before a child can be placed in their home. The home study may be conducted by a licensed adoption agency. The usual total fee for pre- and post-placement services ranges from $1,500-2,500.

It is not required by law that the adoptive parents and the birth mother meet in person and share identities, although some elect to do so voluntarily. The adoptive parents are permitted to assist the birth mother with pregnancy-related expenses, including living expenses. The child can be released directly to the adoptive parents from the hospital, although each hospital may employ different release forms.

The consent to adoption, called a *Surrender of Parental Rights*, can be signed no sooner than 72 hours after the birth. It must be witnessed and approved by a judge in a hearing in which the birth mother appears. The birth parents must be represented by counsel, unless a judge waives that requirement. If the birth parent is under the age of 18 the court will require the consent of the birth parent's parent as well. Once signed, the surrender can only be withdrawn upon proof of fraud or duress and that the child's bests interests would be served by removal from the adoptive parents.

New Hampshire has a putative birth father registry. Putative birth fathers must register prior to the time the birth mother surrenders her parental rights. If he fails to do so, he has lost his right to claim paternal rights.

Agency Adoption. There is no difference regarding the process in which a birth mother signs her surrender in an independent or agency adoption. The information provided above regarding independent adoption (e.g. when the surrender can be signed and before whom) is identical regarding agency adoption.

Some agencies in New Hampshire agree to do identified adoptions. Some agencies also agree to make immediate hospital "at risk" placements with the adoptive parents before the consents are irrevocable.

American Academy of Adoption Attorney members:

Margaret Cunnane Hall; 37 High Street, Milford, NH 03055
Tel: (603) 673-8323 ● www.margaretchall.com ●
m.hall@adoptionattorneys.org
A graduate of the New England Law School, she has been practicing law since 1979. She estimates she has completed 1,200 adoptions in her career. She assists in creating adoptive matches. She is an adoptive parent. She accepts contested adoption cases and handles assisted reproductive technology matters.

NEW JERSEY

Official State Adoption Website:
http://www.state.nj.us/njfosteradopt/adoption/path/

State Adoption Exchange or Related Website:
http://www.adoptuskids.org/states/nj/index.aspx

State laws and procedures:

General Information. New Jersey permits both independent and agency adoption. Advertising is permitted. To file a Petition for Adoption within New Jersey the adoptive parents must reside there, or the child must be born there (making non-resident adoption possible, but the petition must be filed within three months of the child's birth). A Petition for Adoption can also be filed there if the child was surrendered to a New Jersey adoption agency. Normally, independent adoptions are finalized ten-eleven months after the placement of the child with the adoptive parents. Agency adoptions are usually finalized seven to eight months after placement. The adoptive parents are required to appear in court for the final hearing, but out-of-state residents are often permitted to appear by video conferencing.

Independent Adoption. Birth mothers can be introduced to adoptive parents by intermediaries only if the adoptive parents have a completed home study. The intermediary (which includes attorneys) cannot charge a fee for this service. This home study must be conducted by a non-profit adoption agency licensed by the State of New Jersey. The fee varies.

It is not required by law that the adoptive parents and birth mother meet and share identities, although it is often done voluntarily. The adoptive parents are permitted by law to assist the birth mother with pregnancy-related living, medical, counseling and legal expenses. The child can be placed with the adoptive parents directly from the hospital, but some hospitals require that the birth mother must be discharged with the baby, then personally place the child with the adopting parents outside the hospital.

The consent to adoption can be signed any time after birth. The consent is not irrevocable until one of two situations occur. The birth parent can appear before a judge and agree to the termination of parental rights. If this is done, usually it is scheduled between two weeks to three months after the birth. If this is not done, the consent cannot be made permanent until a preliminary hearing, which normally occurs several months after the birth and filing of the Complaint for Adoption.

New Jersey does not have a putative birth father registry. Notice is given to any putative birth father of the pending adoption. He has 120 days after birth, or the date of the preliminary hearing, whichever is first, to either amend the birth certificate to be named as the biological father, or file a paternity action. If he does one of these actions he has the right to object and the court will examine his fitness and the best interests of the child. Although there are other procedures to give notice and terminate parental rights, this is the traditional one. This does not preclude the termination of rights of unknown or unfindable birth fathers.

Agency Adoption. Only licensed non-profit agencies may "place" children for adoption. The information provided above regarding independent adoption is identical regarding agency adoption, except a birth mother's consent to adoption, called a *surrender*, can be taken no sooner than 72 hours after birth. Once executed, it is irrevocable, except for fraud or duress. A birth parent must also be offered, but is not required to accept, three counseling sessions.

Many agencies in New Jersey agree to do identified adoptions. Many agencies will agree to do immediate hospital "at risk" placements.

American Academy of Adoption Attorney members:

Jean M. Cavaliere; 89 Headquarters Plaza N. #1458, Morristown, NJ 07960 ● Tel: (973) 366-2499 ● jeanmcavalierelaw.com ● jean@jeanmcavalierelaw.com A graduate of Fordham University School of Law, she began practicing law in 1986. She has completed more than 600 adoptions (agency, independent and stepparent) the majority of which are newborn placements.

Donald C. Cofsky; 209 Haddon Avenue, Haddonfield, NJ 08033 Tel: (856) 429-5005 ● 209law.com ● dcc@209law.com A past president of the American Academy of Adoption Attorneys and a graduate of the Temple University School of Law, he has been practicing law since 1973. He estimates he has completed more than 1,800 adoptions in his career and completes 100 annually (independent, agency, stepparent, grandparent, international) and also accepts contested adoption cases. He assists in the legal aspects of assisted reproductive technology matters. In 2005 he was named as an Angel in Adoption by the Congressional Coalition of Adoption. He serves on the New Jersey Supreme Court Family Practice Rules Committee for issues related to adoption.

Robin Fleischner; 374 Millburn Ave. #303E Millburn, NJ 07041 Tel: (973) 376-6623 ● adoptsurrogatelaw.com ● r.fleischner@adoptionattorneys.org A graduate of the Yeshiva University, Benjamin N. Cardozo School of Law, she has been practicing law since 1980. She is also licensed to practice in New Jersey. She estimates she has completed more than 1,000 adoptions in her career, and last year completed approximately 50. Her practice is limited to adoptions (typically 75% independent; 25% agency), and of these all are newborn placements. She assists in creating adoptive matches and handles assisted reproductive technology matters. She is a 2015 recipient of the Angel in Adoption award from the Congressional Coalition on Adoption. She is an adoptive parent.

Debra E. Guston; 55 Harristown Road, #106, Glen Rock, NJ 07452
Tel: (201) 447-6660 ● gustonlaw.com ● d.guston@adoptionattorneys.org
A graduate of the Cardozo School of Law, she has been practicing family formation law for close to 30 years. She is the 2017-18 President of the American Academy of Adoption Attorneys and the American Academy of Assisted Reproductive Technology Attorneys. She is a pioneer in New Jersey's LGBT legal community and has been honored by the New Jersey State Bar Association for her legislative efforts. She works in all areas of adoption (agency, independent, foster care, step/second parent and contested adoptions) and also in assisted reproduction. She also works to protect families of special needs children in guardianship actions and immigrant children in special immigrant juvenile matters.

Tara E. Gutterman; 5 Village Dr., Voorhees, NJ 08043
Tel: (215) 748-1441 ● t.gutterman@adoptionattorneys.org

Elizabeth A. Hopkins; 766 Shrewsbury Ave., Tinton Falls, NJ 07724
Tel: (732) 933-7777 ● njadoptioncounsel.com ●
e.hopkins@adoptionattorneys.org
A graduate of the Seton Hall School of Law, she has been practicing law since 1984.

Deborah E. Spivack; P.O. Box 3433, Cherry Hill, NJ 08034
Tel: (856) 857-1155 ● familybuildinglaw.net ●
d.spivack@adoptionatttorneys.org
A graduate of the Widener, University School of Law, she has been practicing law since 1993. She estimates she has completed more than 1,000 adoptions in her career and presently completes 80-100 (agency, independent, foreign re-adoption and intra family/stepparent). She is an adoptive parent. She is an adoptive parent and received the 2105 Congressional Coalition of Adoption Angel Award. She has offices in New Jersey, Pennsylvania and Delaware.

NEW MEXICO

Official State Adoption Website: http://heartgallerynm.org/

State Adoption Exchange or Related Website:
https://www.adoptex.org/adopt-nm-kids

State laws and procedures:

General Information. General Information. New Mexico permits both independent and agency adoption. Advertising is permitted. To file a Petition for Adoption within New Mexico the adoptive parents must be residents, or the child must be born there (making non-resident adoption possible). If it is an agency adoption the Petition for Adoption can also be filed there if the agency having custody of the child is located in New Mexico. Normally, adoptions are finalized four months after the child's placement with the adoptive parents. The adoptive parents are required to appear in court for the final hearing unless good cause can be shown to waive it (such as the distance to travel for out-of-state residents).

Independent Adoption. A pre-placement home study of the adoptive parents is required before the child is placed in their home. The home study may be conducted by a licensed adoption agency or an independent social worker certified by the Children, Youth and Families Department. The fee varies but typical pre- and post-placement services combined range from $2,000 to $3,000.

It is not required by law that the adoptive parents and birth mother meet in person and share identities, although it is done in most cases voluntarily. The adoptive parents are permitted to assist the birth mother with pregnancy-related expenses, including living expenses, although these expenses must be paid directly to the party supplying the related services and not to a third party like the birth mother. The child may be released directly from the hospital to the adoptive parents, although hospitals use various forms for the release.

The consent to adoption, called the Voluntary Relinquishment, can be signed no sooner than 48 hours after the birth. It must be signed before a judge. It is irrevocable upon signing, but for proof of fraud or duress. New Mexico allows for enforceable open adoption agreements.

New Mexico has a putative birth father registry. Putative fathers are divided into two categories. One category is "acknowledged" fathers (men who filed with the registry, filed a paternity action within 10 days of the birth, or satisfied one of an additional list of requirement too numerous to list), and the other category is "alleged" fathers (men who failed to file with the registry). An action to terminate the rights of an alleged father must be filed with the court, but no notice to the birth father is required. If the birth father is in the acknowledged category, however, notice must be given to him of the intent to terminate his parental rights. If he does not object within twenty days his rights are terminated. If he does object, the court will normally examine his conduct/responsibility toward mother and child and the best interests of the child.

Agency Adoption. There is no difference regarding the process in which a birth mother signs her consent to adoption in an independent or agency adoption. The information provided above regarding independent adoption (e.g. when it can be signed, before whom and the legal burden to seek to withdraw a signed consent) is identical regarding agency adoption.

Some agencies in New Mexico agree to do identified adoptions. Some agencies also agree to make immediate hospital "at risk" placements.

American Academy of Adoption Attorney members:

Harold O. Atencio; 3809 Atrisco NW, Suite B; P.O. Box 66468, Albuquerque, NM 87193
Tel: (505) 839-9111 ● atenciolawpc.com ● h.atencio@adoptionattorneys.org
A graduate of the University of New Mexico School of Law, he has been practicing law since 1988. He estimates he has completed more than 500 adoptions in his career.

Lisa H. Olewine; 4801 Lang, Suite 110: P.O. Box 93216, Albuquerque, NM 87199 ● Tel: (505) 858-3316 ● nmadoptionlaw.com ● l.olewine@adoptionattorneys.org
A graduate of the University of New Mexico School of Law, she has been practicing law since 2001. Her practice is limited to adoptions and assisted reproduction. She is a past president of the Adoption and Foster Care Alliance of New Mexico and is an adoptive parent.

Allison P. Pieroni; 3200 Carlisle Blvd. N.E. #219, Albuquerque, NM 87110 ●
Tel: (505) 830-6032 ● apfamilylaw.com ● a.pieroni@adoptionattorneys.org

NEW YORK

Official State Adoption Website: http://ocfs.ny.gov/adopt/

State Adoption Exchange or Related Website: Use above state website.

State laws and procedures:

General Information. New York permits both independent and agency adoption. Advertising is permitted. It is illegal for an intermediary, other than a licensed adoption agency, to receive compensation for locating a birth mother for adoptive parents to create an adoptive match. To file a Petition for Adoption within New York either the adoptive parents, or the child being adopted, must reside there (making non-resident adoption possible). If it is an agency adoption the Petition for Adoption may be filed in New York if the agency having custody of the child is located there. Normally, adoptions are finalized from three to twelve months after the child's placement with the adoptive parents. The adoptive parents and the child are required to appear in court for the final hearing, although some judges may allow out-of-state residents to appear via video-conferencing.

Independent Adoption. A pre-placement home study of the adoptive parents is required before a child can be placed in their home. The home study is used to allow the adoptive parents to be "certified" as qualified adoptive parents. If the adoptive parents have not been certified by the time the placement is to occur, a court may permit the adoptive parents to have physical custody of the child if they file a request for temporary guardianship within five days of having obtained custody. The home study may be conducted by a licensed agency, licensed social worker, state adoption office, or other person approved by the court. The fee varies.

It is not required by law that the adoptive parents and birth mother meet in person and share identities, although some elect to do so voluntarily. The adoptive parents are permitted to assist the birth mother with pregnancy-related medical, legal and living expenses. Living assistance is limited to two months pre-birth and one month post-birth. Assistance in excess of these periods requires court approval. The child can be released from the hospital directly to the adoptive parents, although hospitals use different forms and have different policies.

The consent to adoption can be signed any time after the birth. The consent must be witnessed by a judge or a notary public. Most consents are

328

signed within several days of the birth. If the consent is signed before a judge, it is irrevocable upon signing, but for proof of fraud or duress. If the consent was witnessed by a notary public, the consent may be revoked for a period of 45 days from the time it is signed, but only if a court determines the child's best interests would be served by the child being removed from the adoptive parents.

New York has a putative birth father registry. A putative birth father who registers, who is named on the birth certificate, or who is identified by the birth mother in a written sworn statement, must be given notice, giving him the right to offer evidence that he believes adoption is not in the best interests of the child.

Agency Adoption. The information provided above regarding independent adoption is identical regarding agency adoption, with the following exception: The consent to adoption, called a *surrender* in an agency adoption, may be signed any time after birth. If it is witnessed by a judge the surrender is irrevocable upon signing. The surrender may also be witnessed by a representative of the adoption agency, and one additional witness. If this non-judicial witnessing option is selected, the surrender may be withdrawn by proving the child's best interests would be served, but only until 30 days have elapsed from the time the surrender is signed, and the child must have been placed with the adoptive parents. Once 30 days have elapsed and the child is placed with the adoptive parents, the surrender is irrevocable and can only be withdrawn upon proof of fraud or duress.

Some agencies agree to do identified adoptions. Some agencies also agree to do immediate hospital "at risk" placements.

American Academy of Adoption Attorney members:

Jeanine Castagna; 1225 Franklin Ave., #325, Garden City, NY 11530 ● Tel: (516) 495-7906 ● jcadoptionlaw.com ● j.castagna@adoptionattorneys.org
A graduate of Hofstra Law School, she has been practicing law since 1997. She estimates she has completed more than 500 adoptions in her career and completes 30 annually. She was the recipient of the Congressional Angel in Adoption Award in 2008.

Anne Reynolds Copps; 126 State Street, 6th Floor, Albany, NY 12207 ● Tel: (518) 436-4170 ● coppsdipaola.com ● a.copps@adoptionattorneys.org
A graduate of the Albany Law School of Union University, she has been practicing law since 1982. She estimates she has completed more than 1,000 adoptions in her career. She also handles assisted reproductive technology matters.

Kathleen "Casey" A. DiPaola; 126 State St. 6th Floor, Albany, NY 12207 ● Tel: (518) 436-4170 ● coppsdipaola.com ● k.dipaola@adoptionattorneys.org
A graduate of the Albany Law School of Union University in 2009, she has represented birth parents, adoptive parents and adoption agencies in all types of adoptions, including private, agency, foster care, and contested adoptions.

Robin Fleischner; 11 Riverside Dr. #14MW. New York, NY 10023
Tel: (212) 362-6945 ● adoptsurrogatelaw.com ●
r.fleischner@adoptionattorneys.org
A graduate of the Yeshiva University, Benjamin N. Cardozo School of Law, she has been practicing law since 1980. She is also licensed to practice in New Jersey. She estimates she has completed more than 1,000 adoptions in her career, and last year completed approximately 50. Her practice is limited to adoptions (typically 75% independent; 25% agency), and of these all are newborn placements. She assists in creating adoptive matches and handles assisted reproductive technology matters. She is a 2015 recipient of the Angel in Adoption award from the Congressional Coalition on Adoption. She is an adoptive parent.

Karen A. Foley; 666 Old Country Rd. #305, Garden City, NY 11530
Tel: (516) 795-7752 ● nyadoptlaw.com ● k.foley@adoptionattorneys.org
A graduate of Hofstra University School of Law, she has been practicing law since 1994. She estimates she has completed more than 100 adoptions in her career. She is an adoptive parent.

Gregory A. Franklin; 150 Allens Creek Road, Rochester, NY 14618
Tel: (585) 442-0540 ● afylaw.com ● g.franklin@adoptionattorneys.org
A graduate of the Fordham University School of Law, he has been practicing law since 1984. He estimates he has completed more than 2,200 adoptions in his career. He is an adoptive parent and accepts contested adoption cases.

Laurie B. Goldheim; 20 Old Nyack Turnpike, #300, Nanuet, NY 10954 ● Tel: (845) 624-2727 ● adoptionrights.com ● l.goldheim@adoptionattorneys.org
A graduate of the Boston University School of Law, she has been practicing law since 1990. She estimates she has completed more than 1,200 adoptions in her career and completes 80 annually: 90% independent; 10% agency. She is an adoptee.

Michael S. Goldstein; 62 Bowman Avenue, Rye Brook, NY 10573

Tel: (914) 939-1111 ● adoptgold.com ● m.goldstein@adoptionattorneys.org
A graduate of the Fordham Law School, he has been practicing law since 1982. He estimates he has completed 3,000 adoptions in his career and completes 40 annually: 20% independent; 20% agency; 60% international. He is a Licensed Clinical Social Worker, an adoptive parent of three, the co-founder of Forever Families Through Adoption, Inc. (FFTA) a placement agency in New York, and the recipient of the Congressional Angel in Adoption Award in 2006. He is Hague approved for intercountry adoptions – incoming and outgoing.

Cliff Greenberg; 363 Seventh Ave. #400, New York, NY 10001
Tel: (212) 545-7337 ● greenbergadoption.com ●
c.greenberg@adoptionattorneys.org

Kevin P. Harrigan; 2 Clinton Square #215, Syracuse, NY 13202
Tel: (314) 478-3138 ● k.harrigan@adoptionattorneys.org
A graduate of the Syracuse University College of Law, he has been practicing law since 1978. He estimates that he has completed more than 2,000 adoptions in his career, and completes approximately 100 annually. He was the recipient of the Congressional Angel in Adoption Award in 2007.

Stephen Lewin; 845 Third Avenue # 1400, New York, NY 10022
Tel: (212) 759-2600 ● ilcllaw.com ● s.lewin@adoptionattorneys.org

Frederick J. Magovern; 1539 Franklin Ave., Mineola, NY 11501
Tel: (516) 747-6800 ● fred@nylawexperts.com
A graduate of the Fordham University School of Law, he has been practicing law since 1972. He estimates he has completed more than 1,000 adoptions in his career. He specializes in contested adoption cases. He has been awarded the Congressional Angel in Adoption award.

Cynthia Perla Meckler; 8081 Floss Lane, East Amherst, NY 14051
Tel: (716) 741-4164 ● cpmadopt@gmail.com
A graduate of the SUNY Law School at Buffalo, she has been practicing law since 1980. She estimates she has completed more than 1,000 adoptions in her career.

Rebecca L. Mendel; 801 2nd Ave., 10th Floor, New York, NY 10017
Tel: (212) 972-5430 ● lawrsm.com ● r.mendel@adoptionattorneys.org
A graduate of Benjamin N. Cardozo School of Law, she has been practicing law since 1998. She estimates she completes approximately 75 adopts a year, including independent, agency, adult, step-parent, second parent, and re-adoptions. She also represents birth parents. She accepts contested adoption cases and handles assisted reproductive technology matters. She was awarded Resolve's Hope Award for Advocacy.

Suzanne B. Nichols; 800 Westchester Ave. #641 N., Rye Brook, NY 10573 ●
Tel: (914) 697-4870 ● rlnlaw.com ● s.nichols@adoptionattorneys.org
A graduate of the New York Law School, she has been practicing law since 1985. She is also licensed to practice law in New Jersey. She estimates she has completed more than 1,000 adoptions in her career.

Brendan C. O'Shea; 40 Beaver Street, Albany, NY 12207
Tel: (518) 432-7511 ● gdwo.net ● b.oshea@adoptionattorneys.org
A graduate of the Albany Law School, he has been practicing law since 1980. He estimates he has completed more than 1,500 adoptions in his career and presently completes 85 annually: 20% independent; 75% agency; 5% international. He accepts contested adoption matters.

Douglas H. Reiniger; 801 2nd Avenue, New York, NY 10017
Tel: (307) 690-6625 ● lawrsm.com ● d.reiniger@adoptionattorneys.org
A graduate of the Fordham Law School, he has been practicing law since 1981.

Benjamin J. Rosin; 801 2nd Avenue, New York, NY 10017
Tel: (212) 972-5430 ● lawrsm.com ● b.rosin@adoptionattorneys.org
A graduate of the Columbia University School of Law, he has been practicing law since 1966. He estimates he has completed more than 1,000 adoptions in his career, and last year completed approximately 30 (10 independent; 20 agency). He is an adoptive parent.

Nina E. Rumbold; 116 Kraft Avenue #3, Bronxville, NY 10708
Tel: (914) 779-1050 ● adoptionlawny.com ●
n.rumbold@adoptionattorneys.org
A graduate of the New York University School of Law, she has been practicing law since 1978. She estimates she and her law partner, Denise Seidelman, have completed over 1,000 adoptions in their careers and that they complete 60 adoptions annually: 60% independent; 30% agency; 10% international.

Steven L. Sarisohn; 350 Veterans Memorial Highway, Commack, NY 11725
● Tel: (631) 543-7667 ● sarisohnlaw.com ● s.sarisohn@adoptionattorneys.org
A graduate of the Benjamin N. Cordozo Law School, he began practicing law in 1984. He estimates he has completed approximately 300 adoptions in his career and completes approximately 20 adoptions annually: 85% independent; 15% agency. He does not assist in creating adoptive matches.

Denise Seidelman; 116 Kraft Avenue #3, Bronxville, NY 10708
Tel: (914) 779-1050 ● adoptionlawny.com ●
d.seidelman@adoptionattorneys.org
A graduate of the Washington College of Law, she has been practicing law since 1980. She estimates she and her law partner, Nina E. Rumbold, have completed over 1,000 adoptions in their careers and that they complete 60 adoptions annually: 60% independent; 30% agency; 10% international.

Laurie Slavin; 275 Fair Street #23, Kingston, NY 12401
Tel: (845) 338-0700 ● hudsonvalleyadoptionservices.org ●
l.slavin@adoptionattorneys.org

Mary Walsh Snyder; P.O. Box 11118, Albany, NY 12211
Tel: (518) 225-2776 ● m.walshsnyder@adoptionattorneys.org

Yekaterina "Kate" Trambitskaya; 410 E. 92nd St., New York, NY 10128 ●
Tel: (212) 369-0300 ● spence-chapin.org ●
k.trambitskaya@adoptionattorneys.org

Debbie S. Wolf; 62 Bowman Ave., Rye Brook, NY 10573
Tel: (914) 939-1180 ● foreverfamiliesthroughadoption.org ●
adopt@foreverfamiliesthroughadoption.org
A graduate of New England School of Law, she began practicing law in 1992. She assists in creating adoptive matches. She focuses on agency adoptions: 100% agency, 0% independent. She has been on the Senior Agency Counsel for Forever Families Through Adoption since 2008.

NORTH CAROLINA

Official State Adoption Website: http://www.dhhs.state.nc.us/dss/adopt/

State Adoption Exchange: Use above state website.

State laws and procedures:

General Information. North Carolina permits both independent and agency adoption. Advertising is permitted only by licensed adoption agencies or adoptive parents with completed home studies. To file a Petition for Adoption the adoptive parents must reside there, usually for at least six months, or the minor must be born and resided there for at least six months. Normally, adoptions are finalized approximately six months after the child's placement with the adoptive parents. The adoptive parents and child are usually not required to appear in court for the final hearing.

Independent Adoption. A pre-placement home study ("pre-placement assessment") is required of the adoptive parents before a child is placed in their home. The home study may be conducted by a licensed adoption agency, or in some areas, the county department of social services. The fee varies.

It is required that the adoptive parents and birth mother share identities. Virtually all will also voluntarily elect to meet in person. A copy of the adoptive parents' home study must be given to the birth mother. The adoptive parents are allowed to assist the birth mother with pregnancy-related medical and legal expenses. Assistance with living expenses is normally permitted, but usually for not more than six weeks after birth. The child may be released from the hospital directly to the adoptive parents.

The consent to adoption may be signed any time after the birth by the birth mother. (The birth father can usually sign before birth.) It must be witnessed by a notary or the clerk of the Superior Court. The birth mother has the automatic right to withdraw her consent for a period of 7 days after signing (extended if the 7th day falls on a weekend or court holiday). If the placement occurs before the home study is delivered to the birth mother, she has an additional five business days to revoke her consent after she receives the home study. Once these time periods have elapsed the consent is irrevocable, except upon proof of fraud or duress.

North Carolina does not have a putative birth father registry. Notice must be given to putative fathers and they have 30 days in which to object after notice (40 days if notice given by publication). If he elects to object, he must prove he did all of the following things before the Petition for Adoption was filed: acknowledge paternity; communicate with the birth mother; and provide support.

Agency Adoption. The information provided above regarding independent adoption (e.g. when it can be signed, before whom, and the legal burden to seek to withdraw a signed consent) is identical regarding agency adoption, with one exception: It is not required that the adoptive parents' home study be offered to the birth mother (although it may still voluntarily be offered).

Few agencies within North Carolina agree to do identified adoptions. Some will agree to make immediate hospital "at risk" placements.

American Academy of Adoption Attorney members:

Christopher M. Craig; 149 S. Lexington Ave., Asheville, NC 28801
Tel: (828) 258-2888 ● chriscraiglaw.com ● c.craig@adoptionattorneys.org
A graduate of North Carolina Central University School of Law, he has been practicing law since 2001. He estimates he completes approximately 50-65 adoptions annually, all independent. He assists in creating adoptive matches and he accepts contested cases. He also handles assisted reproductive technology matters. He is an adoptee.

Kelly T. Dempsey; 2301 W. Morehead St. Suite F, Charlotte, NC 28208 ●Tel: (919) 710-8199 ● kdempseylaw.com ● k.dempsey@adoptionattorneys.org
A graduate of North Carolina Central University, she began practicing law in 2005. She estimates she completes 100 adoptions annually. She accepts contested adoption cases and appeals. He also handles assisted reproductive technology matters. She is an adoptive parent of one internationally adopted child and one domestically adopted child.

Amy Wallas Fox; 417 E. Blvd. #101, Charlotte, NC 28203
Tel: (704) 702-0300 ● ncbabylaw.com ● a.fox@adoptionattorneys.org
A graduate of William & Mary Law School, she has been practicing law since 2007. She estimates she completes 50 adoptions annually (independent, ICPC, agency, adult, stepparent. She also handles assisted reproductive technology matters including surrogacy and egg, sperm and embryo donation.

Bobby D. Mills; P.O. Box 1677, Raleigh, NC 27602
Tel: (919) 821-1860 ● herringandmillslawfirm.com ●
b.mills@adoptionattorneys.org
A graduate of the Wake Forest School of Law, he has been practicing law since 1985. He estimates he completes 50 adoptions annually: 50% independent; 50% agency. He does not assist in creating adoptive matches.

Sharon A. Thompson; 113 Broadway St., Durham, NC 27701
Tel: (919) 688-9646 ● nicholsonpham.com ●
s.thompson@adoptionattorneys.org

W. David Thurman; 301 S. McDowell St., #608, Charlotte, NC 28204 ● Tel: (704) 377-4164 ● twbglaw.com ● w.thurman@adoptionattorneys.org
A graduate of the University of North Carolina School of Law, he has been practicing law since 1983. He estimates he has completed 3,000 adoptions in his career and completes 100 annually: 50% independent; 40% agency; 10% international. He does not assist in creating adoptive matches. He accepts contested adoption cases.

Brinton D. Wright; 324 W. Wendover Ave. #170, Greensboro, NC 27408 ● Tel: (336) 373-1500 ● wendoverlaw.com ● brinton@wendoverlaw.com
A graduate of Wake Forest University School of Law, he has been practicing law since 1976. He estimates he has completed more than 1,200 adoptions in his career and completes 60 annually: 85% independent; 10% agency; 5% international. He does not assist in creating adoptive matches. He is an adoptive parent.

NORTH DAKOTA

Official State Adoption Website:
http://www.nd.gov/dhs/services/childfamily/adoption/

State Adoption Exchange: Use above state website.

State laws and procedures:

General Information. North Dakota permits only agency adoption, although identified agency adoptions as done within the state are very similar to independent adoption. Advertising is not expressly permitted or barred by law, so most interpret that as it being permitted. To file a Petition for Adoption within North Dakota the adoptive parents must reside there, or the agency having custody of the child must be located there (permitting non-resident adoption). Normally, adoptions are finalized approximately seven months from the child's placement with the adoptive parents. The adoptive parents and the child are required to appear in court for the final hearing.

A pre-placement home study of the adoptive parents is required before a child can be placed in their home. The home study may be conducted by a licensed adoption agency. The fee typically varies from $7,000 to $8,000 for pre- and post-placement services.

It is not required by law that the adoptive parents and birth mother meet in person and share identities, although some elect to do so. However, if the adoption is designated an "identified adoption," full identities are shared. The adoptive parents are permitted to assist the birth mother with pregnancy-related medical, legal and living expenses. The child may be released directly to the adoptive parents from the hospital if they are licensed as foster parents. Otherwise, a court order is required if the placement occurs prior to the birth mother's termination of parental rights. The latter option is more common in identified adoptions.

The birth mother shows her assent to the adoption by filing a *Petition for Relinquishment* with the court. If she is under the age of 18, a guardian ad litem must be appointed to be sure she understands the proceedings. Her signature must be witnessed by a notary or a representative of a licensed adoption agency. Although the Petition for Relinquishment can be signed and filed before the child's birth, the Petition will not be heard until at least 48 hours after the birth, or the signing of the Petition, whichever occurs later. Once the court has granted the birth mother's Petition for Relinquishment, the child cannot be reclaimed by the birth mother, unless proved to the court within 30 days that fraud or duress was used to obtain her consent.

North Dakota does not have a putative birth father registry. A putative birth father is entitled to notice and if he can't be found notice is given by publication. If he elects to object, the adoptive parents must normally prove he is unfit.

American Academy of Adoption Attorney members:

William P. Harrie; 201 N. 5th Street, Suite 1800; P.O. Box 2626, Fargo, ND 58102 ● nilleslaw.com ● Tel: (701) 237-5544 ● wharrie@nilleslaw.com
A graduate of the University of North Dakota School of law, he has been practicing law since 1986. He is also licensed to practice in Minnesota. He

estimates he has completed 1,000 adoptions in his career and presently completes about 50 annually. He also practices assisted reproductive law.

OHIO

Official State Adoption Website:
http://jfs.ohio.gov/factsheets/FosterCare.pdf

State Adoption Exchange: Use above state website.

State laws and procedures:

General Information. Ohio permits both independent and agency adoption. Advertising is permitted by agencies and families with approved Ohio home studies. To file a Petition for Adoption within Ohio either the adoptive parents must reside there, the child must be born there, or a birth parent must reside there (making non-resident adoption possible). If it is an agency adoption, the Petition for Adoption may also be filed in Ohio if the agency having custody of the child is located there. Normally, independent adoptions are finalized approximately six months after the child's placement with the adoptive parents; agency adoptions normally 6 months to one year. The adoptive parents are required to appear in court for either the final or interlocutory hearing.

Independent Adoption. A pre-placement home study is required before a child can be placed in the adoptive parents' home. Depending upon the policy of the county in which the Petition for Adoption is filed, the home study may be conducted by the state adoption office, a private licensed agency or a person approved by the court. The fee varies.

It is not required by law that the adoptive parents and birth mother meet in person and share identities, although some elect to do so voluntarily. The adoptive parents are permitted to assist the birth mother with pregnancy-related medical and legal expenses, and living expenses not to exceed $3,000 if incurred during the pregnancy and up to 60 days post-birth. The child may be released directly from the hospital to the adoptive parents, although a court order is sometimes required.

The consent to adoption can be signed no sooner than 72 hours after the birth, or the completion of the social work assessment, whichever occurs later. The birth mother must personally appear in court and request placement of the child with the adoptive parents. Once the placement is approved by the court, the child is placed in the custody of the adoptive parents and they may file their Petition for Adoption. Courts in different counties in Ohio differ. Some enter an *Interlocutory Order of Adoption* after the child has been with the adoptive parents for 30 days. This Interlocutory Order then becomes final about six months after the placement. Other counties do not enter an Interlocutory Order and wait about six months after the placement and enter a *Final Decree of Adoption*. The consent of the birth mother becomes irrevocable upon the entry of either the Interlocutory Order, or Final Decree, whichever occurs first. Prior to the granting of either order, the birth mother can withdraw her consent based only upon proving the child's best interests would be served.

Ohio has a putative birth father registry. Putative birth fathers must register no later than 15 days after the birth. If he registers and elects to object a key issue the court will examine is if he supported the birth mother during the pregnancy.

Agency Adoption. The information provided above regarding independent adoption is similar regarding agency adoption, except the birth mother executes a *surrender*, giving custody of the child to the adoption agency. The surrender can be signed no sooner than 72 hours after birth or the completion of the social work assessment, whichever occurs later. It is irrevocable upon signing. If the child is under the age of six months, the birth mother is not required to appear in court.

Some agencies in Ohio agree to do identified adoptions. Some agencies also agree to do immediate hospital "at risk" placements.

American Academy of Adoption Attorney members:

James S. Albers; 88 North Fifth Street, Columbus, OH 43215
Tel: (614) 464-4414 ● alberslawfirm.com ● j.albers@adoptionattorneys.org

Margaret "Peggy" L. Blackmore; 580 S. High St. #120, Columbus, OH 43215 ● Tel: (614) 427-0999 ● mblackmorelaw.com ● p.blackmore@adoptionattorneys.org

Julia A. Cain; 1 Park Center #101, Wadsworth, OH 44281
Tel: (440) 653-3147 ● juliacainlaw.com ● cainlegal@yahoo.com
A graduate of the Ohio State University College of Law, she has been practicing law since 1989. She estimates she completes 30 adoptions annually: 25% independent; 70% agency; 5% international. She assists in creating adoptive matches.

Susan G. Eisenman; 4900 Reed Rd. #204, Columbus, OH 43220
Tel: (614) 326-1200 ● s.eisenman@adoptionattorneys.org
A graduate of the Ohio State University School of Law, she has been practicing law since 1974. She estimates she has completed more than 2,000 adoptions in her career and completes 85 annually: 30% independent; 52% agency; 18% international. She assists in creating adoptive matches. She is an adoptive parent.

Ellen Essig; 4540 Cooper Rd. #304, Cincinnati, OH 45242
Tel: (513) 698-9345 ● essigevans.com ● ee@essigevans.com
A graduate of the Salmon P. Chase College of Law, she has been practicing law since 1986. She estimates she has completed 600 adoptions in her career (mostly independent, interstate and stepparent adoptions) and presently completes about 20 adoptions annually. Additionally, she estimates she has completed 3,000 assisted reproductive technology matters in her career, and presently completes about 100 annually. She was co-counsel in the 2015 U.S. Supreme Court case, *Obergefell v. Hodges*.

Barbara Thornell Ginn; 8595 Beechmont Ave. #103, Cincinnati, OH 45255
● Tel: (513) 277-1478 ● ginnllc.com ● b.ginn@adoptionattorneys.org

Patrick A. Hamilton; 400 S. Fifth St., #103, Columbus, OH 43215
Tel: (614) 464-4532 ● aphamiltonlaw.com ●
p.hamilton@adoptionattorneys.org

John C. Huffman; 540 W. Market Street, Lima, OH 45801
Tel: (419) 227-3423 ● j.huffman@adoptionattorneys.org

Jerry M. Johnson; 400 West North Street, Lima, OH 45801
Tel: (419) 222-1040 ● j.johnson@adoptionattorneys.org
A graduate of the Ohio Northern University School of Law, he has been practicing law since 1975. He estimates he has completed more than 600 adoptions in his career. He accepts contested adoption cases.

Carolyn McKenna; 3411 Michigan Avenue, Cincinnati, OH 45208
Tel: (513) 871-5777 ● c.mussio@adoptionattorneys.org

Lori S. Nehrer; 650 Graham Rd. #106, Cuyahoga Falls, OH 44221
Tel: (330) 928-3373 ● akronadoption.com ● lori@akronadoption.com
A graduate of the Georgetown University Law Center, she has been practicing law since 1985. She estimates she has completed 700 adoptions in her career and completes 80 annually: 40% independent; 59% agency; 1% international. She assists in creating adoptive matches. She is an adoptive parent.

Rosemary E. Pomeroy; 7100 N. High St. #301, Worthington, OH 43085 ●
Tel: (614) 885-2101 ● ebnerpomlaw.com ● r.pomeroy@adoptionattorneys.org
A graduate of the Detroit College of Law, now Michigan State University College of Law, she has been practicing law since 1988. She estimates that she has completed 1,000 adoptions in her career and completes between 50 and 60 adoptions annually. She represents both adoptive families and birth parents. She also represents families in agency adoptions, private adoptions, and international adoptions.

Michael R. Voorhees; 11159 Kenwood Road, Cincinnati, OH 45242
Tel: (513) 489-2555 ● m.voorhees@adoptionattorneys.org
He has been practicing law since 1987. He estimates he has completed 3,000 adoptions in his career and completes 150 annually: 60% independent; 30% agency; 10% international.

OKLAHOMA

Official State Adoption Website:
http://www.okdhs.org/services/adopt/Pages/default.aspx

State Adoption Exchange: Use above state website.

State laws and procedures:

General Information. Oklahoma permits both independent and agency adoption. Advertising is permitted by adoptive parents having a completed home study. To file a Petition for Adoption in Oklahoma either the adoptive parents must reside there, or the child to be adopted must show significant contacts with the state, usually by being born there or having resided there at least six months. Normally, adoptions are finalized approximately 7-12 months after the placement of the child with the adoptive parents. The adoptive parents and the child are required to appear in court for the final hearing.

Independent Adoption. A pre-placement home study of the adoptive parents is required before a child can be placed in their home. It may be conducted by a licensed adoption agency, Department of Human Services, or a person approved by the court. The fee for pre- and post-placement home study services ranges from $750 to $2,000 in some regions and may be higher in others.

It is not required by law that the adoptive parents and birth mother meet in person and share identities, although in some cases it is done voluntarily. The adoptive parents are permitted to assist the birth mother with pregnancy-related expenses, although living assistance may not be provided directly to the birth mother except in very limited circumstances. Prior court approval is required for any assistance exceeding $1,000. The child may be released directly from the hospital to the adoptive parents, although hospital policies differ. Some hospitals accept special release forms, while others require a court order.

The consent to adoption can be signed any time after the birth by the birth mother. (A non-marital father may sign his consent before the birth witnessed by a notary public, which becomes irrevocable 15 days after signing.) The birth mother's consent must be witnessed by a judge. If the birth mother is under the age of 16 the consent of one of the birth mother's parents, or her guardian, is also required. Most consents are signed within 4-5 days of the birth. The consent to adoption is irrevocable immediately upon signing. It may only be withdrawn upon proof of fraud or duress, the adoptive parents' failure to file their Petition for Adoption within nine months, or if a court does not terminate the rights of the alleged father. For the latter situations it must also be proved that withdrawing consent would serve the best interest of the child.

Oklahoma has a putative birth father registry. Notice must be given to birth fathers who are identified by the birth mother, have filed with the registry, who cohabited with the birth mother within the 10 months preceding the birth or signed an Acknowledgment of Paternity at the hospital. The notice will be of an action to terminate his parental rights. If he appears at the hearing and elects to object, he will first have to prove paternity. Then the key issue will usually be if the putative father financially supported the birth mother during the pregnancy to the extent his financial ability permitted. If he claims he had no opportunity to do so, he will have to show he made sufficient efforts to determine if he fathered a child and offered support.

Agency Adoption. There is no difference regarding the process in which a birth mother signs her consent to adoption in an independent or agency adoption. The information provided above regarding independent adoption (e.g. when the consent can be signed, before whom, legal burden to seek to withdraw a signed consent) is identical regarding agency adoption.

Some agencies in Oklahoma agree to do identified adoptions.

American Academy of Adoption Attorney members:

Barbara K. Bado; 1800 Canyon Park Circle, #301, Edmond, OK 73013 ●
Tel: (405) 340-1500 ● badoandbadoattorneys.com ●
b.bado@adoptionattorneys.org
A graduate of the American University, Washington College of Law, she has
been practicing law since 1978.

John T. Bado; 1800 Canyon Park Circle, #301, Edmond, OK 73013
Tel: (405) 340-1500 ● badoandbadoattorneys.com ●
j.bado@adoptionattorneys.org
A graduate of the Baylor University, he has been practicing law since 1971. He
is also licensed to practice in Texas.

Virginia "Ginny" L. Frank; 1434 Spruce #100, 201 N. Broadway #107A,
Moore, OK 73160 ● Tel: (888) 749-0168 ● virginialfrank.com ●
v.frank@adoptionattorneys.org
A graduate of Oklahoma City University School of Law, she has been practicing
law since 1992. She estimates she has completed 4,000 adoptions in her career
and presently completes more than 200 annually, including independent, agency,
interstate, and re-adoptions. She also handles assisted reproductive technology
matters.

Jennifer K. Kern; 15 West 6th St. #2700, Tulsa, OK 74119;
Tel: (918) 587-0101 ● newtonoconnor.com ● j.kern@adoptionattorneys.org
A graduate of University of Tulsa College of Law, she has been practicing since
2003. She estimates she has completed over 250 adoptions in her career and
presently completes legal services for 20-35 annually (65% independent, 33%
agency, 2% intercountry). She assists in creating adoptive matches. She also
accepts contested and appellate cases. She served on the Adoption Review Task
Force of the Oklahoma legislature.

Mark Morrison; 524 W. Evergreen St.; P.O. Box 1623, Durant, OK 74702 ●
Tel: (580) 924-1661 ● m.morrison@adoptionattorneys.org

Peter K. Schaffer; 4334 NW Expressway, #254, Oklahoma City, OK 73116
Tel: (405) 848-3313● p.schaffer@adoptionattorneys.org

A graduate of the Oklahoma City University, he has been practicing law since 1974. He estimates he has completed more than 350 adoptions in his career: 75% independent; 25% agency. He accepts contested adoption cases. He is the recipient of the Outstanding Service to the Public Award, presented by the Oklahoma State Bar Association.

Paul E. Swain III; 406 South Boulder Ave. #423, Tulsa, OK 74103
Tel: (918) 599-0100 ● swainlaw.com ● p.swain@adoptionattorneys.org
A graduate of the University of Oklahoma College of Law, he has been practicing law since 1982. He estimates he has completed over 400 adoptions in his career and completes an average of 20 annually: 65% independent; 35% agency. He assists in creating adoptive matches. He is an adoptive parent. He accepts contested adoption cases. He is on the ICWA Committee of the American Academy of Adoption Attorneys.

Mike Yeksavich; 7122 S. Sherdian #2-353, Tulsa, OK 74135
Tel: (918) 592-6050 ● miketheattorney.com ●
m.yeksavich@adoptionattorneys.org
A graduate of University of Tulsa Law School, he has been practicing law since 1968. He handles approximately 40 adoptions per year (about 70% independent and 30% agency). He assists in creating adoptive matches.

OREGON

Official State Adoption Website:
http://www.oregon.gov/DHS/children/adoption/

State Adoption Exchange: Use above state website.

State laws and procedures:

General Information. Oregon permits both independent and agency adoption. Advertising is permitted if the adoptive parents have a completed home study, are represented by an Oregon attorney, and they have obtained a Certificate of Approval upon the home study by an Oregon agency. To file a Petition for Adoption within Oregon either the adoptive parents, the child to be adopted, or the birth parent whose consent to the adoption is required must reside there for at least six months prior to filing the Petition for Adoption. Normally, adoptions are finalized approximately four to seven months after the child's placement with

344

the adoptive parents. The adoptive parents and the child are usually not required to appear in court at the final hearing.

Independent Adoption. A pre-placement home study of the adoptive parents by a licensed adoption agency is required, as well as ten hours of adoption education. The fee for the pre- and post-placement home study is approximately $3,000-$4,000, plus $200-$300 for the required educational classes.

It is not required by law that the adoptive parents and birth mother meet in person and share identities, although virtually all do so voluntarily. The adoptive parents are permitted to assist the birth mother with reasonable and necessary pregnancy-related expenses. The child may be placed with the adoptive parents directly from the hospital, although each hospital's forms and policies vary.

The consent to adoption can be signed any time after the birth. There is no statutory requirements regarding whom must witness it, so the common practice is to use a notary. Most consents are signed within days of the birth, sometimes in the hospital only 12-24 hours after birth. The birth mother has the right to seek to withdraw her consent until the adoption is final. However, if the birth mother also signs a *Certificate of Irrevocability* (which is commonly done) after having been provided advice from an independent attorney, the consent is irrevocable, except upon proof of fraud or duress, provided that all the following conditions are met: the child is physically placed with the adoptive parents, the Petition for Adoption and home study have been filed with the court, the child's medical history has been obtained, the Certificate of Irrevocability has been explained to the birth mother by her attorney, and the judge signs an order naming the adoptive parents as the temporary guardians for the child.

Oregon does not have a putative birth father registry, although men who file a paternity action (called a "filiation" proceeding) must notify the state Vital Statistics office by filing a *Notice of Initiation of Filiation Proceedings*. Some people incorrectly think of this as a true birth father. Notice must be given to putative birth fathers who have signed a voluntary acknowledgment of paternity with the birth mother, filed a paternity action and filed the required notice with Vital Records, or the birth mother's affidavit states the birth father did one of the following: has supported or attempted to support the child before and/or after the birth; or lived with the child following the child's birth. Putative fathers who did not do the above are not entitled to notice.

Agency Adoption. The information provided above regarding independent adoption is identical regarding agency adoption, except the following. The consent to adoption may be signed any time after birth. It may be witnessed by a notary or a representative of the adoption agency. Once the consent has been signed, and the child has been placed with the adoptive parents, the consent is irrevocable if the birth mother also signed a Certificate of Irrevocability, but for fraud or duress.

Most agencies in Oregon agree to do identified adoptions. Some also agree to do immediate hospital "at risk" placements, where the child is placed with the adoptive parents before the consents are irrevocable.

American Academy of Adoption Attorney members:

Timothy F. Brewer; 590 West 13th Avenue, Eugene, OR 97401
Tel: (541) 683-1814 ● tfbrewer.com ● t.brewer@adoptionattorneys.org
A graduate of the University of Oregon School of Law, he has been practicing law since 1985.

John Chally; 2722 NE 33rd Street, Portland, OR 97212
Tel: (503) 238-9720 ● bckattorneys.org ● j.chally@adoptionattorneys.org

Sandra L. Hodgson; 2722 NE 33rd Street, Portland, OR 97212
Tel: (503) 238-9720 ● bckattorneys.com ● s.hodgson@adoptionattorneys.org

Tabitha Lundberg Koh; 2722 NE 33rd Street, Portland, OR 97212
Tel: (503) 238-9720 ● bckattorneys.com ● t.koh@adoptionattorneys.org

Susan C. Moffet; 916 SW 17th St. #201, Redmond, OR 97756
Tel: (541) 316-7150 ● oregonadopt.com ● smoffet@oregonadopt.com
A graduate of the Northwestern University School of Law at Lewis and Clark College, she has been practicing law since 1987. She estimates she has completed more than 2,000 adoptions in her career: 80% independent; 15% agency, 5% intercountry. Her practice is limited to family formation law through adoptions and surrogacy. She does assist in creating adoptive matches.

Robin E. Pope; 4500 SW Hall Boulevard, Beaverton, OR 97005
Tel: (503) 352-3524 ● robinpope.com ● robin@robinpope.com
A graduate of Lewis & Clark Law School, she has been practicing law since 1981. She estimates she has completed more than 2,000 adoptions in her career. She handles assisted reproductive technology matters.

Erin Robinson; 14171 Bangy Rd., Lake Oswego, OR 97035
Tel: (503) 451-3321 ● attorneyerinrobinson.com ●
e.robinson@adoptionattorneys.org

PENNSYLVANIA

Official State Adoption Website:
http://www.dhs.state.pa.us/forchildren/childwelfareservices/adoptioninpennsylvania/index.htm

State Adoption Exchange or Related Website:
http://www.adoptpakids.org/AdoptionExchange.aspx

State laws and procedures:

General Information. Pennsylvania permits both independent and agency adoption. Advertising is permitted. To file a Petition for Adoption within Pennsylvania either the adoptive parents, the birth parents, or the child must reside there (making non-resident adoption possible). If it is an agency adoption the Petition for Adoption can also be filed in Pennsylvania if the agency having custody of the child is located there. If all parties agree, enforceable post-contact agreements can exist when approved by the court. Normally, adoptions are finalized six months to one year after the child's placement with the adoptive parents. The adoptive parents and the child are required to appear in court for the final hearing.

Independent Adoption. A pre-placement home study of the adoptive parents is required before a child can be placed in their home. An interim placement can be made with court approval, if a home study is not completed but underway, and the social worker recommends that the early placement occur. The home study is conducted by a licensed adoption agency or licensed social worker. The fee varies.

It is not required by law that the adoptive parents and birth mother meet in person and share identities, although many do so voluntarily. The adoptive parents are permitted to assist the birth mother with pregnancy-related medical expenses, although living expenses are not permitted. The child may be released from the hospital directly to the adoptive parents, although hospital forms and policies differ.

The consent to adoption can be signed no sooner than 72 hours after the birth. It must be witnessed by two witnesses. The birth mother has the automatic right to withdraw her consent for 30 days. On the 31st day it becomes irrevocable, except upon proof of fraud or duress. Usually about one to two months after the consent has become irrevocable, a court hearing will confirm the consent and issue an order terminating parental rights.

Pennsylvania has a putative birth father registry, but unlike most registries, it is not integral to the termination of a putative father's rights. Notice is required, unless with due diligence, he can't be found. A petition to terminate parental rights must be filed, and his rights severed if he defaults. If he elects to object, the adoptive parents must prove 4 months of abandonment if the child is a newborn, 6 months of abandonment if an older child, rape of the birth mother, or his inability to parent. A putative birth father can sign a consent to adoption before or after the birth, but may withdraw it within 30 days after the birth, or when he signed the consent, whichever is later.

Agency Adoption. There is no difference regarding the process in which a birth mother signs her consent to adoption in an independent or agency adoption. The information provided above regarding independent adoption (e.g. when the consent can be signed, before whom, legal burden to seek to withdraw a signed consent) is identical regarding agency adoption.

Many agencies in Pennsylvania agree to do identified adoptions.

American Academy of Adoption Attorney members:

Denise M. Bierly; 486 Nimitz Ave., State College, PA 16801
Tel: (814) 237-7900 ● d.bierly@adoptionattorneys.org
A graduate of the Dickenson School of Law of the Pennsylvania State University, she has been practicing law since 1990.

Craig B. Bluestein; 7237 Hollywood Rd., Fort Washington, PA 19034 ● Tel: (215) 646-9000 ● craigslegal.com ● c.bluestein@adoptionattorneys.org
A graduate of the Duquesne University School of Law, he has been practicing law since 1979.

Barbara L. Binder Casey; 527 Elm Street, Reading, PA 19601
Tel: (610) 376-9742 ● ababystepadoption.com ●
office@ababystepadoption.com
A graduate of the University of Pennsylvania Law School, she has been
practicing law since 1978. She estimates she has completed more than 900
adoptions in her career and completes 80-100 annually: 30% independent; 70%
agency. She assists in creating adoptive matches.

Donald C. Cofsky; 660 Two Logan Square, Philadelphia, PA 19103
Tel: (215) 563-2150 ● 209law.com ● dcc@209law.com
A past president of the American Academy of Adoption Attorneys and a
graduate of the Temple University School of Law, he has been practicing law
since 1973. He estimates he has completed more than 1,800 adoptions in his
career and completes 100 annually (independent, agency, stepparent,
grandparent, international) and also accepts contested adoption cases. He
assists in the legal aspects of assisted reproductive technology matters. In 2005
he was named as an Angel in Adoption by the Congressional Coalition of
Adoption.

Debra M. Fox; 355 W. Lancaster Avenue, Haverford, PA 19041
Tel: (610) 896-9972 ● transitionsadoption.com ●
mail@transitionsadoption.com
A graduate of the Temple University School of Law, she has been practicing law
since 1985. She estimates she has completed 1,000 adoptions in her career and
completes 15 annually: 30% independent, 50% agency, 20% international. She
only assists in creating adoptive matches through the agency she directs. She
handles contested adoption cases.

Tara E. Gutterman; 4701 Pine St. J7, Philadelphia, PA 19143
Tel: (215) 748-1441 ● t.gutterman@adoptionattorneys.org
A graduate of the Temple University School of Law, she has been practicing law
since 1991.

Deborah L. Lesko; 373 Vanadium Road, Pittsburgh, PA 15243
Tel: (412) 276-4200 ● leskolawandmediation.com ●
d.lesko@adoptionattorneys.org
A graduate of the University of Pittsburgh School of Law, she has been practicing
law since 1983. She estimates she has completed over 3,000 adoptions in her

career and completes 160 annually: 45% independent; 50% agency; 5% international.

Martin S. Leventon; 1011 Cedargrove Road, Wynnewood, PA 19096 • Tel: (610) 642-7182 • m.leventon@adoptionattorneys.org
A graduate of the Temple University School of Law, he has been practicing law since 1981.

Mary Ann Petrillo; 412 Main Street, Irwin, PA 15642
Tel: (724) 861-8333 • maryannpetrillo.com •
m.petrillo@adoptionattorneys.org
A graduate of the University of Pittsburgh School of Law, she has been practicing law since 1983. She estimates she has completed 1,000 adoptions in her career and completes 50 annually: 60% independent; 20% agency; 20% international. She does not assist in creating adoptive matches. She is an adoptive parent.

Susan Potts; 18 S. New St., West Chester, PA 19382
Tel: (484) 883-4466 • susanpottsesq@gmail.com
A graduate of Widener College of Law, she has been practicing law since 2001. She has 16 years experience representing birth parents, adoptive parents, grandparents and children. She assists in creating adoptive matches. She is an adoptive parent.

Bobbie L. Rabuck; 486 Nimitz Ave., State College, PA 16801
Tel: (814) 237-7900 • bierlyandrabuck.com •
b.rabuck@adoptionattorneys.org

Stuart S. Sacks; 4431 N. Front Street, Harrisburg, PA 17110
Tel: (717) 234-2401 • sasllp.com • s.sacks@adoptionattorneys.org
A graduate of the Washington University School of Law, he has been practicing law since 1973. He is an adoptive parent.

Deborah E. Spivack; P.O. Box 56182, Philadelphia, PA 19130
Tel: (215) 763-5550 • familybuildinglaw.net •
d.spivack@adoptionattorneys.org
A graduate of the Widener, University School of Law, she has been practicing law since 1993. She estimates she has completed more than 1,000 adoptions in her career and presently completes 80-100 (agency, independent, foreign re-adoption and intra family/stepparent). She is an adoptive parent. She is an

adoptive parent and received the 2105 Congressional Coalition of Adoption Angel Award. She has offices in New Jersey, Pennsylvania and Delaware.

Samuel C. Totaro; 2005 S. Easton Rd. #100, Doylestown, PA 18901
Tel: (267) 898-0570 ● curtinheefner.com ● s.totaro@adoptionattorneys.org

RHODE ISLAND

Official State Adoption Website: http://www.dcyf.ri.gov/adoption.php

State Adoption Exchange: Use above state website.

State laws and procedures:

General Information. Rhode Island permits both independent and agency adoption. Advertising is not permitted. To file a Petition for Adoption within Rhode Island the adoptive parents must reside there. If it is an agency adoption the Petition for Adoption can also be filed there if the agency having custody of the child is located there (making non-resident adoption possible). Normally, adoptions are finalized approximately six to eight months after the child's placement with the adoptive parents. The adoptive parents and the child are required to appear in court for the final hearing.

Independent Adoption. A pre-placement home study of the adoptive parents is not technically required before a child is placed in their home, but virtually all Rhode Island adoptive families elect to have one as it is the norm in the state. The post-placement home study may be conducted by the state adoption office but is usually done by private agencies. The fee for both pre- and post-placement home studies is about $1,200-$1,300.

It is not required by law that the adoptive parents and birth mother meet in person and share identities, although some elect to do so voluntarily. There are no specific laws governing whether the adoptive parents are permitted to assist the birth mother with pregnancy-related expenses, including living assistance, so most agencies and attorneys view it as permitted. The child may be released directly from the hospital to the adoptive parents, although this is usually done by discharging the baby to the birth mother or a relative, who in turn places the child with the adoptive parents.

The consent to adoption can be signed any time after the birth. It has no enforceability, however, until the birth mother affirms her desire to consent to the adoption before a judge in a Placement Hearing. This hearing usually occurs about three months after the child's placement with the adoptive parents but can be as late as at the final adoption hearing (when it could be done concurrently), about six months after the placement. Once the court approves the consent at this hearing, state law provides that the consent is irrevocable and can only be withdrawn upon proof of fraud or duress. Once the adoption is finalized by the court (usually six to seven months after the child's placement with the adoptive parents), however, the consent is irrevocable.

Rhode Island does not have a putative birth father registry. A putative father is entitled to notice if his whereabouts are known, and if not, notice by publication is required. Notice will be given of a termination of parental rights hearing, and if he fails to appear and object, his rights will normally be terminated.

Agency Adoption. The information provided above regarding independent adoption is identical regarding agency adoption, except for the following. A pre-placement home study is always required in an agency adoption. The adoption agency can file a Petition to Terminate Parental Rights no sooner that the fifteenth day after the birth, with the birth mother's agreement that her rights be voluntarily terminated. Once the court has issued its order terminating her parental rights she has lost the automatic right to stop the adoption. There are no state laws governing a request to withdraw consent, but case law indicates it can only be done upon proof of fraud or duress.

Most agencies in Rhode Island agree to do identified adoptions. Agencies will sometimes agree to make immediate hospital "at risk" placements but many still use initial foster parent placement.

American Academy of Adoption Attorney members:

William J. Gallogly; 1220 Kingstown Road #201, Wakefield, RI 02879 • Tel: (401) 789-8810 • w.gallogly@adoptionattorneys.org

SOUTH CAROLINA

Official State Adoption Website:
http://www.state.sc.us/dss/adoption/index.html

State Adoption Exchange or Related Website:
http://www.scheartgallery.org/

State laws and procedures:

General Information. South Carolina permits both independent and agency adoption. Advertising is permitted only by adoption agencies and attorneys licensed in South Carolina and prospective adoptive parents with a completed home study. To file a Petition for Adoption within South Carolina either the adoptive parents must reside there, or the child be physically present there. Non-residents can file a Petition for Adoption if the child is present in state at the time of filing, but the placement of a South Carolina child placed with non-residents must be approved by court order prior to placement. (This may be done pre-birth.) If it is an agency adoption the Petition for Adoption can also be filed in South Carolina if the agency having custody of the child is located there. Normally, adoptions are finalized three to six months after the child's placement with the adoptive parents. The adoptive parents and the child are required to appear in court for the final hearing. Other than in adoptions between blood relatives, adoptions by non-residents are normally required to be finalized within South Carolina, rather than the adoptive parents' state of residence.

Independent Adoption. A pre-placement home study of the adoptive parents is required before a child can be placed in their home. The home study is conducted by a licensed adoption agency or social worker approved by the State Department of Social Services to conduct home studies. The fee is approximately $1,500.

It is not required by law that the adoptive parents and the birth mother meet in person and share identities, although a small number elect to do so voluntarily. The adoptive parents are permitted to assist the birth mother with pregnancy-related medical and living expenses. The child may be released from the hospital directly to the adoptive parents, although hospital forms and policies differ.

The consent to adoption can be signed any time after the birth. It may be witnessed by a judge, an attorney not representing the adoptive parents, or a certified adoption worker. Consents are usually signed one to two days after the birth. Once signed, the consent is irrevocable, except upon proof of fraud or duress, and that the child's best interests would be served by being removed from the adoptive parents.

South Carolina has a putative birth father registry, applicable to unnamed fathers not married to the birth mother. If an unnamed putative father does not register before the date of the filing of the Petition for Adoption, his rights are waived. If the birth father is known/named, notice must be given to him, unless he can't be located with due diligence, and he has 30 days in which to object. If he objects, he will have to establish that (assuming the child was placed for adoption when less than six months of age) he lived with the birth mother, or if the baby has been born that he lived with the child, or provided reasonable financial support based upon his ability to provide. (Different standards apply if the child is placed when over six months of age.)

Agency Adoption. There is no difference regarding the process in which a birth mother signs her consent to adoption in an independent or agency adoption. The information provided above regarding independent adoption (e.g. when the consent can be signed, before whom, legal burden to seek to withdraw a signed consent) is identical regarding agency adoption.

Few agencies in South Carolina agree to do identified adoptions. Some also agree to make immediate hospital "at risk" placements, where the child is placed with the adoptive parents before the consents to adoption are irrevocable.

American Academy of Adoption Attorney members:

Emily McDaniel Barrett; 198 Rutledge Ave. #8, Charleston, SC 29403 • Tel: (843) 723-1688 • adoptionlawsc.com • emily@adoptionlawsc.com
A graduate of Cumberland School of Law, she has been practicing since 2000. She estimates she completes approximately 40 adoptions annually: 70% independent; 30% agency. She assists in creating adoptive matches.

Frederick Corley; 1214 King St., P.O. Box 2265, Beaufort, SC 22901 • Tel: (843) 524-3232 • f.corley@adoptionattorneys.org
A graduate of the University of South Carolina School of Law, he has been practicing law since 1976. He estimates he has completed more than 400 adoptions in his career and completes 110 annually: 60% independent; 40% agency. He does not assist in creating adoptive matches.

L. Dale Dove; 125 Hampton Street #200, Rock Hill, SC 29730
Tel: (803) 327-1910 • dove-barton.com • l.dove@adoptionattorneys.org

A graduate of the University of South Carolina School of Law, he has been practicing law since 1983. He is an adoptive parent.

James Fletcher Thompson; 302 E St. John Street, P.O. Box 1853, Spartanburg, SC 29304 ● Tel: (864) 573-5533 ● adoptionsc.com ● jfthompson@thompsonlawfirm.net
A graduate of the University of South Carolina School of Law, he has been practicing law since 1989.

Stephen Yacobi; 408 North Church St. #B, Greenville, SC 29601
Tel: (864) 242-3271 ● scadoptlaw.com ● syacobi@yacobilawfirm.com
A graduate of the University of South Carolina, he has been practicing law since 1980. He estimates he has completed 800 adoptions in his career and presently completes 40 annually.

SOUTH DAKOTA

Official State Adoption Website:
https://dss.sd.gov/childprotection/adoption/

State Adoption Exchange: Use above state website.

State laws and procedures:

General Information. South Dakota permits both independent and agency adoption. The state statutes don't say if adoption advertising is permitted or not, so it is generally presumed to be permitted. To file a Petition for Adoption within South Dakota the adoptive parents must reside there. Out-of-state residents can file their Petition for Adoption in South Dakota if the agency having custody of the minor is located there. Normally, adoptions are finalized approximately six months after the child's placement with the adoptive parents. The adoptive parents and the child are required to appear in court for the final hearing.

Independent Adoption. A pre-placement home study of the adoptive parents is required before a child can be placed in their home. The home study may be conducted by a licensed adoption agency or an independent licensed social worker with a private independent practice certificate who is approved by the South Dakota Department of Social Services. The fees for pre- and post-placement home study services typically varies from $1,000 to $1,500, but can be higher.

It is not required by law that the adoptive parents and birth mother meet in person and share identities, although most all do so voluntarily. The adoptive parents are permitted to assist the birth mother with pregnancy-related expenses, including living expenses, but prior court approval is required. The child may be released to the adoptive parents directly from the hospital, although most hospitals will require written permission from the birth mother identifying the adoptive parents.

The consent to adoption is made by the birth mother filing a Petition for Voluntarily Termination of Parental Rights, which can be signed at birth, but it cannot be filed prior to the fifth day after birth. The court's hearing on the petition can often occur immediately upon filing, or may take as long as about 25 days. The birth mother must have received counseling prior to the hearing, to have occurred at least 15 days prior to the court hearing. The birth mother must appear in court for the court to grant the order that her parental rights be voluntarily terminated. Prior to this hearing the birth mother has the right to withdraw her consent with no legal burden. Once the court has made the order, the consent is irrevocable, although the birth mother has a 30-day appeal period in which she may withdraw her consent if she can prove fraud was employed to obtain her consent.

South Dakota does not have a putative birth father registry. Notice must be given to any putative father identified by the birth mother. If he is unknown, there is a 60-day period in which he must step forward and acknowledge paternity, or his rights will be terminated. For birth fathers who wish to consent, they can appoint a person, often the birth mother, to present his consent at the hearing at which her parental rights are voluntarily terminated.

Agency Adoption. There is no difference regarding the process in which a birth mother signs her consent to adoption in an independent or agency adoption. The information provided above regarding independent adoption (e.g. when the consent can be signed, before whom, legal burden to seek to withdraw a signed consent) is identical regarding agency adoption.

Some agencies in South Dakota agree to do identified adoptions.

American Academy of Adoption Attorney members:

John R. Hughes; 101 N. Phillips Ave. #601, Sioux Falls, SD 57104;
Tel: (605) 339-3939 ● adoptionhelp.net ● j.hughes@adoptionattorneys.org
A graduate of the University of Nebraska College of Law, he has been practicing law since 1982. He estimates he has been involved in several hundred adoptions and related voluntary termination of parental rights proceedings in his career. He assists with independent, agency, interstate, stepparent and adult adoptions, as well as domestication of intercountry adoptions and re-adoptions. His firm assists in creating adoptive matches and he will consider representation in contested adoption cases.

TENNESSEE

Official State Adoption Website: http://tennessee.gov/youth/adoption.htm

State Adoption Exchange: Use above state website.

State laws and procedures:

General Information. Tennessee permits both independent and agency adoption. Advertising is permitted. To file a Petition for Adoption within Tennessee the adoptive parents must be residents for at least six months prior to filing the Petition for Adoption. However, a non-resident may possibly adopt in Tennessee if they obtained guardianship by order of a Tennessee court, and the adoption is filed in the same county as the guardianship. Normally, adoptions are finalized six months after the child's placement with the adoptive parents. The adoptive parents are required to appear in court at the final hearing.

Independent Adoption. A pre-placement home study of the adoptive parents is required before a child is placed in their home. Post-placement supervision may be conducted by a licensed adoption agency. The fee varies but usually does not exceed $1,200. (Some courts will waive the home study requirement, as well as the typical six-month period before finalization if the adoptive parents are related to the child.)

It is not required by law that the adoptive parents and the birth mother meet in person and share identities, although it is voluntarily done in most adoptions. The adoptive parents are permitted to assist the birth mother with pregnancy-related expenses, although living expenses may not be provided beyond 90 days prior to, and 45 days after, the birth, unless a court expressly grants it. The child may be released directly from the hospital to the adoptive parents, although hospital policies differ. Some hospitals simply require a written release, while others require a copy of the birth mother's consent to the adoption.

The consent to adoption, called a *surrender*, cannot be signed before the fourth day after the birth, unless a court waives this period. It must be witnessed by a judge. Once signed, the birth mother has the right to withdraw the consent for a period of three business days. Once the three-day period has elapsed the consent is irrevocable, but for proof of fraud or duress.

Tennessee has a putative birth father registry. The registry must be checked for putative birth fathers ten days prior to filing the Petition for Adoption and the petition to terminate his parental rights. A man who has registered, as well as any man personally named by the birth mother, must be given notice. A primary ground for granting the action to terminate his parental rights is the putative birth father's failure to file a paternity action within 30 days of notice. A putative father may also sign a consent to adoption, or a Waiver of Rights and Notice either before or after the child is born.

Agency Adoption. There is no difference regarding the process in which a birth mother signs her consent to adoption in an independent or agency adoption. The information provided above regarding independent adoption (e.g. when the consent can be signed, before whom, legal burden to seek to withdraw a signed consent) is identical regarding agency adoption.

Some agencies in Tennessee agree to do identified adoptions. Some agencies also agree to make immediate hospital "at risk" placements.

American Academy of Adoption Attorney members:

Lisa L. Collins; 4501 Charlotte Ave. #90744, Nashville, TN 37209
Tel: (615) 269-5540 ● tnadopt.com ● lcollins@tnadoption.com
A graduate of the Vanderbilt University School of Law, she has been practicing law since 1993. She also handles assisted reproductive technology matters.

Dawn Coppock; P.O. Box 388, Strawberry Plains, TN 37871
Tel: (865) 933-8173 ● dawncoppock.com ● d.coppock@adoptionattorneys.org
A graduate of the Wythe School of Law at the College of William and Mary, she has been practicing law since 1987.

Michael S. Jennings; 130 Jordan Drive, Chattanooga, TN 37421
Tel: (423) 892-2006 ● m.jennings@adoptionattorneys.org
A graduate of the University of Georgia School of Law, he has been practicing
law since 1984.

Theodore R. Kern; 800 S. Gay St. #1600, Knoxville, TN 37929
Tel: (865) 637-3900 ● tedkernlaw.com ● t.kern@adoptionattorneys.org
A graduate of the Case Western Reserve School of Law, he has been practicing
law since 1983. He has completed more than 300 adoptions in his career, of all
types. His practice also includes both interstate and contested adoptions. He is
an adoptive parent.

Sharon T. Massey; 221 S. Third Street, Clarksville, TN 37040
Tel: (931) 906-0555 ● sharonmasseylaw.com ●
s.massey@adoptionattorneys.org
A graduate of Nashville School of Law, she has been practicing law since 1998.
She estimates she completes 150 adoptions annually: 40% independent; 40%
agency; 20% international. She does not assist in creating adoptive matches.

Robert D. Tuke; 222 4th Avenue North, Nashville, TN 37219
Tel: (615) 256-8585 ● tntlaw.net ● r.tuke@adoptionattorneys.org
A graduate of the Vanderbilt University School of Law, he has been practicing
law since 1976. He estimates that he completes 20-30 adoptions annually, 80%
of which are independent. He does not assist in creating adoptive matches.

Kevin W. Weaver; 51 Germantown Ct. #112, Cordova, TN 38018
Tel: (901) 757-1700 ● k.weaver@adoptionattorneys.org

TEXAS

Official State Adoption Website:
http://www.dfps.state.tx.us/Adoption_and_Foster_Care/About_Adoption/

State Adoption Exchange or Related Website:
https://www.dfps.state.tx.us/Adoption_and_Foster_Care/Get_Started/Informati on_Meetings/default.asp

State laws and procedures:

General Information. Texas permits both independent and agency adoption. Advertising is permitted only by licensed adoption agencies. To file a Petition for Adoption within Texas either the adoptive parents must reside there, or the child to be adopted must have been born there or reside there (making non-resident adoption possible). The child is required to reside in the state for at least six months before finalization, but this can be waived in exceptional circumstances. If it is an agency adoption the Petition for Adoption can also be filed in Texas if the adoption agency having custody of the child is located there. Normally, adoptions are finalized approximately seven or eight months after the birth or the placement of the child with the adoptive parents. The adoptive parents are required to appear in court for the final hearing, although the court may waive this requirement and allow only one parent to be present.

Independent Adoption. A pre-placement home study, called an "adoption evaluation," is not required before a child can be placed in their home, but it is required prior to the court's order terminating parental rights. The home study may be conducted by a licensed adoption agency or qualified licensed social worker approved by the court. The fee for pre- and post-placement adoption evaluation is typically under $3,000.

It is not required by law that the adoptive parents and birth mother meet in person but it is required that they share identities. The adoptive parents are permitted to assist the birth mother with pregnancy-related medical, counseling and legal expenses. Any other financial assistance may be provided to her only through a licensed adoption agency. The child can be released directly from the hospital to the adoptive parents with the birth mother signing a release form which varies hospital to hospital.

The consent to adoption, called a *relinquishment*, can be signed no sooner than 48 hours after the birth. It must be witnessed by a notary and two witnesses. Most consents are signed within several days of the birth. There are two options in relinquishment forms. One is that it is irrevocable from signing for a period of up to 60 days. During those 60 days the adoptive parents' attorney must have a court terminate the birth mother's rights based upon her relinquishment. Failure to do so will make the consent revocable. The other option is to make the consent revocable for ten days, and any time thereafter the court order may be sought. The only grounds to set aside an irrevocable relinquishment is upon proof of fraud or duress.

Texas has a putative birth father registry. Putative birth fathers must register no later than the 31st day after the birth. Any birth father who registers must be given notice of a termination of a parental rights action. A birth father who is then served with a citation must file his response by the first Monday after the elapsing of 20 days from notice. An alleged/putative father can sign an Affidavit of Waiver of Interest pre-birth and it is irrevocable upon signing.

Agency Adoption. There is little difference regarding the process in which a birth mother signs her relinquishment in an independent or agency adoption. However, a birth mother's relinquishment in an agency adoption is irrevocable upon signing without the 60-day period, after which she has the right to seek to withdraw her relinquishment if a court order terminating her rights was not obtained.

Some agencies in Texas agree to do identified adoptions. Some agencies also agree to make immediate hospital "at risk" placements, allowing the child to be placed before the consents to adoption are final.

American Academy of Adoption Attorney members:

Gerald A. Bates; 3200 River Front Dr., #204, Fort Worth, TX 76107
Tel: (817) 338-2840 ● txadoptions.com ● g.bates@adoptionattorneys.org

Lester R. Buzbee III; 116 S. Avenue C, Humble, TX 77338
Tel: (281) 540-8060 ● l.buzbee@adoptionattorneys.org
A graduate of South Texas College of Law, he has been practicing law since 1977. He estimates he completes 90 adoptions annually: 20% independent; 80% agency.

Carla M. Calabrese; 5944 Luther Lane #875, Dallas, TX 75225
Tel: (214) 939-3000 ● calabreselaw.com ● c.calabrese@adoptionattorneys.org
A graduate of the University of Cincinnati College of Law, she has been practicing law since 1986.

David Charles Cole; 3631 Fairmont St., #201, Dallas, TX 75219
Tel: (214) 363-5117 ● adoptlegal.com ● d.cole@adoptionattorneys.org
A graduate of Pepperdine University School of Law, he has been practicing law since 1987.

Heidi Bruegel Cox; 6300 John Ryan Drive, Fort Worth, TX 76132
Tel: (817) 922-6043 ●gladney.org ● h.cox@adoptionattorneys.org
A graduate of the Texas Tech University School of Law, she has been practicing law since 1986, she focuses on agency adoptions, including private domestic adoptions (approximately 125 per year), adoptions from Texas foster care, and international adoptions. In Texas is it illegal for an attorney or anyone else to match an expectant mother with a prospective adoptive parent, so all placements are completed with agency matching.

Eric C. Freeby; 201 Main Street #801, Ft. Worth, TX 76102
Tel: (817) 338-4888 ● brownpruitt.com ● e.freeby@adoptionattorneys.org
A graduate of University of Arkansas, Little Rock, he has been practicing since 2005. He estimates he completes 375 adoptions annually: 30% independent; 50% agency; 20% international. He does not assist in creating adoptive matches.

Winifred "Winnie" Huff; 5944 Luther Ln. #875, Dallas. TX 75225
Tel: (214) 939-3000 ● calabresehuff.com ● w.huff@adoptionattorneys.org

Dale R. Johnson; 7303 Blanco Road, San Antonio, TX 78216
Tel: (210) 349-3761 ● d.johnson@adoptionattorneys.org

Michael R. Lackmeyer; 1201 S. WS Young Dr. #F, Killeen, TX 76543
Tel: (254) 690-2223 ● adopttexas.net ● m.lackmeyer@adoptionattorneys.org
A graduate of the Baylor University School of Law, he has been practicing law since 1970.

Susan I. Paquet; 201 Main Street, Suite 801, Fort Worth, TX 76102
Tel: (817) 338-4888 ● brownpruitt.com ● s.paquet@adoptionattorneys.org
A graduate of the University of Arizona, she has been practicing since 1983. She estimates she completes 375 adoptions annually: 30% independent; 50% agency; 20% international. She does not assist in creating adoptive matches.

Donald Royall; 13430 Northwest Freeway #270, Houston, TX 77040
Tel: (713) 462-6500 ● adoptiontexas.com ● d.royall@adoptionattorneys.org

Melody Royall; 13430 Northwest Freeway #270, Houston, TX 77040
Tel: (713) 462-6500 ● adoptiontexas.com ● m.royall@adoptionattorneys.org

Steve Watkins; P.O. Box 876, Greenville, TX 75403
Tel: (903) 454-6688 ● watkins-perkins.com ●
s.watkins@adoptionattorneys.org
A graduate of the Texas Tech University School of Law, he has been practicing law since 1980.

Jenny L. Womack; 5495 Beltline Rd, Dallas, TX 75254
Tel: (214) 935-3310 ● womackadoptions.com ●
j.womack@adoptionattorneys.org
A graduate of the University of Texas School of Law, she has been practicing law since 1998. Her practice is focused exclusively on family formation law, including all types of adoptions as well as assisted reproduction matters. She received an Angel in Adoption award in 2009 from the Congressional Coalition for Adoption Institute.

Ellen A. Yarrell; 50 Briar Hollow Lane, #425 W, Houston, TX 77027
Tel: (713) 621-3332 ● e.yarrel@adoptionattorneys.org
A graduate of the University of Texas at Austin School of Law, she has been practicing law since 1979.

Harold Zuflacht; 12000 Huebner Road, #200, San Antonio, TX 78230
Tel: (210) 349-9933 ● h.zuflacht@adoptionattorneys.org

UTAH

Official State Adoption Website: http://dcfs.utah.gov/adoption

State Adoption Exchange: Use above state website.

State laws and procedures:

General Information. Utah permits both independent and agency adoption. Advertising is permitted by adoptive parents. To file a Petition for Adoption within Utah the adoptive parents must reside there, the child is born there, or the child is in the custody of a Utah adoption agency (making non-resident adoption possible). Normally, adoptions are finalized six months after the child's placement with the adoptive parents. The adoptive parents and the child are normally required to appear in court for the final hearing, but counts can waive this requirement for good cause.

Independent Adoption. A pre-placement home study of the adoptive parents is required before a child can be placed in their home, unless a court order is obtained allowing the placement in advance of a pre-placement home study. The home study is conducted by a licensed adoption agency or licensed social worker. The fee for pre- and post-placement home study services is typically $1,000.

It is not required by law that the adoptive parents and birth mother meet in person and share identities, but it is usually done voluntarily. The adoptive parents are permitted to assist the birth mother with pregnancy-related medical, legal, counseling and living expenses. The child may be released directly from the hospital to the adoptive parents, usually via a release form prepared by the adoptive parents' attorney.

The birth mother's consent to adoption can be signed no sooner than 24 hours after the birth. It must be witnessed by a judge or a person appointed by the court. Most consents are signed within three days of the birth. Once signed, the consent to adoption is irrevocable, but for proof of fraud or duress. A birth father's consent may be signed before or after the birth.

Utah has a putative birth father registry. Prior to when the birth mother signs her consent to adoption, the putative birth father must file a paternity action and register notice of that action, as well show as he has paid pregnancy expenses, if the birth father lives in Utah. If he fails to do so before the birth mother's consent is signed, he loses his rights. If he lives outside of Utah, he must meet the same standard, if he knows or should have known prior to the birth mother's consent that the adoption may occur in Utah, but he is given 20 days to do so from the date of such knowledge, or before the birth mother signs her consent, whichever occurs later. If he does not know the adoption may take place in Utah, prior to the birth mother's consent he must comply with the laws of the state where conception occurred or where the birth mother last resided, to establish parental rights.

Agency Adoption. There is no difference regarding the process in which a birth mother signs her consent to adoption in an independent or agency adoption, although the consent may usually be witnessed by a notary and agency representative. The information provided above regarding independent adoption (e.g. when the consent can be signed and the legal burden to withdraw the consent) is identical regarding agency adoption.

Some agencies in Utah agree to do identified adoptions. Virtually no agencies will agree to make immediate hospital "at risk" placements, allowing the child to be placed with the adoptive parents before the consents to adoption are final.

American Academy of Adoption Attorney members:

Dale M. Dorius; 29 S. Main; P.O. Box 895, Brigham City, UT 84302
Tel: (435) 723-5219 ● d.dorius@adoptionattorneys.org

Larry S. Jenkins; 50 East South Temple Street, 4th Floor, Salt Lake City, UT 84111 ●Tel: (801) 366-6060 ● kmclaw.com● l.jenkins@adoptionattorneys.org
A graduate of the J. Reuben Clark Law School at Brigham Young University, he has been practicing law since 1986. He estimates he has completed over 3,000 adoptions in his career and completes 200-300 annually: 30% independent; 65% agency; 5% international. He does not assist in creating adoptive matches. He is a 2005 recipient of the Angel in Adoption award by the Congressional Coalition on Adoption Institute.

Lance Rich; 500 Eagle Tower, 60 E. South Temple, Salt Lake City, UT 84111
● Tel: (801) 350-7621 ● kmclaw.com ● l.rich@adoptionattorneys.org
A graduate of the Michigan School of Law, he has been practicing since 2004. He estimates he completes 200 or more adoptions annually: 30% independent, 65% agency, 5% international. He does not assist in creating adoptive matches.

Derek J. Williams; 10 Exchange Pl. 11th Fl., Salt Lake City, UT 84111 ● Tel: (801) 322-9331 ● scmlaw.com ● djw@scmlaw.com
A graduate of the University of Utah S.J. Quinney College of Law, he has been practicing since 2003. He handles approximately 75 adoptions annually: 75% independent, 25% agency. He does not assist in creating adoptive matches. He accepts contested adoption cases. He is an adoptive parent.

VERMONT

Official State Adoption Website: http://www.projectfamilyvt.org

State Adoption Exchange: Use above state website.

State laws and procedures:

General Information. Vermont permits both independent and agency adoption. Advertising is permitted. To file a Petition for Adoption within Vermont the adoptive parents must be residents. If it is an agency adoption the Petition for Adoption may also be filed in Vermont if the agency having custody of the child is located there (making non-resident adoption possible). Normally, adoptions are finalized approximately seven months after the child's placement. The adoptive parents are required to appear in court for the final hearing.

Independent Adoption. A pre-placement home study of the adoptive parents is required before a child is placed in their home. The post-placement home study may be conducted by a licensed adoption agency or social worker approved the court. The fee for the pre- and post-placement home study varies but is usually $1,750-$2,000.

It is not required that the adoptive parents and the birth mother meet in person and share identities, although it is usually done voluntarily. The adoptive parents are permitted to assist the birth mother with pregnancy-related expenses, including living costs. The child may be released directly to the adoptive parents from the hospital, although each hospital may employ a different release form.

The consent to adoption can be signed no sooner than 36 hours after the birth. It must be witnessed by a judge. Most consents are signed within days of the birth. Once signed, the birth mother has the automatic right to withdraw the consent for 21 days. After the 21-day period has expired, the consent is irrevocable except upon proof of fraud or duress.

Vermont has a putative birth father registry. Putative birth fathers file a notice of their intent to retain parental rights in the probate court. The court then notifies the state registry of the filing, which is cross-checked when a Petition for Adoption is filed.

Agency Adoption. There is no difference regarding the process in which a birth mother signs her consent to adoption in an independent or agency adoption. The information provided above regarding independent adoption (e.g. when the consent can be signed, before whom and the legal burden to withdraw the consent) is identical regarding agency adoption.

Some agencies in Vermont agree to do identified adoptions. Some agencies also agree to make immediate hospital "at risk" placements, allowing the child to be placed with the adoptive parents before the consents to adoption are final.

American Academy of Adoption Attorney members:

Kurt M. Hughes; 131 Main St., P.O. Box 363, Burlington, VT 05402
Tel: (802) 864-9811 ● mhtpc.com ● khughes@mhtpc.com
A graduate of Vermont Law School, he has been practicing law since 1985. He estimates he has completed hundreds of adoptions in his career and presently completes 20-30 annually (independent, agency, adult and stepparent). He accepts contested adoption cases. He handles assisted reproductive technology matters and is the owner of the Vermont Surrogacy Network.

VIRGINIA

Official State Adoption Website:
http://www.dss.virginia.gov/family/ap/index.cgi

State Adoption Exchange: Use above state website.

State laws and procedures:

General information. Virginia allows both independent and agency adoption. Advertising is permitted. To file a Petition for Adoption within Virginia the adoptive parents must reside there, or the birth mother resides in Virginia and the consent to adoption is taken there (making non-resident adoption possible). The Petition for Adoption can also be filed in Virginia if the agency having custody of the child is located there. Normally, adoptions are finalized 4 to 7 months after the child's placement with the adoptive parents in independent adoption, and 9 months in agency adoptions. The adoptive parents and the child are generally not required to attend a final hearing in which the adoption is finalized, as typically the order granting the adoption is signed by the judge simply upon receipt of the social worker's report, without any hearing.

Independent Adoption. A pre-placement home study of the adoptive parents is not mandatory before a child can be placed in the adoptive parents' home, although the birth mother's consent will not be accepted by the court until a home study report to the court has been completed. The home study report to court is usually conducted by a licensed adoption agency, but occasionally is done by a County Department of Social Services.

It is required by law that the adoptive parents and birth mother meet in person, unless all parties waive sharing names. The adoptive parents are permitted to assist the birth mother with pregnancy-related medical, counseling and legal expenses. Living costs may also be provided, but requires written confirmation from her physician that she is unable to work for a medical reason. The child can be released directly from the hospital to the adoptive parents, although each hospital may employ a different release form.

The birth mother's consent to adoption may be signed no sooner than the child's third calendar day of life. It must be witnessed by a judge. (The birth father's consent, married or unmarried to the birth mother, can be signed either before or after the birth, with a 7-day period from the date of signing to revoke.) The courts give preference to adoption matters and try to schedule the signing of adoption consents within ten days of the filing of the petition. Once the birth mother's consent is signed, the birth mother has the automatic right to withdraw her consent for a period of 7 days, unless the child is at least ten days old and the birth mother is represented by her own attorney, then she can waive the 7-day revocation period. The consent cannot be revoked except upon proof of fraud or duress.

Virginia has a putative father registry. Notice of the registry must be given to any putative birth father named by the birth mother. The notice explains the existence of the registry and that he has 10 days from the date of the mailing to file. If the identity or location of the birth father is not ascertainable, then he is not entitled to actual notice but has ten days after birth to register with the registry. If he files with the registry he must be given notice of the adoption. The standard at the hearing is the child's best interests. Birth fathers wishing to agree to the adoption may sign their consent before, or after, the birth before a notary, or may sign a Denial of Paternity.

Agency Adoption. The information provided above regarding independent adoption is identical regarding agency adoption, except for the following. A pre-placement home study of the adoptive parents is required. The consent to adoption, called an *entrustment agreement* in an agency adoption, can be signed any time after birth and is to be witnessed by a notary. The entrustment becomes irrevocable 7 days after execution, upon the child reaching 10 days of age, or when the child is placed with the adoptive parents, whichever is later.

Most agencies will make immediate "at risk" placements.

American Academy of Adoption Attorney members:

Mark Eckman; 311 Maple Avenue, Suite E, Vienna, VA 22180
Tel: (703) 242-8801 ● hagarcenter.org ● m.eckman@adoptionattorneys.org
A graduate of the Catholic University School of Law, he has been practicing law since 1984. He estimates he has completed more than 1,000 adoptions in his career and completes 50 annually: 30% independent; 20% agency; 85% international. He does not assist in creating adoptive matches. Mr. Eckman speaks Spanish, French, German and Italian.

Barbara C. Jones; 7016 Balmoral Forest Road, Clifton, VA 20124
Tel: (703) 222-1101 ● joyfuladoption.com ● b.jones@adoptionattorneys.org
A graduate of the George Mason University School of Law, she has been practicing law since 1988. She estimates she completes 100 adoptions annually: 50% independent, 35% agency, 15% international. She is the co-author of Virginia Lawyer's Practice Handbook: Procedures and Forms.

Robert H. Klima; 9300 Grant Ave. #101, Manassas, VA 20110
Tel: (703) 361-5051 ● vaadoptlaw.com ● r.klima@adoptionattorneys.org
A graduate of the George Mason University School of Law, he has been practicing law since 1978.

Karen S. Law; 42909 Riverstone Court, Ashburn, VA 20148
Tel: (703) 723-4385 ● lawadoption.com ● k.law@adoptionattorneys.org

Thomas Nolan; 304 Hickman Rd., Charlottesville, VA 22911
Tel: (434) 817-4001 ● vawills.com ● nolan@vawills.com
A graduate of the University of Virginia School of Law, he has been practicing law since 1984. He estimates he completes approximately 20 adoptions annually: 50% independent, 50% agency. He does not assist in creating adoptive matches. He is an adoptive parent.

Rosemary G. O'Brien; 109 South Fairfax Street, Alexandria, VA 22314 ●Tel: (703) 549-5110 ● r.obrien@adoptionattorneys.org

Janet Ours; 9306 Grant Avenue, Manassas, VA 20110
Tel: (571) 292-5651 ● oldtownadvocates.com ● jours@oldtownadvocates.com
A graduate of George Mason University School of Law, she has been practicing since 1999. She estimates she completes 25 adoptions annually: 50% independent; 50% agency. She assists in creating adoptive matches.

Stanton Phillips; 1921 Gallows Rd. #110, Tysons Corner, VA 22182
Tel: (703) 891-2400 ● babylaw.us ● stan@babylaw.com
A graduate of the George Mason School of Law, he has been practicing law since 1980. He estimates he has completed 3,500 adoptions in his career and completes 100 adoptions annually: 50% independent; 50% agency. He assists in creating adoptive matches. He handles assisted reproduction, contested adoptions and subsidy issues. He is the recipient of the 2007 Congressional Angel in Adoption award and has served as Chair of the Advisory Council of the Congressional Coalition on Adoption Institute, Chair of the D.C. Superior Court Adoption Rules Committee and as a Trustee of the American Academy of Adoption Attorneys.

Rodney M. Poole; 4901 Dickens Rd., #108, Richmond, VA 23230
Tel: (804) 358-6669 ● pooleandpoole.com ● r.poole@adoptionattorneys.org
A graduate of the University of Virginia, he has been practicing law since 1973. He estimates he has completed 2,500 adoptions in his career and completes 75 annually: 44% independent; 28% agency; 28% international. He does not assist in creating adoptive matches. He is an adoptive parent and a past-president of the American Academy of Adoption Attorneys.

Colleen M. Quinn; 4928 W. Broad Street, Richmond, VA 23230
Tel: (804) 545-9406 ● virginia-adoption-attorney.com ●
quinn@lockequinn.com
A graduate of the University of Virginia School of Law, she has been practicing law since 1988. She estimates she completes 150-200 adoptions annually, 85% independent and 15% agency. She assists adoptive parents in networking, handles contested adoptions and handles all varieties of adoptions. She serves on the Board of Trustees of the American Academy of Adoption Attorneys and was Academy President (2016-17). She is a 2008 recipient of the Congressional Coalition in Adoption's Angel in Adoption award, recipient of the "Leader in the Law" award by *Virginia Lawyer's Weekly* for her adoption and surrogacy work, and named among the "Best Lawyers in America" from 2014 to 2017 by the *U.S. News & World Report*. She is a member of the National Council for Adoption and the LGBT Bar.

Jennifer B. Shupert; 1333 Laskin Rd., Virginia Beach, VA 23451
Tel: (757) 390-3331 ● shupertchaing.com ● j.shupert@adoptionattorneys.org
A graduate of Regent University School of Law, she has been practicing law since 2003. She handles independent, agency, adult, and stepparent

adoptions. She also accepts contested adoption cases and reproductive technology matters.

Please be aware than several AAAA members in neighboring states, particularly Maryland and the District of Columbia, practice in Virginia, including Mark McDermott (DC) and Peter Wiernicki (MD).

WASHINGTON

Official State Adoption Website: https://www.dshs.wa.gov/ca/adoption-and-adoption-support/considering-adoption

State Adoption Exchange or Related Website: http://www.warekids.org

State laws and procedures:

General Information. Washington permits both independent and agency adoption. Advertising is permitted, but only when placed by adoption agencies, attorneys licensed by the State of Washington, or adoptive parents with an approved Washington home study. To file a Petition for Adoption in Washington either the adoptive parents, the child, or the birth mother must reside there (making non-resident adoption possible). Normally, adoptions are finalized two to three months after the placement of the child with the adoptive parents. The adoptive parents are usually required to appear in court for the final hearing, although the court may waive this requirement.

Independent Adoption. A pre-placement home study of the adoptive parents is required before a child may be placed in their home. The home study may be conducted by the state adoption office, a licensed adoption agency, or licensed social worker or other person approved by the court. The fee varies but is usually $500 to $2,000.

It is not required by law that the adoptive parents and the birth mother meet in person and share identities, although most do so voluntarily. The adoptive parents are permitted to assist the birth mother with pregnancy-related expenses with court approval. The child can be released directly from the hospital to the adoptive parents. Some hospitals only require a hospital release form but most others require a court order.

The consent to adoption may be signed before or after the birth. It must be witnessed by a witness selected by the birth parent. Birth parents under the age of 18 must have a guardian ad litem appointed to make sure they understand the proceedings. The consent to adoption becomes effective only after it has been filed and approved by the court, at which point the court terminates the parental rights of the parent. This can occur no sooner than 48 hours after birth, or the signing of the consent, whichever occurs later. Before the court has approved the consent, the birth mother has the automatic right to withdraw her consent without any legal burden. After the court has approved the consent, the consent is irrevocable, except upon proof of fraud, duress or mental incompetency.

Washington does not have a putative birth father registry. Putative birth fathers must be given notice (usually 20 days if by personal service and 30 days if by publication) of a hearing to terminate their parental rights. If they do not object, their rights can be terminated by default. If they do object the court will examine the best interests of the child and whether the putative father failed to perform parental duties showing a substantial lack of regard for his obligations.

Agency Adoption. There is no difference regarding the process in which a birth mother signs her consent to adoption in an independent or agency adoption. The information provided above regarding independent adoption (e.g. when the consent can be signed, before whom and the legal burden to withdraw the consent) is identical regarding agency adoption.

Some agencies in Washington agree to do identified adoptions. Some agencies also agree to make immediate hospital "at risk" placements, allowing the child to be placed with the adoptive parents before the consents to adoption are final.

American Academy of Adoption Attorney members:

David V. Andersen; 5507 35th Avenue NE, Seattle, WA 98115
Tel: (206) 547-1400 ● holmancahill.com ● d.andersen@adoptionattorneys.org

Janna J. Annest; 1000 Second Ave. 30th Fl., Seattle, WA 98104
Tel: (206) 382-1000 ● millsmeyers.com ● j.annest@adoptionattorneys.org
A graduate of the University of Washington School of Law, she has been practicing since 2003. She helps form all types of adoptive families, and her practice includes representation of adoptive parents and birth parents in private, domestic, interstate, kinship, adult, and second-parent adoptions, as well as finalization of international and DSHS adoptions. She is an adoptive parent.

Rita L. Bender; 1301 Fifth Avenue, 34th Fl., Seattle, WA 98101

Tel: (206) 623-6501 ● skellengerbender.com ●
r.bender@adoptionattorneys.org
A graduate of Rutgers University School of Law, she has been practicing law since 1968. She estimates she has completed several thousand adoptions in her career (independent, agency, intercountry, interstate, foster parent adoption and same sex couples). She assists in creating adoptive matches and handles assisted reproductive technology matters. She is an adoptive parent.

Mark M. Demaray; 145 3ʳᵈ Avenue South, #201, Edmonds, WA 98020 ● Tel: (425) 771-6453 ● washingtonadoptionattorney.com ●
m.demaray@adoptionattorneys.org
A graduate of the Lewis and Clark Law School of Portland, he has been practicing law since 1981. He estimates he has completed more than 5,000 adoptions in his career. He assists in creating adoptive matches. He is an adoptive parent.

Marcus J. Fry; P.O. Box 1689, Yakima, WA 98907
Tel: (509) 248-7220 ● lyon-law.com ● m.fry@adoptionattorneys.org

J. Eric Gustafson; P.O. Box 1689, Yakima, WA 98901
Tel: (509) 248-7220 ● northwestadoptions.com ●
e.gustafson@adoptionattorneys.org
A graduate of the Northwestern School of Law of Lewis and Clark College at Portland, he has been practicing law since 1973. He estimates he has completed more than 1,000 adoptions in his career, and last year completed approximately 50 (36 independent; 6 agency; 2 intercountry). He is an adoptive parent.

Michele Gentry Hinz; 33035 52ⁿᵈ Avenue South, Auburn, WA 98001 ● Tel: (253) 740-0667 ● michelehinz.com ● m.hinz@adoptionattorneys.org
A graduate of the University of Washington School of Law, she has been practicing law since 1981. Approximately of her 75% of her practice consists of adoptions (typically 90% independent; 5% agency; 5% intercountry).

Mark R. Iverson; 921 W. Broadway #305, Spokane, WA 99201
Tel: (509) 462-3678 ● adoptionwa.com ● m.iverson@adoptionattorneys.org
A graduate of Gonzaga University School of Law, he has been practicing since 1988. He estimates he completes 300 adoptions annually: 60% independent; 30% agency; 10% international. He assists in creating adoptive matches.

Albert G. Lirhus; 1200 5th Ave, Suite 1550, Seattle, WA 98101

Tel: (206) 728-5858 ● lk-legal.com ● andrea@lk-legal.com
A graduate of the University of Washington School of Law, he has been practicing law since 1973. He estimates he been involved with more than 6,000 adoptions in his career and completes 200 annually: 25% independent; 25% step and second parent, 40% agency; 10% international. He assists in creating adoptive matches. He will consider contested adoption cases.

Raegen N. Rasnic; 1301 Fifth Avenue #3401, Seattle, WA 98101
Tel: (206) 623-6501 ● skellengerbender.com ● r.rasnic@adoptionattorneys.org
A graduate of the University of California, The Hastings College of Law, she has been practicing since 1995.

Joyce E. Robson; 201 St. Helens Avenue, Tacoma, WA 98402
Tel: (253) 572-5104 ● j.robson@adoptionattorneys.org
A graduate of the University of Puget Sound School of Law, she has been practicing law since 1988.

Marie N. Tilden; 4001 Main St. #327, Vancouver, WA 98663
Tel: (360) 695-0290 ● marietilden.com ● m.tilden@adoptionattorneys.org
A graduate of the University of Texas School of Law, she has been practicing law since 1985.

WEST VIRGINIA

State Adoption Office: http://www.wvdhhr.org/oss/adoption

State Adoption Exchange or Related Website:
http://www.adoptawvchild.org

State laws and procedures:

General Information. West Virginia allows both independent and agency adoption. Advertising is permitted. To file a Petition for Adoption within West Virginia the adoptive parents must reside there. Normally, adoptions are finalized six to nine months after the child's placement with the adoptive parents. The adoptive parents and the child are usually required to attend the court hearing in which the adoption is finalized.

Independent Adoption. A pre-placement home study of the adoptive parents is not required. The post-placement supervision may be conducted by a licensed adoption agency or a person approved by the court. The fee varies but is typically under $2,000.

It is not required by law that the adoptive parents and the birth mother meet in person and share identities, although this is sometimes done voluntarily. The adoptive parents are only permitted to assist the birth mother with medical, counseling and legal expenses. Anything outside those categories requires court approval, which is rarely given. The child can be released directly from the hospital to the adoptive parents, although hospital forms and policies vary.

The consent to adoption may be signed no sooner than 72 hours after the birth. It must be witnessed by a notary. If the birth mother is under the age of 18, the consent must be witnessed by a judge. Two consent options can be used. If the consent is an *Irrevocable Consent,* the consent is irrevocable effective immediately. It can only be withdrawn upon proof of fraud or duress. Birth mothers are alternatively permitted to sign a *Conditional Consent*, in which they may give themselves the right to stop the adoption within the conditions set forth in the consent (such as a number of days to reconsider, or if the birth father were to object).

West Virginia does not have a putative birth father registry. Notice must be given to any putative father at his last known address or by publication if unfindable. The notice is of the final adoption hearing. Birth fathers wishing to consent must wait 72 hours, like birth mothers, to sign a consent.

Agency Adoption. There is no difference regarding the process in which a birth mother signs her consent to adoption, called a relinquishment, in an independent or agency adoption. The information provided above regarding independent adoption (e.g. when the consent can be signed, before whom and the legal burden to withdraw the consent) is identical regarding agency adoption. However, a pre-placement home study is required.

Some agencies in West Virginia agree to do identified adoptions. Some agencies also agree to make immediate hospital "at risk" placements, allowing the child to be placed with the adoptive parents before the consents to adoption are final.

American Academy of Adoption Attorney members:

David Allen Barnette; P.O. Box 553, Charleston, WV 25322
Tel: (304) 340-1327 ● d.barnette@adoptionattorneys.org
A graduate of the University of Dayton School of Law of Lewis, he has been practicing law since 1979. He estimates he has completed 1,850 adoptions in his career, and last year completed approximately 45 (10 independent; 15 agency; 20 intercountry). He accepts contested adoption cases.

WISCONSIN

Official State Adoption Website:
http://dcf.wi.gov/children/adoption/default.htm

State Adoption Exchange or Related Website:

State laws and procedures:

General Information. Wisconsin permits both independent and agency adoption. Advertising is permitted if the adoptive parents have a favorable home study. To file a Petition for Adoption within Wisconsin the adoptive parents must be residents. The Petition for Adoption cannot be filed until the investigating agency has written its final report approving the adoption, which is usually six months after placement. After the Petition for Adoption is filed, the finalization hearing is usually one to two months thereafter. The adoptive parents are required to appear in court for the final hearing.

Independent Adoption. A pre-placement home study of the adoptive parents is required before a child is placed in their home. The home study may be conducted by a licensed adoption agency. The fee varies.

It is not required by law that the adoptive parents and the birth mother meet in person and share identities, although it is often done voluntarily. The adoptive parents are permitted to assist the birth mother with necessary pregnancy-related medical, living and legal expenses. However, assistance with living expenses cannot exceed $5,000. The child may be released directly from the hospital only into a licensed foster home. This can be the home of the adoptive parents, if they have a foster home license, which is traditionally part of their pre-placement home study. If so, the child is placed with them in a "legal risk placement." If this is not possible, the child can be placed with them by court order of temporary guardianship.

The consent to adoption is made by means of a *Petition for Voluntary Termination of Parental Rights*, which is filed with the court any time after the birth. The birth mother then appears in court to consent to the termination of her parental rights, which usually occurs two to four weeks after the birth or placement with the adoptive parents. The adoptive parents normally attend this hearing as well, and should have had their initial home study previously filed with the court. The court then signs a *Termination of Parental Rights Order*. Before the court's order terminating parental rights, the birth mother has the automatic right to withdraw her consent. After the court's order, the consent is irrevocable, although there is a 30-day period in which an appeal can be filed to withdraw the consent based upon fraud, duress or to correct a legal error.

Wisconsin has a putative birth father registry, of sorts. Two methods are available to adoptive parents to notify birth fathers. The traditional method is to give notice of a termination of parental rights hearing to any putative birth father named by the birth mother. This can be done regardless of the child's age. The newer method requires notice to all birth fathers of their right to file with the putative birth father registry. If the birth father registers within 14 days of the birth, or 21 days from when notice was received, whichever is longer, he must be given notice of an action to terminate his parental rights. This method is only available when the child is one year of age or less.

Agency Adoption. There is no difference regarding the process in which a birth mother signs her consent to adoption in an independent or agency adoption. The information provided above regarding independent adoption (e.g. when the consent can be signed, before whom and the legal burden to withdraw the consent) is identical regarding agency adoption.

Some agencies in Wisconsin agree to do identified adoptions. Many agencies will agree to make immediate hospital "at risk" placements.

American Academy of Adoption Attorney members:

Lynn J. Bodi; 450 S. Yellowstone Drive; Madison, WI 53719
Tel: (608) 821-8212 ● law4kids.com ● l.bodi@adoptionattorneys.org
A graduate of the University of Wisconsin Law School, she has been practicing law since 1987. She accepts contested adoption cases and also handles assisted reproductive technology matters. She does not assist in creating adoptive matches. In 2011 she was named an Angel in Adoption by the Congressional Coalition on Adoption.

Stephen W. Hayes; N14 W23777 Stone Ridge Drive #200; Waukesha, WI 53186
Tel: (262) 347-2001 ● ghnlawyers.com ● swh@ghnlawyers.com
A graduate of the University of Illinois College of Law, he has been practicing law since 1969. He has completed approximately 4,000 adoptions and completes 100-120 per year: 50% private; 50% agency. He does not assist in creating adoptive matches. He accepts contested adoption cases and handles assisted reproductive technology cases.

Elizabeth A. Neary; N14 W23777 Stone Ridge Drive #200; Waukesha, WI 53188 ●Tel: (262) 374-2001 ● ghnlawyers.com ● ean@ghnlawyers.com
A graduate of Marquette University Law School, she began practicing in 1983. She does not assist in creating matches. She handles independent and agency adoptions and accepts contested cases.

Theresa L. Roetter; 211 S. Paterson St., #340; Madison, WI 53703
Tel: (608) 251-6700 ● annenroetter.com ● t.roetter@adoptionattorneys.org
A graduate of the Marquette University School of Law, she has been practicing law since 1993. She estimates she has completed 500 adoptions in her career and completes 25 adoptions annually: 55% independent; 40% agency; 5% international. She does not assist in creating adoptive matches. She accepts contested adoption cases. She has been named an Angel in Adoption by the Congressional Coalition of Adoption Institute and a Champion of Adoption by the Governor of Wisconsin. She also handles all types of assisted reproduction matters including drafting contracts and establishing parentage.

Victoria J. Schroeder; 385 Williamstowne #103; Delafield, WI 53018 ● Tel: (262) 646-2054 ● v.schroeder@adoptionattorneys.org
A graduate of the University of Wisconsin Law School, she has been practicing law since 1980. She estimates she has completed 1,000 adoptions in her career and completes 75 annually: 14% independent; 85% agency; 1% international. She does not assist in creating adoptive matches.

Judith Sperling-Newton; 450 S. Yellowstone Dr.; Madison, WI 53719 ●Tel: (608) 770-8210 ● law4kids.com ● j.sperling-newton@adoptionattorneys.org

Emily Dudak Taylor; 450 S. Yellowstone Dr.; Madison, WI 53719
Tel: (608) 821-8214 ● law4kids.com ● edudaktaylor@law4kids.com

WYOMING

Official State Adoption Website:
http://dfsweb.wyo.gov/social-services/adoption

State Adoption Exchange: Use above state website.

State laws and procedures:

General Information. Wyoming permits both independent and agency adoption. Advertising is permitted. To file a Petition for Adoption within Wyoming the adoptive parents must be residents. Normally, adoptions are finalized approximately six months after the child's placement. The adoptive parents are required to appear in court for at least one court hearing, either the initial court appearance for an interlocutory decree, or the final hearing to grant the adoption.

Independent Adoption. A pre-placement home study of the adoptive parents is not required before a child is placed in their home. In fact, Wyoming law does not even require a post-placement evaluation, unless ordered by the court. The home study may be conducted by a licensed adoption agency or licensed social worker. The fee for the post-placement home study is typically $1,200-1,500.

It is not required that the adoptive parents and the birth mother meet in person and share identities, although it is often done voluntarily. Wyoming law has no provisions for or against the adoptive parents being permitted to assist the birth mother with pregnancy-related expenses, but some judges require a summary of expenses paid. Typically, adoptive parents can provide pregnancy-related medical, living and legal assistance if needed. Normally, the child may be released directly to the adoptive parents from the hospital, although some adoptive parents prefer that the child be released to an intermediary, often an attorney, to maintain confidentiality.

The consent to adoption may be signed any time after the birth. It must be witnessed by a notary, representative of a licensed adoption agency or a judge. Once signed, the consent is irrevocable except upon proof of fraud or duress.

Wyoming has a putative birth father registry. Notice must be given to any putative birth father identified by the birth mother, as well as any man listed in the registry. The putative birth father has 30 days in which to file a paternity action. He must also be given notice of the action to terminate his parental rights.

Agency Adoption. There is no difference regarding the process in which a birth mother signs her consent to adoption in an independent or agency adoption. The

379

information provided above regarding independent adoption (e.g. when the consent can be signed, before whom and the legal burden to withdraw the consent) is identical regarding agency adoption. However, a home study will be required.

Some agencies in Wyoming agree to do identified adoptions. Some agencies also agree to make immediate hospital "at risk" placements, allowing the child to be placed with the adoptive parents before the consents to adoption are final.

American Academy of Adoption Attorney members:

Douglas H. Reiniger; 320 E. Broadway, Suite 2A; P.O. Box 1215, Jackson, WY 83001 ● Tel: (307) 690-6625 ● lawrsm.com ● d.reiniger@adoptionattorneys.org

Debra J. Wendtland; 2161 Coffeen Ave. #301; Sheridan, WY 82801 Tel: (307) 673-4696 ● wendtlandlaw.com ● deb@wendtlandlaw.com A graduate of the University of Wyoming College of Law, she has been practicing law since 1988. She estimates she has completed approximately 100 adoptions in her career.

Appendix A

NATIONAL AND REGIONAL ADOPTION EXCHANGES

National exchange:

Children's Bureau, Department of Health and Human Services (AdoptUSkids): www.adoptUSkids.org

Regional exchanges:

National Adoption Center: www.adopt.org

Children Awaiting Parents, Inc. (The CAP Book): www.capbook.org

The Adoption Exchange: www.adoptex.org

Northwest Adoption Exchange: www.nwae.org

Adopt America Network: adoptamericanetwork.org

State exchanges:

Chapter 15 (state-by-state review) lists each state's individual adoption exchange.

Appendix B

HELPFUL ORGANIZATIONS, PUBLICATIONS AND WEBSITES

Helpful Organizations:

North American Council for Adoptable Children (NACAC)
Website: www.nacac.org ● Email: info@nacac.org
  Committed to the needs of waiting children and adoptive families.

National Council for Adoption
Website: www.adoptioncouncil.org ● ndfa@adoptioncouncil.org
  An advocate for state laws that promote sound adoption policy. It was responsible for the nation's first photolisting of waiting children, now done by www.adoptuskids.org.

The Child Welfare League of America (CWLA)
Website: www.cwla.org
  An association of agencies that assist more than 2.5 million abused and neglected children and their families each year.

Resolve
Website: www.resolve.org ● Email: info@resolve.org
  A highly respected, non-profit national infertility organization.

The Child Welfare Information Gateway
Website: www.childwelfare.gov ● Email: info@childwelfare.gov
  A service of the U.S. Department of Health and Human Services. It offers a tremendous database of adoption information.

American Academy of Adoption Attorneys
Website: www.adoptionattorneys.org
  A not-for-profit fellowship of adoption attorneys and judges who have distinguished themselves in the field of adoption.

The Donaldson Adoption Institute
Website: www.adoptioninstitute.org • info@adoptioninstitute.org
Its goal is to achieve ethical and legal reforms in adoption.

Organization of Teratology Information Specialists (OTIS).
Website: MotherToBaby.org
Information on all types of fetal drug exposure and consequences.

The American Adoption Congress
Website: www.americanadoptioncongress.org
Dedicated to promoting legislation and public awareness regarding adoptee and birth parent access to identifying information.

Concerned United Birthparents, Inc. (CUB)
Website: www.cubirthparents.org
Focusing on the needs and concerns of birthparents.

The Dave Thomas Foundation
Website: davethomasfoundation.org
Dedicated to the adoption of children in foster care.

Publications:

Adoptive Families Magazine
Website: www.adoptivefamilies.com
Offering articles of tremendous assistance to both new adoptive parents, as well as those whose adopted children are now adults.

Websites:

Adoption101.com (Free and very detailed articles on adoption in an advertising-free setting, with an online adoption bookstore.)

Adoption.com (Despite the many advertisements it carries, there are many excellent articles, and other helpful information provided, making it a helpful resource.)

Appendix C

SAMPLE PHOTO-RESUME LETTER

Hi,

We're Brian and Shelly and we are hoping with all our hearts to adopt. We live in a wonderful suburban community in southern California. Our neighbors are some of our best friends and many of them have young children, or are just starting their families. We are about five minutes to the ocean and we love to spend weekends at the beach. Brian likes to bodysurf while I prefer to sit under an umbrella and read a good book. What we'd really love to be doing is building sandcastles with our child, but we know that day will come. Besides the beach, Brian likes to barbeque and also enjoys playing softball and doing home projects. I like sports like jogging and tennis, but I also like being a homebody and just relaxing at home. Sunday mornings we do the crossword puzzle together and see who can get the most answers – winner gets a massage. (Sometimes I even let him win!)

Brian is a fireman and loves his job. He also feels good about having a job where he can help people and make a difference in our town. My job is not so exciting. I'm the assistant manager of a clothing boutique, but I have fun helping people choose clothes that make them feel good about themselves. I plan to be a stay-at-home mom.

We are working with an adoption attorney/agency, _____, to make sure we do everything correctly. To learn more about us, you can call him/her/them at _____. Many adoptions nowadays are open, allowing us to meet, share identities and get to know each other, so you can be sure you are picking the right parents for your baby. We can't wait to meet you!

Brian and Shelly

Appendix D

SAMPLE "TRADITIONAL" NETWORKING COVER LETTER

Hi!	Hi!
We are hoping to adopt a baby. We are sending you our photo-resume letter with the hope you will keep it on hand, and when the time comes, that you will pass it along to a woman who is facing an unplanned pregnancy and might be considering adoption as a loving option for her child. We are able to help with pregnancy-related expenses. We have selected "open" adoption because it allows adoptive and birth parents to get to know each other before the birth, with no hidden identities. Thank you!	We are hoping to adopt a baby. We are sending you our photo-resume letter with the hope you will keep it on hand, and when the time comes, that you will pass it along to a woman who is facing an unplanned pregnancy and might be considering adoption as a loving option for her child. We are able to help with pregnancy-related expenses. We have selected "open" adoption because it allows adoptive and birth parents to get to know each other before the birth, with no hidden identities. Thank you!

Note: printing two cover letters per page will allow you to cut it in half, giving you two copies. Then affix one to each photo-resume letter, allowing half the cover letter to show from behind it.

Appendix E

SAMPLE "PERSONAL" NETWORKING COVER LETTER

Dear Friends:

We are hoping to adopt a baby and we hope that you can help us. As you may know, there are many couples like us unable to conceive a child who turn their hopes to adoption. Unfortunately, there are more couples waiting to adopt than there are babies. Nowadays, most adoptions are started by the baby's biological mother, learning of a couple who is hoping to adopt, usually from one of her healthcare providers, or a friend.

The process is very open and women considering adoption can meet us in person to decide if they would like to select us as the adoptive parents. That's where you come in! We hope you will help us by *personally* giving a copy of our resume letter (we've enclosed five) to people you know who will keep it on hand for when they may come into contact with a woman with an unplanned pregnancy. Specifically, please give one directly to your family doctor the next time you have an appointment, as well as your OB/GYN. Not their receptionist, but directly to the doctor. Other people you could give it to could be your minister, and any friends you have who work in medical clinics, as counselors, etc. Even where you get your hair and nails done can be great places to get the word out. If you have any questions, please call us. We have an adoption attorney/agency helping us to be sure we do everything correctly.

There is nothing more important to us than having a family, and we thank you for helping us create ours.

Ryan and Robin

Index

From the Author

Thank you for reading *Adopting in America: How to Adopt Within One Year* (2018-2019). I've worked hard to give you great depth and insight into each adoption option, help you select the option uniquely best for you, and increase your chances of success. Most importantly, I want you to go into the option you select with your eyes open. The more educated you are in the adoption process from the very beginning, the better your chances will be to find the best-qualified agency or attorney to assist you, and the more skillful you will be in determining if a particular adoption situation offered to you is one you should elect to pursue.

If you have a comment or question, I'd truly enjoy hearing from you. You can reach me at Randy@RandallHicks.com. I respond to all emails. Perhaps you will even have a suggestion to improve a future edition of this book.

Again, thanks for reading. I sincerely hope you will take a moment to review this book online on Amazon or other online retailer to help others looking for help in adopting. Hearing from actual readers like you is very helpful to prospective adoptive parents who are several steps behind you in their adoption knowledge and can use your insight about books which will best educate and prepare them.

Best wishes,

CPSIA information can be obtained
at www.ICGtesting.com
Printed in the USA
LVHW02s1106250218
567798LV00004B/800/P